THE
Conte

Oral and written dynamics

Janice Carruthers and Maeve McCusker (eds)

PETER LANG

Oxford · Bern · Berlin · Bruxelles · Frankfurt am Main · New York · Wien

Bibliographic information published by Die Deutsche Nationalbibliothek
Die Deutsche Nationalbibliothek lists this publication in the Deutsche Nationalbibliografie;
detailed bibliographic data is available on the Internet at http://dnb.d-nb.de.

A catalogue record for this book is available from The British Library.

Library of Congress Cataloging-in-Publication Data:

The conte : oral and written dynamics / [edited by] Janice Carruthers
and Maeve McCusker.
  p. cm.
  Some essays in French.
  Includes bibliographical references and index.
  ISBN 978-3-03911-870-0 (alk. paper)
  1. Folk literature, French--History and criticism. 2. Fairy
tales--France--History and criticism. 3. Fairy tales--French-speaking
countries--History and criticism. 4. Orality in literature. 5. Oral
tradition--France. 6. Oral tradition--French-speaking countries. I.
Carruthers, Janice, 1964- II. McCusker, Maeve.
  GR161.C58 2009
  398.20944--dc22
                        2009034413

ISBN 978-3-03911-870-0

© Peter Lang AG, International Academic Publishers, Bern 2010
Hochfeldstrasse 32, CH-3012 Bern, Switzerland
info@peterlang.com, www.peterlang.com, www.peterlang.net

Printed in Germany

Contents

Acknowledgements

The editors would like to acknowledge the support of the following in the preparation of this volume: Queen's University Belfast, Wendy Ayres-Bennett, Patrick Caudal, Elizabeth Childs, Mary Gallagher, Graham Speake, Caroline Sumpter, and above all, Steven Wilson; and the following for their support for the Conference which provided the impetus for the volume: The British Academy, Queen's University Belfast, Simon Davies, Denise Toner.

The workshop in Queen's University Belfast, from which many of the articles published here originated, was greatly enlivened by Professor John Conteh-Morgan's energetic and characteristically meticulous reading of Zadi Zaourou's *La Guerre des femmes*, and by his interventions from the floor. Sadly John's untimely death in 2008 meant that this oral contribution, despite his best efforts, was in the end not transformed into text; the absence of this written version, in a volume dedicated to the oral-written dynamic, adds a particular poignancy to the publication.

Contextualising the oral-written dynamic in the French and francophone *conte*

JANICE CARRUTHERS AND MAEVE MCCUSKER

The word *conte* in French is a capacious term, describing a much wider range of narratives than any of its English equivalents (folktale; fairytale; short story; oral tale). Thus it is appropriate, in generic terms, that the parameters of this collection of essays, *Le Conte: Oral and Written Dynamics*, are set broadly, so as to accommodate and reflect something of this variety. Nonetheless, linking each contribution is the fact that the discourse analysed is always 'narrative', if one takes any of the major definitions of narrative,[1] and involves a storyline that draws on one or more of the variations of a particular *conte* existing in oral or written form around the world. The focus is on the French and francophone *conte*, in the sense that the narratives under investigation are, or have been, performed, written or read in the French language.

---

1   Linguistic definitions of narrative discourse tend to emphasise the presentation of a series of events in temporal sequence: for an influential early definition, see W. Labov and J. Waletsky, 'Narrative analysis: oral versions of personal experience', in J. Helm (McNeish) (ed.), *Essays on the Verbal and Visual Arts. Proceedings of the 1966 Annual Spring Meeting of the American Ethnological Society* (Seattle, University of Washington Press, 1967), 12–44; for a more recent linguistic definition, see C. Smith, *Modes of Discourse* (Cambridge, CUP, 2003). For a narratological approach, which has become a standard reference in literary studies, see G. Genette, 'Frontières du récit', *Communications* 8 (1966), 152–163; *Figures III* (Paris, Seuil, 1972); *Nouveau discours du récit* (Paris, Seuil, 1983). Genette sees narrative as depending on the inter-relationship between three elements: story, narrative and narrating (*narration*). See too M. Bal, *Narratology: Introduction to the Theory of Narrative* (Toronto, University of Toronto Press, 1985).

Within this broad francophone setting, the *conte* is embedded in linguistic and cultural contexts that go well beyond the boundaries of France. It forms part of a heritage which spans literary and oral forms of dissemination in both European and postcolonial traditions. For example, many of the narratives function in environments where languages other than French – notably the regional languages of France, and forms of Arabic, Creole or other indigenous languages in the broader postcolonial context – play a very significant role. In Sections 3 and 4, which focus on the language of the *conte* and on its use in postcolonial contexts, the *contes* themselves are often drawn from non-European sources, and even in Sections 1 and 2, where the majority of the narratives could be said to be 'French', the stories more often emanate from much broader European, Middle Eastern and Oriental cultural traditions. To this extent, the corpus represented here bears out Marina Warner's observation that '[t]he nature of the genre is promiscuous and omnivorous […]. Motifs and plotlines are nomadic, travelling the world and the millennia, turning up on parchment in medieval Persia, in an oral form in the Pyrenees, in a ballad sung in the Highlands, in a fairy story in the Caribbean'.[2] Warner's phrase nicely points to the precise focus of our volume: in the transition from the spoken (or the sung) to parchment or print, or indeed, as we shall also explore, in the reverse trajectory, what are the precise faultlines, the slippages, the tensions or the points of convergence that would help to shed light on the dynamic and shifting relationship between the written and the oral, between the communal experience of storytelling and the solitary experiences of writing and reading, between the textual and the corporeal, between what Derrida calls the 'metaphysics of presence' enshrined in the oral performance, and the secondary state of writing?

*   *   *

---

2   M. Warner, *From the Beast to the Blonde. On Fairytales and their Tellers* (London, Chatto and Windus, 1994), xvii.

The research questions explored in published work on the *conte* have stimulated debate across a wide range of disciplines, and many of those questions have important implications for the relationship between the oral and the written. However, within particular disciplines, these questions have tended to take on different resonances, raise different sets of problems, and been attributed different levels of importance. One of the results of this is that the complexities of the dynamic between written and oral have, relatively speaking, been neglected.

Within anthropology, folklore studies and ethnolinguistics, there is considerable focus on issues around the practice, function, structure and significance of oral narrative in oral cultures, and on the use and evolution of particular story types in specific cultural contexts.[3] A second major strand within anthropological research concerns the typology and classification of *contes*. The seminal work on the French *conte*, Delarue and Tenèze's *Le Conte populaire français: catalogue raisonné des versions de France*, gives a detailed account of the narrative sequences for each type, alongside attested variations.[4] The versions analysed by Delarue and Tenèze are both oral and written, both popular and literary, and indeed, it is the latter opposition that is often noted rather than a putative oral-written divide. Anthropologists and ethnolinguists have also debated a number of questions around the language of oral literature. Following on from early work by Parry and Lord which articulated what became known as the 'oral formulaic theory', phenomena such as formulae and parallelisms have been widely explored in oral narrative; the most important study of such features in the French *conte* is that of Ariane de Félice, whose work

---

3   See for example R. Bauman, *Story, Performance and Event: Contextual Studies of Oral Narrative* (Cambridge, CUP, 1986); R. Finnegan, *The Oral and Beyond. Doing Things with Words in Africa* (Chicago, University of Chicago Press, 2007); G. Calame-Griaule, *Contes dogons du Mali* (Paris, Karthala, 2006).

4   P. Delarue and M.-L. Tenèze, *Le Conte populaire français: catalogue raisonné des versions de France* (Paris, Maisonneuve et Larose, 2002).

is based on a corpus of stories from the Berry, Poitou and Haute-Bretagne regions.[5]

However, although orality, language and variation are all central preoccupations in anthropological research, most anthropologists are suspicious of – even hostile to – any methodology where an oral-written divide is posited that might imply the superiority of written modes or literate cultures, or that might group together under vague categories such as 'oral' and 'written' types of discourse that are actually extremely wide-ranging. For example, in her recent volume, *Poétique du conte*, Nicole Belmont explores the sophistication of the poetic techniques deployed by *conteurs/ses* from the oral tradition in the 'creation' of a given *conte* performance within the constraints of the 'espace narratif' of the relevant *conte-type*.[6] Contrary to certain perspectives that might dismiss the oral *conte merveilleux* as a 'simple' genre destined for children, Belmont – implicitly endorsing Peter Brooks's suggestion, in another context, that the folktale and psychoanalysis are inherently compatible, given that psychoanalysis is itself 'a primarily narrative art'[7] – uses Freudian theories of dream analysis to discuss the complex poetics of the oral *conte*.

In literary studies, the *conte* has long occupied an important position. Early scholarship was characterised by an attention to the oral sources of written tales, by an interest in the appropriation and transformation of *contes*, and by the effect and significance of these appropriations in particular literary works. This scholarship was transformed by Vladimir Propp's now classic study, *Morphology of the Folktale* (1928), which was having a strong

---

5   A. de Félice, *Essai sur quelques techniques de l'art verbal traditionnel* (Thèse de doctorat, Université de Paris, 1957); M. Parry, *The Making of Homeric Verse (Collected Papers of Milman Parry)* (Oxford, Clarendon Press, 1971); A. B. Lord, *The Singer of Tales* (Cambridge, Mass., Harvard University Press, 1960).

6   I.e. the narrative schema associated with the particular story. See N. Belmont, *Poétique du conte* (Paris, Gallimard, 1999), 17.

7   P. Brooks, *Reading for the Plot. Design and Intention in Narrative* (Cambridge, Mass. and London, Harvard University Press, 1984), xiv.

influence in French scholarship by the 1960s.[8] Propp moved away from an emphasis on sources and rewriting, to formulate a structuralist approach to the *conte*. He attempted to codify recurrent textual structures in the folktale, identifying a limited number of functions in the *conte merveilleux*. This approach, described as a syntagmatic one – based around chronological order in a linear sequence along a horizontal axis – would in turn inspire important work by figures such as Claude Lévi-Strauss and Algirdas Greimas, who privileged instead the paradigmatic axis, based around a symmetrical matrix-like structure founded on the opposition between, say, Hero, Sender and Object.[9]

Yet, while these structuralist approaches have been hugely influential in the study of the French and francophone *conte*, the precise modalities of the relationship between the oral and the written have been underrepresented in much literary criticism. Valuable work is undoubtedly being carried out in a number of centres in France, notably by the CNRS group working in the Université Stendhal in Grenoble.[10] However this research deals with a very specific genre (the *conte merveilleux* of the eighteenth and nineteenth centuries), and indeed much of the work is conducted according to strictly literary lines of analysis. In an important contribution to one of the recent volumes produced by the Grenoble group, Lewis Seifert attempts to account for the fact that orality has so often been viewed as an 'effet de l'écrit'. He notes the ambiguous and unstable link made in the popular imaginary between the *conte* and orality, and attributes the dominance of the literary to 'la polysémie de la notion même d'"oralité", qui peut désigner à la fois une tradition narrative, la voie de transmission de celle-ci, une situation de contage, sinon l'énonciation au niveau de la

---

8   This influence was initially via its (already belated) translation into English in 1958; the work was translated into French only in 1970.
9   See A. Dundes, 'Introduction to the Second Edition', in V. Propp, *Morphology of the Folktale*, trans. L. A. Wagner (Austin and London, University of Texas Press, 1986), xi–xvii.
10   LIRE: Littératures, Idéologies, Représentations, XVIIIe–XIXe siècles.

narration ou de la diégèse'.[11] Arguably, all of these issues identified by Seifert are equally applicable to writing, which at once designates the act, the
product and the literary tradition. And yet the common, and paradoxical,
sense of the oral as being at once slippery, ephemeral and intangible (in
contrast to the fixity and permanence of text), and at the same time as lack-
ing in artifice, and hence eminently and straightforwardly *representable*,
has dominated literary analysis. To illustrate his point, Seifert shows how,
from the nineteenth century onwards, Perrault's genius became associated
with his perceived skill in faithfully rendering the oral style of nurses and
children in a unique and inimitable writing style; in other words, 'fidèle à
une oralité imitable [Perrault] crée une œuvre écrite inimitable'.[12] Seifert
argues that this privileging of the written remains constant, so that even
in the very valuable work of critics such as Soriano and Mainil, for example, 'il s'agit de la représentation de l'écrit de l'oralité, de l'appropriation
de celle-ci par l'écrit'.[13] Reflecting different disciplinary and theoretical
perspectives to Seifert, both Velay-Vallantin and Delarue and Tenèze also
allude to the 'distortion' of the oral in written texts that supposedly reflect
'oral' origins. Commenting for example on the first 'folktale' in one of
Madame D'Aulnoy's collections, Delarue and Tenèze observe that 'elle
lui donne une forme littéraire qui le fait accepter',[14] while Velay-Vallantin
claims more generally that 'il s'agit moins de réhabililter la culture orale
que de lui substituer une oralité factice, reconstruite, qui rejette, et pour
longtemps, les véritables réctis oraux dans les marges de la culture légitime'.[15]
Meanwhile, in environments associated more strongly with the oral tra-

11 L. Seifert, 'Entre l'écrit et l'oral: la réception des contes de fées "classiques"', in
    A. Defrance and J.-F. Perrin (eds), *Le Conte en ses paroles. La Figuration de l'oralité
    dans le conte merveilleux du Classicisme aux Lumières* (Paris, Desjonquères, 2007),
    21–33, 21.

12 Sainte-Beuve was in this sense, according to Seifert, typical, in his view that 'Perrault
    fait de l'oralité et tout ce qu'elle connote un monument que seule l'écriture peut ériger'.
    Seifert, 'Entre l'écrit et l'oral', 25.

13 *Ibid.*

14 Delarue and Tenèze, *Le Conte populaire français*, 19–20.

15 C. Velay-Vallantin, *L'Histoire des contes* (Paris, Fayard, 1992), 31–32.

dition, written versions of stories also circulated, not least through the *livres de colportage*, which themselves raise complex questions around the oral-written divide, since texts could be read aloud in collective 'readings'. And if theorists such as Jack Goody and Walter Ong proposed the notion of a 'great divide' between oral and print culture, more recent work – and indeed the later writings of Goody and Ong themselves – has nuanced this sense of a dichotomy, given the extent to which the two modes were in fact porous and complicit with each other.[16]

The literary context – in both the European and the postcolonial perspectives – has also been characterised by a strong strain of nostalgia for the disappearance of an uncontaminated oral tradition beyond the reach of print, and for earlier, more authentic forms of knowledge. Although critics such as Ruth Bottigheimer and others have cast doubt on the pristine nature of this oral culture, and queried the extent to which it can be seen as distinct from, and prior to, the literary, this view still has some purchase. Among its earliest and most influential proponents is Walter Benjamin, whose often-cited 1936 essay 'The Storyteller' (first published in French), links the decline of storytelling to the fact that 'experience has fallen in value' as a direct result of the conditions of modernity.[17] As storytelling has subsided, it has been replaced by a new, essentially modern, form of narrative, the novel, the predominant narrative form of print culture and capitalist individualism: 'The birthplace of the novel is the solitary individual, who is no longer able to express himself by giving examples of his most important concerns'.[18] Benjamin's melancholic diagnosis of the rise of bourgeois individualism, and its effects on the communal activity of

16 J. Goody and I. Watt, 'The consequences of literacy', in J. Goody (ed.), *Literacy in Traditional Societies* (Cambridge, CUP, 1968), 27–68; W. Ong, *Orality and Literacy. The Technologizing of the Word* (London and New York, Methuen, 1982), 16–57.

17 W. Benjamin, 'The Storyteller: reflections on the works of Nikolai Leskov', in *Illuminations*, ed. H. Arendt, trans. H. Zohn (London, Fontana, 1983), 83–109, 83–84.

18 Benjamin, 'The Storyteller', 87.

storytelling, has in turn been challenged by a number of critics,[19] who see the relationship as much more complex, and mutually enriching, than Benjamin's essay – now a 'standard line in twentieth century criticism' – would allow.[20]

Research on the *conte* in the colonial and the postcolonial context has, unsurprisingly, been driven in the first instance by anthropologists and ethnologists. If early work still bore the trace of having emanated from the missionary and then the colonial administrator set, later scholarship, which intensified in the 1960s, has been more firmly grounded in the principles of modern French and European ethnography, as exemplified in the work of anthropologists and ethnolinguists such as Veronika Görög-Karady, Marcel Griaule and his daughter, Geneviève Calame-Griaule. It has also been heavily influenced by many of the schools mentioned above (notably by Propp, Lévi-Strauss and Michel Leiris) and by key texts emerging in the anglophone context, such as Ruth Finnegan's *Limba Stories and Storytelling* and *Oral Poetry*, and Isidore Okpewho's *African Oral Literature*.[21] French scholars – and thus, very often, the *contes* of the colonies and ex-colonies of France – have been at the forefront of research carried out in anthropology and ethnolinguistics. As Görög-Karady notes, 'If France's participation in the study of African oral literature has always been important, her contribution constituted almost 25 per cent of all the topical production from 1960 onwards'.[22] Nonetheless, she also notes that the field suffers from a certain marginalisation within France, in that there is still no chair of African oral studies in France, and doctoral students tend to defend

19   See for example I. Kreilkamp, *Voice and the Victorian Storyteller* (Cambridge, CUP, 2005).

20   Kreilkamp, *Voice and the Victorian Storyteller*, 7.

21   R. Finnegan, *Limba Stories and Storytelling* (Oxford, Clarendon Press, 1967), and *Oral Poetry: Its Nature, Significance and Social Context* (Cambridge, CUP, 1977); I. Okpewho, *African Oral Literature. Backgrounds, Character, and Continuity* (Bloomington, Indianapolis, Indiana University Press, 1992).

22   V. Görög-Karady, 'French Study of African Folklore', in P. Peek and K. Yankah (eds), *African Folklore: An Encyclopedia* (London, Routledge, 2004), 138–141, 139.

their theses in other cognate departments such as Comparative Literature, Anthropology or Linguistics.

Literary critics of African and Caribbean literatures have, for their part, often been suspicious of the ethnographic approach, associated by many with an inherently Western or Eurocentric gaze. They have preferred to valorise the *griot* and the *conteur* as figures of resistance, and to highlight the political impetus of the *conte* in literary texts, seeking in these works the traces of what Warner calls 'the irrepressible energy of interdicted narrative and opinion among groups of people who have been muffled in the dominant, learned milieux'.[23] And yet, in an echo of some of the criticisms levelled at Benjamin, writers such as Raphaël Confiant and Patrick Chamoiseau have been criticised for the nostalgia with which they invest the *conteur* in their fiction. Moreover, attempts by critics to scour the written text for evidence of the oral tradition can themselves produce distorted readings, which risk fossilising or romanticising the oral as an unproblematic and essentialised reservoir of folk wisdom.[24] As Eileen Julien cautions, critics have too often attempted to 'identify a Euro-language text's authenticating traces – proverbs, embedded stories, phrases in indigenous languages – naming and cataloguing these elements as though they were ends in themselves or making superficial comparisons that lead to praise or blame'.[25]

It is of course essential to distinguish *between* postcolonial cultures in terms of the specificities of history. The Martinican writer Edouard Glissant draws an important distinction between the role of the oral tradition

---

23   Warner, *From the Beast to the Blonde*, 11.

24   To take just one example from many, A. Bogniaho, in an article which attempts to 'montrer le génie culturel spécifique inspirateur de la littérature orale', presents the oral tradition as being 'née du terroir profond et pour le terroir [...]. Aussi est-elle demeurée vierge, de sorte qu'elle exprime l'identité culturelle des peuples qui la créent et l'utilisent'. See 'Francophonie et diversité littéraire', in A. Huannou (ed.), *Francophonie littéraire et identités culturelles. Actes du colloque du GRELEF (cotonou, 18–20 mars 1998)* (Paris, L'Harmattan, 2000), 29–45, 30.

25   E. Julien, 'Reading "orality" in French-language novels from sub-Saharan Africa', in C. Forsdick and D. Murphy (eds), *Francophone Postcolonial Studies. A Critical Introduction* (London, Arnold, 2003), 122–132, 129.

in 'cultures ataviques' and in 'cultures composées'.[26] While many African
societies, for example, can identify a myth of origins in their folktales,
Caribbean cultures, with their history of transplantation, cultural mixing
and combination, cannot attribute to the *conte* the status of an 'original'
or unproblematically traditional local form. The historical conditions
of their production make the *contes* of 'Old World' Africa and the 'New
World' Americas radically distinct. And, in terms of the contemporary
Antilles, Jean Bernabé cautions against an overly neat dichotomy between
the oral and the written. He criticises the tendency to see the written as
merely a representation of the oral, 'donc une réalité seconde par rapport à
la parole qui, ontologiquement première, est assimilée au verbe divin', but
also warns against the converse view, according to which 'l'écrit occupe
une position hiérarchiquement première par rapport à l'oral'. As he suggests, 'Sortir d'une telle contradiction s'impose, d'autant que l'examen
de la textualité antillaise commande de repenser de façon dynamique les
relations intervenant entre oralité et écriture'.[27] Bernabé points to the
continued absence in the the French Antillean islands of Guadeloupe
and Martinique – which could be described as hyper-literate cultures,
départements d'outre-mer since 1946 and fully assimilated to the French
education system – of a dynamic model of reading *across* the textual-oral
interface.

More generally, it is worth noting that, for all the attention paid
by French critics to the African and Caribbean *conte* in the last twenty
years, a major broad-based theoretical intervention such as Henry Louis
Gates's *The Signifying Monkey* has not been produced.[28] Gates's ambi-
tious monograph traces the folkloric origins of the Afro-American

---

26   E. Glissant, 'Le Chaos-monde, l'oral et l'écrit', in R. Ludwig (ed.), *Écrire la 'parole de
      nuit'. La nouvelle littérature antillaise* (Paris, Folio, 1994), 111–129.
27   J. Bernabé, '*Fènwè* et *wè klè*, le syndrome homérique à l'œuvre dans la parole antillaise',
      in J. Bernabé et al. (eds), *Au Visiteur lumineux. Des îles créoles aux sociétés plurielles.
      Mélanges offerts à Jean Benoist* (Petit Bourg-Schœlcher, Ibis Rouge-GEREC, 2000),
      633–650, 635.
28   H.L. Gates, *The Signifying Monkey. A Theory of African-American Literary Criticism*
      (Oxford, OUP, 1988).

practice of 'signifying', and extrapolates a theory of literary criticism from the relationship between the black vernacular tradition and the Afro-American literary tradition. He shows how the trickster figure so prevalent in these oral traditions (Anancy and Coyote for example, but also Brer Rabbit/Compère Lapin) has resulted in metaphor and irony being placed at the heart of all African-American communication, and particularly literature.

Research within contemporary linguistics on the language of the *conte* has been much less prolific, although there is a perceptible surge of interest in the field. Most current research tends to focus primarily either on the oral or on the written, although the interface between the two is now beginning to enter the debate. Principal areas of interest in oral *contage* include the use of particular linguistic features such as parallelisms to structure the narrative, temporal and aspectual patterns (e.g. tense switching, temporal framing, temporal sequencing), strategies for speech and thought presentation (use of direct speech, free indirect speech etc.), and the syntactic and pragmatic properties of structures such as inversion and detachment.[29] In many cases, patterns observed in the *conte* are analysed alongside patterns in other varieties of oral narrative such as conversational stories, or alongside earlier varieties of storytelling, or, in some cases, in relation to patterns attested in medieval 'texts'.[30] In terms of linguistic research on 'literary' versions of *contes*, the Comparative Literature team in the University of Lausanne is leading the field, notably through the work of Jean-Michel Adam and Ute Heidmann.[31] Their research uses linguistic theory to explore, amongst other issues, questions

---

29   See for example J. Carruthers, *Oral Narration in Modern French. A Linguistic Analysis of Temporal Patterns* (Oxford, Legenda, 2005); N. Guézennec, 'Mémoire et transmission de la tradition orale en Basse-Bretagne. Approches ethno- et sociolinguistiques de la littérature orale, de la mémoire, de l'oral et de l'écrit' (Thèse de doctorat, Université Paris X-Nanterre, 2005).

30   J. Carruthers and S. Marnette, 'Tense, voices and point of view in medieval and modern "oral" narration', in E. Labeau, C. Vetters and P. Caudal (eds), *Sémantique et diachronie du système verbal français* (Amsterdam, Rodopi, 2007), 177–202.

31   For details of recent and current publications, see www.unil.ch/lleuc

of genre, *énonciation* and intertextuality, drawing on texts from a broad historical period and in a number of European languages.

* * *

This volume thus situates itself in a rich research context in terms of scholarship on the *conte* in its written and oral forms, but one where debate about the range of complex issues raised by the oral-written dynamic is certainly under-represented, if not neglected. The primary aim of this volume is to discuss a number of significant aspects of the relationship between oral and written forms of the *conte*: some Chapters deal with sources and influences (written on oral and vice versa), others with the nature of the discourse resulting from an oral-written dynamic (e.g. discourse structure, linguistic features etc.), others still with the oral-written interface as it affects the definition of genre, and others with the role of the oral within the literary or written text (use of storytelling scenarios, the problematics inherent in transcribing/adapting the spoken word etc.).

A second objective is to bring together perspectives on this oral-written dynamic from fields that are rarely brought into dialogue. The Chapters in literary studies treat a broad spectrum of texts from the eighteenth century to the twenty-first, dealing with authors ranging from the canonical (e.g. Perrault, Voltaire, Balzac) to the less well known (e.g. Gueullette, Hearn), and including several postcolonial writers (e.g. Césaire, Dadié, Diop). There are three linguistics chapters (discussing questions around tense/aspect/voice and discourse features such as 'parallelisms'), and one which is on the borderline between literature, linguistics and anthropology. This chronological and typological range allows us to situate the form in socio-cultural terms, and to open up debate around *contes* that are embedded in particular historical, geographical and political contexts: regional (Guézennec); national (Defrance, Perrin, Raynard, Francis, Caudal, Carruthers); European (Bottigheimer, Farrant); postcolonial (Stafford, Gallagher, McCusker, Decourt).

The volume is structured into four broad thematic areas (The Oral-Written Dynamic in Early Modern France; Literary Appropriations and Transformations; Postcolonial Contexts; Storytelling in Contemporary

France – Linguistic Strategies). In Section 1, our focus is on tales of the eighteenth and nineteenth centuries. Richard Francis's analysis of a number of canonical Voltaire *contes*, while insisting on their inherently literary quality, analyses the strategic use of oral narration to bolster the parodic and polemical qualities of his work. Sophie Raynard compares scenes of storytelling in the work of the earliest writer of fairytales, Mme d'Aulnoy, with a number of historical descriptions of 'real life' storytelling, so as to ascertain whether these fictional *mises en abyme* reconstruct a reliable record of the birth of the genre, or rather an idealised fictional imagining of its genesis. Ruth Bottigheimer, meanwhile, challenges widely held assumptions about the oral origins of fairy tales, arguing instead that the genre's origins were inherently literary, and that dissemination was primarily via the print-based media rather than through such figures as the nursemaid or the peasant.

In Section 2, Jean-François Perrin's Chapter examines a collection of *contes* by a little-known writer, Thomas-Simon Gueullette [1683–1766], showing how Gueullette's tales exemplify the hybridity of the form, and reflect – through their attention to technology, science, religious scepticism and the 'Other' – the profound social and ideological transformations of this period. Anne Defrance's Chapter shows how Mme Leprince de Beaumont's explicitly pedagogical rewriting of Cazotte's source tale, *La Patte du Chat*, in her version, *Le Prince Désir*, calls into question the power of orality. Tim Farrant's Chapter tackles the issue of definition, showing how the emphasis on form in definitions of the nineteenth-century *conte* and the *nouvelle* meant that the written became (somewhat questionably) linked to repression, finality and the establishment, while the oral was perhaps too categorically associated with freedom and subversion.

Section 3 is concerned with the function of the *conte* in a postcolonial perspective. Andy Stafford's Chapter looks at two African writers of *contes*, Bernard Dadié from the Côte d'Ivoire and Birago Diop from Senegal, and argues that Fredric Jameson's model of Third World allegory – a model contested by many postcolonial critics – can in fact be a useful way of approaching the work of both writers, so as to keep the political import of their work in the foreground. Mary Gallagher examines the transcription of *contes* by the Anglo-Irish/Greek writer, Lafcadio Hearn. For Gallagher,

Hearn's emphasis on reworking, adaptation, translation and incorporation, processes which are themselves constitutive of Creole culture, are particularly important to this multiply-located writer, and testify to an aesthetic of displacement and mediation in his work more generally. Maeve McCusker's analysis of the appropriation of the *conte* by successive generations of Martinican theorists shows how the form has been harnessed to a range of ideological perspectives. This highly masculine theoretical discourse, she argues, has occluded not only the *conteuse*, but has also overlooked and distorted work done by female critics and anthropologists.

Section 4 opens with Nadine Decourt's Chapter which is situated on the borderline between anthropology, linguistics and literature. Decourt explores the cultural and linguistic issues that arise when attempting to publish a written edition of stories collected from Magrebin women recounting the narratives not only in an oral context, but also in a language which sets up both cultural and linguistic frontiers between the original Arabic and the textual French versions. Caudal, Carruthers and Guézennec explore specific syntactic and stylistic phenomena. Caudal's Chapter focuses on tense usage, and in particular on tense switching, its use in oral storytelling, and its theoretical analysis; Guézennec discusses the use of parallelisms in oral narrative and their significance in terms of defining storytelling in both written and oral forms; and Carruthers uses an analysis of three linguistic phenomena – tense switching, hypotaxis versus parataxis, speech and thought presentation – to discuss the viability of a notion such as the oral-written divide.

*   *   *

Michèle Simonsen, in a 1981 study, noted that France was somewhat behind her European neighbours in formally collecting and recording her *contes*.[32] It was only really in the post-1870 period that this branch of folklore became an established and vibrant discipline, and that specialist journals devoted to folklore and popular traditions were established. Since then,

---

32   M. Simonsen, *Le Conte populaire français* (Paris, PUF, 1981), 21.

the scholarly attention paid to the *conte* has ebbed and flowed; for example, the inter-war period saw a virtual suspension of publishing on the form. It is undoubtedly the case, however, that this present volume, specifically focussed on the interrelationship between the oral and the written, emerges against the general backdrop of a remarkable renewal in both the activity of storytelling (notably the much-vaunted 'renouveau du conte'),[33] and in the level of research activity being carried out in this area. Within such a dynamic practical and academic context, we hope that this collection will prove useful for scholars in the field, that it might stimulate further work on a topic that has suffered from relative neglect, and that it might contribute to the unsettling of some of the conventional binaries which are often used to describe the relationship between the oral and the written (high versus low culture, Western versus non-Western culture, male versus female, power versus resistance, renewal versus nostalgia). The volume cannot, of course, make any claim to full coverage, and inevitably leaves many areas under-represented. We hope, however, that in our discussion of a number of significant aspects of this interrelationship, we have managed to reflect something of the range of approaches to the oral-written dynamic. By locating these approaches within a broad historical and geographical frame, we hope that the volume will instigate and sustain a dialogue within and across fields that too often, to adopt a (second) oral metaphor, do not talk to each other.

---

33   For a very full and varied discussion of this phenomenon, see G. Calame-Griaule (ed.), *Le Renouveau du conte* (Paris, CNRS, 1991).

SECTION ONE

The oral-written dynamic in early modern France

The shadow of orality in the Voltaire *conte*

RICHARD FRANCIS

No one could possibly mistake the Voltaire *conte* for anything other than a sophisticated literary construct aimed at reaching its public through the written page rather than the spoken word. It is true that Voltaire was a gifted *raconteur*, as well as an enthusiastic amateur actor, and it is possible, though by no means certain, that some of his earliest *contes* grew out of improvised performances to entertain the Duchesse du Maine and her circle in the château de Sceaux, but his activity as a published *conteur* did not develop until late in life, when he was in exile and detached from the *mondain* audiences that would have appreciated such performances. The majority of his *contes* emanated from Geneva and Ferney, and were planned from the start as publishing operations. Yet his fiction draws on rich and varied traditions, and the purpose of this Chapter is to consider what he owes to oral narrative traditions, and in what ways he uses oral narration, or its appearance, as a device.

Voltaire's fiction shows signs of a certain mistrust of oral communication. In the first place, it is unreliable. The story of *Les Oreilles du comte de Chesterfield* hinges on a deaf lord who mishears a suppliant's request to be relieved of his 'pauvreté', thinks he wants to be cured of a 'mal à la vessie' and sends him to a surgeon rather than giving him the post he wants.[1] Even wordless communication can do better than this, as witness the success of the deaf mute in *Zadig* who warns the hero and heroine of a plot against them by telling the story in pictures.[2] Secondly, Voltaire finds oral

---

1   Voltaire, *Romans et contes en vers et en prose*, ed. E. Guitton (Paris, Livre de Poche, 1994), 794. This edition has the advantage of presenting the verse *contes* alongside the better-known works in prose.
2   Voltaire, *Romans et contes*, 82.

storytelling of little practical use. In two *contes* he portrays attempts to console the suffering by telling them stories of others suffering from similar problems, only worse, and the attempts prove unsuccessful. In *Les Deux Consolés*, a lady in distress cannot be distracted by a philosopher's tales of the sufferings of queens, discovering in the end – as indeed does the philosopher himself – that time alone is the great healer,[3] and Amaside in *Le Taureau blanc* reacts with irritation to attempts to amuse her with stories while her beloved is under sentence of death. In the latter case, to make matters worse, the narrator is none other than the serpent who tempted Eve; oral narrators can be dangerous seducers and Amaside is tricked into saying things that place her own life at risk.[4] Thirdly, and most seriously, Voltaire was profoundly ambivalent about myths and fables. He discovered this kind of tale, no doubt, through written sources such as Homer, Hesiod and Ovid, but their original source would have been oral tradition. He could enjoy such things if the poetry was good enough,[5] in other words precisely at the point where literary convention takes over from spontaneous orality, but as historian and philosopher he was annoyed at suggestions that they had any kind of truth to communicate. They had little to reveal, in his view, about the early history of nations, and even less about religious truths; in this, the more outlandish stories of the Old Testament differed in no way from Egyptian and Greek myth, and one function of Voltaire's late *conte*, *Le Taureau blanc*, is to further his anticlerical campaign by juxtaposing figures from scripture and mythology in a series of undignified situations. Truth should be sought, not in the unpolished imagination of folk traditions, but in reason and properly documented historiography, which might by comparison look prosaic alongside colourful traditional tales, but that makes it all the more necessary to devise a new type of philosophical fable, respectful of the findings of reason, which would offer an equally entertaining counterblast to old and false traditions. This is what

3   Voltaire, *Romans et contes*, 205.
4   Voltaire, *Romans et contes*, 761–765.
5   See his judgement on Homer in the *Apologie de la Fable*: 'Il ment, mais en grand homme; il ment, mais il sait plaire', *Romans et contes*, 485.

the Voltaire *conte* tries to achieve, and in rejecting traditions that take their origin in oral narrative, it will perforce favour the written.

Eighteenth-century fictional works tend to take great care to define their narratorial situation. Be they first-person or third-person, they spell out whether they are authentic documents rediscovered, collections of letters, narrations written for a specific purpose or recorded oral tales; the scenarios given are, of course, usually fictional, but completely free-standing narrations with no explanatory paratext are relatively rare. This fashion is, of course, related to the emerging novel's drive for respectability and plausibility; Voltaire, who has no pretensions to be a novelist, is less affected than some, but it does afford him a playful and often necessary way of covering his tracks, and most of his fiction has some kind of initial statement of its supposed origins. The advantages of having a defined narratorial situation may perhaps be seen as threefold. First, there is the purely narrative advantage to be gained from the telling of a story from an unambiguous focalising position, which has much to offer in terms of vividness and mimetic plausibility, especially if it involves eyewitness testimony. Second, where the focaliser is intradiegetic, a narrator telling a story in which he or she is a participant, a uniquely intimate approach to character development becomes possible. Finally, a defined narrative voice may be a means of facilitating any polemic purpose that the author may have, either by providing a constructed persona onto whom he may project a body of ideas that it may be convenient for him not to present in his own name, or by allowing him to experiment with the implications of an intellectual position to which he is reluctant fully to commit himself. In a nutshell, the device may be used for purposes of storytelling, characterisation or rhetoric.[6] All of these have some importance for Voltaire, but his concerns are not always those of his novelist contemporaries.

---

6   It may be useful to clarify, in this paper devoted to orality, that the term 'rhetoric' is used throughout in its broadest sense of language being used in any way to persuade. It does not necessarily imply the devices of oratory.

This care taken over defining the narrative persona tends to encourage the pretence that a story, even a written one, is told orally, but such is, of course, not necessarily the case, and in Voltaire's fiction it is very rare that narratives are so presented. One device particularly striking by its absence, for instance, is what we might call the Scheherazade option, in which a series of short stories is strung together by attributing them to one unifying oral narrator telling them for a specific purpose. The recently translated *Thousand and One Nights* was highly fashionable and Voltaire enjoyed using oriental settings, but he makes little use of framework narratives of any kind, and that in itself is enough to limit the scope for an imaginary oral narrator, who can be found only in a very few of his shorter *contes*. The twin works *L'Éducation d'un prince* and *L'Éducation d'une fille*, for instance, use the traditional device of an old man on a winter evening telling a fireside story to children,[7] but it is used ironically; one of these stories is a philosophical fable and the other a mildly libertine tale, neither of which would be suitable fare for children. Tellingly, both are verse *contes*, and it is here rather than in prose that Voltaire is prepared to use the pretence of oral narration. The conventional language of Voltairean verse is far removed from the language of oral narration, which suggests that he is prepared to present his works as oral narration only when there is little possibility of the reader taking the claim seriously.[8] In major fictions, such as *Zadig*, *Candide*, *L'Ingénu* and *La Princesse de Babylone*, the genres that Voltaire has in mind, either as models or targets for satire, are seventeenth-century novels and the romances of Ariosto, as much as more recent works that follow the fashion for defining narratorial situation; that too has its part to play in restricting any pretence of orality.

Working in a similar direction is Voltaire's relatively limited use of first-person narration. Again, there is no necessary relationship between first-person narration and oral narration; many eighteenth-century novels

---

7   Voltaire, *Romans et contes*, 378, 385.
8   Voltaire does, however, use oral narration within the verse *conte* as a kind of *exercice de style*. In two such works, *Les Trois Manières* and *Le Dimanche ou Les Filles de Minée* he portrays three girls of contrasting character vying with each other by telling stories in contrasting verse metres.

related in the first person are unambiguously presented as written documents and could not be anything else. Yet first-person narration, by the sense of immediacy that it generates and the attention it can focus on narrating persona and narratorial situation, readily accommodates the pretence of oral narration, and the two are often fruitfully coupled; *Manon Lescaut*, in the world of the novel, is an obvious example. Again, however, this particular type of defined narratorial situation is primarily useful to the novelist, whose concern tends to be with entering into the mind of his protagonist; Voltaire, whose concerns are with rhetoric rather than characterisation, has different priorities. None of his major *contes* are wholly couched in the first person; the relatively brief *Scarmentado* is the only one to use first-person narration for a complete fictional biography in the style of so many contemporary novels, and it shows no trace of orality; the narratorial situation is undeveloped, it is explicitly a written rather than a spoken text and its highly disciplined, sardonic style, so obviously a dry run for that of *Candide*, shows little sign of oral influence.[9] Voltaire simply does not seem comfortable with intradiegetic focalisation. The idea of building one of his characters into a central focalising persona who can, as it were, change the telling of a story into a conversation with the reader, or admit the reader into his intimate feelings, has little to contribute to the essentially rhetorical aims of Voltaire's fiction. Although there is clearly no simple or necessary relationship between the presence of such a character and an effective impression of oral narration, the absence of any such character does restrict the emergence of any such impression.

For all that, the narrating persona in the Voltaire *conte* is far from unimportant; in fact it is crucial. In the broadest sense of the word, these *contes* are works of rhetoric, whose function is polemic and whose material is tendentiously and ironically slanted so as to guide the reader's intellectual response. The narrator is the rhetorician manipulating the reader; he is not often named, not always presented in a clear relationship to the diegesis, and can sometimes show signs of deliberate ambiguity in the way

---

9   Its full title is *Histoire des voyages de Scarmentado, écrite par lui-même.*

he is represented.[10] Yet he is always strongly characterised by his style, and those readers who know Voltaire only through the ironic playfulness of his major *contes* might be tempted to conclude that this is the style of Voltaire himself, and perhaps to detect orality in the thought that this is Voltaire himself talking to the reader. Such a conclusion would be justified to the extent that the relative informality of the *conte* allowed Voltaire freer play than many of the grander genres that he also cultivated. Yet ultimately this is a simplistic view; Voltaire is a stylistic virtuoso capable of writing in many voices according to his choice of genre, and the nature of the narrating persona he adopts varies considerably between and even within *contes*.

It is revealing, in this context, that the *contes* in which he makes most use of first-person narration are precisely those in which the narrative element is least important and the rhetorical function is most to the fore. *Pot-pourri*, *L'Homme aux quarante écus* and the *Histoire de Jenni*, late works characterised by great flexibility of narratorial mode, are the best examples. Yet even here, first-person narration is only one mode among several; episodes so narrated alternate, often without apparent reason, with third-person narration or dialogue scenes. All three of these *contes* are, in fact, primarily means of staging philosophical dialogues, in which the narrative interest is minimal. Their use of dialogue adds a touch of orality to them, of course, but the dialogue tends to be literary and conventional in character, so it is little more than a touch, and in any case it is orality used for discursive rather than narrative purposes, hence it lies somewhat outside the scope of the present study. In general terms, we may perhaps draw the provisional conclusion that, though Voltaire is less interested in character development than his novelist contemporaries, he shares their concerns for vivid storytelling, and his intense desire to make a rhetorical appeal to the reader, to influence the reader's way of thinking, makes it important for him to build a relationship between reader and narrating persona which

10   In the occasional instances where a narrator is named, he tends to be a shadowy extradiegetic figure, the naming of whom offers little to the reader's perception of the story he is purported to relate. Dr Ralph in *Candide* is a typical example.

shares something of the immediacy of oral communication. It is no more than a shadow of orality, perhaps, but shadows can be important.

If we turn to the use made of oral narration as a device within the *conte* for embedding secondary narrations, rather than as the central narratorial mode, we find something much more substantial. Voltaire's *contes* represent oral narration in a variety of ways and for a variety of purposes, and the rest of this paper will attempt to categorise some of them. The most obvious device that should be mentioned is the interpolated tale, a substantial narration embedded in a written narrative purporting to be related orally to the central hero, usually involving a completely separate set of characters but often providing a variation on themes established by the central narration. This is a popular device in the novel; *Manon Lescaut* will serve again as an example. But it is, on the whole, conspicuous by its absence from Voltaire's *contes*, not only because they tend to be too short to encompass such things, but also because the diffusion of interest inherent in long interpolations is rarely conducive to sharp polemic focus. Interpolated tales are acceptable in works written as entertainments for a leisured public not unduly worried about structure, and even in that context they have their risks. If Voltaire uses interpolations, they are usually short, maybe of only tangential relevance to the central narrative, but always with a polemic point. This is just the kind of interjection that one might expect to find in a good wide-ranging but unstructured conversation between intelligent people, and to this extent we may detect a link with the world of orality.

Such interpolations can be analysed in terms of how sharply they are distinguished from the central narration, ranging from formal interventions with a clearly signalled change of narrator to anecdotes inserted into conversations. If we start with the former, it is worth noting that Voltaire often uses an oral narrator if he wishes to include a fable or allegory in a longer *conte*. One of Voltaire's most sharply anticlerical texts, the *Relation de la mort du jésuite Berthier*, after narrating the said Jesuit's death, brings him back from purgatory to relate an encounter with the allegorical figures of the seven deadly sins,[11] and the *Éloge historique de la raison*, relating the progress of the allegorical figures of Truth and Reason through history until the relatively congenial present day, is presented as an oral narration in the form of a speech by a provincial academician.[12] Very little is made here of the oral framework, but it is the only one of Voltaire's prose *contes*, as opposed to the verse *contes* mentioned earlier, where the basic narratorial situation purports to be oral, and again the highly conventionalised nature of the material makes it hard to take the claim of orality seriously.[13]

The most extensive purportedly oral narrations in Voltaire's *contes* take the form of what we might call 'catch-up narrations'. They occur principally where the main story line is complex, involving characters in separations followed by reunions at which they tell each other what they have been doing while separated. This is, of course, a device much used in the novel, a genre that Voltaire's longer *contes* often parody, and the way the device is used gives clues to his parodic aims in each text. In *Zadig*, we find it during the hero's absence from Babylon, when he is informed of events in the city by a series of oral narrations from the brigand Arbogad, the fisherman and Queen Astarte, each of which cumulatively reveals part of the picture to Zadig. Apart from their expository function, these narrations form an *exercice de style* with their contrasting tone; Arbogad's is a boastful, cynical account of his brigandry, in which the anarchy in Babylon, though of crucial importance to Zadig, figures only incidentally.[14] The fisherman's account of his misfortunes in Babylon's civic upheavals begins as a pathetic monologue akin to a theatrical soliloquy and continues in a dialogue with Zadig which draws on the well-established romanesque topos of two unfortunate characters each claiming to be more unfortunate than the other.[15]

---

11   Voltaire, *Romans et contes*, 317.

12   Voltaire, *Romans et contes*, 774.

13   The title is the only evidence we have that this is meant to be a speech, and the sole hint of oral presentation in the body of the text is the curt initial statement: 'Vous m'ordonnez de vous faire l'éloge de la Raison', there being no indication of who the 'vous' might be.

14   Voltaire, *Romans et contes*, 99–100.

15   Voltaire, *Romans et contes*, 101–103.

The focus here is still on the plight of the fisherman, a little man caught up in a revolution; it tells Zadig little of the fate of Astarte herself, which must wait till her own narration, the fullest and most substantial, delivered with queenly dignity. But her dignity, and with it the pretensions of the standard novel heroine, is subverted by her failure to inspire, by her speech, the respect of her captor, the Prince of Hyrcania; she too emerges as an ordinary woman suffering in difficult times, and gaining little from her royal rank.[16] These narrations are part of the gentle parody of prevailing modes of the novel that runs through this *conte*, and their three different angles on the sufferings of individuals at times of civic disorder introduce a satirical theme that will move centre stage in *Candide*. Also, incidentally, they are a relatively rare example of Voltaire achieving differentiated characterisation by manipulation of narratorial mode. *Zadig* further uses the catch-up narration to develop another satirical theme, that of the difficulty of achieving justice. On several occasions, an oral exchange of narratives is required to correct a misleading impression or to answer an accusation; Zadig does so at some length in the celebrated story of the escaped dog and horse, whom he identifies through their tracks without having actually seen them,[17] more briefly, to justify his killing of Missouf's lover,[18] and again at the closing tournament to explain how Itobad has stolen his armour.[19] The difficulty of arriving at a complex truth is one of the main themes of this *conte*, and the juxtaposition of oral testimonies is an effective device for exploring it.[20]

16 'J'avais toujours entendu dire que le ciel attachait aux personnes de ma sorte un caractère de grandeur qui, d'un mot et d'un coup d'œil, faisait rentrer dans l'abaissement du plus profond respect les téméraires qui osaient s'en écarter. Je parlai en reine, mais je fus traitée en demoiselle suivante. L'Hyrcanien, sans daigner seulement m'adresser la parole, dit à son eunuque noir que j'étais une impertinente, mais qu'il me trouvait jolie'; Voltaire, *Romans et contes*, 108.

17 Voltaire, *Romans et contes*, 68–70.

18 Voltaire, *Romans et contes*, 86.

19 Voltaire, *Romans et contes*, 121.

20 A further example of the truth emerging through oral testimonies, though with only a limited narrative element, is the trial scene in which the crucial witness to the exchange of a contract is a mute stone; Voltaire, *Romans et contes*, 89.

In *Candide* we again find parody of the novel with its frequent use of catch-up narrations, but linked even more closely with the theme of the individual's sufferings in an unjust world. Candide in his wanderings is constantly separated from and reunited with friends and associates, who with each reunion bring news of fresh disasters. Pangloss and the Baron, twice each, Cunégonde, Paquette and Giroflée all have their lurid tales to tell, and in the story of la Vieille we find Voltaire's closest approach to a full-blown interpolated tale, in which a new character's extended account of her past life gives a fresh angle on this harrowing catalogue of man's inhumanity to man by exploring man's inhumanity to woman.[21] Its length, however, makes it the exception rather than the rule in this *conte*, where most interpolations are short, sometimes extremely so, as in the case of the brief tales told by six exiled kings to explain their presence at the carnival of Venice.[22] The purpose of this brevity is clear: to emphasise the shock effect of the new sufferings that each tale presents. Here is how one of the six kings tells his story; the others are all in parallel form:

> Je m'appelle Achmet III; j'ai été grand sultan plusieurs années; je détrônai mon frère; mon neveu m'a détrôné; on a coupé le cou à mes vizirs; j'achève ma vie dans le vieux sérail, mon neveu le grand sultan Mahmoud me permet de voyager quelquefois pour ma santé; et je suis venu passer le carnaval à Venise.[23]

The short, paratactic clauses and shifting tense usage of this brief narration project an effective impression of orality in this grim tale, where the complete lack of detail or of any attempt to soften the horror of events is typical of *Candide*. There are clear advantages in presenting this as part of a dinner party conversation, which lends itself to brief narratives and to the presentation of even serious material with a certain lightness of touch. Such bluntness also has its part to play in the parody of the novel, as may be seen at the first reunion of Candide and Pangloss: the latter has just stated that Cunégonde is dead, and Candide proceeds to enquire:

---

21   Voltaire, *Romans et contes*, 234–241.
22   Voltaire, *Romans et contes*, 288–289.
23   Voltaire, *Romans et contes*, 288.

> Mais de quelle maladie est-elle morte ? Ne serait-ce point de m'avoir vu chasser du beau château de monsieur son père à grands coups de pied ? – Non, dit Pangloss, elle a été éventrée par des soldats bulgares, après avoir été violée autant qu'on peut l'être.[24]

His narration continues with more shocking details of warfare and pillage. The contrast between Candide's naïve assumption that the lady died for love of him like the heroine of a novel and the harsh reality of affairs could hardly be more marked, and the contrast of tone between the two speakers, Candide high-flown and literary where Pangloss is blunt and down to earth, plays its part in the effect.

As the story switches between the central narrator and various oral first-person narrators, it becomes possible to vary narratorial tone. Voltaire to some extent avails himself of this; as in *Zadig*, style of narration does occasionally have things to reveal about character. Pangloss's pedantry emerges in the genealogy he provides for his syphilis,[25] Cunégonde demonstrates her sexual ambivalence in the way she couples a certain relish in recounting her sexual adventures with a total lack of any sense that this might devalue her as a novel heroine,[26] the Baron reveals his homosexuality without actually naming it and la Vieille, with her constant refrain stressing the commonplace nature of the ills that afflict her, demonstrates her resilience and abiding love of life. Yet there are, as ever, limits to how far Voltaire seeks to characterise by dialogue, and the prevailing tone remains that of the central narrator. As an illustration, in the passage quoted above, Candide alludes to having been 'chassé à grands coups de pied' from the Baron's castle, but the phrase is actually first used by the central narrator, who tells us at the outset how the Baron 'chassa Candide du château à grands coups de pied dans le derrière',[27] and like a leitmotif it recurs in the speech of Paquette[28] and Pangloss,[29] who cannot be supposed to be quoting

---

24   Voltaire, *Romans et contes*, 216.

25   Voltaire, *Romans et contes*, 216.

26   'Une personne d'honneur peut être violée une fois, mais sa vertu s'en affermit'; Voltaire, *Romans et contes*, 228.

27   Voltaire, *Romans et contes*, 208.

28   Voltaire, *Romans et contes*, 280.

29   Voltaire, *Romans et contes*, 300.

anybody. For Voltaire, the humorous effect of the repetition outweighs any desire to provide each character with a consistent mode of speech; a full account of narratorial mode in Voltaire would indeed reveal that deliberate inconsistency is often a feature of it. This perforce limits the uses he can make of oral narration.

In *L'Ingénu*, there are no catch-up narrations, despite there being an excellent opportunity for one in the long separation of the hero and heroine; the central narrator simply follows the two characters in their separate adventures, and at their reunion the stories they tell each other are elided. Even in the potentially pathetic scene in which the dying Saint-Yves confesses to the Ingénu her violation by Saint-Pouange, everything is done succinctly by summary and indirect speech.[30] This change in technique relates to the changed target of Voltaire's parody; *Zadig* and *Candide* allude to the seventeenth-century novel, the *Thousand and One Nights* and Prévost's *Cleveland*, while *L'Ingénu* attacks the sentimental novel of Richardson and Rousseau by means of holding itself at a certain distance from the potentially pathetic scenes it portrays; the suppression of dialogue helps the detached central narrator to maintain overall control. *L'Ingénu* contains only two significant oral narrations, the hero's tale of his first love in Canada, one of the few exotic touches in the portrayal of this Huron well on the way to becoming a Frenchman,[31] and Gordon's story of the prodigal son who arrests his own parents, a harrowing tale told as part of a discussion of the corrupt nature of the society of the time.[32] Neither of these is of any length.

In *La Princesse de Babylone*, we find examples of a related technique in which a first-person spokesman gives a traveller a brief oral account of the history of a country where he has just arrived. This is of particular value in this *conte*, where the hero and heroine pursue each other all over

---

30   'Ces paroles tendres et terribles ne pouvaient être comprises; mais elles portaient dans tous les cœurs l'effroi et l'attendrissement: elle eut le courage de s'expliquer. Chaque mot fit frémir d'étonnement, de douleur et de pitié tous les assistants'; *Romans et contes*, 549.
31   Voltaire, *Romans et contes*, 495.
32   Voltaire, *Romans et contes*, 545–546.

the world, but it is striking that Voltaire confines the device to societies being presented in a positive light; it is used for a portrayal of Catherine the Great's Russia[33] and of England,[34] as well as of the imaginary ideal society of the Gangarides;[35] the ideal society of Eldorado in *Candide* is presented in exactly the same way.[36] When the society in question is one that Voltaire wishes to criticise, such as Rome[37] and especially France,[38] he avoids using any such spokesman, presenting his observations through the words of the central narrator. One can only speculate on the reason for this, but it may be that in positive social portrayals he needs to suppress the detached irony that tends to characterise his narratorial mode, and he finds it easiest to do this by displacing the narration to a venerable representative of the society concerned.

Such narrations tend to feature as part of a dialogue, which is not surprising given the important part played in Voltaire's *contes* by philosophical dialogue; as we have seen, some of the later ones such as *L'Homme aux quarante écus* and *Les Oreilles du conte de Chesterfield* are little more than a series of dialogues held together by a relatively weak narrative framework. Yet it is within such dialogues that another form of oral narration comes into its own, the anecdote told to illustrate a point. With his well-known mistrust of metaphysics, Voltaire liked to clinch an argument with concrete examples rather than abstractions, and the amusing brief anecdote allows him to do so very effectively, well within the spirit of eighteenth-century salon conversation. The device allows a story to be told with extreme succinctness and wit, and gives much scope for tendentious slanting. In *Micromégas*, for instance, the eponymous space traveller from Sirius asks one of the tiny human scientists he encounters why a certain war is being fought. The scientist replies:

33   Voltaire, *Romans et contes*, 589.
34   Voltaire, *Romans et contes*, 594–596.
35   Voltaire, *Romans et contes*, 571–572.
36   Voltaire, *Romans et contes*, 256.
37   Voltaire, *Romans et contes*, 599.
38   Voltaire, *Romans et contes*, 602–603.

Il s'agit [...] de quelques tas de boue grand comme votre talon. Ce n'est pas qu'aucun de ces millions d'hommes qui se font égorger prétende un fétu sur ce tas de boue. Il ne s'agit que de savoir s'il appartiendra à un certain homme qu'on nomme *Sultan*, ou à un autre qu'on nomme, je ne sais pourquoi, *César*. Ni l'un ni l'autre n'a jamais vu ni ne verra jamais le petit coin de terre dont il s'agit; et presque aucun de ces animaux qui s'égorgent mutuellement n'a jamais vu l'animal pour lequel ils s'égorgent.[39]

There is a world of difference between this and the properly sourced and researched historical narration that Voltaire might have wished to write in other genres; in the subversive world of the *conte*, the value of this technique is clear, and such anecdotes, explicitly delivered by a defined 'je' to a defined 'vous', clearly gain from the convention of being presented orally. The device can be used for a variety of purposes, not always wholly satirical; here, for instance, is a version of Harvey's account of human procreation, taken from *L'Homme aux quarante écus*:

Le célèbre Harvey, qui le premier démontra la circulation, et qui était digne de découvrir le secret de la nature, crut l'avoir trouvé dans les poules: elles pondent des œufs; il jugea que les femmes pondaient aussi. Les mauvais plaisants dirent que c'est pour cela que les bourgeois, et même quelques gens de cour, appellent leur femme ou leur maîtresse *ma poule*, et qu'on dit que toutes les femmes sont coquettes, parce qu'elles voudraient que les coqs les trouvassent belles. Malgré ces railleries, Harvey ne changea point d'avis, et il fut établi dans toute l'Europe que nous venons d'un œuf.[40]

Though mildly satirical of the *esprit de système* involved in this particular scientific debate, and despite the tone of elegant sexual banter springing straight from the world of salon conversation, this is basically respectful of Harvey, and Voltaire's aim is scientific popularisation as much as satire.

Some of these anecdotes can be very brief indeed, amounting to little more than allusions to a story rather than actual narrative. This is especially the case when the story is a well known one with which Voltaire can expect his public to be familiar; in such cases the slanting of the story is more important than the story itself, which can readily be elided. In *Candide*, for instance, all Voltaire needs to do with the story of the scapegoating of

39   Voltaire, *Romans et contes*, 41.
40   Voltaire, *Romans et contes*, 647.

Admiral Byng after the battle of Minorca is summarise it in two wither-
ing lines: 'Il n'a pas tué assez de monde; il a livré un combat à un amiral
français, et on a trouvé qu'il n'était pas assez près de lui'.[41] Similarly, in *Le
Taureau blanc*, when the Witch of Endor tells the stories of the menagerie
of Biblical animals in her charge – Balaam's ass, Eve's serpent, Jonah's whale
and others – all she needs to do is mention them without going into detail,
and her dismissive tone fosters the disrespectful attitude to Biblical narrations that Voltaire is trying to develop in this *conte*.[42] With this degree
of brevity and ellipsis, one may wonder whether it is appropriate to call it
narrative at all; implied narration might be a better term. The allusiveness
of such a passage, however, is again redolent of conversation.

Whatever else it has achieved, this investigation will have demonstrated
the wide variety of narrative devices used in the Voltairean *conte*. Far from
being the careless throwaway that it was once thought to be, it is a highly
sophisticated genre full of calculated effects, and any extended study of
Voltaire's manipulation of narrative modes should take full account of
this. There is certainly scope for such an investigation, which is of course
far beyond the aims of the present study, but the very variety of devices
surveyed should give pause to any attempt to revive the old view of the
Voltairean *conte* as a hasty improvisation, and every step it takes away from
improvisation is likely also to be a step away from the spontaneity of orality.
Whatever Voltaire's skills as an oral *raconteur*, there is a limit to his willing-
ness to use the pretence of oral narration as a device in his *contes*, largely
because he is in reaction against the kind of stories most usually associated
with oral narration, the deceptive fable and the first-person narration in

41   Voltaire, *Romans et contes*, 278.
42   'Le serpent est celui qui persuada Eve de manger une pomme, et d'en faire manger à
son mari. L'ânesse est celle qui parla dans un chemin creux à Balaam, votre contemporain. Le poisson qui a toujours sa tête hors de l'eau est celui qui avala Jonas il y a
quelques années. Ce chien est celui qui suivit l'ange Raphaël et le jeune Tobie dans le
voyages qu'ils firent à Ragès en Médie, du temps du grand Salmanazar. Ce bouc est
celui qui expie tous les péchés d'une nation. Ce corbeau et ce pigeon sont ceux qui
étaient dans l'arche de Noé, grand événement, catastrophe universelle que presque
toute la terre ignore encore'; Voltaire, *Romans et contes*, 741.

the novel. If he draws on these modes of narration, it is usually in such a way as to subvert them and to discourage the reader from developing any kind of belief in them. Yet even though he has little interest in the advances made by the novel in terms of mimesis and characterisation, he values vivid, attention-grabbing storytelling, not only for its rhetorical possibilities but also for its own sake. The appearance of orality, as a means of achieving these objectives, is too useful to ignore, and his skill at ironic allusiveness, fostered in the world of salon conversation, contributes to the appearance. If few of his *contes* purport themselves to be oral narrations, the device figures frequently as a means of presenting shorter narrations embedded within longer *contes*, either in the form of episodes in complex plots or anecdotes to illustrate a point, and the tone of the oral narrator confers an immediacy and point even to texts where there is no specific pretence to orality. The study of such narrations, of which just a small selection has been presented here, can throw considerable light on Voltaire's objectives both as a polemicist and as a parodist of narrative modes.

Mises en scène de l'oralité dans les récits-cadres de Mme d'Aulnoy: les enjeux

SOPHIE RAYNARD

Mme d'Aulnoy est non seulement la créatrice du conte de fées littéraire en tant que genre, mais elle présente aussi l'avantage d'avoir mis en scène plusieurs situations de contage dans les récits-cadres de ses contes.[1] Dans cette étude, nous nous proposons de comparer ces scènes imaginées par Mme d'Aulnoy dans la fiction aux quelques situations authentiques de contage qui nous sont rapportées ou décrites dans la non-fiction par ses contemporains afin de voir s'il y a bien concordance. Les mises en scène de Mme d'Aulnoy sont-elles effectivement une reconstitution du phénomène de la naissance du conte de fées dans les salons ou à la cour, ou bien sont-elles plutôt censées représenter la situation idéale de contage? Ultimement, il s'agira pour nous de dégager les enjeux de ces mises en abyme du contage chez Mme d'Aulnoy.[2]

---

1   Elle a inséré le premier conte de fées en date dans son roman *Hypolite, Comte de Duglas* (1690).
2   P. Hannon offre une analyse théorique très pertinente de la mise en abyme dans les contes de fées féminins. Elle perçoit la mise en abyme de la situation d'énonciation comme caractéristique de l'esthétique des conteuses (par rapport à celle des conteurs): voir la section intitulée 'Fairy-tale aesthetics' dans P. Hannon, *Fabulous Identities* (Amsterdam, Rodopi, 1998), 157–163. Son interprétation est résolument féministe: elle y voit une mise en scène du corps symbolique des salonnières. Nous avons décidé ici de nous pencher exclusivement sur les rapports entre oralité et source livresque, c'est pourquoi nous ne reprenons pas les propos de P. Hannon, mais son ouvrage est incontournable sur la question générale de la mise en abyme dans le conte de fées. Elle joue notamment avec les expressions presque interchangeables de 'mise en abyme', 'mise en scène' et 'mise en spectacle', qui révèlent le rapport étroit qui peut exister entre les deux modes d'énonciation: l'oral et l'écrit.

Examinons pour commencer les scènes que nous savons s'être passées dans la réalité. Nous possédons d'abord le témoignage de la marquise de Sévigné, qui dans sa lettre du 6 août 1677[3] rapporte à sa fille une situation elle-même rapportée par un tiers, son amie Mme de Coulanges. Celle-ci aurait été témoin d'un nouveau jeu de société: 'des contes avec quoi l'on amuse les dames de Versailles; cela s'appelle les *mitonner*' rapporte Mme de Coulanges, et tente alors de reconstituer pour la marquise la scène dont elle a été témoin. 'Elle nous *mitonna* donc', dit Mme de Sévigné, 'et nous parla d'une île verte, où l'on élevait une princesse plus belle que le jour; c'étaient les fées qui soufflaient sur elle à tout moment. Le prince des délices était son amant. Ils arrivèrent tous deux dans une boule de cristal alors qu'on y pensait le moins. Ce fut un spectacle admirable. Chacun regardait en l'air, et chantait sans doute:

> Allons, allons, accourons tous,
> Cybèle va descendre'.[4]

Ce témoignage rapporté par la spectatrice et transmis à l'écrit par l'épistolière est pour nous très précieux parce qu'il nous renseigne sur l'apparition *orale* du conte de fées: celui-ci se présente avant tout comme un jeu de société mondain destiné à agrémenter la conversation. Mme de Coulanges en effet lui 'parla' d'une île verte: elle ne lui conta pas un conte figé. Aucune source écrite n'est mentionnée ni par Mme de Sévigné ni par Mme de Coulanges. L'origine du conte est sans importance: au niveau de l'énonciation, tout semble s'être passé à l'oral. Sur ce phénomène du récit offert comme prestation orale, Roger Duchêne rapporte une anecdote intéressante qui concerne un contemporain illustre de Mme de Sévigné: 'Bourdelot, dans une lettre de 1641, affirme que Condé se faisait lire "dès les six heures du matin jusqu'à huit heures du soir", soit pour se donner une excuse à ne pas parler, soit "qu'effectivement il eût de la passion pour ces sortes de livres

---

3   M. de Rabutin Chantal Sévigné, Marquise de, lettre 596, à Madame de Grignan, 6 août 1677, dans R. Duchêne (éd.), *Correspondance* (Paris, Gallimard-Pléiade, 1973–78), II, 515–517.

4   Sévigné, dans Duchêne (éd.), *Correspondance*, II, 516.

[les romans] qui lui donnaient matière de rêver profondément".[5] Ainsi nous apprenons que le Grand Condé lui-même se passionnait de lectures romanesques quand il n'était pas en train de s'illustrer héroïquement au combat. Ceci nous rappelle qu'il était de coutume chez les grands de ce monde de se *faire lire* plutôt que de lire et qu'on préférait *écouter* que *parler*. Ainsi donc on se faisait lire comme on se serait fait jouer un spectacle pour se divertir. La lecture offerte comme divertissement signifie pour celui qui écoute à la fois une économie de parole et un service reçu.

Maintenant pour revenir à l'exemple de Mme de Sévigné, semblablement, ce qui frappe dans la description de la scène de contage, c'est que notre épistolière est capable par la spontanéité de sa prose (grâce au recours aux discours direct et indirect libre) de re-mettre en scène l'expérience du contage. Le récit devient ainsi théâtre vivant et par là se transforme en fiction sous sa plume. Mme de Sévigné nous donne à voir ce qu'elle n'a pas vu elle-même et son récit nous engage au point que l'impression de vécu semble au lecteur plus forte qu'elle ne l'a été aux participants eux-mêmes. Son récit est de fait devenu la référence sur le sujet de la naissance mondaine du conte de fées et non pas le compte-rendu du témoin de la scène lui-même, Mme de Coulanges.

Dans son article sur la signification du romanesque chez Madame de Sévigné, Duchêne a suggéré que les apparitions répétées de la terminologie romanesque dans les *Lettres* trahiraient la vision romanesque que Mme de Sévigné se ferait de la réalité.[6] Il utilise justement cette même anecdote de l'épisode versaillais du conte de fées raconté par la marquise pour généraliser sur la propension des mondains à 'créer par la parole un monde en marge du réel, quoique dans son prolongement'.[7] Et du reste leurs rapports ambigus entre imaginaire et réalité reflètent également ce que nous voyons se passer dans le conte entre oral et écrit. 'Il y a de la vie au roman un va-et-vient qui repose sur le même plaisir de changer les réalités en les racontant',

---

5   R. Duchêne, 'Signification du romanesque chez les mondains: l'exemple de Madame de Sévigné', *Revue d'histoire littéraire de la France* 77 (1977), 578–594, 580.
6   Duchêne, 'Signification du romanesque', 578.
7   Duchêne, 'Signification du romanesque', 580.

remarque Duchêne, et ce terme de 'va-et-vient' nous semble particulièrement adéquat pour désigner la dynamique qui existe entre oralité et source
livresque dans le conte de fées.[8] Nous pourrions ainsi dire que de même
que Mme de Sévigné applique à la réalité un schéma romanesque, Mme
d'Aulnoy applique à la réalité un schéma merveilleux. Toutefois Duchêne
nous avertit que 'parce que le romanesque appartient à la culture mondaine,
il n'est pas, lui, employé sur le mode sérieux'. Il précise ainsi: 'Elément de la
"galanterie", il sert à égayer agréablement le récit et suppose une distance
critique entre lui et la personne qui l'emploie'. Il faut donc jouer le jeu pendant la lecture, mais bien le considérer comme tel une fois le livre fermé. De
fait, Duchêne explique que '[l]'erreur de Bélise dans *Les Femmes savantes*
est de croire sérieusement reconnaître le roman dans la réalité'.[9] Aussi nous
ne pouvons que concourir avec ce critique en remarquant que, de même,
l'erreur des personnages provinciaux du récit-cadre de Mme d'Aulnoy, *Le
Nouveau Gentilhomme bourgeois*, commettent l'erreur de prendre la féerie
au sérieux et par là se ridiculisent (tout autant que leurs modèles comiques
moliéresques).[10] Semblablement, nous souhaitons préciser qu'il est essentiel de ne pas prendre au sérieux l'artifice de l'oralité dans les contes de fées
de Mme d'Aulnoy. Aussi conclurons-nous avec Duchêne que les allusions
romanesques[11] dans le style langagier des mondains ne sont que 'les mots

8   Pour illustrer sa théorie du va-et-vient entre fiction et réalité, Duchêne mentionne aussi
     les deux exemples suivants: 'Les relations de Mlle de Scudéry et de ses amis donnent
     naissance aux "chroniques du samedi" tenues par Pellisson, avant d'être transposées
     pour devenir quelques-unes des pages les plus célèbres de *Clélie*. Inversement les sur-
     noms reçus du *Grand Cyrus* par Mme du Plessis-Guénégaud et ses amis sont repris
     par eux quand ils se rencontrent à Fresnes, et les aident à voir autrement la réalité ou
     du moins à la décrire différente'. Duchêne, 'Signification du romanesque', 581.
9   Duchêne, 'Signification du romanesque', 585.
10   Dans *Les Contes nouveaux ou Les Fées à la mode* (1698).
11   Barchilon, l'un des grands spécialistes de Mme d'Aulnoy, déclare en effet: 'Les contes
     de fées de Mme d'Aulnoy se lisent comme des romans raccourcis écrits principale-
     ment pour adultes'. Dans J. Barchilon, *Le Conte merveilleux français de 1690 à 1790:
     cent ans de féerie et de poésie ignorées de l'histoire littéraire* (Paris, Champion, 1975),
     38.

de code d'un milieu qui imprègne l'état d'esprit du temps'.[12] Le recours à la mise en scène serait effectivement chez Mme d'Aulnoy un phénomène de convention stylistique plutôt que de création pure. Il relèverait de ce goût mondain prononcé pour la fiction théâtro-romanesque (on pense notamment aux opéras de Quinault et de Lully qui sont adaptés de romans et qui sont aussi un genre nouveau alors très en vogue). Comme l'a remarqué Duchêne, c'est presque toute la prose mondaine qui se trouve contaminée par l'influence romanesque. Cet exemple de Mme de Sévigné l'illustre bien: le style du conte de fées semble déteindre sur sa prose; plus encore en racontant le conte de fées, on le vit virtuellement. Le reste du commentaire le prouve: 'Ce conte dure une bonne heure. Je vous en épargne beaucoup, en considération de ce que j'ai su que cette île verte est dans l'Océan; vous n'êtes point obligée de savoir exactement ce qui s'y passe. Si c'eût été dans la Méditerranée, je vous aurais tout dit, comme une découverte que M. de Grignan eût été bien aise d'apprendre'.[13] Ici, le ton ironiquement badin de l'épistolière nous invite en effet à jouer le jeu de la fiction pour mieux l'apprécier.

Nous mentionnerons un autre témoignage authentique de cette pratique mondaine de contage, donné quelque vingt ans plus tard, en 1695, cette fois par l'une des premières conteuses, Mlle Lhéritier, et sa description du phénomène concorde bien avec celle de Mme de Sévigné. L'information vient incidemment dans ses *Œuvres meslées* au début du conte 'Marmoisan,'[14] qu'elle adresse à Mademoiselle Perrault, et où elle décrit comment elle se serait elle aussi mise au conte, alors en pleine vogue: 'Je me trouvai il y a quelques jours, Madame, dans la compagnie de personnes d'un mérite distingué où la conversation tomba sur les Poèmes, les Contes et les Nouvelles. On s'arrêta beaucoup à raisonner sur cette dernière sorte d'ouvrage;

---

12   Duchêne, 'Signification du romanesque', 587.

13   Sévigné, lettre 596, à Madame de Grignan, 6 août 1677, dans Duchêne (éd.), *Correspondance*, II, 516.

14   M.-J. Lhéritier de Villandon, 'Œuvres meslées' dans *Contes. Mademoiselle Lhéritier, Mademoiselle Bernard, Mademoiselle de La Force, Madame Durand, Madame d'Auneuil*, éd. R. Robert (Paris, Champion, 2005 [Paris, Jean Guignard, 1696]), II, 43‒44.

on en examina de divers caractères, en vers et en prose [...]. On en raconta quelques-uns et cela engagea insensiblement à en raconter d'autres. Il fallut en dire un à mon tour [...]'.[15]

Ici, c'est dans le contexte d'une discussion salonnière sur un sujet de poétique que le contage a lieu, comme illustration pratique en quelque sorte. Nous soulignerons la distinction socio-culturelle de l'auditoire participant, sur laquelle la conteuse insiste, et qui est en tout conforme à celle décrite par Mme de Sévigné. Or ces deux témoignages authentiques que nous venons de rapporter sont bien différents de la situation reproduite en image par Perrault dès 1695 dans son manuscrit de contes en vers (reprise en 1697 dans sa collection de contes en prose). Le frontispice de ses contes évoque en effet la scène d'une paysanne en train de filer au coin du feu et racontant à des jeunes enfants des 'contes de ma mère l'oye'. Qu'en est-il alors de la représentation de la conteuse par Mme d'Aulnoy? Est-elle conforme à la représentation mondaine aristocratique qui nous a été donnée dans les deux exemples authentiques que nous venons d'évoquer, ou bien véhicule-t-elle ce mythe de l'oralité folklorique que nous trouvons chez Perrault?

La critique toujours en vigueur s'accorde pour dénoncer la fausse réalité décrite par Perrault[16] – à savoir l'origine directement folklorique de ces

---

15   Lhéritier de Villandon, *Œuvres meslées*, éd. R. Robert, 43–44.
16   J. Roche-Mazon, 'Les Fées de Perrault et la véritable Mère L'Oye', *Revue hebdoma-daire* 41 (1932), 345–360; P. Delarue, 'Les Contes merveilleux de Perrault. Faits et rapprochements nouveaux', *Arts et traditions populaires* 1 (1954), 1–22; et 2 (1954), 251–274; M.-L. Tenèze, '"Si Peau d'Âne m'était conté ...". À propos de trois illustra-tions des *Contes* de Perrault', *Arts et traditions populaires* (avril–déc. 1957), 313–316; R. Robert, *Le Conte de fées littéraire en France de la fin du XVIIe à la fin du XVIIIe siècle* (Paris, Champion, 2002 [1982]); L. Marin, 'Les Enjeux d'un frontispice', *L'Esprit créateur* 27.3 (1987), 49–57; J. Brody, 'Charles Perrault, conteur (du) moderne', dans L. Godard de Donville et R. Duchêne (éds), *D'un siècle à l'autre. Anciens et modernes. Actes du XVIe colloque du C.M.R. 17* (Marseille, CMR 17, 1987), 79–90; R. Zuber, 'La Voix de la conteuse et le goût du merveilleux', *Commentaires* 40 (1987–88), 752–755; G. Verdier, 'Figures de la conteuse dans les contes de fées féminins', *XVIIe siècle* 180 (1993), 481–499.

contes[17] – et beaucoup ont essayé de trouver les 'enjeux'[18] de ce frontispice ambigu quant à la représentation de la conteuse en vieille paysanne. Il s'agira maintenant pour nous d'essayer de dévoiler les enjeux de 'l'appareil liminaire' des contes de Mme d'Aulnoy pour interpréter cette figure de la conteuse selon elle.[19] Cet appareil consiste dans un frontispice, mais aussi et surtout dans les dédicaces et les récits-cadres de ses contes; aussi l'analyserons-nous dans son ensemble, à la manière des critiques qui ont analysé les seuils des contes de Perrault pour en trouver une interprétation cohérente.

I L'Oralité mise en question dans les 'préfaces' des contes de Mme d'Aulnoy

I.1 Le Frontispice des Contes nouveaux

Gabrielle Verdier a admirablement bien analysé le frontispice du recueil en tête du tome trois des *Contes nouveaux ou Les Fées à la mode*, 1698.[20] Ce frontispice selon elle a un statut particulier et diffère de façon significative dans ses enjeux de celui de Perrault. Il représente la 'Madame D...' de la page de titre: 'non plus la simple paysanne mais une sorte de sibylle, comparable par ses attitudes et son costume aux sibylles de Michel-Ange'.[21] C'est une femme à l'allure antique, mais qui traverse les âges car elle porte des lunettes afin de *lire* le livre ouvert qu'elle tient à la main, et Verdier d'ajouter que ce

---

17 N. Jasmin réitère les théories de R. Robert sur le passage de l'oral à l'écrit en ce qui concerne le conte de fées français de la période. Voir N. Jasmin, *Naissance du conte féminin. Mots et merveilleux: les contes de fées de Madame d'Aulnoy, 1690–1698* (Paris, Champion, 2002), troisième partie.

18 Pour reprendre le terme du titre de l'article-clé de Louis Marin sur le sujet.

19 Pour reprendre l'expression de François Rigolot dans son article théorique sur les préfaces.

20 Verdier, 'Figures de la conteuse', 481–499.

21 Verdier, 'Figures de la conteuse', 486.

livre est ouvert, ce qui signifie que la lectrice – plus savante que la fileuse traditionnelle tenant une quenouille au lieu d'un livre – peut en saisir le contenu. D'autre part, le titre du livre est le titre même du premier recueil de Mme d'Aulnoy, 'Contes des fées', avec pour sous-titre le titre du premier conte de ce recueil, 'Gracieuse et Percinet'. Or ce conte traite précisément d'une guenon 'raisonnante', qui 'répondait comme une sibylle à cent questions spirituelles et savantes'.[22] Aussi Verdier conclut-elle que c'est dans le rôle que l'auteur a voulu attribuer à la conteuse que ce frontispice à la sibylle proposé par Mme d'Aulnoy diffère de celui de Perrault. Et à la suite de Louis Marin, qui décrivait la scène de Perrault comme celle d'une 'énonciation *orale*', Verdier précise que la scène de Mme d'Aulnoy, quant à elle, 'si elle représente bien la "narration" des contes, c'est celle de leur *lecture*'.[23]

L'oralité se présente donc dans le frontispice de Mme d'Aulnoy sous la forme d'une lecture à voix haute d'un texte écrit. C'est du reste ainsi que le contage se fait dans la plupart des scènes encadrant le récit de ses contes: quelqu'un *lira* un conte à une assemblée exclusive et très attentive à partir d'un *cahier*. Verdier remarque aussi que la bouche de la sibylle du frontispice de Mme d'Aulnoy est fermée, contrairement à celle de la paysanne de Perrault, ce qui souligne selon elle 'la source littéraire, livresque du récit'. L'oralité de la situation de contage chez Mme d'Aulnoy se limite donc à la manière dont est lu un texte et ne représente en aucun cas la nature des origines de ce texte. Examinons maintenant les paratextes dans les recueils de contes de Mme d'Aulnoy pour confirmer cette hypothèse de l'oralité restreinte à la lecture à voix haute.

I.2 Les Dédicaces

Le tome premier des *Contes des fées* s'ouvre avec une dédicace 'À son altesse royale Madame', où la conteuse fait appel à la 'bonté' et la 'générosité merveilleuse' de sa dédicataire, qu'elle assimile ensuite à une fée au vu

---

22   Verdier, 'Figures de la conteuse', 486.
23   Marin, 'Les Enjeux', 51.

précisément de ces attributs 'merveilleux'.[24] La dédicataire devient même le modèle du personnage féerique: 'Ce sont sans doute de grandes princesses comme vous, Madame, qui ont donné lieu d'imaginer le royaume de féerie: on s'est persuadé qu'il fallait qu'il y eût des génies particuliers qui eussent pris soin de ces personnes incomparables, en qui tout est merveilleux'. Avec ses contes, Mme d'Aulnoy se propose modestement de divertir son altesse, et si Madame voulait bien lire ses contes, elle lui ferait ainsi un honneur infini et la comblerait plus que 'si toutes les fées de l'univers [lui] avaient fait part de leurs précieux dons'.

Cette construction d'un univers féerique propre à établir le contexte des contes à venir se poursuit ensuite avec l'évocation du lieu choisi pour le contage ou la lecture. En effet, le château et le domaine de Saint-Cloud ont souvent été décrits par les contemporains – notamment par Donneau de Visé dans le *Mercure galant* en 1677 et 1680 – comme étant ce qu'il y a de plus remarquable et rivalisant avec Versailles. Pour Mme d'Aulnoy, nul doute qu'il s'agit du cadre rêvé pour une re-mise en scène des contes de fées. Il est évident qu'en choisissant le domaine sublime de Saint-Cloud comme cadre principal de l'énonciation et de la réception de ses contes de fées, notre conteuse montre de façon symbolique que la caractéristique naturellement enchantée de ce cadre est le contexte idéal de l'acte de contage.[25] C'est ce cadre qui inspire la féerie, et non la féerie qui incite à la mimesis dans la réalité. Ce serait donc le phénomène inverse de l'anecdote au sujet de la duchesse du Maine qui cherchait dans ses loisirs à reconstituer un cadre artificiel ressemblant au monde de féerie et se faisait vainement appeler 'la grande fée'. Une des pionnières dans la critique sur le conte de fées, Mary Elizabeth Storer, commente en effet cette extravagance de la duchesse en

---

24 M.C. Le Jumel de Barneville, Comtesse d'Aulnoy, *Contes nouveaux ou Les Fées à la mode* par Mme D** [1698], dans *Madame d'Aulnoy. Contes des fées suivis des Contes nouveaux ou Les Fées à la mode*, éd. N. Jasmin (Paris, Champion, 2004), I, 149–150.

25 Sur *Saint-Cloud*, Jasmin note: 'Bien des romans du temps sont de même encadrés par le récit de promenades mondaines entre gens de bonne compagnie, fournissant le cadre idéal à la lecture de contes ou nouvelles. On citera, parmi bien d'autres, la *Psyché* de La Fontaine (1669) ou la *Célinte* de Mlle de Scudéry (1661)'; Jasmin, *Naissance du conte féminin*, 382, note 4.

ces termes: 'On vivait des Contes de fées avant d'en raconter'.[26] Dans *Saint-Cloud*, c'est au contraire la réalité merveilleuse (Madame et son domaine) qui inspire la fiction féerique.

Une autre épître dédicatoire, adressée de nouveau à Madame, vient faire écho à la première dédicace. Saint-Cloud y est évoqué comme 'l'heureux séjour', 'un palais enchanté', où Madame règne en maîtresse des lieux:[27]

> C'est là, que sous les pas d'une si chère hôtesse,
> En dépit des hivers, les fleurs naissent sans cesse.
> Les nymphes, les sylvains sortent de leurs forêts,
> Et viennent envier ou louer ses attraits.
> Vous verrez les beautés dont les dieux l'ont ornée,
> Ce que n'eût jamais fait la plus puissante fée.[28]

En somme, Madame surpasse même dans la réalité les fées que Mme d'Aulnoy a mises sur la scène et vient lui présenter: il s'agit là de l'ultime compliment qu'un auteur puisse faire à sa dédicataire, à savoir lui présenter sa création littéraire comme indigne d'elle tout en l'offrant quand même. Encore une fois nous voyons la nature purement rhétorique d'un tel recours stylistique, si ce n'est que dans le cas du conte de fées, la métaphore féerique devient plus astucieuse car on joue avec les mots en les prenant à la lettre. C'est dans ce contexte de compliment élégamment tourné que le premier récit-cadre *Saint-Cloud* commence, ne venant que reconfirmer la fonction merveilleuse du lieu dans la lecture de ses contes de fées.[29]

26   M.E. Storer, *Un épisode littéraire de la fin du XVIIème siècle: la mode des contes de fées, 1685–1700* (Genève, Droz, 1972), 12.

27   Dans le tome second des *Contes nouveaux ou Les Fées à la mode* de Mme d'Aulnoy.

28   Aulnoy, *Contes nouveaux*, éd. N. Jasmin, 725.

29   Aulnoy, *Contes des fées*, éd. N. Jasmin, 379–381.

I.3 Les Récits-cadres des contes de Mme d'Aulnoy: l'exemple de Saint-Cloud

Saint-Cloud est le texte qui offre le meilleur exemple de mise en scène de l'oralité car il le fait par le biais d'une mise en abyme extrêmement éloquente. Voici comment il se présente:

> Après avoir éprouvé tout ce qu'un long hiver a de plus rigoureux, le retour de la belle saison invita plusieurs personnes d'esprit et de bon goût d'aller à Saint-Cloud. Tout y fut admiré, tout y fut loué [...]. Madame D..., qui s'était lassée plus vite que le reste de la compagnie, s'assit au bord d'une fontaine. 'Laissez-moi ici', dit-elle, 'peut-être que quelque sylvain or quelque dryade ne dédaignera pas de venir m'entretenir.'[30]

Ce récit-cadre est ce qui fait l'originalité de Mme d'Aulnoy dans son usage de l'enchâssement. Ce n'est pas que le procédé en soi soit complètement original à l'époque de notre conteuse: Boccace, Marguerite de Navarre, Straparole et Basile, avant elle, ont déjà eu recours à cet artifice afin que leurs devisants puissent tour à tour narrer un conte. Mais ce qui est nouveau chez Mme d'Aulnoy, c'est qu'elle préfère encadrer ou insérer un récit dans un autre plutôt que d'offrir une succession de contes. En bref, la conteuse pratique la superposition plutôt que la juxtaposition selon le principe de la mise en abyme, et c'est pourquoi son exemple est particulièrement significatif pour notre propos. Selon Nadine Jasmin, en effet, 'ce dispositif narratif présente d'abord l'intérêt de mettre en scène l'oralité sous toutes ses formes, à travers les lectures diversifiées de lecteurs, de conteurs ou de récitants parfois fort proches de Mme d'Aulnoy, telle cette Madame D... s'avouant auteur des *Contes de fées* qu'elle lit à son auditoire attentif'.[31]

À ce titre, nous dirons donc que *Saint-Cloud* se présente comme le 'prologue' au premier recueil de contes, *Contes des fées*, car il y a assimilation de l'auteur (Madame D**, la signature des deux recueils de contes) et de la *persona* ('Madame D...', le personnage-auteur de *Saint-Cloud*).[32] En effet

---

30   Aulnoy, *Contes des fées*, éd. N. Jasmin, 379.

31   Aulnoy, *Contes des fées*, éd. N. Jasmin, 102–103.

32   Nous empruntons à François Rigolot cette terminologie nuancée de 'l'appareil préfaciel d'une œuvre littéraire': 'c'est surtout entre le prologue et la préface qu'il existe une différence théorique notable, la préface se constituant comme discours hors-texte

M. de Saint-P... dit plus loin à Madame D... pour la divertir dans sa solitude:
'Je vais vous donner les *Contes des fées* qui vous occuperont agréablement'.
Or Madame D... refuse sous le prétexte qu''il faudrait [qu'elle] les [eût] pas
écrits pour [la] laisser au moins prévenir par les grâces de la nouveauté', et
elle assure qu'elle peut rester là seule sans se trouver 'désœuvrée'.[33] Ainsi
Madame D... avoue ouvertement être l'auteur des contes qu'on lui propose
comme divertissement valable pour celui qui ne les aurait pas lus, mais en
tant qu'auteur, elle préfère se proposer une autre occupation, dont la teneur
n'est révélée que par la suite. En effet, elle rétorque à la comtesse de F...
qui regrette que Madame D... ait manqué le spectacle merveilleux que la
compagnie venait de faire durant la promenade que 'ce qui vient de [lui]
arriver [...] ne l'est pas moins'. Et Madame D... de raconter alors que dans
sa courte solitude elle a eu l'honneur de recevoir la visite de la Nymphe de
Saint-Cloud, qui lui a récité des vers admirables. Une marquise s'empresse
aussitôt de l'envier en ces termes: 'Vous êtes trop heureuse [...] d'être dans
un commerce si agréable, tantôt avec les muses, tantôt avec les fées!'. 'Vous
ne pouvez pas vous ennuyer, poursuit-elle, et si je savais autant de contes
que vous, je me trouverais une fort grande dame'.[34]

Le souhait qu'exprime l'auditrice distinguée de Mme d'Aulnoy en dit
long sur la façon dont l'entreprise de création littéraire était considérée par
les mondains aristocrates. Il s'agit en effet de la minimiser en la qualifiant
plutôt de 'savoir' inné ou à peine cultivé. De fait, le seul talent invoqué ici
est celui d'une mémoire exceptionnelle seule capable de donner lieu à une
restitution orale ou écrite. La mémoire de Mme d'Aulnoy a effectivement
été célébrée si l'on en croit les éloges dont elle a fait l'objet. Storer rapporte

---

(parole d'auteur, d'éditeur, de commentateur, de traducteur, etc.) alors que le prologue
fait déjà partie du texte (l'annonceur n'y est pas l'auteur lui-même mais son masque
narratif promu en présentateur)'; F. Rigolot, 'Prolégomènes à une étude du statut de
l'appareil liminaire des textes littéraires', *L'Esprit créateur* 27.3 (1987), 7–18, 12. Cette
définition du prologue est particulièrement pertinente dans le cas de *Saint-Cloud*,
où apparaît la 'Madame D...', *persona* de Madame D** (signature de Mme d'Aulnoy
sur la couverture de ses recueils).

33 Aulnoy, *Contes des fées*, éd. N. Jasmin, 379.
34 Aulnoy, *Contes des fées*, éd. N. Jasmin, 381.

en effet les propos flatteurs de La Porte et La Croix sur la conversation de Mme d'Aulnoy: 'Tout le monde recherchait avec empressement sa société pour jouir de son entretien. Rien n'échappait à sa pénétration; et elle répondait avec la plus grande précision sur quelque matière qu'elle fût interrogée. Elle avait l'art de rendre la conversation la plus stérile, par ses réparties ingénieuses et les remarques historiques qu'elle savait placer à propos'.[35] Charles de Mayer, l'éditeur du *Cabinet des fées*, renchérit en disant de Mme d'Aulnoy qu'elle avait beaucoup lu, que sa mémoire était excellente, 'que [p]ersonne ne savait mieux amener l'anecdote, et la faire sortir par l'à-propos', enfin que '[s]a facilité pour la composition était égale à celle de la conversation'.[36] Du reste, l'éloge de la mémoire se trouve évoqué par Mme d'Aulnoy elle-même dans son roman *Hypolyte, comte de Duglas* comme introduction au conte de fées, 'L'Île de la félicité', qui va être raconté. Le héros éponyme est dit être 'utilisé' par son compagnon 'pour entretenir les dames'; 'sa conversation est assez agréable' dit ce dernier et de l'enjoindre aussitôt de 'rappeler dans sa mémoire un conte approchant de ceux des fées'.[37] Dans ces deux méta-textes offerts par Mme d'Aulnoy – *Saint-Cloud* et le récit-cadre de 'L'Île de la félicité' – l'origine des contes en question reste obscure, et ne semble en aucun cas importer:[38] qu'elle soit orale ou littéraire, les talents que l'on reconnaît au conteur sont de nature orale. Dans sa performance, celui-ci doit faire preuve de mémoire et être capable d'improviser.

Quels sont maintenant les enjeux spécifiques de la mise en abyme du contage? Nous emprunterons d'abord à Anne Defrance son commentaire

---

35   Storer, *Un épisode littéraire*, 23, source tirée de l'*Histoire littéraire des femmes françaises*, II, 106–305.

36   'Notice des auteurs qui ont écrit dans le genre des Contes de fées' dans le *Cabinet des fées*, XXXVII, 43.

37   Aulnoy, *Contes des fées*, éd. N. Jasmin, 129.

38   M.L. Tenèze rapporte dans son article une citation de Stith Thompson qui s'applique tout à fait à notre propos: 'Une fois qu'un conte imprimé est devenu partie intégrante de la tradition orale, le fait de son origine écrite *n'est plus d'aucune importance psychologique*'. En bref, Tenèze explique que c'est le propre du conte que de revenir à l'oralité, peu importe la nature de ses origines. Le phénomène de va-et-vient entre oral et écrit est donc particulier au conte; 'Si Peau d'Âne', 316.

pour montrer l'invraisemblance patente de la situation de *Saint-Cloud* où
'Madame D...semble restituer de mémoire les quarante vers qui sont censés
avoir été prononcés par la nymphe quelques minutes plus tôt'. Or, nous
dit-elle, 'le narrateur "oublie" de dire si elle les lit ou si elle les récite'. Voici
alors comment Defrance tente d'interpréter cette scène invraisemblable:
'De deux choses l'une en effet: ou bien elle a composé ces vers pendant
le temps où la compagnie a poursuivi sans elle la promenade, ou elle les
a appris par cœur pour impressionner la galerie, et elle feint de les avoir
composés (et retenus) en très peu de temps. Quoi qu'il en soit, tout est fait
pour escamoter le recours à l'écrit et pour donner, par l'illusion de l'oral,
celle de la plus totale facilité de style'.[39] De ce commentaire, auquel nous
souscrivons tout à fait, nous retiendrons l'expression 'illusion de l'oral', pour
prouver notre hypothèse selon laquelle Saint-Cloud, par ses attributs naturellement merveilleux, représente effectivement le cadre idéal de contage et
non nécessairement le *locus* vraisemblable à de telles scènes de contage qui
se sont probablement faites dans des conditions plus prosaïques, dans un
salon ou dans une ruelle, et que l'auteur a préalablement répétées comme
avant toute performance.

Pour conclure sur ces exemples de mise en abyme de l'oralité dans
les préfaces aux contes de Mme d'Aulnoy, nous dirons donc qu'elles nous
éclairent à la façon de méta-textes sur les questions d'oralité et d'écriture.[40] L'acte de contage, tout comme la conversation, nous y est présenté
comme un exercice de style consistant moins en la *transmission d'une
information* spécifique qu'en la *manière agréable et divertissante* dont cette

---

39   A. Defrance, 'Écriture féminine et dénégation de l'autorité: les contes de fées de
      Madame d'Aulnoy', *Revue des sciences humaines* 238 (1995), 111–126, 121, note 29.

40   Citation de François Rigolot à l'appui: 'En termes de la théorie des "actes de langage"
      il faudrait souligner l'aspect *performatif* du discours préfaciel et, plus généralement,
      de tout l'appareil paratextuel. L'émetteur du message liminaire ne se contente pas de
      "déclarer": il prescrit. Son autorité est telle qu'il se croit autorisé à doubler la voix de
      l'auteur, bien plus: de se l'approprier. Grammaticalement cette autorité est marquée
      par l'emploi de la première personne dont le *dire* devient naturellement un *faire*';
      Rigolot, 'Prolégomènes', 11. Cette remarque nous autorise il nous semble à assimiler
      le 'je' de la phrase finale au 'Madame D...' de Saint-Cloud en ce que ce lapsus est
      révélateur de cette prise d'autorité de la part de la narratrice.

information est transmise, d'où la possibilité de bâcler la fin, comme il a été reproché souvent aux femmes auteurs de le faire une fois que le jeu menace de lasser, et comme la clôture du dernier recueil de Mme d'Aulnoy l'illustre bien: 'Il faudrait bien du temps pour écrire tout ce qui [se] passa. Je crains déjà d'avoir abusé de la patience du lecteur, je finis avant qu'il me dise de finir'.[41]

Ce dernier exemple où la conteuse se met elle-même en scène expose les limitations du récit en tant que rapport d'un fait réel. Il trahit en effet le fait que l'on ne peut jamais dans aucun récit rendre totalement compte de ce qui s'est véritablement passé ou dit *en vrai*. La fiction a l'avantage de pouvoir enjoliver la réalité, de n'en retenir que ce qu'il y a de dramatique et d'intéressant à lire, écouter ou regarder. Aussi la reconstitution de la réalité est-elle supérieure à la réalité elle-même, en ce qu'elle a la capacité de n'en garder que la substance valable et de le purger de l'insignifiant. Donner l'illusion de l'oralité à l'écrit revient à offrir à son public une performance virtuelle: il a l'avantage de n'en restituer que les grands moments. En gros, c'est présenter un morceau choisi de l'oralité vraisemblable. De même chez Mme d'Aulnoy la mise en abyme ne sert pas à reconstituer une scène de contage selon les règles de la vraisemblance. C'est seulement l'illusion, plus que la vraisemblance, qui est nécessaire pour donner une impression de naturel, de talent inné et non cultivé par le travail ou les répétitions (telles celles qu'un acteur doit endurer avant de donner le spectacle). La mise en abyme ici permet de créer le mythe de l'auteur amateur pour effacer l'aspect professionnel et laborieux du métier et n'en montrer que le génie conteur qui s'illustre mieux à l'oral à cause de l'illusion de la spontanéité.

Certaines conteuses ont été plus douées que d'autres à se forger cette réputation. Mme d'Aulnoy, bien qu'ayant eu un succès littéraire incontestable comme auteur de romans, mémoires et contes, a voulu donner l'impression qu'elle a été avant tout supérieure en tant que devisante en

---

41 Aulnoy, *Contes des fées*, éd. N. Jasmin, 1049.

direct.[42] Storer rappelle que quand elle fut élue membre de l'Académie des Ricovrati de Padoue, 'on la surnomma Clion, l'*Éloquente*, car elle aimait à conter; cela lui venait naturellement, sans qu'elle ne fît rien pour perfectionner son style ni pour polir ses ouvrages. Aussi écrivit-elle beaucoup plus de contes qu'aucun autre auteur'.[43] N'ayant depuis aucun moyen d'illustrer son génie oral – particulièrement ses qualités légendaires de mémoire et d'improvisation – le meilleur expédient qu'elle ait pu trouver pour le faire habilement à l'écrit, c'est précisément par le recours à la mise en abyme de la situation de contage, où elle a su représenter la conteuse en oratrice talentueuse faisant l'admiration de son auditoire par ses talents innés. Il ne faut donc pas se fier à ses mises en scène de contage oral pour reconstituer le contexte d'énonciation et de réception des contes car il n'est qu'une mise en abyme de la situation réelle, qui a nécessité sans aucun doute un travail de composition préalable dans l'imagination ou à l'écrit, peu importe, mais un travail ou plutôt la maîtrise d'un art comme Madame d'Aulnoy le fait dire à l'un des personnages principaux de sa nouvelle-cadre *Don Gabriel Ponce de Leon*: '[J]e ne laisse pas d'être persuadée qu'il y a de l'art dans cette sorte de simplicité et j'ai connu des personnes de fort bon goût, qui en faisaient quelquefois leur amusement favori' [438]. Et tout le monde – interlocuteurs ridicules comme honnêtes hommes – de renchérir sur cette

---

42   Les qualités que l'éditeur du *Cabinet des fées* a attribuées à Mme d'Aulnoy sont aussi confirmées par le témoignage direct de son amie et consœur Madame de Murat: 'J'ay fort connu Mme Daulnoy; on ne s'ennuyoit jamais avec elle, et sa conversation vive, et enjouée, étoit bien au-dessus de ses livres; aussi ne se faisoit-elle pas une étude d'écrire, elle écrivoit comme je fais par fantaisie, au milieu et au bruit de mille gens qui venoient chez elle, et elle ne donnoit d'application à ses ouvrages qu'autant que cela la divertissoit. Voilà une petite digression que vous me pardonnerez, je croy, parce qu'elle vous fera connoitre le caractere d'une personne dont l'esprit a été connu et estimé de beaucoup de monde' (citation extraite du *Journal* manuscrit de Mme de Murat dans ses *Ouvrages*, 173–174, et rapportée par Storer, *Un épisode littéraire*, 24). Cette désinvolture apparente nous rappelle la situation décrite dans le récit-cadre de *Saint-Cloud* où Madame D... profite d'un moment de répit et d'isolement quand le reste de la compagnie poursuit sa promenade pour composer de nouveaux contes de fées ou tout au moins pour trouver de l'inspiration auprès d'une muse.

43   Storer, *Un épisode littéraire*, 24, source tirée de Vertron, I, 426.

affirmation que la facilité et la spontanéité ne sont qu'illusoires: elles ne sont qu'une impression que la bienséance mondaine ordonne aux auteurs (surtout de petits genres) de donner si l'on veut recevoir les compliments auxquels on aspire. Chez les mondains, imiter le style oral à l'écrit, c'est vanter ses qualités oratoires naturelles. Mme de Sévigné l'a merveilleusement fait dans ses lettres, et nous avons voulu montrer ici que Mme d'Aulnoy a su le faire aussi à sa manière dans les récits-cadres de ses contes à travers la mise en abyme du contage.

A new history for fairy tales

RUTH B. BOTTIGHEIMER

I Disciplinary background

A key and long enduring belief about fairy tales holds that they were created by illiterate peasants and passed along orally by similarly illiterate peasants until they were gathered and written down by literate authors. It is often assumed that the form in which informants recounted fairy tales to folklorists in the nineteenth and twentieth centuries faithfully mirrored the form in which the tales themselves had existed centuries, or even millennia, earlier.

Understanding the position of folk and fairy tales within the study of folklore requires an understanding of their history vis-à-vis the discipline of folklore. In the 1880s and 1890s, the formative years of the study of folklore, folk and fairy tales were the principal object of study, as articles, addresses to the annual assembly, and letters to the editor in *Folk-Lore* and other national journals of folklore attest. A generally polite battle simmered between those who argued for the importance of print in the history and spread of 'folklore' and those who posited the folk as sole authors and as oral disseminators of folklore. For the oralists, print's only role lay in contaminating the folk's pure tales. In these early disputes, oralists generally carried the day, and with their victory came theoretical baggage: the absence of any evidence that certain kinds of tales existed before the 1500s was proof positive that such tales had been part of an undocumented oral tradition. In other words, an absence of documentary evidence proved the existence of an oral presence.

A century later, however, the province and concerns of folklore had vastly expanded and had adopted the evidence-based paradigms characteristic of modern research in the social sciences. Folk and fairy tales, the entity that had precipitated the study of the lore of the folk, became 'folk narrative'. Folklore generalists maintained an interest in folk narrative, and continued to address it with the theoretical approach and the research tools that had grown from late nineteenth- and early twentieth-century oralist researchers. Twentieth-century anthropological studies of illiterate, aliterate, and preliterate cultures, where individuals communicated tribal and family histories from one generation to another, lent weight to oralists' beliefs that folk and fairy tales, too, had been communicated by word of mouth over equally long periods of time.

Twentieth-century anthropological studies of exotic cultures thus confirmed, or at least appeared to confirm, conclusions reached by nineteenth-century nationalistically coloured folklore studies. Anthropologically oriented folk narrativists came to regard orally told tales gathered in the field as authentic, while labeling tales by known authors such as Giovan Francisco Straparola (c. 1480–c. 1557), Giambattista Basile (c. 1575–1532), Charles Perrault (1628–1703), and Marie Catherine d'Aulnoy (c. 1650–1705) as literary contaminations of pure oral tradition. Folklorists recognised Jacob (1785–1863) and Wilhelm (1786–1859) Grimm's fairy tales as having been edited,[1] but generally viewed them as less contaminated by literarisation. Social historians, psychologists, and literary critics and historians, having adopted these positions, perpetuate the views of folklorists that were codified by Laurence Gomme in his 1890 presidential address to the Folk-Lore society's membership.[2]

---

1   See J.M. Ellis, *One Fairy Story Too Many* (Chicago, University of Chicago Press, 1983).
2   See *Folk-Lore* 2 (1891), 1–30.

II Defining tales about fairies and fairyland, folk tales, and fairy tales

The paragraphs above conceal problematic assumptions, chiefly the definition of the English term 'fairy tale'. 'Fairy tale' conventionally appears without further explanation, just as the French and German terms *contes de fées, Märchen, Volksmärchen*, and *Zaubermärchen* are routinely used without precise definition. Although overlapping, none of these terms coincides perfectly with any of the others. I shall begin, then, by attempting to establish a more precise set of working definitions.

Expansible boundaries and flexible requirements for the genre complicate defining 'fairy tales'.[3] In broad parlance, 'fairy tales' refer to the stories in the Grimms' *Kinder- und Hausmärchen* (Nursery and Household Tales). The Grimms' collection, however, included a broad variety of sub-genres, most of which were actually *folk* tales of one sort or another. However, the fact that the collection became popular in English as 'Grimm's [sic] Fairy Tales' introduced a terminological confusion with far-reaching consequences for people's understanding of the nature and history of fairy tales themselves.

'Fairy tales' as a term has long been interchangeable with three fundamentally different sorts of narratives: tales about fairyland and fairies, folk tales, and fairy tales. Each of the three subgenres has its own history, cast of characters, style, and subject matter. The plots of each typically lead to characteristically different sets of narrative conclusions. Furthermore, the individual histories of each of the sub-genres has been indiscriminately and undiscriminatingly applied to the others. In particular, the millennia long history of folk tales has been grafted onto the briefer histories of tales about fairies and fairyland as well as onto fairy tales. Before proceeding

3   See R.B. Bottigheimer, 'Fairy tales and folk tales', in P. Hunt (ed.), *International Companion Encyclopedia of Children's Literature 1* (London, Routledge, 2004 [1996]), 261–274.

further, therefore, it will be useful to establish distinguishing characteristics for each.

Tales about fairies and fairyland, generally lengthy and stylistically
elaborate narratives, detail the adventures of fairy as well as of human
protagonists. Fairy and human characters pass into and out of each other's
worlds, each of which operates according to distinctive natural laws. The
fourth dimension of the human world functions as expected, but in fairyland, time proceeds at a radically different pace. Consequently, a human's
passage to and from fairyland can produce disastrous results, as it does in
Mme d'Aulnoy's 'L'Isle de la Felicité' (The Island of Happiness). Having
spent a year in fairyland with his fairy beloved, the princely hero is granted
leave to visit his homeland, with the proviso that he not dismount from
his fairyland horse. But he does so, in order to help an old man, and in that
instant he breaks the protective connection with fairyland that was meant
to protect him from suffering the results of its accelerated passage of time
while he is in the human world. Fairyland is equally maleficent in Mme
d'Aulnoy's 'Le Nain jaune' (The Yellow Dwarf), whose titular fiend captures
a beautiful princess and kills her adoring lover. Despairing, the princess
kills herself, and she and her lover achieve immortality as two palm trees
that forever incline towards each other, interweaving their fronds.

Though often called 'fairy tales', tales like 'The Island of Happiness'
and 'The Yellow Dwarf', with their highly developed plots and their parallel human and fairy worlds, are more properly designated 'tales about
fairyland and fairies'. In historical terms, their long documented existence
began before the age of print and continued to provide amusement for both
courtly and common listeners and readers in the early modern period.

'Folk tales' include a variety of sub-genres, such as animal tales, tales of
origins, warning tales, jests, and burlesques. Human beings who figure in *folk*
tales are generally people from daily life (husbands and wives, preachers and
doctors, soldiers and beggars, servants and tricksters) rather than kings and
queens. In terms of plot, the poor protagonists of folk tales frequently gain
wealth only to lose it at the tale's conclusion. Generally brief, a great many
folk tales are documentably ancient, with early versions recorded in the
ancient world. In the seventeenth century, Perrault's 'Ridiculous Wishes', a
'folle & peu galante fable' as he called it, retold a folk tale already hundreds

of years old, told by La Fontaine before him, and that would be told by many others in both similar and different forms in later centuries:

> Once upon a time Jupiter visited a poor woodcutter and gave him three wishes. While his wife was hatching grand schemes, he idly wished for a sausage, which instantly appeared. His wife, angered by losing one chance to wish for gold, pearls, rubies, diamonds, and fine clothes, irritatedly rebuked her husband, at which he exploded into a wish that the sausage stick to her nose. That came immediately to pass, so that the much chastened woodcutter had to use his third and last wish to rid his wife of the disastrous sausage.[4]

Typical of folktales, the poor couple ended up, in economic terms, exactly where they began.

'Fairy tales' differ both from tales about fairies and fairyland and from folk tales. Fairy tales have happy endings, whether the heroes and heroines are princes, princesses, country peasants, or born into urban poverty. In a fairy tale that begins with and principally concerns princes or princesses, royal protagonists generally experience a social fall that plunges them into poverty and suffering, during which they prove themselves in one or more adventures that involve magic and *from* which they emerge triumphant, resolving all problems in a dazzling wedding to an appropriately royal spouse. This ancient and comfortably gratifying plotline had existed in various literary forms for millennia, but in the Middle Ages magic – sometimes religious and sometimes secular – was added to the mix. Romances, composed of individual episodes strung one after the other in endless narratives, proliferated. When mass readership became a commercial factor in the late 1400s, abbreviated romance forms developed, and from these came far briefer tales in which magic propelled a suffering prince or princess into a wedding to another royal in a happy resolution. In terms of its history, this kind of restoration plotline consistently revolving around the eventual restoration of a royal protagonist to royal status is only a few centuries old. Such fairy tales can reasonably be called 'restoration fairy tales'.

---

4   'Les Souhaits ridicules. Conte. A Mademoiselle de La C... .' (A[ii]) in Perrault, *Contes de Perrault. Fac-similé de l'édition originale de 1695–1697*, ed. J. Barchilon (Genève, Slatkine Reprints, 1980).

A second group of fairy tale plots begins with a dirt-poor protagonist. In the earliest such tales, a poor hero's or heroine's adventures, successfully managed with the help of magic, lead to a marriage with royalty and material wealth, which together end their stories as a happily-ever-after idyll. The plotline of poverty, magic, marriage, and money in that order exists nowhere in the ancient or medieval world.[5] Newly created in Renaissance Venice, it is distinctly, and distinctively, modern.[6] Since tales in this group regularly involve the social rise of a poor protagonist, they can be distinguished from restoration fairy tales by the term 'rise fairy tales'.[7] They first appeared in Giovan Francesco Straparola's *Piacevoli Notti* (2 vols, 1551, 1553 Pleasant Nights); their numbers increased dramatically as old rise fairy tales were edited and new ones were created in the nineteenth and twentieth centuries. In the latter stage, however, material wealth as a sign and measure of life success diminished in literary importance, with a royal marriage itself becoming the sole denominator of a fairy tale happy ending.

To recapitulate: the three subgenres have histories of different lengths. Folk tales have existed for more than two thousand years; tales about fairies and fairyland a bit less than a thousand years; and restoration and rise fairy tales a little less than 500 years. The three subgenres also play out in different kinds of locations, typically with differing casts of characters and differing outcomes.

5   This proposition has elicited strong opposition from folklorists. See *I[nternational] S[ociety for]F[olk] N[arrative]R[esearch] Newsletter* 2 (2007), 17–26.

6   R.B. Bottigheimer, *Fairy Godfather. Straparola, Venice, and the Fairy Tale Tradition* (Philadelphia, University of Pennsylvania Press, 2002).

7   Bottigheimer, *Fairy Godfather*, 5–27.

III A new history of fairy tales

The traditional and still widely held definition of folk fairy tales (*Volksmärchen*) as pure and authentic and of literary fairy tales (*Kunstmärchen*) as contaminated and inauthentic is highly problematic. On the contrary, an increasing body of evidence suggests that the canon of European fairy tales was initially created by self-aware authors; that folk origins were not posited for these works until the late eighteenth century; and these literary texts were first edited into folk forms in the nineteenth century for nation-forming and educational purposes.

A thumbnail sketch of the history of European fairy tales that reflects the understanding of the genre outlined above begins in Renaissance Venice, picks up pieces in Baroque Naples, is codified in late seventeenth-century Paris, is moralised in the mid-eighteenth century and then spread throughout Europe first in French and subsequently in local languages, and is folklorised in early nineteenth-century Germany.[8] In this history of European fairy tales, the authors principally responsible for the formation of the fairy-tale canon were not legion, unlettered, and anonymous, but few, well-read, and documentable: Giovan Francesco Straparola in Venice, Giambattista Basile in Naples, Marie-Jeanne Lhéritier, Charles Perrault, Marie-Catherine d'Aulnoy, and Charlotte-Rose de la Force in Paris, Jeanne-Marie Leprince de Beaumont in London, and Jacob and Wilhelm Grimm in Germany. The overwhelming majority of European fairy tales known today derive directly or indirectly from these few authors' works, with an ancillary body of orientalised tales adapted from Antoine Galland's *Mille et une nuits*.

Europe's fairy-tale authors produced purposefully crafted texts, but it can be argued that each did so for individually differing purposes. Straparola produced a consumer commodity for the Venetian book market that ranged

---

8 R.B. Bottigheimer, 'Fairy tales, old wives, and printing presses', *History Today* 54.1 (2004), 38–44. For a detailed treatment of the same subject see R.B. Bottigheimer, *Fairy Tales. A New History* (Albany, SUNY Press, 2009).

from servant and artisan to noble financier; Basile parodically inverted
educational content and ideals of courtesy for contemporaries who shared
his educational background; Mlle Lhéritier and Mme d'Aulnoy reworked
Italian plots into long tales that continued an existing French fictional
style; Perrault reworked Italian plots into brief tales that broke new stylistic
ground; Mme Leprince de Beaumont assembled new literary models of
bourgeois morality and *honnêteté* from the elements of existing stories; the
Grimms further edited these and other narratives into a moral and social
vision for a national readership.[9]

As far as dissemination is concerned, the tales composed by the hand-
ful of named authors moved from their points of origin (Venice, Naples,
Paris, London, Berlin), which were also centres of print, and spread via
commercial trade routes that carried print products from one urban center
of population to another. At the local level chapbook peddlers carried fairy
tales along with a variety of other print products into the countryside surrounding Europe's towns and cities.[10]

Two important consequences follow logically upon the print-based
history posited here. The first is that literary texts preceded folkloric oral
performances of these tales;[11] the second is that printed texts underlie
oral performances.[12] As far as oral transmission is concerned, it might be

---

9   See R.B. Bottigheimer, 'Marienkind (KHM 3): a computer-based study of edi-
     torial change and stylistic development within Grimms' Tales 1808–1864', *ARV
     Scandinavian Yearbook of Folklore* 46 (1990), 7–31; and R.B. Bottigheimer, *Grimms'
     Bad Girls and Bold Boys: The Social and Moral Vision of the Tales* (New Haven and
     London, Yale University Press, 1987).

10   R. Schenda, *Volk ohne Buch. Studien zur Sozialgeschichte der populären Lesestoffe
     1770–1910* (Frankfurt, Klostermann, 1970); *Vom Mund zu Ohr. Bausteine zu einer
     Kulturgeschichte volkstümlichen Erzählens in Europa* (Göttingen, Vandenhoeck and
     Ruprecht, 1993).

11   A. Wesselski, *Versuch einer Theorie des Märchens* (Reichenberg in Böhmen,
     Sudetendeutscher V. F. Kraus, 1931).

12   K. Pöge-Alder, *Märchen als mündlich tradierte Erzählungen des Volkes? Zur
     Wissenschaftsgeschichte der Entstehungs- und Verbreitungstheorien von Volksmärchen
     von den Brüdern Grimm bis zur Märchenforschung in der DDR* (Frankfurt, Peter
     Lang, 1994), 17–23; Abd-El-Hameed Hawwas, 'A prologue tale as manifesto tale:

noted in passing that no documentation whatsoever exists to show that more than three oral tellings of what we in the modern world call a 'fairy tale' have ever existed between a book source and a subsequent witnessing of an oral telling of that tale. No footnote is possible here, since this statement is based on an absence of documentation. But any and every claim that a given fairy tale descended unchanged from an ancient past through repeated oral tellings is an imagined and invented history.

The invented history of oral transmission was formulated by Wilhelm Grimm in successive forewords to successive editions of the *Kinder- und Hausmärchen* between 1812 and 1857; his and his brother Jacob's writings about *Märchen* (brief tales) were given iconic status in Germany and beyond by their national and scholarly prominence. When twentieth-century anthropologists observed oral practices (such as tellings of apparently ageless traditions of family and tribal oral histories) in non-, pre-, or aliterate cultures, their findings were credulously, but mistakenly, applied to the practices of European storytellers who lived within literate and lettered print cultures, whether or not they themselves were able to read. The case of sources for stories told by illiterate storytellers was extensively explored by Rudolf Schenda (1930–2000), who for decades studied relationships between printed materials and oral tellings. His most focused treatment of the subject, in *Vom Mund zu Ohr* (1993, From Mouth to Ear), led him to describe '[t]he mediation of literary information via a literate person (schoolmaster, pastor, or chapbook seller) who read aloud to people unable to read for themselves [as] a *semi-literate* process'.[13] This history of fairy tales is at variance with nearly two centuries of scholarship, whose dominant direction Jacob and Wilhelm Grimm set in their *Kinder- und Hausmärchen* (Nursery and Household Tales) forewords. Nearly all nineteenth- and twentieth-century scholars and commentators accepted

---

establishing a narrative literary form and the formation of the Arabian Nights', *Marvels and Tales* 21.1 (2007), 65–77; C. Trinquet, 'On the literary origins of folkloric fairy tales: a comparison between Madame d'Aulnoy's "Finette Cendron" and Frank Bourisaw's "Belle Finette"', *Marvels & Tales* 21.1 (2007), 34–49.

13   R. Schenda, 'Semiliterate and semi-oral processes', trans. R. Bottigheimer [from *Vom Mund zu Ohr* (1993) 127–140], *Marvels & Tales* 21.1 (2007), 127–140, 127.

the Grimms' assertions that the fairy tales in their collection had had a long oral existence before being committed to paper, despite the fact that – as the Grimms themselves tacitly acknowledged – they had no firm evidence for their declaration.[14]

IV Early proponents of print history in the history of fairy tales

Despite the heterodoxy of this history of European fairy tales, there exists a respectably long and scholarly tradition of (principally) German-language research that supports these propositions. One early and cautiously voiced hypothesis for modifying the Grimms' position arose in an 1867 Göttingen dissertation by a young Herr Brakelmann, who proposed that Straparola's tales were part of a written tradition.[15] Others – like Moses Gaster, Joseph Jacobs, and W. R. Halliday, all of whom opposed the general belief that fairy tales originated in oral tradition among the folk – aired their views in the 1880s and 1890s in conjunction with the emergence and organisation of national societies for the study of folklore, which at that time meant, in effect, the study of folk and fairy tales.[16] By and large, however, *their* conceptualisations of the history of European fairy tales were rejected by the larger, more traditional, and more nationalistic forces in the study of folklore.

14   In forewords and epilogues to the *Kinder- und Hausmärchen* from 1812 to 1856 the
       Grimms implied the existence of Märchen of the sort they included in their volume
       in the ancient world and in the medieval period. However, they were never able to
       provide ancient examples of fairy tales, only of folk tales.
15   F.W.J. Brakelmann, *Giovan Francesco Straparola da Caravaggio* (Göttingen, E.A.
       Huth, 1867).
16   M. Gaster, 'The modern origin of fairy tales', *Folk-Lore Journal* 5 (1887), 339–351; J.
       Jacobs, 'The folk', *Folk-Lore* 4 (1893), 233–238; J. Jacobs, 'The problem of diffusion:
       rejoinders', *Folk-Lore* 5 (1894), 129–149.

Nonetheless, doubt persisted. In the 1920s the German folklorist Hans Naumann offered a two-culture vision of society in which fairy tales, first created by a literate elite, subsequently trickled down to the people.[17] A few years later the Czech-born comparatist Albert Wesselski, basing his work on print culture, published a global account of the origins and dissemination of fairy tales. Wesselski had the misfortune to live and work in the same period in which National Socialism was emerging as a potent force in a Germany whose unnuanced and unquestioning celebration of its folk resulted in an effective silencing of Wesselski's cogently argued views.[18]

Nearly two generations passed before evidence supporting the literary origins of fairy tales and their print dissemination was again investigated. In the magisterial *Vom Mund zu Ohr*, Rudolf Schenda presented the results of his study of the relationships between oral tellings and literary or print sources in the enormous and sometimes overlapping folk narrative repertoires of Italy, France, and Germany. Thirty years of research from 1970 to 2000 led Schenda to conclude that print was the single most important instrument for the dissemination of fairy tales.

Manfred Grätz similarly demonstrated the power of print processes with a stunning documentation of the wholesale movement of French-language fairy tales to Enlightenment Germany in the course of the eighteenth century.[19] And in her 1995 *Märchen und mittelalterlilche Literaturtradition*, Maren Clausen-Stolzenburg expanded the historical purview by working out literary relationships between high literature and fairy tales beginning in the middle ages and continuing into the nineteenth century.[20]

17 H. Naumann, *Primitive Gemeinschaftskultur. Beiträge zur Volkskunde und Mythologie* (Jena, E. Diederichs, 1921).

18 For more on Wesselski, see Pöge-Alder, *Märchen*.

19 M. Grätz, *Das Märchen in der deutschen Aufklärung. Vom Feenmärchen zum Volksmärchen* (Stuttgart, Metzler, 1988).

20 M. Clausen-Stolzenburg, *Märchen und mittelalterlilche Literaturtradition* (Heidelberg, C. Winter, 1995).

A print-based history of the fairy-tale genre has neither simple nurse-maids nor illiterate peasants as points of origin or as means of transmission.[21] It is an alternative history that presupposes and, more importantly, has evidence for, educated authors, literary texts, printers, publishers, translations and piratings, and an overall historical and documentable drift from literate classes to middling and artisanal consumers.[22]

V Charles Perrault's statements about fairy tales

But what of the literate authors mentioned here? What do they say about their own writings? What words do they use? In earlier work I argued that Charles Perrault had compiled his 'Peau d'Âne' from bits and pieces taken from Straparola and Basile, a discussion based on textual comparisons.[23] There is much additional evidence within Perrault's writings that confirms fairy tales' literary origins. For instance, in 1695 Charles Perrault addressed 'Mademoiselle de la C***' in the foreword to 'Les Trois Souhaits ridicules' (The Three Ridiculous Wishes), a folk tale he had just published. (See above for its content.) Perrault took it up now as part of his efforts to show that modern French tales had the same elevating instructional qualities that ancient Greek tales had had. Perrault spoke of the style in which he had

---

21   The illiteracy of nineteenth-century informants was often imputed or invented, contradicting actual fact. One particularly egregious example is that of Blind Stromberg, who lost his sight at the age of ten after copious reading in his boyhood. See G. Herranen, 'A big ugly man with a quest for narratives', in A.L. Siikila (ed.), *Studies in Oral Narrative* (=*Studia Fennica* 33 (1989)), 64–69.

22   R.B. Bottigheimer, 'France's first fairy tales: the rise and restoration narratives of "Les Facetieuses Nuictz du Seigneur François Straparole"', *Marvels & Tales* 19.1 (2005), 17–31.

23   R.B. Bottigheimer, 'Perrault au travail', in A. Defrance and J.-F. Perrin (eds), *Le Conte en ses paroles: la figuration de l'oralité dans le conte merveilleux du Classisme aux Lumières* (Paris, Desjonquères, 2007), 150–159.

rendered the tale with the verb 'inventer', proposing that what a person invents to tell a story is more important than the story's actual substance.[24] For her part, Catherine Bernard used the same word, 'inventer', but did so to discuss the story itself. In her *Ines de Cordoue* (1696), she had one character say that they would give Inès the rest of the day to invent the story that she was to present the following day.[25]

'Composer' was another word that Perrault used to describe what an author did with respect to tales like those he was working on. When he pretended to 'Mademoiselle', Louis XIV's niece, that not he but his son had prepared the stories of the 1695 manuscript of *Histoires, ou Contes du temps passé*, he wrote that nobody should find it strange that a child had taken pleasure in *composing* the stories of the collection.[26] Perrault repeated the same sentiment in the 1697 print edition. What might Perrault have meant by choosing this verb? Might he have borrowed the term from a culinary context, where it means assembling ingredients and as it did in the seventeenth century? It goes without saying, but it must be emphasised, that in cookery the constituent ingredients in a dish that one composes already exist. If the constituent narrative components were similarly pre-existent, what might they actually comprise in the case of fairy tales? Three significant elements – the editorial history of individual tales, the publishing history of Straparola's collection in France, and the distribution history of Basile's collection by the French-born Neapolitan publisher Antonio Bulifon – suggest that bits and pieces from their pre-existing works had

24 C'est la maniere
   Dont quelque chose est inventé,
   Qui beaucoup plus que la matiere
   De tout Recit fait la beauté ...
   Griselidis, nouvelle, avec Le Conte de Peau d'Asne et celuy des Souhaits ridicules. Quatrième édition (Paris, J.B. Coignard, 1695 [rpt. with *Contes de Perrault*, 1695]), 4.

25 'L'on donna à Inès le reste du jour pour inventer le conte qu'elle devoit faire le lendemain', *Griselidis, nouvelle*, 9.

26 'On ne trouvera pas estrange qu'un Enfant ayt pris plaisir a composer les contes de ce recueil ...' (l. 3^{r-v}).

been assembled,[27] as is easily demonstrated by a textual analysis of Perrault's 'Peau d'Âne' in comparison with Straparola's 'Tebaldo' (Night 1, Story 4) and Basile's 'L'Orsa' (Day 2, Story 6).[28]

When Perrault wrote about fantastic tales told for amusement (*histoires dépourvuës de raison*), and the ordinary people (*les moindres familles des particuliers*) who told such tales to instruct their young children, he used the verb *imaginer*. This Perrauldian phrase has been used so often to prove the existence of the telling of fairy tales among the poor (*les moindres familles*)[29] that it is worth examining Perrault's statement in detail. Read in context, the *contes* to which Perrault refers in general terms in the Preface to his 1695 *Griselidis* are ones parents tell to impart a praiseworthy and instructive moral (*une moralité loüable & instructive*).[30]

27 S. Magnanini, 'Postulated routes from Naples to Paris: the printer Antonio Bulifon and Giambattista Basile's fairy tales in seventeenth-century France', *Marvels & Tales* 21.1 (2007), 78–92, esp. 82–89.

28 R.B. Bottigheimer, 'Before *Contes du temps passé* (1697): Charles Perrault's "Grisélidis" (1693), "Souhaits ridicules" (1693), and "Peau d'Asne" (1694)', *Romanic Review* 99.2 (2009), 175–189.

29 For instance in her introduction to the tales of Mme d'Aulnoy, Nadine Jasmin cites Perrault's statement in the preface to the 1695 printing of 'Griselidis. Nouvelle' together with 'Peau d'Asne. Conte' and 'Les Souhaits ridicules. Conte' as 'nos aïeux ont inventé [ces contes] pour leurs enfants' (21) in discussing his *Histoires, ou Contes du temps passé*. That is, she conflates the two disparate traditions represented by the first collection of three tales (which derives respectively from popular print editions of the single story Griselda, higher-end print collections which formed the basis for 'Peau d'Asne', and the elevated print tradition that had most recently Lafontaine's version of the 'Souhaits ridicules') and the second collection of the eight tales in *Histoires, ou Contes du temps passé* (six of which derive from higher-end print productions and two of which are very likely his own composition). In so doing Jasmin assumes and implies that the tales of Perrault's *Histoires, ou Contes du temps passé* also grew from an oral tradition that was passed on when parents told them to their children. What is obviously problematic is that Perrault did *not* write that poor parents had told their children the tales that were in his *Histoires*, nor did he say that parents told their children the tales that were in the three-tale 1695 collection.

30 Perrault, *Griselidis etc.* (1695). Préface à iiij.

Nowhere does Perrault say that the tales he included either in his 1695 *Griselidis*, his 1695 manuscript collection, or his 1697 *Histoires* were the same ones told in humble homes. Instead he wrote that the stories in his manuscript were *like* (my emphasis) those told, that they give a picture (*image*) of what happens in those humble homes. And what happens in those humble homes is that people *imaginent*, that is, they make up, contrive, devise, invent, imagine, believe, conceive, fancy, put into images, stories that are themselves devoid of reason. They do so in order to teach their children what they need to know because they have not yet developed the capacity to reason. And what does Perrault proceed to declare that these not-yet-reasonable children need to know? They need to recognise and to learn how to behave towards those people whom Heaven has destined to govern them.[31] We need not attempt to parse the socio-political significance of Perrault's complex statement. What is abundantly evident is that he did not say that the tales in his 1695 manuscript were those that 'les moindres familles' told. Nor is there any reason that those families would have known the kinds of tales Perrault put into the 1695 manuscript collection or into the 1697 *Histoires*, unless they, like Perrault, had had access to a copy of Basile's *Pentamerone* or to Straparola's *Facétieuses Nuictz*. The Italianist Suzanne Magnanini has shown that although in theory an occasional *moindre famille* might have encountered a French-language copy of Straparola's tales, they would have remained completely ignorant of Basile's tales before the 1680s, by which point the French-born Antoine Bulifon had built up a publishing business in Naples, had republished Basile's *Pentamerone*, and was in the process of introducing it into Parisian circles.[32]

---

31   A Mademoiselle 1695 MS: 'Il est encore vray que ces contes donnent une image de ce qui se passe dans les moindres familles des particuliers ou la loüable impatience d'instruire des enfans fait imaginer des histoires depourvues de raison pour s'accommoder a ces mesmes enfans qui n'en ont pas encore mais a qui convient il mieux des connoistre comment vi–(l. 4ʳ)vent les Peuples qu'aux personnes que le Ciel destine a les conduire?' (l. 4ᵛ).

32   Magnanini, 'Postulated routes from Naples to Paris'.

VI Conclusion

Fairy tales, as we use the term in the modern world, whether in French, German, or English terminology, is a relatively modern concept.[33] Even newer is a concept that distinguishes restoration and rise fairy tales based on the social level of their heroes and heroines.[34] This article, in offering distinguishing terminological definitions of folk tales, tales about fairies and fairyland, restoration fairy tales, and rise fairy tales on the one hand, and in challenging assumptions about fairy tales' folk origins and oral dissemination on the other hand, might be viewed solely in terms of its revisionist point of view. But, in fact, treating fairy tales and tales about fairies and fairyland as literary creations opens new avenues of inquiry into a much-studied area. For instance, analysing Perrault's first fairy tale, 'Peau d'Asne', in conjunction with Straparola's and Basile's precursor tales, revealed that the specific and identifiable elements that were newly added to those already in Straparola's and Basile's tales, such as 'les trois robes', 'couleur du Temps', 'couleur de la Lune', et 'couleur du Soleil'[35] exemplify and identify Perrault's personal style.[36] What might a similar analysis of Perrault's 'Belle au bois dormant' with the texts of Basile's 'Sole, Luna e Talia' and the French *Perceforest* and its Catalonian analogues tell us about his use of precursor texts and the precise nature of his editing?

Many of the *conteuses* produced fairy tales and tales about fairyland whose plots resemble and reprise earlier Italian tales by Straparola and Basile. Straparola's tales had been printed in France in the thousands in a minimum of 16 printings in the sixteenth and seventeenth centuries, and many of those books were still extant in the late seventeenth century, to

---

33 R. Schenda, 'Telling tales – spreading tales: change in the communicative forms of a popular genre', trans. R.B. Bottigheimer, in R.B. Bottigheimer (ed.), *Fairy Tales and Society: Illusion, Allusion, and Paradigm* (Philadelphia and London, University of Pennsylvania Press, 1986), 75–94.

34 Initially introduced in Bottigheimer, *Fairy Godfather*, 5–27.

35 *Peau d'Asne*, 11, 12, 13.

36 R.B. Bottigheimer, 'Perrault au travail', 155.

judge from Mme de Murat's statement that everybody was mining 'Strapa-role' for plots.[37] But what about the fact that Perrault and contemporary *conteuses* produced many *contes* that give evidence of having been based on tales in Basile's, but not Straparola's collection? That puzzling problem, promisingly explored by Suzanne Magnanini, now appears to have a solution indicating that at least one copy of Basile's *Cunto de li Cunti* was physically present in Paris.

The likelihood that Basile's *Cunto de li Cunti* was present in Paris, and more precisely the conclusion that Marie-Jeanne Lhéritier and Charles Perrault had a copy of it (which a textual analysis of a number of their tales reveals) allows an exploration of undocumented literary relationships. For instance, was Mme d'Aulnoy's utilisation of Basilean precursor tales mediated through Perrault's publication (or perhaps his oral delivery) of 'Les Fées' or did she have direct access to Basile's *Cunto*? Attempting to date Mme d'Aulnoy's composition by using privilege, registry, and publishing dates provides a beginning, but motifs and plot elements buried in Basilean tales, whether in the apparent precursor or in other tales in his collection, have the potential to confirm a given Parisian author's direct acquaintance with and use of Basile's text, or of a knowledge of Basilean material mediated through Perrault's and/or Mlle Lhéritier's introduction of Basilean tale elements into French. If these pieces of indirect evidence weren't sufficient to nail down either the presence of Basile's book or the knowledge of its contents in 1690s Paris, there is the evidence provided by the title chosen by Mlle de la Force for her collection of tales *Les Contes des contes*, a near translation of Basile's title along with the reworking of a Basilean tale to produce her 'Rapunzel'-prototype, 'Persinette'. Textual examinations directed towards understanding which *conteuses* had direct access to Basile's *Cunto de li Cunti* might also illuminate working literary relationships and help us to map functional book-borrowing and book-sharing friendships in late 1690s Paris.

---

37   H.J. de Castelnau, Comtesse de Murat, 'Avertissement', *Histoires sublimes et allégoriques* (Paris, F. and P. Delaune, 1699), n.p.

Ancillary and fascinating questions also implicate seventeenth-century socio-cultural history and the history of ideas. For instance, it is impossible to find a copy of Basile's *Cunto de li Cunti* that was acquired in the seventeenth or early eighteenth century still in French public library holdings. What accounts for this remarkable absence? Is it possible that copies of the *Cunto* once formed part of Louis XIV's Royal Library, and that they were later removed? What does this tell us about early processes of moralisation that affected eighteenth-century editings of fairy tales as they made their way into German educational channels and then into publishing vehicles that bore them to a broad German adult readership?

Positing literary rather than nursemaid or peasant origins for 1690s French fairy tales challenges deeply held and foundational views about the origins and history of European fairy tales. It suggests new questions to be asked about those fairy tales. It unites social context to literary texts. And it views Europe's folks in European terms, as an integral part of an overarching literate culture, with which they interacted directly and indirectly.

SECTION TWO

Literary appropriations and transformations

Definition, repression, and the oral-literary interface in the French literary *conte* from the 'folie du conte' to the Second Empire

TIM FARRANT

> *Lorsqu'on fait un conte,*
> *c'est à quelqu'un qui l'écoute*[1]

Telling is the essence of the tale – etymologically and actually, its very being.[2] It has to have a narrator, and a listener or a reader. The central role of the oral, and of the oral-literary interface, has been explored in many studies.[3] Yet much literary scholarship on the *conte*, in particular on its

---

1   Diderot, *Ceci n'est pas un conte* in *Œuvres romanesques*, ed. H. Bénac (Paris, Classiques Garnier, 1961), 793.

2   'Tale' and 'tell' derive from OHG 'zala' and 'zellen', 'conte' and 'conter' from 'compter' and the Latin 'computare'. For simplicity, I shall use 'tale' as the English equivalent of 'conte'.

3   W. Ong, *Orality and Literacy: The Technologizing of the Word* (London, Methuen, 1982); V. Propp, *Les Racines historiques du conte merveilleux*, trans. L. Gruel-Apert, pref. D. Fabre and J.-C. Schmitt (Paris, N.R.F.-Gallimard, 1983 [1946]); J. Bellemin-Noël, *Les Contes et leurs fantasmes* (Paris, PUF, 1983); F. Marotin (ed.), M. Lioure (pref.), *Frontières du conte* (Paris, Éditions du Centre National de la Recherche Scientifique, 1982); M. Simonsen, *Le Conte populaire* (Paris, PUF, 1984); S. Loiseau, *Les Pouvoirs du conte* (Paris, PUF, 1992); C. Velay-Vallantin, *L'Histoire des contes* (Paris, Fayard, 1992); N. Belmont, *Poétique du conte. Essai sur le conte de tradition orale* (Paris, Gallimard, 1999); and J. Perrot (ed.), *Les Métamorphoses du conte* (Brussels, Peter Lang, 2004) in various ways draw on the *conte* as a viva voce form, from a sociological, historical and/or anthropological viewpoint.

written derivatives, the *nouvelle*[4] and the 'short story',[5] has been obsessed
with definition – as if the hearer, the audience, did not exist, and the *conte*
had its being in isolation, removed from conditions of production and
reception, remote from its oral origins, devoid of ideology and social
function, a virtually Platonic form whose main purpose was to be
analysed, categorised and contained.[6] Whether in the 'shortness' sought
in 'short stories', in Forster's arithmetical absurdities (where novels begin
at 50,000 words, and stories presumably stop at 49,999),[7] the *conte* has
risked becoming an adjunct to the writers who define it, rather than what

4   In the nineteenth century *conte* and *nouvelle* were used interchangeably: Cf.
     D. Bryant, *Short Fiction and the Press in France, 1829–1841* (Lampeter, Edwin Mellen
     Press, 1996), 5–8; and F. Vernier, '*Nouvelle*, laboratoire expérimental? L'impossible
     définition', in V. Engel and M. Guissard (eds), *La Nouvelle de langue française aux
     frontières des autres genres, du Moyen Âge à nos jours* (Ottignies, Quorum, 1997),
     158. *Nouvelle* implied oral narrative: 'la majorité des nouvelles du XIXe siècle sont
     des textes *contés*, c'est-à-dire que les auteurs laissent une place importante à la parole
     d'un narrateur, conservant et restituant le ton de ce qui est parlé'; R. Godenne, *La
     Nouvelle* (Paris, Champion, 1995), 56. M. Guissard, *La Nouvelle française. Essai de
     définition d'un genre* (Louvain-la-neuve, Bruylant Academia, 2002), 83–87, stresses
     the role of orality.
5   Term invented by B. Matthews, 'The philosophy of the short-story', in *The London
     Review*, 5 July 1884, reprinted in C.E. May (ed.), *The New Short Story Theories* (Athens,
     Ohio, Ohio University Press, 1994), 73–80. Cf. F. Garcier, 'Du nom au genre: le cas
     de la *short story*', *La Licorne* 22 (1992), 19–27, esp. 19–20.
6   See, for example, A. Jolles, *Formes simples* (Paris, Seuil, 1972 [1930]); A. Fonyi,
     'Nouvelle et subjectivité'; V. Hell, 'L'Art de la brièveté'; H. Böll-Johansen, 'Une
     théorie de la nouvelle', *Revue de littérature comparée* 5.4 (Oct.–Dec. 1976), Special
     Issue on 'Problématiques de la nouvelle', 355–375, 389–401, 421–432; I. Reid, *The
     Short Story* (London, Methuen, 1977); and R. Godenne, *La Nouvelle* and *Études
     sur la nouvelle de langue française* (Geneva, Slatkine, 2005), a position still found in
     A. Pasco, *Nouvelles françaises du dix-neuvième siècle* (Charlottesville, Rookwood,
     2006), 1–2. M.-L. Pratt, 'The short story: the long and the short of it', in May (ed), *The
     New Short Story Theories*, 91–113, is a notable exception, as are P. Cogman, *Narration
     in Nineteenth-Century French Short Fiction* (Durham, University of Durham Modern
     Languages Series 22, 2002), and F. Place-Verghnes's *Jeux pragmatiques dans les 'Contes
     et Nouvelles' de Guy de Maupassant* (Paris, Champion, 2005).
7   E.M. Forster, *Aspects of the Novel* (Harmondsworth, Penguin, 1966), 13.

it is: the founding mode of social discourse.[8] This article will explore the sources of that questionable stress on form, linking definition to repression and the written, and the oral to freedom and subversion in the rise of the French literary *conte* to prominence between 1830 and 1852. And it will take the word *conte* permissively, as it was understood in its widest sense at the time, to cover a whole range of fictions from short to long, including those called *nouvelles*,[9] and even novels, united by an emphasis on writing 'oral telling': that is, presenting in written form a supposedly initially oral narrative.

8   See e.g. Ong, *Orality and Literacy*, 74–75, 174–177. Derrida, following Rousseau and Lévi-Strauss, explores (but unlike them, questions) *parole*'s primacy over *écriture* (*De la grammatologie*, Paris, Éditions de Minuit, 1967), whilst G. Jean asserts that 'la parole du conte est d'abord *dans* le conte. Elle est également et indissociablement *dans* le conteur'; *Le Pouvoir des contes* (Tournai, Casterman, 1990 [1981]), 185. Jolles cites Arnim's insistence that the *conte* should incite its audience to *raconter* (*Formes simples*, 177); and Chapter 1 of R. Clements and J. Gibaldi, *Anatomy of the Novella* (New York, New York University Press, 1977) explores the exemplary and entertainment roles of the Renaissance *novella* in conversation (6–8 et seq.). But, treating the fundamental pedagogic role of the *conte* in the nursery school, S. Loiseau stresses that 'avant d'être un objet, objet pédagogique ou objet d'étude, *le conte est une pratique* [...] pratique orale, mais aussi pratique sociale, le conte ne se comprend vraiment que dans son contexte qui est un contexte où la tradition orale est vivante, où le conteur répond à un besoin social (se retrouver au sein d'une corporation, d'une communauté, se distraire) [...]. Les contes sont initiation, et incitation, totales, à l'humain'; *Les Pouvoirs du conte*, 12, 19; a seriousness and substantiveness of purpose presented also by G. Jean, *Le Pouvoir des contes*, 178–184. As Propp demonstrates, via its connection with rite, the *conte* is a founding form not just of social discourse but also of social intercourse (see *Les Racines historiques du conte merveilleux*, 20–27, 64–69; Jean, *Le Pouvoir des contes*, 34–35; Velay-Vallantin, *L'Histoire des contes*, 219, 335), instrumental in both socialisation and social repression (Velay-Vallantin, *L'Histoire des contes*, 320).

9   See n. 4 and K. Ackermann, *Von der philosophisch-moralischen Erzählung zur modernen Novelle. 'Contes' und 'nouvelles' von 1760 bis 1830* (Frankfurt-am-Main, Klostermann, 2004), esp. 'Die Auflösung der Opposition *conte* vs *nouvelle*', 72 et seq.

I

In the French nineteenth century, the canonical definition is Baudelaire's:

> Le roman [...] est un genre bâtard dont le domaine est vraiment sans limites [...]. La nouvelle, plus resserrée, plus condensée, jouit des bénéfices éternels de la contrainte: son effet est plus intense; et comme le temps consacré à la lecture d'une nouvelle est bien moindre que celui nécessaire à la digestion d'un roman, rien ne se perd de la totalité de l'effet.[10]

This famous statement gives a determinant emphasis. It implies that characterising, understanding, even creating the *conte*, and its shadow, the *nouvelle*, depends mainly on repression, on setting limits. Earlier comments had been strikingly more dynamic,[11] but Baudelaire makes form a matter of constraint. His remark on 'la totalité de l'effet' is echoed by others on poems,[12] and by his fusion of poetry and prose in the *Petits poèmes en prose*. And one step behind Baudelaire lies Poe, whom Baudelaire had

---

10   Baudelaire, 'Théophile Gautier', *L'Artiste* 4, 13 March 1859, in *Œuvres complètes*, ed. M. Ruff (Paris, Seuil, 1968), 464.

11   Cf. e.g. J. Janin: '[...] il n'en est pas de la nouvelle comme du roman. La nouvelle, c'est une course au clocher. On va toujours au galop, on ne connaît pas d'obstacles; on traverse le buisson d'épines, on franchit le fosse, on brise le mur, on se brise les os, on va tant que va son histoire', 'Le Piédestal', *Revue de Paris* 43 (1832), 103; L. de Bruno, *Léoncel ou l'émigré, nouvelle historique* I (1800), xiiij: 'elle [la nouvelle] n'admet aucun épisode, ni rien qui puisse en arrêter la marche. C'est exactement un récit qu'on suppose être fait ou pouvoir se faire de mémoire' (and thus, by implication, oral); Godenne, *La Nouvelle*, 76.

12   Letter to A. Fraisse, 18 Feb. 1860: 'parce que la forme est contraignante, l'idée jaillit plus intense. [...] Quant aux longs poèmes, nous savons ce qu'il en faut penser; c'est la ressource de ceux qui sont incapables d'en faire de courts. / Tout ce qui dépasse la longueur de l'attention que l'être humain peut prêter à la forme poétique n'est pas *un* poème'; Baudelaire, *Correspondance*, eds C. Pichois and J. Ziegler (Paris, Gallimard-Pléiade, 1973), I, 676.

translated,[13] and another canonical characterisation of the tale. Dismissing the less formed if more authentically oral narrative of his contemporaries,[14] Poe stresses the tale's advantages over the novel, in particular those of 'unity of impression', and of being 'read at one sitting': 'All high excitements are necessarily transient [...] without unity of impression, the deepest effects cannot be brought about [...]. As the novel cannot be read at one sitting, it cannot avail itself of the immense benefit of *totality*.'[15]

> [La nouvelle] a sur le roman à vastes proportions cette immense avantage que sa brièveté ajoute à l'intensité de l'effet. Cette lecture, qui peut être accomplie toute d'une haleine, laisse dans l'esprit un souvenir bien plus puissant qu'une lecture brisée, interrompue souvent par les tracas des affaires et le soin des intérêts mondains. L'unité d'impression, la *totalité* d'effet est un avantage immense qui peut donner à ce genre de composition une supériorité toute particulière, à ce point qu'une nouvelle trop courte (c'est sans doute un défaut) vaut encore mieux qu'une nouvelle trop longue.[16]

---

13   *Histoires extraordinaires* (1856 [*Revue de Paris*, Mar.–Apr. 1852]); *Nouvelles histoires extraordinaires* (1857); *Les Aventures de Arthur Gordon Pym* (1858) and *Eurêka* (1863); *Histoires grotesques et sérieuses* (1863). The history of these translations is covered in a series of articles by W.T. Bandy, culminating in 'Baudelaire et Edgar Poe', *Revue de littérature comparée* 41 (1967), 180–194. Cf. C. Pichois and J. Ziegler, *Baudelaire*, trans. G. Robb (London, Vintage, 1991), *passim.*, esp. 144–146, 182–183, 216–219. But even parts of Baudelaire's criticism touched on translation or plagiarism: M. Zimmerman, 'Baudelaire, Poe and Hawthorne', *Revue de littérature comparée* 39.3 (1965), 448–450.

14   Irving's *Tales of a Traveler* or John Neal's magazine stories: review of N. Hawthorne, *Twice-Told Tales*, in E.A. Poe, *Selected Writings*, ed. D. Galloway (Harmondsworth, Penguin, 1967), 446–447. Neal's tales 'ramble too much', according to Poe, 'and invariably break down just before coming to an end, as if the writer had received a sudden and irresistible summons to dinner'; the interest of many of Irving's narratives is 'subdivided and frittered away, and their conclusions are insufficiently *climactic.* There is not one of the series [*Tales of a Traveler*] which can be commended as a whole'.

15   Poe's emphasis: *N. Hawthorne, Twice-Told Tales*, in *Selected Writings*, 446; Cf. *The Philosophy of Composition*, 482.

16   Baudelaire, *Notes nouvelles sur Edgar Poe*, in *Curiosités esthétiques*, ed. H. Lemaître (Paris, Classiques Garnier, 1962), 630.

These oft-quoted remarks have been highly influential.[17] Like, perhaps even
more than, Baudelaire's 'roman…bâtard' declaration, they been taken as pre-
scriptive, and found their echo, in subsequent writers, in a stress on unity,
coherence, limitation – into an excessive emphasis on form. Baudelaire
takes Poe's 'tale' (the equivalent of *conte*, and the term Poe consistently
uses) and makes it into *nouvelle*, with its more formal, written implications,
or, in his translations, into *histoires*. He mentions 'lecture […] toute d'une
haleine', but the breath is merely figurative, the reception mainly passive,
whilst Poe's talk of a sitting suggests much more an occasion defined in
time in place, and a story both written and oral. Baudelaire reconfigures
Poe, whose statement can be taken as permissive, not restrictive; concerned not with definition but with discourse; not with theory but with
practice, with how tales are actually told and heard or read. The stress on
'a single sitting' (in Baudelaire's rendering, the 'lecture accomplie toute
d'une haleine'), expresses the shared nature of the narrative experience, one
where narrator and audience are equal partners; one which emerges from,
or is in the process of emerging from, the realm of the oral into the literary,
yet retaining something of its viva voce origins: an acknowledgement that
stories (if not the 'histories' they recount) are recounted in real time (even
if only the fictional real time of the printed frame story). Is Poe's 'single sitting', indeed, even a definition, a setting of the terms and of the end(s) of
narrative? Is it not rather a characterisation, a post-factem if not yet quite
posthumous appreciation of a still vibrant mode of social discourse?[18] In

17   See R. Hobbs, *From Balzac to Zola: Selected Short Stories* (London, Duckworth,
     Bristol Classical Press, 1992), 14–18; R.F. Marler, 'From tale to short story' in May,
     The New Short Story Theories, 165–191, esp. 171, 175; R. Godenne, 'Pistes pour une
     étude de la nouvelle au XIXe siècle', in B. Alluin and F. Suard (eds), *La Nouvelle:
     Définitions, Transformations* (Villeneuve d'Ascq, Presses Universitaires de Lille, 1990),
     105; D. Grojnowski, 'De Baudelaire à Poe: l'effet de totalité', in J. Gratton and J.-P.
     Imbert (eds), *La Nouvelle hier et aujourd'hui* (Paris, L'Harmattan, 1997), 29–40, esp.
     36; Guissard, *La Nouvelle française*, 55.
18   If Marler ('From tale to short story' in May (ed.), *The New Short Story Theories*) sees
     tale and short story as two distinct genres in nineteenth-century America, in France,
     the written pseudo-oral *conte* persisted throughout the period and beyond, as we
     shall see. Cf. section III and n. 54 below.

what is a seminal reformulation, determined by his own poetic (mystical, unifying, transcendent) agendas, Baudelaire, drawing on Poe, turns what was still, whether oral or written, a social practice, the *conte*, into something more formal and literary, the *nouvelle*, and makes expression a matter of containment. His comments have switched the points for subsequent discussion, and set critics chasing the Will o' the Wisp of definitions and of absolutes. Yet there are, of course, no absolutes in aesthetics, and literary judgements are never innocent. Baudelaire's remarks will now be seen in the context of contemporary conceptions and practice of the *conte*, and of wider debates.

II

It is telling that Baudelaire's encounter with Poe occurs at a key period of transition in French history, between the end of the July Monarchy and the early Second Empire; between the rise of Realism with Courbet and Champfleury in 1846, and what it might be tempting to see as its Classical and Imperial (indeed, *avant la lettre*, formalist) riposte, the Art for Art's sake movement and Parnassianism. Baudelaire is emblematic as posterity's memory of altogether bigger cultural conflicts, between Realism and Idealism, progress and reaction, the popular and the elite (conflicts which Baudelaire himself in some ways embodied).[19] And although the turn of the 1840s and 1850s is pivotal in those conflicts, it is but one moment in a recurrent struggle between tradition and modernity, high and low culture,

---

19   See Pichois and Ziegler, *Baudelaire*, trans. Robb, esp. ch. 13 and 233–234, 273, 298–299; G. and J. Lacambre (eds), *Champfleury: son regard et celui de Baudelaire* (Paris, Hermann, 1990).

expressed through the *conte*, which reaches back at least to the late seventeenth century, to Perrault and the *Querelle des anciens et des modernes*.[20]

In 1830s France these conflicts had gained a particular point of focus in the *conte*. The phenomenon of the years between 1830 and 1833 known as the *folie du conte*[21] crystallises in the realm of prose fiction the tensions between high and low culture, the establishment and the avant-garde, institutions and popular practice, which found other forms of expression elsewhere.[22] The *folie du conte* was an unconscionable expansion, a carnivalesque explosion, of the number of and variety of *contes* written and published during a corresponding slump in the book trade (and in the wider economy) in the early years of the July Monarchy;[23] or rather, a series of explosions, a string of multiple fictional insurrections aimed at literary establishment and convention. Charles Louandre was still speechless fifteen years later:

> Autour du roman se sont groupés une foule de genres accessoires,[24] nouvelles, contes, *Contes démocratiques*, *Contes bleues*, *Contes bruns*, *Contes de toutes les couleurs*, *Contes vrais*, *Contes bizarres*, *Contes de bord*, *Contes drolatiques*, *Contes philos-*

20   See M. Soriano, *Les Contes de Perrault: culture savante et tradition populaire* (Paris, Gallimard, 1968).

21   See R. Guise, 'Le Roman-feuilleton (1830–1848): naissance d'un genre' (Thèse de doctorat, Université de Nancy, 1975; Lille, Service de Reproduction des Thèses, 1985), Pt. I ch. 3, esp. section 4; P. Berthier, *La Presse littéraire et dramatique au début de la Monarchie de juillet (1830–1836)* (Villeneuve d'Ascq, Presses Universitaires du Septentrion, 1997), 1119–1133.

22   The interface was not only oral and literary but also visual and musical. As taste in prose fiction moved from the historical novel to the *conte* (often historical, as we shall see), so taste in painting moved from the *grandes machines* of Vernet and Delaroche to landscape and more intimist and genre works. In theatre, the historically-epic becomes domestic, in Hugo's sublimely-grotesque shutting of Don Carlos in a cupboard (*Hernani*) or in Vigny's small-scale, private-life treatment of the drama of Chatterton. Cf. C. Rosen and H. Zerner, *Romanticism and Realism. The Mythology of Nineteenth-Century Art* (London, Faber and Faber, 1984), esp. chs 2, 6.

23   See T. Farrant, *Balzac's Shorter Fictions* (Oxford, OUP, 2002), 84, n. 5, 6, 7.

24   A label one can hardly endorse, for all that it may long have constituted the traditional story of the novel. It was from the *conte*, more than from the *roman historique*,

ophiques, etc., histoires, tableaux de mœurs, œuvres individuelles ou collectives, *keepsake, abeilles, sachets*, etc., où les nouvelles et les contes ont été entrelacés de vers et illustré d'arabesques et de vignettes. L'avènement de ce nouveau genre est marqué par le *Livre des Cent-et-un*, qui du moins a encore le mérite de contenir, au milieu de beaucoup de futilités, quelques articles sérieux. A ce livre succédèrent *Les Cent-et-une Nouvelles Nouvelles des Cent et un*. On en arriva bientôt au *Salmigondis* et à *Babel* et, quand cette veine fut épuisée, on inventa des bizarreries nouvelles, des livres pour lesquels on ne peut trouver aucune définition dans les divers genres de littérature, et dont les sujets même sont tellement insaisissables, que les auteurs ont été obligés de créer pour eux des titres de fantaisie. *Le Salmigondis* fut remplacé par *Un autre monde* et le *Voyage où il vous plaira*.[25]

'Des bizarreries nouvelles, des livres pour lesquels on ne peut trouver aucune définition dans les divers genres de littérature': the very word *folie* is enough to indicate how much this 'madness' was at odds with the institutions of hegemonic power.[26]

On one level, of course, writing and publishing *contes* was undeniably sane: briefer than novels, capable of appearing individually in newspapers and reviews or grouped, often seemingly randomly, in apparently impro-vised collections, they could be written and brought out quickly, with mini-mum material risk. They offered much greater freedom of operation than longer forms like the novel. But on another level, writing *contes* was risky. The *conte* was, according to the conservative critic Nisard,[27] 'quelque chose

---

that the century's great novelists, Balzac, Dumas, Sand, and, later, Flaubert emerged, along of course, with storytellers like Mérimée.

25 C. Louandre, 'Statistique littéraire. De la production intellectuelle en France depuis quinze ans. Dernière partie. Littérature ancienne et étrangère, Poésie, Roman, Théâtre', *Revue des deux mondes* 20 (1847), 671–703, 684–685; typography standardised.

26 For all that, for contemporaries, its primary meaning was 'engouement', 'craze'. Although there were *contes* which actually supported hegemonic power, such as those which appeared in the Royalist keepsakes (Balzac's *Le Départ*, for example, in *L'Émeraude*, 1832), even these could be seen as counter-hegemonic, given that to be an *ultra* was to be in opposition in the July Monarchy's early years.

27 Despite his later prominence as a member of the *Académie française* (1850), influen-tial critic and government inspector, Nisard was at this time simply a jobbing critic at the *Revue de Paris*.

qui n'a pas la force d'être un roman':[28] 'something' defined only negatively, in relation to a not yet entirely respectable genre, the novel. To associate oneself with the *conte* was to avow one's creative weakness, to be linked with an inferior genre, indeed, almost a non-genre.[29]

Behind this view lay bigger cultural battles about the novel, literature, and language – over who, and what, which genres and subjects,[30] have *droit de cité* and *droit à la parole*. Nisard's damning of the *conte* with faint praise of the novel is a stratagem for containing a strikingly vibrant, polymorphic form. If the novel had proved its substance and seriousness during the later Restoration in the work of Scott and his French acolytes, its ability to treat large social conflicts through litmus individuals in *Waverley* (1814), *The Heart of Midlothian* (1818) or Balzac's *Les Chouans* (1829), by 1830 the historical novel was running out of steam: Mérimée's *Chronique du règne de Charles IX* (1829) breaks down in chapter 8, refusing authoritative authorial discourse, decentralising into a supposedly spoken dialogue between the reader and the author. It was a sign of things to come. Not only in the historical novel was there no longer a Grand Narrative – the plot had been lost in society at large. The Restoration's king and kinship had been supplanted by nascent individualism and a bourgeois monarchy with an exhortation to get rich quick, and *contes*, narrators, and their discourses were proliferating in the journals and reviews – a liberalisation accompanied by a brief relaxing of press censorship. To write *contes* at this time was to seize the right to speak for oneself, to refuse containment and definition, to reject the hierarchy represented by the conventional generic structure which Nisard (here implicitly) so reveres, to challenge authority with an implicitly populist oral form. It was the *conte* which was associated with viva voce vibrancy and authenticity, the expression

---

28 'D'un commencement de réaction contre la littérature facile', *Revue de Paris* 57 (December 1833), 211–218, 217.

29 The negativity was widespread: see e.g. the anonymous 'De la littérature conteuse', *Gazette de France*, 8 June 1833; Bryant, *Short Fiction and the Press in France*, 35 et seq.

30 This conflict was to peak in the 1840s: L. Dumasy, *La Querelle du roman-feuilleton* (Grenoble, Université Stendhal, 1999).

of real contemporary voices. Its major multi-authored collections emerge symbiotically with contemporary panoramic writing: *Les Cent-et-Une Nouvelles Nouvelles des Cent-et-un* (1833) from *Paris ou le Livre des Cent-et-un* (1831), a mélange of documents and *témoignages* as much as tales, where Nodier's *Bibliomane* rubs shoulders with Jal's *Les Soirées d'artistes*; both series were charitable collective efforts by the 161 (not 101) contributors to support their publisher Ladvocat. Hybridity is the watchword, the ethos is community and the contemporary (*Paris* ...), yet also complicity, sharing confidences, membership of some exclusive, even masonic, club (the Cent-et-un).[31] The more overtly narrative collections, *Le Livre des conteurs, Le Salmigondis, contes de toutes les couleurs* (both 1833) develop this ethos, stressing diversity, authenticity, community, and the supposedly live narrative voice. These voices are of course fictions, but also expressions of confusion, of historical dislocation, submissions of inevitable brevity in place of absent unity and plenitude: fictions of community created to blank out fragmentation. *Contes* of this time stress the supposedly authentic, first-hand account, heard from the horse's mouth. Balzac's *Un Épisode sous la Terreur* (1830) or *Le Colonel Chabert* (1832); Mérimée's *L'Enlèvement de la redoute* (1829) or *Une Partie de trictrac* (1830) relate often turbulent moments from recent real experience.[32] And they emphasise the oral: the literary *conte* as surrogate for live narrative, whose vivacity and authenticity is underlined: 'cette profusion de pensées, de formules, de contes, de documents historiques [...] le phénomène oral, qui, bien étudié, bien manié, fait la puissance de l'acteur et du conteur.'[33]

---

31   Balzac's *Histoire des Treize* (1833–35) builds on this ethos, especially in its last fiction, *La Fille aux yeux d'or.* Cf. C. Massol, *Une poétique de l'énigme. Le Récit herméneutique balzacien* (Geneva, Droz, 2006), 299 et seq.

32   Balzac, *La Comédie humaine*, eds P.-G. Castex et al. (Paris, Gallimard-Pléiade, 1976–81), VIII, 421–431; III, 298–302; Mérimée, *Théâtre, romans et nouvelles*, eds J. Maillon and P. Salomon (Paris, Gallimard-Pléiade, 1978), 1330–1332, 1374–1375.

33   *Une conversation entre onze heures et minuit* in H. de Balzac, P. Chasles, C. Rabou, *Contes bruns*, ed. M. Milner (Marseilles, Éditions des autres, 1979 [1832]), 5–6; later reused, with much greater exploitation of the oral-literary interface, in *Autre Étude de femme* (1842). See Farrant, *Balzac's Shorter Fictions*, 132 et seq; 261–264.

We can see, then, that two key features, the 'literary' interfacing of the oral, and the account of the turbulent recent historical past, stand in for, indeed surpass, a contemporary newspaper, legal, administrative and official print culture which is by implication dull.[34] Balzac's *Contes drolatiques* (1832), exploiting a vibrant Renaissance literary model recently brought to prominence in the late Restoration,[35] promise 'une dragme de joyeulsetez par ce tems ou l'ennuy tumbe comme une pluie fine qui mouille'.[36] For Balzac, the *conte drolatique* was an antidote to modernity, and to its defining malady, ennui. Mérimée's *La Vénus d'Ille* (1837), in contrast, is a veritable dialogue of different voices, a cacophony of conversations and putative oral narratives supposedly reported and transcribed by the authorial narrator:[37] his Catalan guide's initial mention of the Venus; the relentless babble of the archaeologist Peyrehorade; the exclamations of the local youths it injures; the bluster and anguish of its victim, Alphonse; the anguished accounts of servant and of his widow, 'cette malheureuse jeune personne, devenue folle'.[38] Society's institutional representatives cannot explain away or counter nature's untamed forces (neither the narrator – Mérimée himself, appointed *Inspecteur-général des monuments historiques* in 1834 and, like Nisard, later an official of the Imperial regime – nor Peyrehorade, whose repeated pompous Classical interjections come to seem like a kind of madness), any more than they can account for exotic cultural practices

---

34   See, for example, Balzac's own pen-portrait of *Le Petit Mercier* in *Œuvres diverses*, eds R. Chollet et al. (Paris, Gallimard-Pléiade, 1990 [*La Caricature*, 16 Dec. 1830]), 830–833; the *Scènes contemporaines sur l'administration des ponts et chaussées*, La Pandore, 3 Apr. 1830, or Flaubert's *Une leçon d'histoire naturelle, genre commis* (1837; unpublished in his lifetime. Republished in *Écrits de jeunesse*, ed. M. Nadeau, Lausanne, Société Coopérative Éditions Rencontre, 1964), 133–138.

35   With the Academy's setting of its 1828 prize essay on sixteenth-century French literature, won by Saint-Marc Girardin's and Philarète Chasles's *Tableau de la marche et des progrès de la littérature française au XVIe siècle*.

36   *Contes drolatiques, Premier dixain, Prologue*, in Balzac, *Œuvres diverses*, I, 8.

37   The tale is a reworking of other texts and real experience, a number of details deriving from Mérimée's own life: see Mérimée, *Théâtre romans et nouvelles*, 1478–1483.

38   *La Vénus d'Ille* in Mérimée, *Théâtre romans et nouvelles*, 755. The phrase both suggests and casts doubt on the reliability of her witness.

in the Corsican story *Mateo Falcone*. The fantastic, the exotic, the worlds of dream and madness, all act as focuses of counter-hegemonic discourse in the July Monarchy *conte*, all challenging monologic, uni-perspectival world-views, the claim that reality has only one face.

This is doubtless why Nisard is so anxious to rubbish the *conte*, to void it of *force*, at a time when it was so manifestly vibrant. A similar operation would be performed by Nettement, a decade later, in his study on the *roman feuilleton* (1844), and in the interim by Sainte-Beuve, in his article 'De la littérature industrielle'.[39] Behind these responses lies a struggle for cultural dominance, expressed by a debate about what authentic expression is: whether it is written or oral, whether it takes the form of *conte* or novel.[40] By placing the *conte* outside the generic system, Nisard denies it institutional status, but at the same time, if unwittingly, attests its vivacity, authenticity and vigour. And, beyond this, these *conte*/novel struggles echo larger ones about the centre of cultural gravity in July Monarchy France: about whether its lies with oral or written culture, with the people or with the elite, with those in power or those in opposition.[41] Coinciding as it does with the waning of the *folie du conte*, the 1833 *Loi Guizot* establishing a primary school in every commune and a secondary school in the *chef-lieu* of each department can be seen as pivotal in the oral-literary interface, beginning the transition from mass orality to mass literacy, and with it, but

39 *Revue des Deux Mondes*, IV, 19, 1 Sept. 1839. Saint-Beuve's article can be seen as the stepping-stone from Nisard's December 1833 article and the next major intervention, Nettement's *Études critiques sur le feuilleton-roman* (1847). See also Dumasy, *La Querelle du roman-feuilleton*.

40 There is an echo of this a decade later, in Balzac's *La Muse du département* (1843), where mockery of Dinah, the lady of letters and eponymous *muse*, is arguably a misreading of women's superiority in viva voce as opposed to written narrative. Cf. F. de Lagenevais, 'Le Roman dans le monde', *Revue des deux mondes* 13.2 (1843), 586–614. Cf. also Sand's choice of oral narrative, in a novel which is effectively a giant frame-story, *Mauprat* (1837). The oral-written interface is a *conte*/novel interface, too.

41 Debates pursued particularly in the realm of education, the *Loi Guizot* (1833) introducing compulsory primary education for boys. Cf. R. Grevet, *L'Avènement de l'école contemporaine en France (1789–1835)* (Villeneuve d'Ascq, Presses Universitaires du Septentrion, 2001), chapter 10.

also, as was intended, an inculcating of law and order and proper respect for the powers that be.

The battle-lines in these struggles, however, were never straightforwardly congruent with political interests or clear-cut: from the ancien régime to the Restoration, salons (like cafés, restaurants and *pensions*) were focuses of reflection, as Balzac's *Le Dernier Souper*[42] (1828), *Le Père Goriot* and *Autre Étude de femme* (1842) attest.[43] Mme d'Abrantès comments, in memoirs largely relaying conversations, 'depuis la révolution, nous avons toujours eu deux décompositions par faction.'[44] If the *conte*, and its literary surrogate, the written tale, is, from the start of (and arguably throughout) the century synonymous with authenticity, in the shape of supposedly viva voce narrative,[45] it is, with the exception of the *conte moral*, generally counter-hegemonic – even if the balance of hegemonic power shifts. We see this in examples as diverse as Napoleon's *Le Souper de Beaucaire* (1793), a dialogue querying the authority of the Republic over dissident Avignon;[46] or Chateaubriand's *René* (1802). René tells a story that pits him against society's repressive received ideas – this within the framework of a larger text, the *Génie du Christianisme*, asserting the values of mysticism above the merely rational, foreshadowing the way in which, later, the fantastic would be pitted against the real in the early 30s, at the height of the *conte fantastique*. The numerous soldier-narratives by Mérimée and Balzac already mentioned (*L'Enlèvement de la redoute*, *Une Partie de trictrac*, *Le Colonel Chabert*, the collaborative *Contes bruns*), Vigny's *Servitude et grandeur militaires* (1835) all use oral narrative, the interaction between frame and

---

42   Now *Les Deux Rêves*, part of *Sur Catherine de Médicis* (1842–46).

43   Cf. A. Vaillant, J.-P. Bertrand and P. Régnier, *Histoire de la littérature française du XIXe siècle* (Paris, Nathan, 1998), 18–22.

44   Mme d'Abrantès, *Mémoires* (London, Edinburgh and Paris, Nelson, n.d.; first published 1831–35), chapter 62, 2. 284.

45   Place-Verghnes in *Jeux pragmatiques* (96–152, esp. 129–138) gives a persuasive analysis of the pragmatics of oral narrative in the later case of Maupassant.

46   See C. Frayling (ed.) *Napoleon Wrote Fiction* (Salisbury, Compton Press, 1972), 113–135.

narrator and audience, to question moral standpoint,[47] or even the nature of truth itself. Gautier's *Les Jeunes France* (1833) builds on the oral-based, word-spinning idiom exploited by contemporary so-called anti-novels[48] to question any mono-perspectival vision of reality.[49] But, by 1848, the political and cultural initiative was passing from the first-generation Romantics and Bohemians who were society's *poil à gratter* to the emergent Realists. Tellingly, the landmark Realist story collection, the first edition of Champfleury's *Contes* (1847), opens with the text-for-text confronting of a Romantic account of the heroine's life and a Realist one. It highlights the gulf between Romantic perceptions of reality, and an altogether grittier account; between Romantic language, and Realist language;[50] between a stylised, formalised view of life, and the realities of life itself.

III

It is this collision between the *conte* as word-spinning, freewheeling, vibrant, spoken narrative, and its surrogate, the *nouvelle* as something written, literary, more formal and more contained that is crystallised in Baudelaire's idealist, absolutist definition. Its antithesis, ideological and aesthetic, is a writer Baudelaire and his mentor Gautier detested: George Sand. Sand,

---

47 E.g. *Histoire du cachet rouge* and *La Veillée de Vincennes* in *Servitude et grandeur militaires*, ed. F. Germain (Paris, Classiques Garnier, 1965) 53, 80.

48 E.g. Janin, *L'Âne mort et la femme guillotinée* (1829); and Nodier, *Histoire du roi de Bohême et de ses sept châteaux* (1830).

49 Gautier's *Celle-ci et celle-là* and *Le Bol de punch* contain particularly striking examples of the oral-literary interface, switching from authorial narrative to dialogue in mid-flow, the latter citing and recycling prominent contemporary literary works; *Les Jeunes France. Romans goguenards* (Paris, Éditions des autres, 1979 [1833]), 145, 217, 222.

50 Champfleury, *Contes*, ed. G. Secchi (Rome, Bulzoni, 1973), 72–73; a procedure already exploited in Musset's *Lettres de Dupuis et de Cotonne. Œuvres complètes*, ed. P. Van Tieghem (Paris, Seuil 1979), 879–880.

seen by Baudelaire as 'cette latrine'[51] and similarly by Gautier ('La copie
est une fonction chez Madame Sand')[52] embodies not only a menacingly
feminine fertility but also a dangerously uncontainable discursiveness, dangerous because it obeys few generic rules and preaches doctrines of love,
progress and reconciliation which Baudelaire thought evil and absurd.[53]
In the years around 1850, when Baudelaire was refashioning Poe's tales
as *nouvelles* and his nominally oral narratives as art, Sand was doing the
reverse, writing landmark works (*François le champi* [1848] and *Les Maîtres
sonneurs* [1853]) which were expressions and celebrations of the oral in the
literary. To notions of definition, containment and finality, Sand opposes
freedom, authenticity, and lack of constraint; not the least striking feature
of these narratives is that they are of novel length, but written as *contes*,
as supposed transcriptions of *Veillées*, evenings of peasant storytelling in
the Berry.[54]

51   Cf. *Fusées. Mon cœur mis à nu. Pauvre Belgique*, ed. A. Guyaux (Paris, Folio, 1986),
      99.
52   G. Sand, *François le Champi*, ed. A. Fermiger (Paris, Folio, 1976), 9.
53   For a different but complementary interpretation, see P. Dayan, 'Baudelaire at his
      latrine: motions in the *Petits poèmes en prose* and in George Sand's novels', *French
      Studies* 48.4 (1994), 416–424.
54   Balzac had done something similar in *Le Médecin de campagne* (1833), a novel which
      is effectively a cycle of *contes*; Cf. Farrant, *Balzac's Shorter Fictions*, 155–157. The *Veillée*,
      popular from at least the eighteenth century in the form of the didactic narrative
      exemplified by Genlis's *Veillées du château* (1784, and frequently republished) was
      also directed at adults (E.-J.-A. Neveu-Derotrie, *Veillées villageoises, ou Entretiens sur
      l'agriculture moderne mis à la portée des habitants des campagnes*, Rennes, 1834; A. de
      Saint-Priest, *Veillées politiques, ou considérations sur l'état et les besoins de la France*,
      1829), specified by calling or region (*Veillées maritimes, miltaires, normandes*, Luzel's
      Veillées bretonnes, 1879), and sometimes only nominally oral: the title *Veillée* was a
      signal to sit comfortably and pay attention as to a real live narrator, or a sign that
      the publication was intended to be read out loud in company, as in the numerous
      periodicals which, from mid-century, included *Veillée* in their title. The oral-literary
      interface is perhaps most extraordinarily embodied in the paradoxically-named *Veillées
      littéraires illustrées* (1849–56) which included a hotchpotch of contemporary and
      older novels and stories, only some of which were oral.

Sand's quest is far from picturesque. The messages of *François le Champi* or of *Les Maîtres sonneurs*, which relate the tribulations of adopting a rural foundling (literally 'field-boy') or the brutal rivalries of country musicians, are expressed by the medium. For the transposition of the oral *conte* into literature expresses a conception and practice of art at the opposite pole from Gautier's and Baudelaire's insistence on the perfection of the art-work, its uselessness and remoteness from life. Sand's art is not superior but subservient to, part of life, expressed via orality, spontaneity and the interaction that comes from communal storytelling. Orality is central to *François le Champi*: art is only a means to an end, which is why the spoken is superior to the literary, and the art work is only relative, an attempt. For Sand, in art as in life, it is more important to journey than to arrive (the antithesis of the narrative or moral finality expressed in the *conte*'s supposed need to make an exemplary 'point', or in Baudelaire's obsession with death),[55] and the art-work is more valuable as a 'tentative' than completed artefact. 'Les chefs-d'œuvre ne sont jamais que des tentatives heureuses. Console-toi de ne pas faire de chefs-d'œuvre, pourvu que tu fasses des tentatives consciencieuses.'[56] Seeking 'par quelle rapport l'art, sans cesser d'être l'art pour tous, peut entrer dans le mystère de la simplicité primitive, et communiquer le charme répandu dans la nature', the narrator (Sand) recites Nodier's *Histoire du chien de Brisquet* like a musician's warm-up, explaining: 'C'était un trait pour ma voix, écrit par Charles Nodier, qui essayait la sienne sur tous les modes possibles; un grand artiste, à mon sens, qui n'a pas eu toute la gloire qu'il méritait, parce que, dans le nombre varié de ses tentatives, il a fait plus de mauvaises que de bonnes.'

This sense of the *conte* as a popular oral form, part of a vibrant social context, was to lead Sand, like others, most relevantly Champfleury,[57] to collect, celebrate and transcribe popular oral narrative whilst Baudelaire was doing the reverse – transmuting Poe's orality into art. For all three

---

55 Cf. Dayan, 'Baudelaire at his latrine'.
56 *François le Champi*, 'Avant-propos', ed. Fermiger, 51–52.
57 Cf. G. and J. Lacambre, *Champfleury: son regard et celui de Baudelaire*; A. Asfour, *Champfleury: Meaning in the Popular Arts in Nineteenth-Century France* (Frankfurt, Peter Lang, 2001), chapters 1 and 2.

writers, if for different reasons and in differing ways, these activities were retreats from politics, responses to the disappointment of 1848. (Champ-fleury was consoled by the *Légende du Bonhomme misère*).[58] It is one of the ironies of literary history that the resultant ideological vacuum was filled not from below, but from above – or rather, in literature as in poli-tics, by a manipulation of the people by the elite – in the collection and management of popular narrative in the *Histoire des livres populaires et de la littérature de colportage* (1854), by Nisard, the very mouthpiece of 1830s condemnation of the *conte*.

Nisard intends to *punir* as well as *surveiller.* In addition to aping the antiquarianism quintessentially embodied by Scott's *Minstrelsy of the Scot-tish Border* (1803), *Tales of my Landlord* (1816–19)[59] or the collections of the brothers Grimm,[60] seeking to preserve for the future 'les divertissements intellectuels et les préceptes de morale que cette littérature a donnés au peuple pendant deux ou trois siècles', he aims to 'faire apprécier au public quelle influence fâcheuse a dû avoir sur les mœurs et l'esprit du peuple le colportage abandonné à lui-même, et, au contraire, quel bien pour-rait faire une telle industrie réglée par la vigilance de l'administration.'[61] Others, notably Villemarqué, and in his wake Champfleury and Luzel,[62]

---

58   Asfour, *Champfleury: Meaning in the Popular Arts*, 75.

59   First trans. Mme F.-A. Collet, 1821.

60   It is noteworthy that, like Scott, the Grimms began with ballads (*Über den altdeutschen Meistergesang*, Göttingen, 1811) before moving to *contes: Kinder- und Hausmärchen* was first published in 1812 (v. 1) and 1814 (v. 1); a third 3 vol. Berlin edition followed between 1819 and 1822. But *Les Veillées allemandes, chroniques, contes, traditions et croyances populaires* did not appear in French translation until 1838. Only after 1860 does popular publication of Grimm's tales really take off.

61   Nisard, *Histoire des livres populaires et de la littérature de colportage*, i.i.

62   Villemarqué's first collection of Breton ballads, the *Barzaz Breiz*, appeared in 1839, *Contes populaires des anciens Bretons* in 1842, and *Les Romans de la table ronde et les contes des anciens Bretons* in 1860. Champfleury's *De la littérature populaire en France. Recherches et variations sur la légende du Bonhomme Misère* came out in 1861 (having been preceded by collecting and publishing on popular images and artefacts: Cf. Asfour, *Champfleury: Meaning in the Popular Arts*, 61); Luzel's *Légendes chrétiennes de la Basse-Bretagne* in 1881, and *Contes populaires de la Basse Bretagne* in 1887.

took in their collection of popular oral literature an ostensibly different view, restricting their activities to those of benign cultural preservation (sometimes embellishment).[63] But, whether consciously or not, all are emblematic of the absorption of the traditional and contemporary *conte* into the establishment, part of a wider appropriation and neutralising of popular art and of the popular (and indeed of politics) under the Second Empire by the powers that be: a process paradoxically begun by for the nineteenth-century French *conte* by Nisard, but which would only achieve completion with the arrival of the contemporary literary *conte* on school syllabuses after 1871.

---

63 A charge levelled chiefly at La Villemarqué. For a succinct account, see D. Laurent, 'La Querelle du *Barzaz Breiz*' in J. Balcou and Y. Le Gallo (eds), *Histoire littéraire et culturelle de la Bretagne* (Paris, Champion-Coop Breizh, 1997), 346–354.

Une interface paradoxale au XVIIIe siècle: conte merveilleux et bibliothèque des savoirs chez Thomas-Simon Gueullette

JEAN-FRANÇOIS PERRIN

'Le baron Roger, gouverneur du Sénégal sous Charles X rapporte qu'un griot, inspiré par sa présence alors qu'il était en train de raconter la fable du lion et de la hyène, eut l'idée de faire demander à Lyon par Hyène, en français:– Monsieur le commandant, comment vous portez-vous? Le succès d'hilarité fut tel que cette répartie resta inscrite dans son répertoire, et remporta toujours le même succès.'[1] Cette anecdote de Claude Brémond pourrait d'une certaine façon résumer les questions qui seront posées dans ce Chapitre, sur le génie de l'actualisation qui caractérise l'art du conteur. Un génie qui, dans le cas rappelé par cette courte histoire, manifeste la capacité du genre à réussir l'intégration d'un élément emprunté à la culture du colonisateur, à la langue de l'Autre. Ce que cette anecdote nous enseigne, les travaux des spécialistes du genre le montrent aussi à leur façon; par exemple, les travaux sur les *Mille et une nuits* ont montré que leur conte-cadre résultait d'une longue histoire de montage et d'hybridation associant des éléments narratifs émanant d'aires géographico-culturelles distinctes.[2] C'est cette dynamique auto-actualisante du genre qui sera mon sujet de réflexion dans ce Chapitre, à partir d'un recueil de contes du XVIIIe siècle

---

1   J.-F. Roger, *Fables sénégalaises recueillies du Oualof* (Paris, Nepveu, 1928), cité dans C. Brémond, 'L'Étymologie des contes', *Féeries* 3 (2006), 183–213, 192.

2   Voir surtout E. Cosquin, 'Le Prologue-cadre des *Mille et une nuits*, les légendes perses et le livre d'Esther', *Études folkloriques* (1922), 293–347; et C. Brémond, 'Préhistoire de Schéhérazade', dans J.-L. Joly et A. Kilito (éds), *Les Mille et une nuits. Du texte au mythe* (Rabat, Publications de la faculté des lettres et sciences humaines, 2005), 19–42.

sur lequel je travaille pour une édition critique,[3] et où je découvre une étonnante poétique du montage et de l'hybridation de scénarios et de récits venus des secteurs les plus variés et quelquefois les plus inattendus de la bibliothèque: des dictionnaires aux relations des voyageurs, des nouvelles italiennes au Coran, de Lucrèce aux traités de démonologie, etc. C'est cette poétique du montage actualisant ou intégratif et à ses enjeux qui servira de problématique pour ce Chapitre, à partir de trois exemples tirés du second recueil de contes orientaux de Gueullette, les *Aventures du mandarin Fum-Hoam, Contes chinois.*[4]

Thomas-Simon Gueullette est né en 1683 et mort en 1766; il exerçait une charge de substitut du Procureur du Roi au Châtelet de Paris, et consacrait ses loisirs aux Belles-Lettres. Son amour du théâtre est suffisamment connu pour n'y point insister;[5] mais outre ses contributions d'auteur et d'historien dans ce domaine,[6] il s'occupe également d'édition: par exemple, les *Contes et fables indiennes de Bidpaï*, dans la traduction de Galland (1724), ou *Le Petit Jehan de Saintré*, ou encore les *Divertissements de la princesse Aurélie* de Segrais, etc. Mais pour ses contemporains, Gueullette est surtout un bon conteur d'histoires orientales: Lenglet-Dufresnoy place ainsi les *Contes Tartares, Mogols* et *Chinois*, immédiatement après les *Mille et une nuits* et les *Mille et un jours* dans sa fameuse *Bibliothèque des romans* (1734).[7] Lorsque Gueullette publie ses *Mille et un quarts d'heure* (sic), alors

3   J.-F. Perrin, C. Bahier-Porte, M.F. Bosquet, R. Daoulas, C. Ramirez (éds), *Les Contes merveilleux de Thomas-Simon Gueullette* (Paris, Champion, 2009).

4   Je renverrai à l'édition originale: *Les Aventures merveilleuses du mandarin Fum-Hoam. Contes chinois*, 2 tomes (Paris, J.-B. Mazuel, 1723).

5   Voir J.E. Gueullette, *T.S. Gueullette, un magistrat du XVIIIe siècle* (Paris, Droz, 1938); et J.E. Gueullette, *Notes et souvenirs sur le Théâtre-Italien au XVIIIe siècle, publiés* (Paris, Droz, 1938).

6   C'est à partir d'une documentation réunie par Gueullette, familier des Riccoboni et des acteurs italiens, que les frères Parfaict ont réalisé leur *Histoire de l'ancien théâtre italien* (1753).

7   N. Lenglet Du Fresnoy, 'Contes des fées et autres contes merveilleux', article XI du *Bibliothèque des romans*, dans *De l'usage des romans où l'on fait voir leur utilité et leurs différents caractères, avec une bibliothèque des romans accompagnée de remarques critiques sur leur choix et leur édition* (Amsterdam, Vve de Poilras, 1734), 285.

que la vogue des contes orientaux relaie celle des contes de fées, leur succès lui crée une notoriété attestée par de nombreuses rééditions et traductions dans les principales langues européennes (ses productions ultérieures sont également rapidement traduites). Cette audience sera durable: presque toute sa production 'merveilleuse' est reprise dans le *Cabinet des fées*, et un indianiste comme Loiseleur-Deslongchamps cite encore ses contes avec précision en 1838,[8] comme le fera encore Clouston en Angleterre à la fin du XIXe siècle,[9] et plus tard Victor Chauvin au début du XXe siècle.[10] En Angleterre, tous ses contes orientaux sont traduits et quelquefois réédités à partir de 1725 jusqu'à 1785 comme l'indique Martha Pike-Conant dans son ouvrage classique sur le conte oriental en Angleterre au XVIIIe siècle (1908);[11] mais l'intégralité de ses contes orientaux est à nouveau traduite par Henry Weber en 1812 dans son anthologie des *Tales of the East* republiant les contes originaux traduits en Occident et leurs imitations les plus connues.[12] On peut enfin signaler son influence sur un écrivain comme Beckford, puisque c'est aux *Conte mogols* que celui-ci a emprunté pour son *Vathek*, le fameux motif des damnés aux poitrines transparentes laissant voir un cœur embrasé.[13]

8   A.-L.-A. Loiseleur-Deslongchamps, 'Essai historique sur les contes orientaux et sur les Mille et une nuits' ('Introduction aux Mille et une nuits'), dans *Les Mille et une nuits* (Paris, Édition du Panthéon littéraire, 1838) – particulièrement intéressant pour les emprunts de Gueullette aux recueils de nouvelles ou aux sources médiévales.

9   W.A. Clouston, *Popular Tales and Fictions. Their Migration and Transformation* (Edinburgh et London, W. Blackwood, 1887). Notamment sur les sources des *Contes tartares*, I, 16; II, 39, 216, 217.

10   V. Chauvin, *Bibliographie des ouvrages arabes ou relatifs aux Arabes publiés dans l'Europe chrétienne de 1810 à 1855*. 12 tomes (Liège, H. Vaillant-Carmanne, 1892–1922).

11   M. Pike-Conant, *The Oriental Tale in England in the Eighteenth Century* (London, Cass, 1966 [1908]), 32–36.

12   H. Weber, *Tales of the East* (Edinburgh, J. Ballantyne, 1812), III.

13   'Suléiman éleva ses deux mains [...] en signe de supplication, et le Calife vit que son sein était d'un cristal transparent, au travers duquel on découvrait son cœur brûlant dans les flammes'; voir W. Beckford, *Vathek: Conte arabe* (Paris, Poinçot, 1787 [Paris, J. Corti, 1992]), 214. Cf. T.S. Gueullette, *Contes mogols* (Paris, Les Libraires associés, 1765), II, 50 (XXIIe soirée): 'Hélas me répondit le second, sans cesse bourrelés par le souvenir de nos mauvaises actions, voyez en quel état nous sommes. Alors

À la différence de Galland ou Pétis de la Croix, Gueullette n'a aucune connaissance des langues orientales, mais il a lu ses prédécesseurs avec attention et maîtrise une importante documentation, notamment la fameuse *Bibliothèque orientale* de d'Herbelot. Les *Contes chinois* constituent son second recueil oriental; ils sont publiés en 1723 et plusieurs fois réédités. Leur structure narrative repose sur le principe de la métempsycose: le conteur est censé avoir expérimenté toutes sortes d'avatars humains ou animaux, et leurs aventures, dont la mémoire lui est restée,[14] font la matière de ses récits. Montesquieu a imité le procédé dans son *Histoire véritable* laissée impubliée,[15] et chacun sait que Crébillon en a fait le principe narratif de son *Sopha* (1742).

À l'imitation des *Mille et une nuits* ou des *Mille et un jours*, les *Contes chinois* s'inscrivent dans un récit-cadre; l'enjeu est moins dramatique que dans les *Mille et une nuits*, il est politico-religieux: le roi de Chine Tongluk aime Gulchenraz, une princesse géorgienne en exil, mais la religion est un obstacle à leur mariage; elle est musulmane et il est idolâtre; elle est monothéiste et il croit à la métempsycose; elle ne l'épousera que s'il jure de la laisser libre de pratiquer sa religion en Chine (Gueullette fait semblant d'ignorer que le bouddhisme n'est pas la religion dominante en Chine, en quoi d'ailleurs il paraît s'inscrire dans l'affabulation 'orientaliste' dénoncée par Edward Saïd);[16] quoi qu'il en soit, le roi jure aussitôt ce qu'elle

---

déboutonnant leurs vestes, j'aperçus à travers de leur peau, qui était transparente comme un cristal, leurs cœurs environnés d'un feu qui les brûlait sans relâche, et sans pourtant les consumer; et je reconnus alors d'où procédaient les différents mouvements de rage et de désespoir qui paraissaient peints sur leur visage.'

14   Suivant le modèle pythagoricien légué par Diogène Laërce et ironiquement mis en scène par Lucien sous la forme d'un récit en Ière personne: *Le Songe du coq*.

15   Entre 1728 et 1734? Le projet d'avis 'Le Libraire au lecteur' renvoie explicitement au recueil de Gueullette.

16   Mais il se peut qu'il y ait là une sorte de jeu partagé avec le lecteur un peu cultivé du temps, car il suffisait d'ouvrir le dictionnaire pour savoir qu' 'il y a quatre principales religions à la Chine. L'ancienne, qui est celle de l'État, et qui ne reconnaît qu'un Dieu, souverain, maître du Ciel et la Terre; sans idoles ni statues. L'idolâtrie est la seconde, elle y fut apportée par Fohe ou Fohi, philosophe indien, 32 ans avant la naissance de Jésus-Christ. Il y a aussi un fort grand nombre d'athées. Enfin la religion chrétienne

demande, tout en suggérant que le mandarin Fum-Hoam est bien capable de la convertir puisqu'il a prétendu que sous peu 'Chinois et Géorgiens seraient soumis à la même divinité';[17] il propose qu'elle rencontre le mandarin et que s'il échoue à la convertir, lui-même se convertira à la religion musulmane et fera détruire temples et statues de la religion chinoise. Sur quoi Gulchenraz lui accorde sa main. Rencontrant ensuite le Mandarin, la reine se dit désireuse d'apprendre de lui les aventures curieuses dont on le crédite; il accepte, tout en avouant redouter son incrédulité puisqu'elle méprise le dogme de la métempsycose qui fonde la vraisemblance de ses récits; elle le lui accorde par hypothèse, comme une sorte de provisoire *suspension of disbelief* à l'égard de ce qu'il va raconter. Il annonce alors qu'il a vécu partout dans le monde, sous des formes très opposées et de 'tout sexe', et selon diverses religions; il a conservé le souvenir des choses qu'il a vues chez autrui ou lui-même vécues. La reine promet d'écouter avec plaisir, et d'éviter d'interrompre ses récits par des réflexions; elle les réserve pour la fin de ses récits. Les séances se dérouleront en soirée, avant le souper. Il y aura quarante-six soirées.

Cet article propose d'examiner comment ce recueil de Gueullette travaille à fabriquer du conte merveilleux à partir de séquences prélevées dans trois régimes de discours de savoir bien spécifiques chacun dans leur genre, mais que rassemble peut-être un certain rapport affiché à la visée de la vérité: la relation de mission en terre étrangère, le traité démonologique, l'orientalisme savant.

Le premier hypotexte consiste dans une reprise d'un chapitre d'un récit de mission: la *Nouvelle relation de la Gaspésie* par le père LeClerq (1691).[18]

---

y a pénétré [...]'; *Dictionnaire de Trévoux* (Paris, J.-M. Gandouin, 1732), art. 'Chine'. Déjà Bayle observait à l'article 'Brachmanes' (en citant le père le Gobien), que leur quiétisme est combattu en Chine: c'est contre cette ridicule doctrine (la doctrine de 'Fo', i.e. Bouddha) que les philosophes chinois déploient toute la force de leur éloquence. Ils regardent l'indifférence parfaite comme un monstre dans la morale, et comme le renversement de la société civile.

17 Gueullette, *Contes chinois*, I, 57.
18 Père C. LeClerq, 'De la croyance des Gaspésiens, touchant l'immortalité de l'âme', dans *Nouvelle Relation de la Gaspésie* (Paris, A. Auroy, 1691), 310–329.

L'ensemble de cette relation est comparable dans son propos et sa facture aux *Lettres édifiantes* des jésuites: c'est à la fois un document ethnographique et une entreprise apologétique. Il s'agit d'une peuplade américaine, les Micmacs, caractérisée par un attachement au symbole de la croix, et dont les capucins, pour cette raison, ont prioritairement entrepris l'évangélisation en s'employant à rectifier leurs croyances animistes. Le chapitre XII utilisé par Gueullette, concerne précisément ces croyances comme l'indique son titre, et le père LeClerq en rapporte la légende fondatrice: dans un temps reculé, des hommes de la tribu s'en sont allés au pays des âmes pour obtenir le retour de celle du fils de l'un d'entre eux. Y étant parvenus au terme d'une série d'épreuves, ils ont ramené cette âme parmi les hommes, mais la maladresse d'une vieille femme a fait qu'elle s'est échappée. En effet dans cette croyance, les âmes des morts tiennent à demeurer au pays des âmes. Ce mythe semble transmettre une expérience d'ordre chamanique et on en trouverait des équivalents dans bien des cultures traditionnelles. LeClerq quant à lui, a orienté son chapitre dans un sens apologétique; il commence ainsi en posant que ce peuple ignore les idées épicuriennes sur la mortalité de l'âme ou les idées pythagoriciennes sur la métempsycose, lesquelles ramènent toutes deux selon lui, l'homme à l'animal; or la légende qu'il rapporte est imprégnée d'animisme, puisqu'au pays des âmes, les objets eux-mêmes sont animés. Sa version est donc entremêlée de commentaires exprimant aussi bien le caractère fabuleux du récit que la nécessité de modifier la religion qu'il fonde, pour amener cette peuplade amatrice de croix vers le vrai Dieu et la vraie Croix.

Qu'est-ce que Gueullette fait de ce récit? Sur le plan narratif, il le recopie quasi littéralement, sans rien toucher d'essentiel à la structure ni même à la lettre; le titre change en revanche puisque cette séquence des *Contes chinois* (fin XXIVe–XXVe soirées) s'intitule: *Aventures du sauvage Kolao*.[19] Il ne transpose ni les noms, ni les coutumes ni le lieu; il indique même sa source en note.[20] En revanche, il efface toutes les interventions

---

19   Gueullette, *Contes chinois*, II, 29.

20   '(Pour) le récit du sauvage Kolao, il y a toute apparence qu'il est né dans le Canada vers l'embouchure du fleuve de St. Laurent. Le père Chrétien le Clerc, récollet missionnaire,

du père LeClerq dans son récit, gommant ainsi la critique chrétienne de la Fable. Néanmoins, une part des enjeux religieux réapparaît dans un autre élément de la structure: du point de vue du Mandarin, ce récit témoigne comme tous les autres, de la réalité de la métempsycose, qui peut déporter l'âme d'un Chinois vers un avatar vivant au Canada. Évidemment, la princesse auditrice suggère ironiquement en fin de récit que ce voyage soi-disant réel du métempsycosiste au pays des âmes paraît passablement fabuleux:[21] la possibilité du débat est ainsi suggérée, du moins pour le lecteur du père LeClerq ou celui qui prendrait au sérieux la discussion philosophique sur les enjeux du récit.

La deuxième sorte de texte utilisée dans ces *Contes chinois* concerne un récit que tout le monde aujourd'hui connaît grâce aux frères Grimm. C'est la légende du joueur de flûte de Hameln (ou Hamelin), cet enchanteur qui débarrasse une ville des rats qui l'avaient envahie, mais qui trompé par les habitants au moment de sa rétribution, se venge en entraînant tous leurs enfants vers le fleuve pour les y noyer. Cette légende fait aujourd'hui partie du patrimoine universel, mais je ne crois pas qu'elle ait été si connue auparavant. La première version en français que nous en ayons se trouve dans un traité de démonologie bien connu à l'Âge classique: *Le Monde enchanté* de Balthazar Bekker, chapitre XIX. *Que l'on ne doit point ajouter*

---

dit que le voisinage de Québec est un pays appelé Gaspé, situé dans des montagnes, des bois et des rochers, près la rivière de Mizamichiche, habité par des sauvages appelés Porte-Croix, parce qu'ils furent guéris d'une maladie pestilentielle par le respect qu'ils portèrent à la croix qu'un homme beau par excellence leur présenta pendant leur sommeil, et qui leur ordonna de porter à la main, sur la chair, ou sur leurs habits, ce signe de leur salut'; Gueullette, *Contes chinois*, II, 29.

21   Le Mandarin clôt cette séquence par son suicide après la fuite de l'âme de son fils, 'laissant (ses) camarades très affligés d'une catastrophe [...] qui les privait du plaisir d'apprendre avec encore plus de certitude des nouvelles du pays des âmes, et dans quelle classe étaient celles de leurs pères et de leurs frères', sur quoi l'auditrice commente: 'Effectivement, ces pauvres misérables perdaient beaucoup [...] ce jeune garçon leur eût fait de jolis contes'; Gueulette, *Contes chinois*, II, 45–46. La princesse ne développe pas la contradiction patente entre l'existence d'un pays des âmes désincarnées et heureuses de l'être et la doctrine classique du cycle des réincarnations; mais le lecteur cultivé du temps peut facilement y suppléer!

foi à la sortie des enfants de Hamelen et à l'esprit de Zacharie (d'après l'édition de 1694); auparavant, il y en a eu plusieurs versions en latin.[22] Ce
récit à cette époque donné pour vrai ou du moins vraisemblable, est censé
attesté par ce qu'en figurent les vitraux de l'église de Hameln en Basse-
Saxe, ainsi qu'une inscription sur la Porte neuve datant à deux cents ans
l'enlèvement de cent trente enfants, ce qui serait encore corroboré par
des vers au mur d'un couvent faisant remonter l'affaire à 1284. Le propos
de Bekker est de démystifier la superstition avec les armes de la raison et
de la vraie religion (il est protestant). En l'occurrence, il ne rapporte la
légende de Hameln que pour attaquer la vraisemblance des trois preuves
que je viens de rappeler. Sa version est donc rationaliste et critique, quoique
d'un point de vue chrétien (il croit à la réalité de l'efficacité trompeuse du
démon). Son propos apologétique est au fond comparable à celui du père
LeClerq; proche également de l'attitude des missionnaires jésuites dans les
Lettres édifiantes, rigoureusement rationalistes quand il s'agit de critiquer
les 'superstitions' des religions adverses, mais sans guère d'esprit critique
quand il s'agit de relater les miracles opérés par la vraie foi parmi les païens
du Nouveau Monde. Mais la réception des traités de démonologie par les
Lumières n'est pas moins paradoxale:[23] d'une part, ils sont un élément de
culture générale (Voltaire les cite facilement comme il cite d'ailleurs l'Écriture Sainte et les Pères),[24] d'autre part ce qui en circule dans le public, ce

22   B. Bekker, *Le Monde enchanté* (Amsterdam, P. Rotterdam, 1694), 364–366: 'Que
       l'on ne doit point ajouter plus de foi à la sortie des enfants de Hamelen et à l'esprit
       de Zacharie'.

23   N. Jacques-Chaquin, 'La Passion des sciences interdites: curiosité et démonologie
       (XVè–XVIIIè siècles)', dans S. Houdard et N. Jacques-Chaquin (éds), *Curiosité et
       Libido Sciendi de la Renaissance aux Lumières* (Paris, ENS, 1998), I, 73–107.

24   'Le fait est que, du temps de Bekker, ministre du saint Évangile (comme on dit en
       Hollande), le diable avait encore un crédit prodigieux chez les théologiens de toutes
       les espèces, au milieu du XVIIe siècle, malgré Bayle et les bons esprits qui commençai-
       ent à éclairer le monde. La sorcellerie, les possessions, et tout ce qui est attaché à cette
       belle théologie, étaient en vogue dans toute l'Europe, et avaient souvent des suites
       funestes'; Voltaire, *Dictionnaire philosophique*, dans *Œuvres complètes*, éd. L. Morand
       (Paris, s.éd, 1877–1885), art. 'BEKKER, ou du Monde enchanté, du diable, du livre
       d'Énoch, et des sorciers'.

sont les récits 'fantastiques' dont ils abondent;[25] d'où un statut équivoque: ils participent de la démystification rationaliste du surnaturel, mais leur matière nourrit aussi ce qu'on pourrait appeler l'envers 'fantastiquant' des Lumières. L'histoire des enfants de Hameln circule dans ce contexte idéologique quasi aporétique caractéristique de la tension au fil du XVIIIe siècle, entre Lumières et Illuminisme. Entre 1710 et la fin du siècle, elle est portée par trois supports (outre Bekker lui-même): le premier est l'*Histoire des imaginations extravagantes de M. Oufle* de l'abbé Bordelon (1710)[26] où elle est rapportée en note assez longuement d'après Bekker (274–277) comme appui érudit à l'une des croyances du héros (ce M. Oufle est quelqu'un qui croit tout ce qui est écrit, particulièrement quant au surnaturel); le second est l'anthologie des *Voyages imaginaires*, où l'on retrouve au t. 36, le roman de Bordelon avec la note en question.[27]

Le troisième support est précisément la version des *Contes chinois*. Elle apparaît à la XLIVe soirée, dans le cadre de l'*Histoire du prince Kader-Bilah*. Gueullette a certainement travaillé avec la version de Bekker. Ici, son travail de réécriture à tous les niveaux du texte est beaucoup plus complexe que dans le cas précédent. Il y a trois aspects significatifs qui signalent une pratique d'hybridation de discours ou de régimes de discours hétérogènes voire hétéroclites. Premier point: l'ancrage géographique n'est plus la Basse-Saxe mais Ispahan, et très précisément l'Ispahan de Chardin, auquel renvoie d'ailleurs une note en bas de page: 'Le chevalier Chardin, dans le huitième volume de ses voyages en Perse, page 148, dit avoir vu des vestiges de cette tour, et qu'elle s'appelait la tour des quarante filles, par la raison

25 Voir surtout la thèse de doctorat d'Emmanuelle Sempere, *De la merveille à l'inquiétude: le registre du fantastique dans la fiction narrative du XVIIIè siècle* (Thèse de doctorat, Université de Paris 3, 2006), à paraître aux Presses Universitaires de Bordeaux, 2009.

26 L. Bordelon, *Histoire des imaginations extravagantes de Monsieur Oufle* (Amsterdam, E. Roger, P. Humbert, P. de Coup et les frères Châtelain, 1710), note du chapitre 25.

27 L. Bordelon, *L'Histoire des imaginations extravagantes de Monsieur Oufle*, dans *Voyages imaginaires, songes visions et romans cabalistiques* (Amsterdam et Paris, s.éd., 1789), XXXVI, 274–277.

ci-dessus alléguée'.[28] Dans la version des *Contes chinois*, si l'enchanteur Giouf (un nain contrefait et non un géant 'd'une grandeur extraordinaire et effroyable' comme dans la version de Bekker), noie bien les rats au son de son flageolet, le châtiment du marché de dupe ne vise pas les enfants de la cité mais les plus belles filles des notables que la mère de Giouf, la ginne Mergian Bannou (une géante cette fois), enferme à l'état de fantômes dans une tour dite des 'quarante jeunes filles' aux abords de la ville. Or, il existe bien à Ispahan, une tour des quarante jeunes filles, dont nous pouvons lire cinq lignes de description chez Chardin, dans l'édition de 1711, au tome et à la page indiqués par Gueullette en note: ainsi, parmi les quatre tours principales de la forteresse d'Ispahan, l'une 'qui est au midi, s'appelle, écrit Chardin, la Tour des quarante filles, parce qu'on croit qu'il y revient des esprits en forme de jeunes filles, à cause de quoi cette tour n'est pas habitée comme les autres; personne n'ose y coucher'. L'on pourrait ajouter que le fleuve Zenderou où sont noyés les rats persans est réel comme l'est la Weser dans la version de Bekker.

Second volet de cette réécriture: le personnage du joueur de flûte est dédoublé: d'une part un nain difforme, d'autre part sa mère la Ginne géante qui prend en charge la vengeance. Cette Ginne ne provient ni de Chardin ni de l'imagination de Gueullette, elle vient de la *Bibliothèque orientale* de d'Herbelot, bible de l'orientalisme au XVIIIe siècle. Gueullette cette fois, est peu prolixe à son sujet en bas de page, se bornant à porter l'explication du mot 'ginne': 'génie femelle';[29] cependant, il a certainement utilisé ce que d'Herbelot offre à son article *Mergian*: 'ce mot, qui signifie en arabe le corail est aussi devenu le nom propre de plusieurs personnages véritables ou fabuleux. Mergian Banou est le nom d'une fée ou enchanteresse, de laquelle il est fait souvent mention dans les romans orientaux. Elle était de la race des Péris, c.a. des géants [...] de la belle espèce. C'est du nom de cette fée que nos anciens romans ont formé celui de Morgane la Déconnuë'.[30]

---

28   Gueullette, *Contes chinois*, II, 246.
29   Gueullette, *Contes chinois*, II, 249.
30   B. d'Herbelot, *Bibliothèque orientale* (Paris, Compagnie des Libraires, 1697).

Le troisième aspect de la réécriture consiste en certaines modifications de la structure narrative de la légende initiale, liées à la présence dans l'intrigue d'un prince en quête de la réalisation de son destin: celui-ci a lu jadis dans une bibliothèque, un livre où sont évoquées la tour d'Ispahan et l'aventure des rats et des jeunes filles: il a pris cela pour une fable et ne s'en est pas préoccupé; mais après la mort de sa femme, les circonstances lui font reprendre cette lecture, et son approche change: d'une part, tant de témoignages semblent attester la vérité des faits racontés que son incrédulité vacille; d'autre part, la fin du récit semble l'appeler à cette tour d'Ispahan pour tenter l'aventure de la délivrance des quarante jeunes filles. Il s'agit donc d'une métalepse narrative, le lecteur de ce récit devenant un protagoniste potentiel.[31] Arrivé à Ispahan et s'étant rendu à la tour, il reconnaît les lieux et y trouve effectivement la lame d'or aux inscriptions oraculaires prédite par le livre; alors peut s'ensuivre le récit de la délivrance mouvementée des quarante jeunes filles, qui occasionnera parallèlement celle des trente-neuf héros pétrifiés pour avoir auparavant échoué. On retrouve là un motif de conte traditionnel.[32]

Gueullette hybride donc des scénarios séparés dans la synchronie du monde des récits à son époque, tout en procédant (conte oriental oblige) à l'''orientalisation' systématique de la donnée transmise dans Bekker. On pourrait avancer trois enjeux de cette opération: le premier serait une articulation de la pratique du conteur au discours savant contemporain (Huet, Galland) sur les origines orientales de la féerie et du merveilleux

---

31 Ce type de métalepse n'est pas étranger au conte de fées antérieur. Voir par exemple le conte du *Rameau d'or* (Mme d'Aulnoy): le prince Torticolis enfermé dans une vieille tour, y découvre un livre et des vitraux animés où il se voit représenté et dont il suit les instructions.

32 On le trouve par exemple dans la séquence III (K) du conte type 707 'L'Oiseau de vérité': 'la sœur (le 3è frère) fait cesser l'enchantement des frères; K5: ainsi que de nombreux autres seigneurs qui les avaient précédés dans ces quêtes'. Voir P. Delarue et M.-L. Tenèze, *Le Conte populaire français. Catalogue raisonné des versions de France* (Paris, Maisonneuve et Larose, 2002), I, 639. Voir *La Princesse Belle Étoile* (Mme d'Aulnoy).

occidentaux;[33] c'est d'ailleurs un thème qui apparaît dans l'article 'Mergian' de d'Herbelot où la ginne passe pour l'origine de la fameuse fée du cycle des *Amadis*. On lirait donc dans cette séquence des *Contes chinois* un retour aux sources un peu ironique du conteur? Pourquoi pas après tout? Mais on pourrait facilement renverser la thèse et soutenir que le discours savant est ici devenu matière de merveilleux, opérateur de féerie. Ce qui m'amène au second point: qu'arrive-t-il dans ce recueil aux récits prétendant à la vérité? Quelle est à cet égard la signification de la mobilisation explicite d'un élément toponymique avéré par Chardin? Tout lecteur de Chardin sait le soin qu'il prend à se distinguer de ses prédécesseurs ignorants de la langue persane et soupçonnés d'inventer une bonne part de leurs récits; mais voici aussi ce qu'écrit Galland dans son *Voyage au Levant*: 'vous n'y aurez point trouvé de ces événements surprenants qui engagent agréablement un lecteur [...] Mais sachant que vous n'avez point le goût dépravé de ceux qui préfèrent des historiettes grossièrement déguisées à des récits véritables et fidèles, je me persuade que ma sincérité ne vous aura point déplu';[34] ainsi le journal de voyage comme genre serait capable de dire la vérité: on est ici au coeur des débats du siècle sur la capacité des formes narratives dominantes (histoire ou roman) à dire mieux que le vraisemblable;[35] une échappée, celle des écrivains modernes, consiste à fabriquer des récits dénonçant leurs propres procédures de fictionnalisation. C'est ce que fait Gueullette: on se souvient que le prince Kader Billah passe de l'incrédulité à la crédulité active dans son interprétation du livre qui recèle son destin: imaginons à sa place un lecteur de Bekker, et disons alors que les *Contes chinois* en ces séquences mais en bien d'autres aussi, hybrident et font travailler ensemble des régimes discursifs *a priori* antinomiques dans leur rapport au mensonge et à la vérité. On verrait se nouer ici sur un mode sceptique, l'articulation de sa pratique de la composition (oxymoronique et paradoxale) avec les

33   Voir J.-F. Perrin, 'L'Invention d'un genre littéraire au XVIIIè siècle: le conte oriental', *Féeries* 2 (2004–2005), 9–28.

34   A. Galland, *Le Voyage à Smyrne*, éd. F. Bauduen (Paris, Chandeigne, 2000), 22.

35   Voir sur ce point M. Hobson, *The Object of Art* (Cambridge, CUP, 1982), 45–138; et R. Démoris, *Le Roman à la première personne. Du Classicisme aux Lumières* (Genève, Droz, 2002), 178–190.

débats esthétiques du temps. Mais on voit bien aussi les tensions idéologiques qui sont ici en jeu.

Le troisième régime discursif travaillé dans ces *Contes chinois*: le régime théologico-philosophique constitue explicitement un enjeu central du recueil, puisque l'autobiographie du mandarin 'métempsycosiste', doit conduire la princesse musulmane à une conversion. Au cours des quarante-six soirées du recueil, la princesse a eu l'occasion de noter brièvement quelques contradictions du type de celle que j'ai relevée à propos du voyage au pays des âmes,[36] mais il n'y a jamais eu de discussion sur le fond. Tout change vers la fin du recueil, le Mandarin se révélant en réalité Alroamat, le frère de la princesse, qui n'a feint la foi des Chinois que pour convertir – non la princesse (elle est sa sœur) – mais leur roi; il a forgé ses récits 'dans le goût' des 'contes extravagants' des mandarins, ce sont de pures fictions, la métempsycose n'existe pas.[37] C'est alors qu'il abandonne le régime narratif pour entrer dans un régime argumentatif, cette fois destiné au roi de Chine: d'une part un argumentaire rationaliste et critique contre la croyance en la métempsycose, et d'autre part une apologie du dogme musulman. Or cet argumentaire et cette apologie sont tous deux intégralement citationnels, et sans doute relativement repérables pour tels à l'époque par un lecteur un peu cultivé. L'apologie de l'Alcoran et de Mahomet est intégralement un montage de citations prélevées dans divers articles de la *Bibliothèque orientale*,[38] citations visiblement choisies par Gueulette pour ce qu'elles exhibent de récit fabuleux dans le discours censément argumenté de son convertisseur: voici un exemple du discours d'Alroamat:

---

36   Par exemple après une séquence d'annonce de la date de la mort d'un avatar du Mandarin par un revenant reconnaissant: 'Voilà des événements assez singuliers, dit la reine de la Chine; ils m'ont fait d'autant plus de plaisir qu'ils combattent un peu votre système de la transmigration; mais je ne veux pas vous arrêter pour si peu de chose; continuez, sage Fum-Hoam, et apprenez-moi ce que vous devîntes ensuite. Le mandarin rougit à ce petit reproche et poursuivit [...]'; Gueulette, *Contes chinois*, I, 124–125.

37   Gueulette, *Contes chinois*, II, 322 *et seq.*

38   Articles 'Alcoran', 'Afu' et Afou', 'Nouh alNabi, Noé', 'Nemrod', 'Feraoun', 'Hegrah', 'Abrahah', 'Zacoum', 'Meviz agagiet'.

(Dieu) punit les impies par les châtiments les plus terribles: n'est-ce pas lui qui pour châtier l'orgueil de Caïcaous, ordonna au moucheron de pénétrer jusqu'aux membranes de son cerveau, et de lui causer une douleur si insupportable qu'il était obligé de se faire battre la tête avec un maillet? N'est-ce pas lui qui fit flotter sur la mer le corps de Ferraoun avec sa cuirasse de fer, pour faire connaître à son peuple qu'il l'avait délivré d'un ennemi si terrible dont il ignorait la mort.[39]

Voici l'une des sources dans d'Herbelot:

Le Nembrod des Hébreux [...], est le même que Caïcaous, second roi de la seconde dynastie de Perse, nommée des Caïanides [...]; après l'épisode de la tour de Babel par laquelle Nemrod a défié Dieu, comme celui-ci restait rebelle, Dieu envoya des nuées de moucherons qui firent fuir les partisans qui lui restaient [...] (quant à lui) un de ces moucherons étant entré par les narines de Nembrod, pénétra jusqu'à une des membranes de son cerveau, où grossissant de jour en jour il lui causa une si grande douleur, qu'il était obligé de se faire battre la tête avec un maillet pour pouvoir prendre quelque repos, et qu'il souffrit ce supplice pendant l'espace de quatre cents ans. (art 'Nemrod')

Et voici l'autre:

Les Israéliens après avoir passé la mer, ne furent pas encore délivrés de toute sorte de crainte, car ne sachant pas que Pharaon fût péri dans les eaux, ils appréhendèrent qu'il ne fit préparer des vaisseaux pour la passer, et ne les poursuivît jusque dans le désert: c'est pourquoi, disent les musulmans en continuant leurs fables, Dieu fit venir au-dessus de l'eau à la vue de leur camp, le corps de Pharaon qui fut reconnu à la cuirasse de fer qu'il portait, et ce miracle de faire flotter un corps chargé de fer les assurant de plus en plus de la protection de Dieu, leur ôta toute sorte d'inquiétude. (art 'Feraoun')

Quant à l'argumentaire contre la métempsycose, il est pour l'essentiel celui de la tradition épicurienne, tel qu'il se répète jusqu'aux libertins érudits du XVIIe, depuis ce qu'a écrit Lucrèce au livre III du *De Natura rerum* (v. 741 *et seq.*); voici ce que dit Alroamat:

---

39   Gueullette, *Contes chinois*, I, 332–333.

Comment suivant leurs principes, veulent-ils pouvoir se ressouvenir dans un corps de ce qui s'est passé dans un autre?[40] Si cela était, et que l'âme passât ainsi de corps en corps, elle serait bien malheureuse d'être assujettie aux inclinations dominantes de celui où elle réside. Car enfin les bêtes féroces conservent toujours la triste et cruelle semence de leur espèce; la ruse et la malice sont héréditaires aux renards et aux singes; la fuite et la timidité est le partage des daims et des cerfs;[41] et c'est bien avilir l'âme que de dire qu'elle ne puisse pas changer les habitudes du corps où elle se trouve.[42] Selon quelques histoires de vos mandarins, les hommes sont irraisonnables, pendant que la farouche espèce des bêtes, ainsi que je vous l'ai fait voir, est douée d'un raisonnement très sensé;[43] ah! seigneur, vous avez trop d'esprit pour croire de pareilles puérilités, mais entraîné par les préjugés de l'éducation, vous n'avez jamais

40 L'argument remonte à Lucrèce: 'Si l'âme est immortelle et qu'au moment de la naissance, elle se glisse dans le corps, pourquoi notre vie antérieure ne nous laisse-t-elle aucun souvenir? Pourquoi ne conservons-nous aucune trace de nos anciennes actions?'; *De la nature, Livre III*, v. 670 *et seq.*, trad. H. Clouard (Paris, Garnier-Flammarion, 1964). Il est repris (d'un point de vue chrétien) par Lactance: 'O miram et singularem Pythagorae memoriam. O miseram oblivionem nostrum omnium, qui nesciamus qui ante fuerimus', *Institutions divines, Livre III*, ch. 18, cité par Bayle, *Dictionnaire*, art. 'Pythagoras', note M.

41 Gueullette paraphrase encore ici un argumentaire lucrétien: 'D'où vient que le lion conserve toujours la férocité, le renard la ruse, le cerf la crainte, et qu'enfin toutes les sortes d'animaux gardent les premières inclinations de leur espèce dès le moment qu'ils commencent à être formés? [...] En vain prétendrait-on que des âmes, qui de leur nature sont immortelles, changeassent d'inclination en changeant de corps'. Voir Lucrèce, *De la nature, Livre III*, v. 741 *et seq.*, trad. J.-B. de Boyer d'Argens, dans *Mémoires secrets de la République des Lettres ou le théâtre de la vérité* (Genève, Slatkine, 1967), II, 178–179.

42 Gueullette condense l'argument lucrétien: 'Si l'âme était immortelle, et que la transmigration dans les corps fût ordinaire, tous les êtres qui jouissent de la vie n'auraient aucune inclination, ni habitude particulière de leur espèce, puisque leur âme en serait indépendante' (*ibid.*).

43 Allusion probable aux fables animalières de Bidpaï: *Contes et fables indiennes*, dont Gueullette éditera la traduction par Galland en 1724. Mais il retrouve aussi la suite de l'argumentaire lucrétien: 'Si l'âme était immortelle, & que la transmigration dans les corps fût ordinaire, tous les êtres qui jouissent de la vie n'auraient aucune inclination, ni habitude particulière à leur espèce, puisque leur âme en serait indépendante. Le chien d'Hyrcanie fuirait devant le cerf, l'épervier craindrait la colombe, les hommes seraient aussi irraisonnables que les bêtes, *et les animaux pourraient être doués d'une grande sagesse et d'une connaissance très sensée*' (*ibid.*) (je souligne).

voulu raisonner sur la religion de vos pères; est-il possible que vous soyez persuadé
avec le peuple, que la nature immortelle des âmes soit soumise à un corps qui est la
nourriture des vers, et que parmi la multitude innombrable des âmes, il naisse une
émulation précipitée pour la préférence de s'introduire dans un corps qui vient d'être
formé, à moins que, par l'accord fait entre elles, il ne soit convenu que la première
arrivée ait le droit d'être la première reçue dans un corps qui en a besoin.[44] La mort,
suivant ce raisonnement, ne serait qu'un nom redoutable, et toutes ses attaques seraient indifférentes: il serait égal à l'homme de faire de bonnes ou de mauvaises actions
(ce qui répugne à la nature).[45]

Non content de monter en épingle les éléments fabuleux de la Révélation
prêchée par son convertisseur exalté (et à l'époque de Fontenelle et de
Montesquieu, c'est là révéler la textualité narrative dans la parole préten-
due révélée – le monothéisme musulman servant d'écran à l'attaque contre
l'autre monothéisme), Gueullette fait encore utiliser un argumentaire maté-
rialiste par un fanatique censé défendre le point de vue religieux; dans ces
contradictions *signalées* (ou ce persiflage ostensible) l'on trouve volontiers
l'hybridation oxymoronique ou paradoxale évoquée ci-dessus; mais on peut
rêver parallèlement sur les liens implicites qui relient ce discours hybride
avec celui du père LeClerq qui, je le rappelle, ouvre son chapitre sur la
religion de ses Gaspésiens par une double attaque contre le matérialisme
philosophique et le pythagorisme, tous deux révoqués devant la seule religion qui rappelle l'âme à sa divinité. La fabrique du conte chez Gueullette
s'avère ainsi opératrice d'hybridation et peut-être de transmutation des
discours reçus: orientalisme savant, débat sur la métempsycose (qui est un

---

44   Cf. Lucrèce: 'Au reste, n'est-il pas ridicule de se figurer que les âmes sont en faction
     pour animer précipitamment les plaisirs de Vénus, & qu'elles ne manquent pas de se
     trouver au moment de la formation des animaux? Est-il possible que des substances
     éternelles s'empressent si fort de s'emparer de quelques infortunés membres mortels,
     et qu'elles se disputent la préférence de s'introduire dans les corps? Il doit sans doute
     y avoir entre elles quelque traité, dans lequel il est stipulé que la première qui arrivera,
     & qui sera la plus diligente, aura le droit d'être reçue dans le corps'; Lucrèce, *De la
     nature, Livre III*, v. 777 *et seq.*, trad. Boyer d'Argens (*op.cit.*).
45   Gueullette, *Contes chinois*, II, 325–327.

thème bien répandu au XVIIIe),[46] éléments de libertinage philosophique et contre-argumentaire chrétien (sous voile musulman): toute une actualité littéraire et idéologique dont le conte oriental de Gueullette se saisit pour en faire matière de fiction critique.

L'on peut constater, en étudiant les recueils de Gueullette, que s'y déroule, en synchronie, une sorte de mime de ce que l'histoire des contes développe en diachronie – soit un processus d'actualisation permanente dont rend bien compte ce jugement de Claude Brémond: 'il n'y a pas de contes originels, mais des contes progressivement construits par intégration et naturalisation d'éléments thématiques empruntés à d'autres sources.'[47] Dans l'histoire du conte littéraire français depuis le XVIIe siècle, ces sources sont souvent des contes ou des segments de contes, et quelquefois aussi elles proviennent du roman ou de l'opéra; dès cette époque de son invention comme genre littéraire, le conte de fées se produit en contrepoint d'autres genres, emboîté dans des nouvelles ou de petits romans, associé à un essai ou à de la poésie, etc. Chez Gueullette cette dimension-là est aussi présente et ses emprunts aux fabliaux, aux *exempla*, aux recueils de nouvelles italiennes, à Straparole, etc. ont bien été repérés; néanmoins, ce n'est pas le plus intéressant chez lui car la meilleure part de son matériau narratif provient d'une documentation didactique et savante, qu'il s'agisse de ses canevas, des noms des personnages, des discours et maximes qu'ils prononcent, etc.: son art consiste essentiellement en une poétique sophistiquée du montage d'éléments narratifs disparates collectés sur tous les rayons de la bibliothèque. Gueullette travaille avec l'encyclopédie de son temps qu'il aborde comme une textualité généralisée des savoirs et des croyances dont il casse les ordonnances, mélange les pages et recompose les textes, en questionnant les savoirs par les fictions, les discours par les récits, les croyances par les fables, et vice versa, selon un point de vue profondément sceptique. À cet égard, le succès de ses recueils, sans doute dû pour une part à ce qui

---

46 Voir J.-F. Perrin, 'Petits Traités de l'âme et du corps: les contes à métempsycose (XVIIè–XVIIIè siècle)', dans R. Jomand-Baudry et J.-F. Perrin (éds), *Le Conte merveilleux au XVIIIè siècle* (Paris, Kimé, 2002), 123–139.

47 Brémond, 'L'Étymologie des contes', 199.

s'y transmet d'une très ancienne matière narrative écrite et orale, doit sans doute être analysé aussi comme lié à l'émergence d'un nouveau public avide de l'Autre et de l'Ailleurs, affamé de science et de technique, prêt à questionner jusqu'à un certain point ses propres croyances, mais partagé pour longtemps encore entre crédulité et incrédulité à l'égard des merveilles et des curiosités qu'on lui conte. Sur le plan de l'histoire du genre, ce recueil nous parle d'une transmutation en cours.

Du conte 'parodique' au conte pédagogique: *Le Prince Désir* de Mme Leprince de Beaumont

ANNE DEFRANCE

Exposant son programme dans l'Avertissement qui introduit *Le Magasin des enfants*,[1] Mme Leprince de Beaumont, gouvernante chargée de l'éducation de jeunes Anglaises, déplore que les livres mis entre leurs mains soient trop souvent inadaptés à leur âge, y compris les contes de fées, qu'elle trouve en général pernicieux. Elle juge bon, pourtant, d'en rédiger et de les intégrer à ses leçons, rendant ainsi au jeune public ce qui était considéré par les détracteurs du genre féerique, dès son origine, comme un ridicule enfantillage d'adulte et ramenant les contes à leur oralité première. Elle récuse alors tout emprunt: 'je n'en ai pas lu un seul que je puisse raccommoder selon mes vues'.[2]

D'aucuns se sont laissés prendre à cette dénégation, mais comme d'autres contes du recueil, *Le Prince Désir*, qui ouvre le second tome (X^e dialogue – 8e journée), a une source: il est inspiré par *La Patte du chat, conte zinzimois*, premier texte de Cazotte, publié anonymement quinze ans

---

1   Madame Leprince de Beaumont, *Le Magasin des enfants, ou Dialogues d'une sage gouvernante avec ses élèves de la première distinction, dans lesquels on fait penser, parler, agir les jeunes gens suivant le génie, le tempérament et les inclinations d'un chacun. On y représente les défauts de leur âge; l'on y montre de quelle manière on peut les en corriger; on s'applique autant à leur former le cœur qu'à leur éclairer l'esprit. On y donne un abrégé de l'histoire sacrée, de la fable, de la géographie, etc., le tout rempli de réflexions utiles, et de contes moraux pour les amuser agréablement; et écrit d'un style simple et proportionné à la tendresse de leurs années*, éd. E. Biancardi (Paris, Champion, 2008 [Londres, s.éd., 1756–1780]), Avertissement, 969. Nous utiliserons les abréviations *M.E.* pour le titre de l'ouvrage, et Av. pour l'Avertissement de l'auteur au lecteur. Les chiffres romains renvoient, si nécessaire, aux numéros des 'Dialogues'.

2   *M.E.*, Av., 968.

plus tôt.[3] Son auteur est alors étudiant à Paris; introduit dans la bonne société, il fréquente certainement des cercles littéraires. Grand lecteur de contes, il les affectionne et se livre pourtant à une dévalorisation ludique de la féerie: pratique paradoxale commune aux auteurs qui, à partir d'Hamilton et surtout dans les années 1740, exploitent de manière voyante le potentiel parodique inhérent au genre.

Si Mme Leprince de Beaumont critique également le merveilleux, ses intentions sont tout autres: elle le juge néfaste quand il n'est pas 'joint nécessairement à la fin qu'on doit offrir aux enfants, l'acquisition des vertus et la correction des vices'.[4] Dans la longue expansion du titre de son recueil qui regroupe un ensemble de séances pédagogiques présentées comme 'dialogues' entre une gouvernante (Mademoiselle Bonne) et ses jeunes élèves de cinq à treize ans, l'auteur annonce la fonction qu'elle assigne à ses '*Contes moraux*': ils sont faits pour 'amuser agréablement' les enfants, l'ensemble étant écrit 'dans un style simple proportionné à la tendresse de leurs années'. Mais tous 'tendent au même but' que ses histoires (adaptées en grande partie de la Bible): 'convaincre incontestablement de la nécessité de pratiquer' les maximes du livre divin, 'convaincre que leur bien-être en cette vie dépend de la docilité à suivre ces maximes'.[5] Le contexte de ces contes et leur vocation apologale implique une stratégie argumentative travaillée par l'oralité, dupliquée au sein de ce conte particulier par les conversations entre héros/élève et fée/pédagogue.

Nous comparerons donc *Le Prince Désir* avec sa source, *La Patte du chat*, en démêlant d'abord les fondements de ce choix, puis en analysant les principales modifications que Madame Leprince de Beaumont a imposées au texte initial. Nous examinerons la manière dont elle résout le paradoxe apparent d'une réécriture qui exhibe les limites du discours éducatif et questionne, plus encore que son modèle inavoué, les pouvoirs de l'oralité.

---

3   J. Cazotte, *La Patte du chat, conte zinzimois*, éd. A. Defrance, dans A. Defrance et J.-F. Perrin (éds), *Hamilton et autres conteurs* (Paris, Champion, 2008 [à Tilloobalaa [Paris], s. éd., 1741]). Nous utiliserons l'abréviation *P.C.* pour *La Patte du chat* de Cazotte. Nous devons le signalement de cette source à Georges Décote.

4   *M.E.*, Av., 969.

5   *M.E.*, Av., 973.

I Pourquoi ce conte?

L'élection du conte source trouve sa justification dans la fiction cadre, avec qui la version de Mme Leprince de Beaumont entretient un fort rapport thématique: l'orgueil, vice très attaqué par les moralistes du XVIIe siècle, y est condamné dans les deux textes. Mademoiselle Bonne choisit ses histoires en fonction de ses élèves, or l'une d'elles, Lady Spirituelle, la seule qui réagisse au conte après audition, a raconté antérieurement à la petite compagnie comment elle aimait être louée par autrui et se moquer des ignorantes.[6] Plus tard elle a dit sa douleur d'avoir surpris une conversation condamnant sa méchanceté et son orgueil de 'démon'.[7] Cette scène mortifiante a suscité sa prise de conscience et motivé sa décision immédiate de tout entreprendre pour se corriger.[8] Ce récit confirme la créance de l'auteur en une idée défendue par Locke dans ses *Pensées sur l'Éducation* (1693), ouvrage très favorablement reçu en Angleterre et diffusé dans toute l'Europe, selon laquelle l'honneur et le sentiment de la honte constitueraient des ressorts éducatifs non négligeables dès la prime enfance.

L'intrigue du conte est centrée sur une rééducation similaire, à laquelle le bonheur du Prince Désir (*alias* Amadil chez Cazotte) est suspendu. La guérison du héros et ses bénéfices sont d'autant plus spectaculaires pour les jeunes auditrices que le défaut incriminé, l'amour-propre, a trouvé dans ce conte une figuration amusante: le jeune homme est affublé par maléfice d'un nez très long qu'il refuse pourtant de reconnaître comme tel. Après de nombreuses avanies, il finit par maudire son nez, qui raccourcit immédiatement, tandis que les obstacles au bonheur général sont instantanément anéantis.

Aussi les jeunes élèves de Mademoiselle Bonne peuvent-elles, selon leur maturité, trouver matière à méditer sur cette double démonstration

---

6   *M.E.*, I, 989.

7   *M.E.*, II, 991.

8   La gouvernante notera plus tard, peu avant le conte qui nous occupe, que Lady Spirituelle a considérablement progressé en un mois (*M.E.*, VI, 1050).

orale par l'exemple, la première consistant en un récit vrai, spontané, une histoire vécue par l'une d'elles, la seconde, en une fiction bien plus colorée et plus amusante, narrée par l'éducatrice, fiction à prendre avec distance et sollicitant l'intelligence de l'interprétation. Dans le conte, le héros doit parvenir seul à la prise de conscience, sans que personne ne lui révèle la condition à laquelle est attachée la fin de ses malheurs, ainsi en a décidé leur auteur, un personnage opposant. Les personnages auxiliaires sont donc prisonniers d'une double contrainte: suggérer sans dire, guider le jeune prince sans faire tout le travail à sa place. Sa laborieuse et ingénieuse rééducation, qui constitue l'essentiel de l'intrigue, offre donc de quoi intéresser celle qui prône, à la suite de Fénelon, une pédagogie participative, et entend non faire avaler mais 'digérer' ses leçons. C'est bien ainsi qu'opère Mlle Bonne, qui laisse les enfants s'accuser eux-mêmes de leurs défauts sans les accabler, les félicitant au contraire de leur aveu.

Mme Leprince de Beaumont, dans l'*Avertissement* inaugural, promet d'ailleurs aux éducateurs qu'en suivant son exemple et en adaptant son recueil, ils pourront en faire profiter tous les élèves, même les plus difficiles:

> Je conjure ici les personnes chargées du soin de l'éducation, de suppléer à ce qui manque à mon travail: qu'elles refondent ce qu'elles trouveront obscur; qu'elles le traduisent, l'abrègent et le tournent de tant de côtés qu'il s'en trouve un qui soit à la portée de leurs élèves. Que les difficultés ne les arrêtent point, une expérience de trente années m'autorise à leur répondre du succès. Je puis les assurer avec vérité que depuis ce grand nombre d'années, je n'ai pas trouvé un seul enfant incurable ...[9]

La pratique de l'adaptation textuelle prônée ici (refonte, traduction, simplification, censure, malaxage) est précisément celle que l'auteur a imposée, sans le dire, au conte de Cazotte, comme aux autres contes réécrits.[10] Réécrivant ce récit de formation, elle met en abyme sa propre démarche pédagogique, et tant mieux si le héros est un cas extrême (de tous les personnages de contes souffrant du même défaut, il remporte en effet la palme de l'aveuglement et de la surdité): par assimilation, son histoire pourra

9   *M.E.*, Av., 981.
10   L. Seifert, 'Madame Le Prince de Beaumont and the infantilisation of the fairy tale', *French Literature Series* 31 (2004), 25–39.

d'autant mieux convaincre de la validité de la méthode, et de son extension possible aux cas les plus rebelles.

II Censure et invention compensatoire

L'asservissement du récit à un message moralisant facile d'accès entraîne donc trois opérations essentielles conjointes: simplification de l'intrigue, censure des éléments inadaptés, et ajout de nouveaux. La longueur du texte source (126 pages in-12) impose d'emblée un raccourcissement conséquent (*Le Prince Désir* est dix fois moins long) mais c'est surtout sa complexité qui appelle amendement. La diversité de ses thèmes, sa narration non rectiligne, la polyvalence des interprétations qu'il peut susciter sont autant d'éléments indésirables, et sans conteste nocifs aux yeux de Mme Leprince de Beaumont.

Chez elle comme chez Cazotte, la particularité physique dont le héros est affublé résulte d'une malédiction proférée par un enchanteur. Dans *La Patte du Chat*, ce dernier est un libertin, qui, après avoir abandonné sa maîtresse, la fée Bleuâtre, la persécute. Jaloux de son nouvel amant, il l'éloigne d'elle, la punit et dote leur fils Amadil d'un long nez, avant de renouer avec elle et de lui faire un enfant. Amadil apprend tardivement cette histoire – et le lecteur avec lui – de la bouche de Bleuâtre qui lui révèle son identité. Dans le long récit rétrospectif de ses aventures amoureuses, elle ne lui cache ni son goût pour le plaisir, marqué dans ses jeunes années, ni le rêve érotique qui l'a précipitée dans les bras du futur père d'Amadil: on conçoit aisément que l'épisode ait été censuré par la conteuse. Il faut donc trouver une autre motivation au motif du long nez qu'elle entend conserver, car l'organe est à la fois symptôme, symbole visible du défaut moral et instrument de la thérapie: c'est en portant atteinte, de diverses manières, à ce nez, que les personnages auxiliaires du conte-source mettront le prince sur la voie de la lucidité.

L'immoralité des personnages du premier conte justifie la principale modification que Mme Leprince de Beaumont fait subir à l'intrigue initiale: la réinvention complète de l'histoire parentale, qui occupera toute la première partie de son conte. Il est assez courant, dans le genre, de présenter d'abord rapidement le couple parental avant d'introduire les aventures de sa progéniture. Cazotte ne se prête pas au jeu, multipliant les dyschronies: récits alternés des aventures des deux héros, encastrement d'histoires qui délivrent un autre éclairage sur des événements dont on n'avait pas soupçonné l'origine, ellipses ayant pour fonction de taquiner la curiosité. Techniques narratives bannies par Mme de Beaumont: le jeune public doit pouvoir suivre facilement et concentrer son attention sur le sens du propos, que dirige ostensiblement l'éducatrice. L'intrigue de *La Patte du chat* commence *in medias res* par le récit d'un méfait dont longtemps le lecteur va croire qu'il est la seule origine des malheurs d'Amadil. Cet épisode inaugural justifie le titre du conte: Amadil, lors d'une cérémonie publique se déroulant à la cour de la reine mère de la jeune Amandine qu'il aime en secret, écrase malencontreusement la patte du chat chéri de cette reine, ce qui lui vaut d'être banni du royaume. On apprendra tardivement que l'animal n'est autre que le méchant génie libertin qui a affublé Amadil d'un long nez, et qu'une fée a puni par une métamorphose animale. Et comme l'on saura alors que Bleuâtre a conduit de loin la destinée de son fils, on émettra éventuellement l'hypothèse d'une petite vengeance de la mère sur l'ex-amant, par l'écrasement de la fameuse patte. Mais à la première lecture, on n'y peut voir qu'un accident absurde, lié à une succession de circonstances qui font boule de neige, dans laquelle entre en compte – discrètement, mais en début de chaîne – ce nez maudit. En effet, Amadil jette des regards enamourés à Amandine assise un peu plus loin, mais elle ne peut apercevoir qu'un seul de ses yeux: Amadil étant assis de profil, son autre œil est caché par son appendice nasal. Curieuse de vérifier aussi dans cet œil-là l'effet qu'elle produit sur le prince, elle se penche dangereusement et tombe. C'est en se précipitant pour la rattraper que se produit l'accident fâcheux, avant qu'Amadil ne recueille Amandine dans ses bras. Une héroïne aussi audacieuse et peu respectueuse des bonnes manières est loin d'être un modèle à suivre pour les jeunes élèves de Mlle Bonne et les lectrices. Le conte de Mme Leprince de Beaumont commence donc de toute autre manière: un roi, ne pouvant épouser une princesse enchantée, va trouver une fée qui lui révèle qu'il lui suffit de marcher sur la queue (non plus la patte) du chat de cette princesse pour dissoudre le sortilège. Après plusieurs essais infructueux, le roi le surprend pendant son sommeil, ce qui provoque l'immédiate métamorphose de l'animal en enchanteur. Furieux, ce dernier annonce au roi qu'il se mariera et aura un fils qui sera malheureux jusqu'à ce qu'il reconnaisse (comme chez Cazotte) que son nez est trop long. Il lui interdit de dévoiler ce mauvais sort et son remède. Le mariage a lieu, et le roi meurt avant la naissance de son fils, Désir.

Ce premier épisode du conte mixe donc plusieurs motifs présents à l'origine: les amours contrariées des parents, l'écrasement de la patte/queue du chat-enchanteur, la vengeance de celui-ci sur l'enfant et enfin la recette permettant de lever le maléfice, compliquée par l'interdit de parole. Mais la distribution des rôles est différente: ce n'est plus le fils mais le père qui écrase le chat, l'animal ayant changé de propriétaire d'un conte à l'autre (par économie de personnages secondaires, la future belle-mère du prince a disparu). La scène de la patte/queue écrasée prend alors une autre fonction: de méfait et maladresse qu'elle était dans le conte de Cazotte, élément catastrophique déclencheur de malheurs, elle s'inverse en épreuve positive permettant la levée du maléfice. Le lecteur n'est aucunement renseigné sur l'origine de l'enchantement de la princesse future mère du héros, le motif de la colère de l'enchanteur (est-il amoureux de cette princesse? l'a-t-il été, comme chez Cazotte?), celle de sa métamorphose en chat. Tous ces silences privent de sens le mauvais sort jeté à l'enfant. L'univers féerique, dans ce contexte, est réduit à n'être qu'une mécanique absurde et les puissances suprêmes, de simples incarnations d'un destin opaque opprimant les êtres soumis à leurs caprices. Cette vision n'est d'ailleurs pas incompatible avec la tradition des contes de fées qui ont souvent mis en scène les décisions arbitraires de puissances supérieures s'acharnant contre d'innocents nouveau-nés, ou déplaçant le châtiment de quelque défaillance d'un parent sur sa progéniture.

Cet épisode inventé n'est pourtant pas si immotivé qu'il le paraît. On notera qu'il est calqué sur le schéma des épisodes suivants empruntés à Cazotte: les aventures du père tout comme celles du fils, chez Mme Leprince, contiennent un mariage contrarié par un maléfice, avec mode d'emploi du remède. En donnant un ordre chronologique au récit, elle fait donc passer sa propre 'invention' en premier, en produisant l'impression que l'histoire filiale est calquée sur l'histoire parentale, alors que c'est l'inverse. En réécrivant cette dernière, elle transforme le héros, fils de deux amants persécutés par un rival jaloux, en fils légitime, issu d'un mariage en bonne et due forme, et elle rend à la figure paternelle sa dignité (dans le premier conte, le père était métamorphosé en concombre).

Elle supprime donc tout ce qui lui semble immoral et inutile à l'économie d'un récit censé faire la démonstration des effets néfastes de l'amour-propre, et elle insiste lourdement sur la rééducation du jeune homme, qui occupe l'essentiel de sa réécriture. Les relations amoureuses (celles du couple parental puis des héros) sont réduites chez elle à n'être que purement fonctionnelles et ne sont évoquées qu'en termes convenus. Modifiant la scène originelle du conte de Cazotte dont elle ne conserve que le motif de l'agression du chat, la déplaçant de sa patte à sa queue – castration symbolique explicite –, l'auteur a voulu tenir ses jeunes lectrices à l'écart de la représentation des chemins retors de la passion amoureuse dont les contes antérieurs et les romans faisaient leur miel (séductions, tromperies, jalousies, etc.). Elle attaque d'ailleurs plusieurs fois ces genres narratifs dans le recueil, comme lectures néfastes aux jeunes gens, et censure tout ce qui a trait aux émois des héros, au développement de leurs sentiments et aux peintures de la galanterie mondaine dont le texte de Cazotte était empli. La séparation des amants, certes douloureuse, y agissait comme révélateur de la passion féminine et comme stimulant émotionnel pour le couple héroïque; cette économie complexe du désir et du sentiment, qui confond méfait structurel et bénéfice libidinal, relève sans doute de ce que Mme Leprince de Beaumont dénonçait comme 'dangereux' dans son *Avertissement*.

Ce double souci d'économie d'une narration assujettie à un message moral univoque et conduite par un principe d'unité (d'action et d'intérêt), explique aussi la suppression de tout ce qui, dans le conte premier, n'était pourtant pas incompatible avec une intention moralisante. Il s'agit de tous les développements ayant trait à la satire de la société et des mœurs de son temps. La seule tare sociale retenue est la flatterie des courtisans: elle lui attribue la responsabilité de l'illusion qui scelle longtemps les yeux du prince Désir. La critique des flatteurs, qui trouve son répondant dans celle des mauvais maîtres gâtant les enfants, est l'un de ses thèmes de prédilection, très développé par Fénelon, son modèle, qui avait inspiré d'autres auteurs de contes (Moncrif et surtout Caylus).

La deuxième séquence du *Prince Désir*, qui a pour sujet la mauvaise éducation du héros, de sa naissance à sa nubilité, insiste sur ce sujet. L'auteur, usant du discours rapporté, s'attarde sur l'énoncé indirect des arguments accumulés par les courtisans d'abord pour consoler la mère attristée par le défaut physique du bébé, puis pour flatter le jeune prince en le lui cachant. Il s'agit ici de trouver une cause extérieure aux aveuglements de l'amour-propre. Ces discours délétères soulignent les dangers du verbe sur de jeunes esprits. Cazotte ne s'intéresse pas à ce sujet, pas plus qu'à l'éducation d'Amadil. Quand les dames camayeules flatteront la vanité du jeune homme, leurs propos joueront alors le rôle d'obstacle supplémentaire à sa quête amoureuse, et contribuent à la satire du libertinage féminin. C'est le moment choisi par le narrateur pour révéler enfin le secret longtemps caché au lecteur:

> Il est temps de dissiper l'obscurité des destinées de ce prince. Il ne devait être heureux que lorsqu'il serait convaincu de l'excessive longueur de son nez. Cette conviction n'était pas aisée à acquérir; plus un défaut est apparent, plus l'amour-propre subtilise pour le cacher. Dans l'enfance, quand nos yeux peuvent à peine apercevoir un ridicule qui nous singularise, ce trompeur habile commence à répandre sur nos yeux l'illusion qui doit nous abuser toute la vie; nous nous familiarisons avec elle, insensiblement elle devient plus forte, elle croît avec nos lumières, et les offusque toujours. Il eût été à souhaiter pour Amadil que la nature entière d'intelligence lui eût parlé du ridicule de son nez: peut-être encore l'eût-elle aigri sans le persuader.[11]

Pour Cazotte, qui joue ici les moralistes, l'amour-propre est inné, et puise d'abord en lui-même ses nutriments, avant que le monde extérieur n'y ajoute son influence néfaste. Même si 'nous naissons tous avec des défauts',[12] celui-ci est présenté dans le conte de Mme Leprince comme acquis: c'est par l'éducation qu'il s'est ancré dans le cœur du héros, ce sera par ce moyen qu'on l'en extirpera.

---

11   *P.C.*, 1039–1040.
12   *M.E.*, VI, 1049.

Mme Leprince s'est également passée des personnages secondaires qu'elle estime incompétents pour divulguer le message moral univoque sur lequel elle entend concentrer l'attention de ses lecteurs. Pour remplir ce rôle, elle ne garde que le personnage de la fée, qu'elle dissocie totalement du personnage de la mère (les deux personnages ne se connaissent d'ailleurs pas). Si Amadil en a été séparé dans son jeune âge malgré elle, celle-ci n'a eu de cesse de guider ses pas, plaçant sur son chemin une série d'intermédiaires ayant pour rôle de l'amener à la prise de conscience, sans révéler le secret: elle 'suscite de petits désagréments pour l'instruire', ayant tous rapport avec la longueur de son nez (la scène de l'écrasement de la patte peut alors être replacée en tête de cette série par le lecteur). Mais cette mère n'est pas poussée par quelque prétention morale, elle entend simplement fournir à son fils le moyen de réparer le méfait imposé arbitrairement à toute la famille, et à elle en premier. Son sort est entre les mains de son fils, mais l'épreuve, c'est d'abord elle qui la passe, en faisant preuve d'imagination et d'ingéniosité pour contourner l'interdit de parole et amener Amadil à la découverte. Mme Leprince de Beaumont, qui donne à la gouvernante de son *Magasin des enfants* un rôle similaire à celui de la fée, a écarté toute possibilité d'assimilation à un personnage de mère disqualifiée par sa vie passée. Préférant rendre les flatteurs de la cour responsables de la mauvaise éducation de Désir, la conteuse fait également disparaître rapidement son personnage maternel du récit, confiant le rôle exclusif de l'auxiliaire à une vieille fée, déjà présente chez Cazotte sous le nom de la Fée aux Glaçons, mandatée par la fée-mère du héros. Ici, la première n'est aux ordres de personne, elle prend les commandes des aventures de Désir après la survenue de l'obstacle (l'enlèvement de la princesse) jusqu'à la réparation du méfait. Cette partie du conte, la plus importante, se divise en deux épisodes: la scène de la grotte (la rencontre entre la vieille fée et Désir), dans laquelle l'oralité (le dialogue) occupe un rôle prépondérant, et la scène du château de cristal (la rencontre entre Désir et sa princesse, agencée par la fée, où l'expérience personnelle l'emportera sur le discours magistral).

La figure de la pédagogue que le conte fait intervenir activement a beau être vieille, laide et jugée ennuyeuse par Désir, c'est une figure autonome, généreuse et au bout du compte efficace: c'est à elle seule qu'il devra son bonheur, elle se sera montrée capable de réparer l'influence d'un environnement corrupteur et défaillant. Chez Cazotte, la fée aux Glaçons, son modèle, n'est pas tout entière positive: surgie dans un désert glacial, elle médit des parents du héros et se vante de facéties peu glorieuses, revendiquant même la responsabilité des fadaises dont sont emplies les œuvres littéraires contemporaines (et auxquelles Cazotte n'hésite pas à ajouter les siennes).[13] La critique de l'auteur est, ici comme souvent, à multiple détente: une telle stratification, une telle polysémie ne peuvent convenir aux buts que s'est fixé Mme Leprince de Beaumont, qui rhabille plus joliment le personnage féerique, pour le mettre aux normes de l'univers manichéen qu'elle construit.

III L'Acharnement thérapeutique ou les vertus de la répétition

La scène de la grotte débute par une invention qui a d'ailleurs fait l'objet d'une illustration de Marillier pour *Le Cabinet des fées* de 1786:[14] la vieille, ouvrant la porte à Désir, tente de mettre ses lunettes qui ont des difficultés à tenir sur son nez, parce qu'elle l'a 'trop court', et tous deux s'exclament ensemble: 'Ah! quel drôle de nez'.[15] Elle se prétend petite parleuse et déclare détester les longs discours alors qu'elle assomme le héros de ses bavardages interminables. Autant d'illustrations de l'aveuglement sur soi, qui ont pour fonction de tendre un miroir au personnage, encore incapable d'interpréter ces signes, comme le montre sa réflexion silencieuse:

---

13   Le conte qu'il publiera un an plus tard s'intitulera ironiquement *Les Mille et une fadaises, Contes à dormir debout.... À Baillons, chez l'Endormy, à l'image du Ronfleur.*

14   [C.-J. Mayer], *Le Cabinet des fées, ou Collection choisie des contes des fées, et autres contes merveilleux* (Amsterdam et Paris, Serpente, 1786), tome 35, 169.

15   *M.E.*, X, 1105.

'Il faut être bien sot, pour ne pas connaître ses défauts: voilà ce que c'est d'être née princesse; les flatteurs l'ont gâtée, et lui ont persuadé qu'elle parlait peu' [...] il admirait surtout une femme de chambre, qui, à propos de tout ce qu'elle voyait, louait sa maîtresse sur sa discrétion: 'Parbleu, pensait-il en mangeant, je suis charmé d'être venu ici. Cet exemple me fait voir combien j'ai fait sagement de ne pas écouter les flatteurs. Ces gens-là nous louent effrontément, nous cachent nos défauts, et les changent en perfections; pour moi je ne serai jamais leur dupe, je connais mes défauts, Dieu merci'. Le pauvre Désir le croyait bonnement, et ne sentait pas que ceux qui avaient loué son nez se moquaient de lui, comme la femme de chambre de la fée se moquait d'elle, car le prince vit qu'elle se retournait de temps en temps pour rire.[16]

Ainsi, le message moral est diffracté: l'auteur le met dans toutes bouches, aussi bien celle des personnages que du narrateur. On notera qu'ici, c'est le héros qui, en pensée, énonce le premier la maxime qu'il doit encore s'approprier. Une interjection ('parbleu'), ainsi qu'une exclamation ('Dieu merci') confèrent à cette pensée un tour oral: cette parole retenue est fondatrice et laisse entendre que Désir est à la croisée des chemins, entre aveuglement et lucidité (dans les deux contes, sa réflexion ne deviendra opérationnelle que si elle est autocritique et proférée à voix haute). Le personnage de la femme de chambre, inventé par la conteuse, redouble l'exemple: son comportement valide la maxime formulée précédemment et met en abyme l'erreur du prince, lui tendant un nouveau miroir. La même leçon sera encore répétée dans la scène suivante, puis commentée après le contage par Spirituelle et Mlle Bonne. Le lecteur de l'*Avertissement* a été informé de la créance de l'auteur en une telle pédagogie: 'J'ai lieu d'espérer qu'à force de répéter les mêmes vérités, sous des formes diverses, elles s'inculqueront [...] d'une manière ineffaçable'.[17]

16   *M.E.*, X, 1106–1107.
17   *M.E.*, Av., 972.

IV Pouvoirs et limites de l'oralité

Chez Cazotte, le bavardage de la fée aux Glaçons, tout aussi ennuyeux, visait d'une part à malmener l'amour-propre d'Amadil, d'autre part à lui fournir un exemple vivant d'aveuglement causé par ce défaut (tout comme chez la conteuse), mais le 'babil' de la fée ne donnait lieu à aucune réflexion critique du prince (ni du narrateur), qui eût pu témoigner d'un quelconque éveil de sa lucidité. L'ennui puis le sommeil étaient finalement venus à bout de l'exaspération d'Amadil. Par comparaison entre les deux textes et les autres contes du *Magasin*, on ne peut qu'être frappé de la place importante qu'occupe, dans ce conte de Mme Leprince, le dialogue reproduit au style direct, entre la fée et le héros. Chez Cazotte, Amadil n'émettait qu'une seule réaction indignée aux propos désobligeants tenus sur son nez, noyés dans la féérique logorrhée. Chez Mme Leprince, l'échange de répliques, vrai duel de paroles, est très serré et le mot 'nez' revient une ou deux fois dans chacune: Désir est beaucoup plus réactif et plus rapidement exaspéré qu'Amadil. Pourtant, dans les deux contes, l'épisode se clôt sur un échec, que consacre la fuite du héros, motivée chez Cazotte par un cauchemar, chez Mme Leprince par les brimades. Nouvel avantage accordé ici au discours, mais accusation d'une stratégie discursive inefficace: Désir supporte ces vexations tant qu'il a besoin de la fée pour satisfaire sa faim. Le lecteur est ainsi préparé à la leçon de l'épisode suivant, dans lequel il sera prouvé que la conscience intime de l'intérêt personnel est le ressort déterminant de l'éducation. L'auteur, dans l'*Avertissement* du recueil, avait montré les limites d'une rhétorique de la répétition:

> On répète continuellement aux enfants: rien n'est plus vilain que de mentir, de se mettre en colère, d'être gourmand, désobéissant. Qui ne croirait que ces vices sont très rares dans le monde, eu égard aux soins qu'on se donne pour en éloigner les enfants? Ils devraient les avoir en horreur, et ils les auraient effectivement, si au lieu de faire entrer les maximes qu'on leur a débitées à ce sujet dans leur mémoire, on les avait fait pénétrer jusqu'à leur raison.[18]

---

18 *M.E.*, Av., 970.

Dans les deux textes, l'épisode démontre aussi l'impuissance d'une certaine forme d'oralité, celle de la 'leçon' faite de principes abstraits, de reproches assénés. Les éducateurs devront donc trouver d'autres moyens que l'énonciation de préceptes moraux et leur pure et simple redite, pour convaincre leurs élèves obtus de leur vérité et de leur bien-fondé. L'inefficacité d'une certaine rhétorique nous renvoie à l'interdit de révélation inaugural: croyant malignement œuvrer contre l'intérêt du héros en l'édictant, le méchant enchanteur n'aurait-il pas distillé, au final, un principe fondamental de bonne pédagogie? Quoi qu'il en soit, cet élément essentiel de l'intrigue dénonce en fin de compte, quoique indirectement, la naïveté de la créance en l'efficience de tout discours de vérité.

Dans le dernier épisode du conte de Cazotte, où cette question est ouvertement discutée, Amadil est conduit près d'Amandine endormie magiquement par une bonne fée qui annonce au héros qu'il peut espérer la posséder. Posté dans le jardin du château de cette nouvelle Belle au Bois Dormant, le visage collé à sa fenêtre, il peine à la distinguer à travers les vitres talquées: la longueur de son nez le gêne. Il s'évertue trois jours et trois nuits à mieux la voir, ce qui fait sourire le narrateur: 'on lui a reproché quelque part de n'avoir pas cassé les vitres, sans doute que cet expédient merveilleux ne lui vint pas à l'esprit'.[19] Cazotte a lu les romans de son temps et sait que le sommeil d'une belle, réel ou feint, est une occasion dont savent profiter les galants. Ce trait d'humour est un coup supplémentaire porté contre un héros paré au début de toutes les qualités, et dont l'image s'est progressivement lézardée au fil des épisodes, sous l'effet de mises en scène qui l'ont placé en posture grotesque au point de le transformer en parfait benêt. Une telle dégradation de la figure héroïque n'est évidemment pas de mise chez la conteuse. Survient dans *La Patte du chat* la prise de conscience tant attendue:

> Enfin l'amour [...] dessilla les yeux de l'amour-propre; il commença à s'apercevoir que sans la longueur du nez, il verrait facilement. Dès qu'il eut fait le premier pas, le reste fut bien aisé à faire; tout ce qu'on lui avait dit sur son ridicule lui revient à l'esprit. 'Peste soit du nez', s'écria-t-il; il n'eut pas le temps de prolonger l'imprécation,

---

19   *P.C.*, 1052.

le ridicule dont il se plaignait était déjà tombé parce qu'il était reconnu, et son nez était devenu beaucoup mieux fait qu'un nez ordinaire.[20]

L'efficacité de la parole éducative opère avec retard, ramenée à la mémoire sous l'effet du besoin. Le dénouement est grotesquement accéléré: la princesse se réveille, la mère du héros fait son apparition, le père démétamorphosé jaillit de son plant de concombres, le mariage a lieu, et le chat ex-enchanteur s'enfuit désespéré. Les personnages principaux ne font aucun commentaire, le narrateur ne tire pas davantage la morale de l'histoire. Cazotte avait promis en titre du chapitre que 'l'on apprendra[it], entre autres choses, comment il faut s'y prendre pour étrangler net un conte':[21] on ne pouvait mieux faire.

Mme Leprince de Beaumont modifie légèrement l'épisode. Elle en efface totalement l'esprit parodique, avant de clore le récit par une moralité qu'elle laisse à sa fée le soin de formuler. À travers les vitres du palais où elle est enfermée, Mignonne, bien éveillée, tend la main à son prince. Plus actif que son contemplatif prédécesseur, il tente de briser la glace, de lui parler, de lui baiser la main, mais en vain: toujours ce nez! 'Il s'aperçut pour la première fois de son extraordinaire longueur, et le prenant avec sa main pour le ranger de côté: "Il faut avouer, dit-il, que mon nez est trop long"'.[22] On aura noté la différence de formulation de la formule apocalyptique, sésame de la rédemption. Cazotte nous avait annoncé une 'réflexion', or le 'peste soit du nez!' d'Amadil n'est qu'une imprécation exaspérée. Elle suffit pourtant à mettre un terme, de manière très formelle, au maléfice. Chez Mme Leprince, la phrase fatidique est plus tempérée. Si sa tournure impersonnelle lui donne l'air d'une concession quelque peu réticente et lui ôte l'énergie attendue d'une illumination par l'évidence, elle rend compte au moins de la victoire du bon sens pratique sur l'obstination obtuse. Son ton presque détaché est le témoignage d'une reddition – fût-elle laborieuse – de la raison. Par ailleurs, le verbe choisi ('avouer') est révélateur du modèle religieux sous-jacent qui travaille l'énoncé: celui de la contrition. Faute avouée

20   *P.C.*, 1052.
21   *P.C.*, 1048.
22   *M.E.*, X, 1108.

est ici totalement pardonnée. La conteuse n'a pourtant pas totalement rangé au placard la formule lapidaire d'imprécation proférée par Amadil, elle l'a seulement déplacée dans l'épisode précédent: 'Peste soit de la vieille avec mon nez! dit le Prince en lui-même' avant de prendre la fuite.[23] Cette relégation à une étape antérieure d'un énoncé pourtant fondamental du récit source prouve que la conteuse a parfaitement perçu son caractère déplacé, son insuffisance pour rendre compte d'un amendement réel.

Un lecteur qui ignorerait les dates de publication de ces deux contes aurait de bonnes raisons de prendre l'épilogue de *La Patte du chat* pour une parodie du *Prince Désir*. Pourtant, on est surpris de constater que seul le premier conte a souligné la part de la mémoire verbale dans la pseudo-conversion du héros et admis l'efficacité, fût-elle tardive, des discours éducatifs. Cela peut s'expliquer par le fait que la gouvernante n'accuse pas directement ses élèves de leurs défauts, les incitant plutôt à s'en confesser publiquement. Mais la surprise la plus considérable réside dans la moralité du second conte, énoncée par la fée qui dresse le constat d'échec des efforts rhétoriques des pédagogues:

> Dans le moment le palais de cristal tomba par morceaux, et la vieille, qui tenait Mignonne par la main, dit au prince: 'Avouez que vous m'avez beaucoup d'obligation; j'avais beau vous parler de votre nez, vous n'en auriez jamais reconnu le défaut, s'il ne fût devenu un obstacle à ce que vous souhaitiez. C'est ainsi que l'amour-propre nous cache les difformités de notre âme et de notre corps. La raison a beau chercher à nous les dévoiler, nous n'en convenons qu'au moment où ce même amour-propre les trouve contraires à ses intérêts.'[24]

La vieille fée dévoile son identité: elle est allégorie de la Raison, cette faculté qu'il faut mettre en œuvre chez l'enfant, plutôt que la mémoire, pour une éducation morale réussie, aux dires de l'auteur de la *Dédicace*. Une Raison qui précise le message donné dans l'*Avertissement*, avouant ici ses propres limites, les conditions très restreintes de son efficacité. Dans les éditions du XVIIIe siècle, l'absence de guillemets conforme aux usages de l'époque, dans les deux dernières phrases citées, accroît l'impression de fondu-enchaîné

---

23   *M.E.*, X, 1106.
24   *M.E.*, X, 1108.

des voix: ces propos de la fée auraient pu être prononcés par Mlle Bonne, qui clôt ensuite le conte, entérinant l'effet durablement profitable de cette 'leçon'. L'insuffisance thérapeutique du discours de vérité est confirmée une dernière fois par le commentaire immédiat de Spirituelle: 'Ma Bonne, est-il possible qu'on ne connaisse pas ses défauts?'. La jeune auditrice fait alors preuve de la même défiance à l'égard d'un conte merveilleux que le père de Désir envers le sortilège jeté par l'enchanteur: 'Si mon fils a le nez trop long, dit-il en lui-même, à moins qu'il ne soit aveugle ou manchot, il pourra toujours le voir, ou le sentir'.[25] La suite du conte a montré comment il se trompait, or cela n'a pas suffi à convaincre complètement la jeune fille, qui avait pourtant antérieurement fait preuve d'une immédiate lucidité en surprenant des critiques à son encontre. La gouvernante est donc obligée d'insister à nouveau sur la cause de l'aveuglement du héros, en l'appliquant virtuellement au cas de sa jeune élève, qui se sait laide:

> Si quelque sot flatteur vous disait que vous êtes jolie, d'abord vous penseriez qu'il se moque de vous; mais s'il vous répétait cela plusieurs fois, vous commenceriez à le croire: il est fort aisé d'oublier ses défauts, à moins qu'on n'ait une bonne amie qui nous en avertisse.[26]

La parole regagne donc, *in fine*, de son pouvoir auparavant tellement menacé. Elle doit cette victoire à la rhétorique de la *variatio* dont l'auteur a déjà beaucoup chanté les louanges, et à l'enchâssement du récit dans un modèle dialogal. Multipliant les analogies de situations, ce dialogue maître/ élève ajoute aux effets spéculaires inclus dans le récit et à sa dimension parabolique. Mlle *Bonne* occupe ce rôle de la *bonne* amie des enfants, mais la formulation indéfinie (*'on* ait...*une* bonne amie') prête à la généralisation. La vérité du conte est finalement validée dans la mesure où l'est précisément cette capacité extensive qui lui confère sa vertu exemplaire.

La parodie, très présente dans le conte source, semble s'être finalement frayé une voie souterraine dans la réécriture de Mme Leprince de Beaumont, et sans doute à son insu. Retour du refoulé, en quelque sorte. La première

25 *M.E.*, X, 1104.
26 *M.E.*, X, 1108.

séquence du *Prince Désir*, qui dessine à grands traits l'histoire parentale, n'est pas mue par une intention satirique ni par cet esprit de dérision dont témoigne un Cazotte étrangleur de conte. Pourtant, plusieurs ingrédients d'un conte de fées ostensiblement parodique sont réunis dans la première séquence inventée par l'auteur féminin: rapidité du récit enchaînant des événements absurdes vécus par de purs fantoches asservis aux besoins fonctionnels d'une intrigue minimaliste, montage de topoï génériques décharnés, mariage parental conditionné par la réussite d'une épreuve d'une ridicule facilité (il suffit bêtement au roi d'attendre le sommeil du chat pour pouvoir lui écraser la queue). Autre trace émergeante de la censure dont a fait l'objet le conte de Cazotte et qui opère un effet boomerang: la leçon dispensée dans l'épilogue n'est pas loin de faire l'éloge de la toute puissance du désir amoureux, de sa suprématie sur la raison, alors même que les représentations du désir dans le conte initial ont été soigneusement enfouies, malgré l'exhibition du prénom allégorique du héros. Enfin, dernier paradoxe, le caractère inopérant de la parole féerique, que la fée elle-même souligne en faisant l'éloge de la supériorité d'un autre ressort éducatif, menace la crédibilité du discours pédagogique et la nécessité de l'oralité. Mais en même temps, l'énonciation de tels propos, performance verbale qui couronne magistralement le conte, constitue un acte de maîtrise oratoire ayant pour effet de compenser l'échec même de la parole en le faisant passer pour une étape nécessaire de la démonstration: superbe récupération de l'incompétence relative des fées de Cazotte, et sauvetage *in extremis* du merveilleux. Enfin, l'écriture du conte et du dialogue qui le suit fixe à jamais la leçon et la met potentiellement en perpétuelle circulation, l'ouvrant à la répétition des relectures ou à la reformulation inventive de ceux qui voudront raconter ce conte à d'autres enfants.

On peut attribuer le tremblé de tels effets à l'ambiguïté de la position de Mme Leprince de Beaumont en ce qui concerne le genre du conte, forcément insuffisant en soi, étant, aux dires de Mlle Bonne, 'une chose fausse, qu'on écrit, ou qu'on raconte pour amuser les jeunes gens,'[27] la parole la plus puissante et la seule véritable étant la parole divine que répercute

27   *M.E.*, III, 993.

l'histoire sainte, 'la seule [histoire] sur laquelle il n'est pas permis de douter'.[28] Le conte ne peut constituer tout au plus qu'une étape dans le long travail pédagogique fait de multiples reformulations. De même que dans les Dialogues le précepte moral renforce son efficacité à s'enrichir d'allers-retours divers entre particulier et général, vécu des auditrices et fiction, la Vérité renforce la sienne à s'adosser au mensonge de la Fable.

Le récit de la création du monde, raconté dans le IVe dialogue par l'une des élèves, s'était clos sur un sombre épilogue, celui de l'exclusion d'Adam et Ève du jardin d'Eden. Un conte forgé très ostensiblement sur la même trame, conte à l'issue dysphorique, avait aussitôt apporté une variation. Spirituelle, toujours elle, avait compris que le péché d'Ève avait à voir avec son propre défaut, l'orgueil, mais elle s'était encore plus sentie concernée par le conte, narré fort à propos et en sa direction par la gouvernante. *Le Prince Désir*: nouvelle variation, lointain écho, modulation vocale plus légère et plus rassurante?

---

28 *M.E.*, III, 1008.

SECTION THREE

Postcolonial contexts

The Creole folktale in the writing of Lafcadio Hearn: an aesthetic of mediation

MARY GALLAGHER

A large part of the critical confusion and fascination surrounding the extraordinarily peripatetic, fin-de-siècle, anglophone writer Lafcadio Hearn is due to the impossibility of locating him within any single literary or cultural tradition. Although he cannot accurately be classified as an American, Creole, Japanese, or Anglo-Irish writer, his œuvre does fall into three distinct periods, the Ohio period, the French Creole period, and the Japanese period, and the dominant aesthetic of his life's labour could best be described as one of mediation. One specific dimension of Hearn's 'Caribbean' work perfectly illustrates this aesthetic: namely his collecting of Creole folktales and his authoring of works that incorporate or assimilate 'contes créoles'. Moreover, this aspect of his œuvre highlights the interface between orality and writing and, more specifically, between folklore and various genres of writing, including such literary sub-genres as travel writing or ethnography.

I Lafcadio Hearn's Creole gravitation

In order to understand the cultural originality and significance of Lafcadio Hearn as a writer, and in order to situate and appreciate his approach to the Creole folktale, it is imperative to recall certain highly pertinent aspects of Hearn's bio-bibliography. Taken together, the following details allow us to make sense not just of his involvement with Creole culture, but more specifically of his aesthetic of mediation. Patrick Lafcadio Hearn was the middle son of three boys born in 1850 to a Greek mother and an Anglo-Irish father who was a peripatetic surgeon in the British army. The father's career brought him *entre autres* to the Ionian Sea, where he met his Greek wife. When his father was subsequently posted to the Caribbean, the young Hearn, whose elder brother had died in infancy, was brought at the age of about two to Dublin by his parents. Less than two years after the family's arrival in Ireland, Hearn's father left his wife and she in turn abandoned her second son to her Irish in-laws and returned to Greece. Both of Lafcadio's parents subsequently remarried and had second families. Having been educated privately in Dublin to the age of about eleven by a paternal grand-aunt who had converted to Catholicism, and then at a Catholic seminary school in the north of England, Hearn moved to the United States in 1869 at the age of nineteen. After about a year, he established himself in Cincinnati, where he found work as a newspaper reporter. In Ohio, he gravitated towards the Mississippi levee, writing in particular of the way of life and of the folk culture in the ghettoes of mostly black and impoverished 'roustabouts' or port workers. He also specialised, however, in the sensational coverage of ghoulish and sordid stories.

Having spent over six years in Cincinnati, Hearn moved to New Orleans, where he established himself as a journalist on the *New Orleans Democrat* and later on the *Times-Democrat*, furthering his literary reputation by much less sensationalist material and treatments than in his Ohio writing. He was especially drawn to the distinctive cultural cachet of the French quarter, and to a type of literary journalism that included both commentaries on, and translations of, the most remarkable writing emerging in France. Hearn's passionate interest in the French language would lead him, indeed, to translate several of the most significant French writers of his own time, including Anatole France, Maupassant, Flaubert, Gautier, and Loti. It was in New Orleans too that Hearn stopped signing himself by his first given name Patrick, shortened by his Ohio acquaintances to Paddy, and adopted his undoubtedly more literary – and certainly more foreign or exotic sounding – second given name, Lafcadio. We also owe to his New Orleans period, in addition to the literary journalism and the translations, two compendia of tales from various distant and exotic literary traditions entitled *Stray Leaves from Strange Literatures* and *Some*

Chinese Ghosts, a novella entitled *Chita*, a Creole recipe book, and a book of Creole proverbs, *Gombo Zhèbes*.[1] Hearn's introduction to this latter work which he qualifies as an 'essay at Creole folklore' bears witness to his quite intensive research into the Creole language as spoken throughout the French Creole world at the time.

One of the most striking aspects of Hearn's American writings, both in Ohio and in New Orleans, is their ethnographic orientation with all that this implies. Historically, notions of observer-participation and of the 'otherness' of the observed culture, an otherness usually associated with spatio-temporal distance, are fundamental to the development of ethnographic discourse. This cultural 'otherness' was typically construed in Hearn's day in evolutionist terms: as primitive or originary, for example. However, the novelty of Hearn's ethnographic interest and indeed the basis of its anticipation of modern, or even post-modern ethnography was its focus on (sub-)cultures – such as the Creole culture of New Orleans – that were neither (conventionally) primitive nor traditional nor distant, but rather contemporary, urban, and at hand. They were, moreover, predominantly oral cultures, and studying them necessarily involved the study of folklore.

Apparently following the call of some deep fascination with the various cultural and linguistic questions raised by Creole culture, which is axiomatically the culture of interface, Hearn left New Orleans in 1887 for a long trip round the Caribbean, undertaking a travel-writing commission

---

1   The works by Hearn referred to in the course of this article are the following: *Gombo Zhèbes: A Little Dictionary of Creole Proverbs* (New York, Will H. Coleman, 1885); *Stray Leaves from Strange Literature* (Boston, James A. Osgood & Co., 1904); *Some Chinese Ghosts* (Boston, Roberts Bros, 1887); *Chita: A Memory of Lost Island* (New York, Harper and Bros, 1889); *La Cuisine créole: A Collection of Culinary Recipes* (New York, Will H. Coleman, 1885); *Youma* (New York, Harper & Bros, 1890); *Two Years in the French West Indies* (Oxford, Signal Books, 2001 [New York, Harper & Bros, 1890]); *Trois fois bel conte*, trans. Serge Denis, preface C.-M. Garnier (Paris, Mercure de France, 1939); *Contes créoles II (inédits)*, collected by L. Hearn, transcribed and trans. L.-S. Martinel (Lamentin-Martinique, Ibis rouge, 2002); *One of Cleopatra's Nights and other Fantastic Romances by Théophile Gautier* (New York, R. Worthington, 1882).

from *Harpers Magazine*. The islands of the Caribbean, and particularly the Lesser Antilles, were, to a much greater extent than New Orleans, the crucible or laboratory par excellence of Creole culture and a site of particularly intense *métissage*. Upon his return from that Caribbean cruise, Hearn found it impossible to settle back into the United States, and so after a very short period he returned to Martinique where he would remain for almost two years before finally giving up on the Tropics. His protracted Caribbean adventure resulted in four principal publications: the *magnum opus* that marries travel writing, folklore, ethnographic sketches, and ethnographic fiction, entitled *Two Years in the French West Indies*, the novella *Youma* about a slave girl, and two volumes of folktales, published posthumously.[2] In 1890, within a few months of his definitive departure from the Caribbean, Hearn undertook another trip, again commissioned by Harpers, although very ambiguously so, via Canada to Japan, where he would spend the remaining fourteen years of his life.

Even in this thumbnail sketch, we can discern many details that might have predisposed Hearn to an interest in the *conte créole*. First of all, as an explanation of his general Creole tropism there is the biographical leitmotif of colonial displacement or deterritorialisation followed by reterritorialisation, a leitmotif with strong associations of foreignness, difference, contact, interrelation, recombination, and *métissage*, all of these dynamics being embodied in the mixed marriage from which Hearn himself issued. Secondly, there is the clear francotropism that motivated his extensive literary translation from the French, and that was confirmed by the move from the anglocentric culture of Ohio to the at least partly francocentric culture of New Orleans. Thirdly, there is the ethnographic penchant for noting and studying popular culture, and for gravitation towards cultures regarded as marginal, 'other', or 'exotic'. Fourthly, there is Hearn's profound attraction to stories coloured by the pi(g)ment of ethnic and racial difference, in particular by various shades of black. It was this combined chromatic and cultural attraction that no doubt led Hearn to marry in Cincinnati the daughter of a liberated Kentucky slave who was also known as a skilful

2   See note 1 for bibliographical details.

raconteuse. Fifthly, there is the proof provided in Hearn's New Orleans writings of his interest in, and mastery of, the Creole language. And finally, there are Hearn's own literary aspirations, especially his manifest writerly interest in prose narrative as witnessed by his journalistic predilection for dramatic storylines, by his insertion into his travel writing of short narrative cameos, and also by his more sustained creative experimentation in the novella genre in *Chita* and *Youma*.

II Mediating the Creole folktale

Apart from being overdetermined by his own background and origins, Hearn's interest in Creole culture, a culture based on displacement and (re) combination, is entirely consonant with the dislocation or the ex-centricity manifested on the generic level by most – if not all – of his writing or poetics. We could point here to the fact that his fascination with ethnography and folklore respectively finds an outlet in journalism or in travel writing rather than in ethnographic or anthropological journals *per se* or in serious folklore scholarship, just as his literary aspirations are expressed more in literary translation or adaptation than in original composition. For example, his first serious book-length literary publications are *One of Cleopatra's Nights and Other Fantastic Romances*, published in New York in 1882, which consists in translations of the writing of Théophile Gautier, and *Stray Leaves from Strange Literature*, published in 1884, and which is a volume of tales re-translated into English from the French version established by French scholars from the original (Oriental) text. Hearn's relation to writing is thus one of displacement, translocation, or mediation, rather than of originality. He creates rather more by translation or modulation than by invention, in other words.

A particularly clear example of Hearn's poetics of mediation is provided by his work as a collector of Caribbean folktales. He returned from his longer Martinican sojourn with the material that would find its way into two volumes of Creole folktales. These tales were noted by Hearn in two separate notebooks, and were subsequently discovered and published many decades after his death. The first of these two collections, *Trois fois bel conte*, comprises six of the thirty-four tales that Hearn seems to have collected in the Caribbean. The second volume, *Contes créoles II*, comprises ten tales. In all cases, it was the Creole version of the tale that Hearn collected, and it was the posthumous editor, rather than Hearn himself, who provided the French translation. The editor of the first volume, Charles-Marie Garnier, had tried unsuccessfully to meet Hearn during a visit to Tokyo in 1900. Having failed to make contact with the writer directly, Garnier began a brief correspondence with him. Although he requested from Hearn a Japanese tale for publication, he was given instead a small waxed notebook containing a list of thirty-four titles of Creole folktales, along with the Creole text of just six full tales. Hearn's covering letter is thin on the actual circumstances of his gathering of the six folktales in question. He emphasises rather the value of the tales now that Martinique is, as he puts it, 'gone for ever'.

> J'ai recueilli un nombre de contes créoles, très baroques, qui sont à la fois amusants et dignes de l'attention de quelques folkloristes. Je puis vous envoyer le texte mais je n'ose point entreprendre la traduction. À Paris, sans doute, vous trouverez quelque Martiniquais pour vous aider avec le texte; et la traduction sera facile. [...] Ce que je vous offre ne se trouve pas facilement ailleurs, car la Martinique est finie pour jamais. C'est comme un manuscrit de Pompei – maintenant – ce petit recueil de contes: un tout petit cahier.[3]

Garnier kept the manuscript containing the six tales until well after World War I, when he met the Martinican, Serge Denis, whose native knowledge of Creole and whose philological expertise equipped him for the task of editing and translating the Creole tales. Denis's preface is most informa-

---

3   L. Hearn, *Trois fois bel conte*, 8–9 (in C.-M. Garnier's preface to the book). The quotation is from Hearn's letter to Garnier, dated October 1903, less than a year before his death in Sept 1904. The reference to Pompei is an allusion to the 1902 eruption of the Mont Pelée in Martinique, a disaster that wiped out the town of Saint-Pierre, widely regarded at the time as the jewel of the French Caribbean.

tive about Hearn's use of French and of Creole, which Denis identifies as somewhat unnatural in places, and sometimes over-corrected. The volume appeared as *Trois fois bel conte*, with a preface by Garnier and an incisive introduction by Denis.

In 1988 a second notebook of folktales in Creole was found in Japan in the possession of a relative of Hearn's by the University of Tokyo emeritus professor Sukehiro Hirakawa. When Louis Solo Martinel, a Martinican student of Comparative Literature was introduced to Hirakawa in Japan, the professor showed him this notebook containing the Creole text of ten Caribbean folktales and encouraged the Martinican to prepare it for publication. The result was an edition of Hearn's *carnet* entitled *Contes créoles 2*, published in 2001 by the Caribbean publisher, Ibis Rouge. Like *Trois fois bel conte*, this volume presents annotated transcriptions of the original Creole version of the tales along with the French translation. Martinel also presents two studies on Hearn as a collector of folklore and on Creole oral culture ('oralité').

These two posthumous volumes are extremely valuable in that they document not just the folktales in circulation in Martinique at the end of the nineteenth century, but also the detail of the Creole language as it was spoken at that time, whatever the inaccuracies and infelicities of Hearn's transcription, and whatever doubts these might raise as to Hearn's own (re)writing initiatives either in the course of the transcription process or subsequent to that process. Certainly, the two volumes allow us to speculate on his rather labyrinthine poetics of transcription, translation, and rewriting, and the comments of his two posthumous editors are very valuable in this context. However, given both our considerable forensic distance from the actual genesis of Hearn's collection and given the limitations of the present study, an arguably more fruitful and certain line of inquiry concerns instead the integration of the *conte créole* into Hearn's own writing, specifically into his Caribbean magnum opus, *Two Years in the French West Indies*, published in 1890 in New York by Harper and Brothers.

III Generic creolisation: ethnographic sketches and (folk) narratives

Two Years in the French West Indies is the major work that emerged from Hearn's Caribbean gravitation. Many of the texts that it gathers had previously been published in *Harper's Magazine* or other periodicals. The book comprises two sections: the 'Martinique Sketches' and the much shorter 'Mid-Summer Trip to the Tropics', which recounts Hearn's cruise around the Caribbean prior to his long sojourn in Martinique. The Sketches number fourteen in all: eleven of these have French titles (including 'La Vérette', which is a local contraction of 'la vérole' and 'La Pelée', a contraction of 'Le Mont Pelée'). Two other titles are clearly in Creole ('Pa Combiné, Chè!' and 'Bête-ni-pié'), while the title 'Yé' consists in a proper name which is more likely to be read as Creole (especially in relation to the next (hyper-French) title 'Lys').[4] All the titles given to the 'Sketches' by Hearn are thus in a language foreign to the English text. In addition to this linguistic combination (of French or French Creole with English), a linguistic diversity which is carried through to almost every page of the text, there is also a certain generic creolisation at work in the 'Martinique Sketches'. For some of the 'sketches' are in reality stories, and one of these stories is a traditional Creole folktale. Other sketches contain stories as 'inserts', and in at least four cases these narrative 'inserts' are, in fact, versions of traditional folktales.

This generic *métissage* of travel writing (traditionally itself a mixture of the traveller's narrative and of descriptive writing), on the one hand, and folk narrative, on the other, produces an interface within the 'Sketches' between a modern written genre and a traditional oral one. This interface is registered, moreover, and grossly exaggerated by the manner in which the

---

4   The titles of the 'Martinique Sketches' are as follows: I Les Porteuses, II La Grande Anse, III Un Revenant, IV La Guiablesse, V La Vérette, VI Les Blanchisseuses, VII La Pelée, VIII Ti Canotié, IX La Fille de Couleur, X Bête-ni-Pié, XI Ma Bonne, XII 'Pa Combiné, Chè!', XII Yé, XIV Lys.

'Martinique Sketches' were translated for the French reading public about twenty years after Hearn's death, and some time after his Japanese work had won him a strong reputation among French Orientalists. The translation of the 'Sketches' was published by Mercure de France in two stages. The first volume, *Esquisses martiniquaises*, a literal translation of the English title, appeared in 1924 and contained the first six sketches from *Two Years*. This volume was followed in 1926 by a second, entitled *Contes des tropiques*, containing the remaining eight 'Martinique Sketches'. The translator was Marc (alias Mary-Cécile) Logé, a particularly prolific translator who also executed the French translations of Hearn's Japanese work.[5]

The French translation, via the title given to the second volume (a title that hides the fact that this is, in fact, a second installment of the 'Sketches'), suggests a clear generic distinction between sketches and tales. The two different titles – on the one hand, the literal translation of the original title *Esquisses martiniquaises*, and the invented title *Contes des tropiques* on the other – create expectations of two rather different works: anthropological or journalistic impressions in the first case, and folktales in the second; descriptive prose on the one hand, and on the other, literary or folk narrative. This generic distinction is underlined by the specificity of the Martinican reference in respect of the *Esquisses martiniquaises*, and the much more vague, orientalist or exoticist reference to mere latitude in the case of the *Contes des tropiques*. It could be said that the term 'Tropics' is not an invention on the part of the translator, since it features in the title of the second shorter text of *Two Years*, the 'Midsummer trip to the Tropics'. However, the reference to the 'conte' is exclusively the translator's (or her publisher's) initiative. Moreover, the reference of Hearn's chosen term 'Sketches' is primarily visual, which is not surprising given Hearn's obsession with the visual, perhaps a compensatory obsession in a man who lost the sight of one eye in an unfortunate schoolyard accident during

---

5   The two titles are: *Esquisses martiniquaises*, trans. M. Logé (Paris, Mercure de France, 1924) and *Contes des tropiques*, trans. M. Logé (Paris, Mercure de France, 1926). See also my critical editions of the two translations published under the titles *Esquisses martiniquaises I* and *Esquisses martiniquaises II* (Paris, L'Harmattan, 2003).

adolescence. In contrast, the reference of the 'conte' is primarily to the ear ('conter' means to recount).

The clear generic dichotomy which is suggested by the fact of having these two separate and differently entitled volumes translate a single work, highlights a fundamental principle of Hearn's poetics, one that is arguably at the heart not just of the generic specificity of the 'conte' as it features in his work, but also of the ethnographic specificity of the Creole condition, namely the principle of combination. The chief creative energy of Creole culture, of the Creole language, of the Creole individual or people, and indeed, of the Creole *conte*, inheres in the encounter of two or more different, if not opposed, elements. Similarly, in the poetics of *Two Years in the French West Indies*, Hearn mixes narrative and description, traditional *conte* and sketch, transcribed oral folk narratives and original written narratives, and in the first part of the volume, the 'Midsummer Trip to the Tropics', travelogue and diary.

Faithful as this suggestion of generic plurality might be to Hearn's aesthetic in the 'Sketches', the unsuspecting reader of *Contes des tropiques* is bound to have been surprised by the overall tenor of that volume. The first and longest sketch of the *Contes* is an extremely long and tedious text, mainly descriptive. It does recount the author's ascent of the Mont Pelée, the volcanic mountain that towers over much of Martinique, but this narrative, overloaded as it is with naturalist observations, hardly suffices to make of the sketch a *conte*. In fact the majority of the sketches in the second volume of the translation are only sporadically narrative. Only 'Ti canotié', 'Yé', and to a lesser extent 'Lys' are virtually entirely constituted by a single unified narrative, and only in the case of 'Yé' is this narrative a 'conte' or folktale in the traditional sense. 'Ma bonne', it is true, does include a brief Creole folktale (the Pimento tale, or 'Zhistouè Piment', recounted in Creole in Hearn's text). Another sketch, 'La Guiablesse', switches without warning or metadiscursive framing from the narrative of Hearn's encounter with the ghost stories of Martinican folk culture, such as the folktale about Baidaux, briefly summarised in Hearn's text, to a narrative that itself reads exactly like a traditional folktale, but that is not explicitly presented as such. The story of Le Père Labat recounted by Hearn in the sketch entitled 'Un Revenant' incorporates two competing versions of the tale of Missié Bon, the one a popular folk version, the other presenting the supposedly (historically) accurate truth about Missié Bon. The sketch entitled (in Creole) 'Ti Canotié', on the other hand, is a contemporary cautionary tale. It is interesting, however, that when Hearn indulges his creative verve by inventing a dramatic story about the drowning of two young Martinican boys who swim out to greet the tourist ships, he gives his story this Creole title. 'Zhistouè piment', 'Yé', and – to a lesser, much abbreviated extent – the Baidaux and the Missié Bon stories take the form of the traditional *conte*. Both of the former (and longer) tales, presented as authentic folktales, are narratives of hunger and deprivation in a family setting, and indeed both tales feature in full in the manuscripts of the *contes créoles* collected by Hearn.

IV The oral and written interface: Hearn's meta-discourse

As we have already seen, Hearn himself did not prepare for publication the folktales that appeared posthumously in the two collections published under his name. Neither collection incorporates any metadiscursive indications from Hearn that might explain, for example, how he came to hear the various tales or what he might have made of them. Certainly, his editors, especially Serge Denis, do make an effort to decipher the extent of Hearn's own input into the transcription of the tales. Denis, for example, bases this effort on Hearn's often idiosyncratic or unusual use of Creole and also on a comparative reading of the English version of 'Yé' contained in the eponymous sketch in *Two Years*, on the one hand, and the Creole version contained in Hearn's notebook, on the other. Conversely, in *Two Years*, Hearn does indicate how he came to hear both 'Yé' and 'Zhistouè piment'. Moreover, in 'Ma bonne', he offers both the Creole version of the latter tale and its English translation, whereas in 'Yé' he only provides his own (English) version of the eponymous folktale. In both cases, the actual *conte* is framed by the author in such a way as to integrate it into the general

ethnographic project of the 'Martinique Sketches'. 'Zhistouè piment', a tale
of a culinary disaster, is inserted into a sketch ('Ma Bonne') about Martinican cuisine, and more specifically about the naive simplicity and goodness
of Hearn's housekeeper, Cyrillia, who recounts the story to Hearn.[6] 'Yé',
meanwhile, is framed by a rather general introduction on Hearn's practice
as a collector of folklore and by a closing section on the socio-historical
signficance of the plot and characterisation of this particular tale.

In his 'Martinique Sketches', Hearn presents himself at the outset of
'Yé' both as audience and as writer, as a receiver and also as a transmitter
of Creole folklore.[7] He stresses his status as a witness to, and translator of,
oral culture, and also acknowledges his reliance on primary sources. He
thus thematises his relation as a writer to the folklore that he is collecting,
explaining that he regularly gathers folktales from a variety of informants.
However he also admits that he sometimes has recourse to secondary, literate intermediaries able to write out the texts directly or from memory
(usually in shorthand), whereas Hearn himself must have them dictated
to him slowly, painstakingly (Hearn's poor eyesight may have presented a
supplementary reason for his preference for third-party scribes). Moreover,
when outlining the disadvantages of dictation, he acknowledges the risk
of deformation and especially the risk of adversely affecting the spontaneity of the narrative. Most of Hearn's acknowledged Martinican informants are not so much *conteurs* as *conteuses*. They include Cyrillia who told
him the 'Pimento Story'; his landlady in St Pierre, Mman Robert, a cigar
seller; and Adou the daughter of his landlady in the mountains. They have,
moreover, little or no association with plantation culture, since Hearn's
preferred location as observer-participant is urban, in small villages or in
the capital, Saint-Pierre.

---

6   'Cyrillia told me a story about this infernal vegetable', *Two Years*, 276.
7   'Almost every night, just before bedtime, I hear some group of children in the street
     telling stories to each other [...]. I am particularly fond of listening to the stories,
     – which seem to me the oddest stories I ever heard. I succeeded in getting several
     dictated to me, so that I could write them; – others were written for me by creole
     friends, with better success [...]. I submit a free rendering of one of these tales, – the
     history of Yé and the Devil'; *Two Years in the French West Indies*, 313.

Although Hearn explains in his sketch that the story of Yé is part of a cycle of folktales all centred on the same character, and that this particular tale is particularly representative of the cycle as a whole, he does not see fit to study the poetics of the *conte*: he does not, for example, point out the various elements of this particular story that are emblematic of the Creole folktale: the preponderance of orality; the importance of the supernatural; the prevalence of repetition, of magic, of scatology. Rather, after recounting it, he reads the tale sociologically or ethnologically, interpreting its significance as an expression of the collective Martinican psyche, of the damage done by slavery, of the legacy of paternalism, namely collective male irresponsibility, etc.[8]

Hearn's metadiscursive emphasis on the processes of oral transmission and transcription is important and perhaps even seminal for the development of French Caribbean writing. Certainly, the traditional enunciative context of the Creole folktale has become crucial to its contemporary cultural value. In other words, its epitomisation of oral culture has been fully exploited by the theoreticians of the *créolité* movement. In fact, though, it is not so much the *conte* that this movement reveres as the mediator of this cultural form, that is, the *conteur*. The *conteur* is the *maître de la parole*,[9] and Martinican novelist Patrick Chamoiseau's second novel entitled *Solibo Magnifique* is entirely centred on the eponymous character's role as *conteur* and on the erosion and eventual demise of this role.[10] On a more general level, much contemporary Caribbean writing is overdetermined by its negotiation of the relation between oral and written culture, and, in particular, by its recuperation and translation of the value of the spoken Creole word,

---

8 'Poor Yé! – you still live for me only too vividly outside of those strange folk-tales of eating and drinking which so cruelly reveal the long slave-hunger of your race'; *Two Years*, 319.

9 On the relation between oral and written culture in the Caribbean context, see R. Ludwig (ed.), *Écrire la parole de nuit: la nouvelle littérature antillaise* (Paris, Gallimard, 1994).

10 See P. Chamoiseau and R. Confiant, *Lettres créoles: tracées antillaises et continentales de la littérature 1635–1975* (Paris, Hatier, 1991). See also P. Chamoiseau, *Solibo Magnifique* (Paris, Gallimard, 1988).

i.e. its articulation or amplification of the resonances of Creole orality within the written text. For Chamoiseau, the role of the writer or *marqueur de la parole* is parasitical to a certain extent, but he is also, more gratifyingly, a *passeur*, a mediator between oral and written culture and a conservationist or archivist of oral culture. We could call Hearn a *marqueur de parole* 'avant la lettre',[11] and yet his outsider-observer status makes his position with respect to orality and writing, memory and tradition, infinitely less ambiguous or less painful than that of native Caribbean writers,[12] since the charge of attrition or betrayal of the oral tradition does not apply to him in the same way. Moreover, the fact that he is a sallow-skinned, culturally indeterminate anglophone outsider makes his mediation much less oppressive than that of an outsider identified with the cultural primacy of the French language.

It is important to note that Hearn's reworking, adaptation, translation, and incorporation of the folktale reflects or re-actualises the constitutional basis of Creole culture. For there is a sense in which the primacy and authenticity with which oral culture is invested in many cultural contexts, for example in the African context – an authenticity based on its perceived originary character – are significantly mitigated in the Caribbean. This is partly because of the violence and oppression that occasioned the emergence of Creole language and culture and that compromised it, partly because of the deracination and belatedness of the new composite language and culture. In other words, the newness of this oral culture means that it cannot be reasonably constructed as (purely) traditional or originary. Hearn does, however, seem to view Creole oral culture as primitive in the sense of being undeveloped. Indeed, for Hearn, one of the attractions of Creole culture is that it is 'primitive' in the sense of being childlike. This does not mean that he is blind to its specificity or to its composite being. Indeed, in moments of ethnological oxymoron he is capable of distinguishing between various

---

11   L. S. Martinel uses this term in his first essay on Hearn at the end of *Contes créoles II*, 'L. Hearn: marqueur de paroles', 109–127.

12   On this painful positioning of the Caribbean writer of the spoken word, see D. Chancé, *L'Auteur en souffrance: essai sur la position et la représentation de l'auteur dans le roman antillais contemporain (1981–1992)* (Paris, PUF, 2000).

examples of Creole culture in terms of their relative degree of 'purity'. For example, in his preface to *Gombo Zhèbes*, the book of Creole proverbs that he wrote in New Orleans, he criticises the Frenchified Creole that he regards as adulterated, writing disapprovingly: 'I have sometimes heard the pure and primitive Creole [...] called "Congo" by colored folks of the new generation'.[13] The word 'Congo', used in this sense, refers to relative closeness to the African origin. It is perhaps significant in this context that the tales highlighted by Hearn typically foreground children and that the Martinicans whom he portrays in most detail have extremely childlike traits. Given Hearn's own dramatic, not to say traumatic childhood, it is tempting to see various lines of identification and transfer at work in his preference for what he regards as a 'childlike' culture.

V The language of interface: Hearn's use of Creole

Apart from folktales, transcriptions of other types of folklore, including especially proverbs, recipes, and songs abound in the 'Martinique Sketches'. Their presence, like that of the folktales, necessarily involves a double process of translation: both from oral to written language and from one language to another (Creole and French into English). In this sense, both the English translation of 'Zistouè Piment' that is given alongside the Creole version in 'Ma bonne', and also that transcribed Creole version – which at times involved Hearn himself in the choice of an orthography for transcribing French Creole – could be regarded as reinforcing the reflexivity and mediational tenor of Hearn's discourse on Creole culture. For, in transliterating the spoken language of this – more or less exclusively oral – culture, his own work is enacting a kind of dislocation, displacement, mediation, and recomposition, all processes at the heart of the Creole condition.

---

13   Hearn, *Gombo Zhèbes*, xvi.

The written form of any traditional *conte*, proverb or song bespeaks an act of transliteration or translation, that is, a displacement or shift. However, this displacement is redoubled when the language being transliterated is an almost exclusively oral language, i.e. Creole. What is Hearn doing, then, when he inserts individual Creole sentences, phrases, expressions or just words in his English text? For the studding of Hearn's English with original Creole terms is, in fact, one of the most striking stylistic aspects of all of Hearn's 'Martinique Sketches'.[14] Is this feature simply intended to inscribe local colour? Is it simply intended as evidence of the authenticity of Hearn's fieldwork and of his linguistic acumen and flexibility? Or does this intensely macaronic style not reflect one of the central principles of his poetics: a penchant for displacement, multilinearity, and combination?

It is important to note that Hearn's deployment of Creole in the text mediates not just an-other language, a different language foreign to the main language (English) of the text, but a language at once related to and different from a second ('foreign') language also incorporated into the English text, that is, French. And of course, the key to this second distinction is precisely the orality of Creole. For example, the fundamental difference between the French word 'fruit' and the Creole word 'fouitt' is the different pronunciation of several phonemes, the missing 'r', the 'ou' for 'u', and the sounding of the (double) 't'. In his preface to *Gombo Zhèbes*, Hearn comments in some detail on the Creole language, on its grammar and on the relation of its lexis to the French lexis and particularly on the question of pronunciation. He also comments frequently in *Two Years* on the sound of the Creole language and indeed of the different Creoles spoken in different parts of the Caribbean.

14   For example: 'While Cyrillia is busy with her *canari*, she talks to herself or sings. [...] Occasionally at such times she will break the silence in the strangest way, if she thinks I am not too busy with my papers to answer a question:–
– "Missié?" – timidly –
– "Eh?"
– "Di moin, chè, ti manmaille dans pays ou, toutt piti, piti – ess ça pâlé Anglais?" (Do the little children in my country, the very, very little children – talk English?)';
Two Years, 210.

Although we can conclude that Hearn had a rather extraordinary grasp of the French language, there is evidence, both textual and anecdotal, to suggest that he was considerably more at home with reading and listening than with producing either written or spoken French. This is evident not so much from the published translations, as from his gradually increasing tendency to write an English studded with French and/or Creole expressions and exclamations, usually of a highly idiomatic nature. One of his biographers writes that 'in spite of his extraordinary mastery of the subtleties of the French language, he always spoke French with an atrociously bad accent'.[15] According to his friend Krehbiel, an eminent musicologist, 'He had a very bad ear' and was 'organically incapable of humming the simplest tune'.[16] While his allegedly bad ear may have prevented him from speaking with a good accent, it didn't prevent him from hearing and transcribing what he heard around him very convincingly. His difficulty may have been not so much in his ear as somewhere between his ear and his larynx. This point, whose demonstration depends precisely on the interface between orality and writing, may seem to be a trivial one, but it assumes a lot of importance when discussing Hearn's practice, limitations, and merits as a collector of folklore (did he get others to transcribe the folklore or did he write it down himself?) or as a translator (did he translate the original text or did he use somebody else's cribs?).

The presence of the Creole folktale in Hearn's 'Martinique Sketches' raises many further questions which cannot be answered or even considered in the space of the present study. For example, in order to appreciate fully the significance of the *conte créole* in Hearn's poetics, it needs to be compared with the role played later on by the Japanese folktale. More specifically, we could study the relative presence of traces of orality or of the Japanese language in Hearn's renderings of such tales. Finally, we could speculate as to the meaning of Hearn's deployment of translation, adaptation, transformation as his preferred literary genres. Does this not

15   N. Kennard, *Lafcadio Hearn* (New York, Appleton & Co. Ltd, 1912), 98.
16   H.E. Krehbiel's chapter 'Hearn and negro music' in his *Afro-American Folksongs: A Study in Racial and National Music* (New York, G. Schirmer, 1914), 37–40.

indicate a deficiency of imagination or of invention on his part? Why did he – throughout his entire writing life indeed – limit himself so much to borrowing, or inhabiting the fictions, the stories, etc. invented and inhabited by others? Did his writing succeed in cancelling an apparent creative deficit or does it at least represent an attempt to cancel it? How does this writing, this transcription, translation, or rewriting, represent, as certain critics including the Englishman Roy Foster and the American Frederick Starr would suggest,[17] a search for location, for a place or an identity? Does it not rather confirm, as the contemporary Martinican writers Raphael Confiant and Patrick Chamoiseau imply, the author's essentially protean and multiple identity?[18]

To conclude, I would suggest that the significance of Hearn's association with the Caribbean Creole folktale is located on at least three levels. First of all, he was, clearly, a significant collector and curator of this oral tradition. Secondly, I would read the fact that he did not himself get around to translating or publishing the tales that he either transcribed himself or that he had transcribed for him, not as an indication of saturation, as a failure of literary stamina, or as a sign of a disenchantment with the Tropics. Rather, I see it as indicating that he was interested not so much in the *conte créole* per se but in its integration into his own writing. And he had probably said all that he wanted to say about these tales, and done all that he wanted to do with them in integrating them into his own writing to the extent that he already did in *Two Years*. He was then ready to move on again. It is, in other words, the actual insertion of these pieces into Hearn's project as a whole that situates then their significance within

17   R. Foster, in his Foreword to P. Murray, *A Fantastic Journey: the Life and Literature of Lafcadio Hearn* (Sandgate, Kent, Japan Library, 1993), suggests that Hearn's life represents a search for location, while F. Starr in his Introduction to *Inventing New Orleans: Writings of Lafcadio Hearn* (Jackson, University Press of Mississippi, 2001), notes that 'It is no surprise that Hearn fitted in nowhere and spent his entire life searching for a place he could call home'; xiii.

18   R. Confiant notes that 'Hearn invented what today we might call "multiple identity" or "creoleness"'; 'Lafcadio Hearn: the magnificent traveller', Foreword to the Signal Books edition of *Two Years*, ix–xii, xii.

Hearn's *imaginaire*, illuminating in the process several crucial dimensions of his poetics. Thirdly, that poetics can be shown to be based on multiple levels of difference, displacement, and cross-fertilisation: culturally, linguistically, in terms of narrative voice and structure, socially, and possibly most crucially, in terms of the crossover between immediate transmission and mediated transmission, between *parole* and *écriture*, between voice and text. In inscribing in his English text the oral culture not just of the Caribbean, but of the French Caribbean, by insetting little jewels and cameos of Creole, a language itself differentiated from French in its status as a new, mixed, displaced language, and as an oral language with a different sound, Hearn gains his creative energy from the linguistic counterpoint between French and Creole, and from the interface of *l'écrit* and *l'oral*, eye and ear.

Mastering the word: appropriations of the *conte créole* in Antillean theory

MAEVE MCCUSKER

I

The relationship between the oral and the literary traditions in the French Caribbean is usually characterised as complex, painful, even hostile. While literature, because of its permanence and prestige, might be seen as the privileged mode of expression, writers from the Antilles continually strain towards the immediacy of orality, albeit within the secondary space of textuality. At the metaliterary level this can be seen, for example, in the sheer number of interviews published with French Caribbean writers, and in the extent to which the *parole* of the author has inflected critical responses to his or her writing, as well as the reception of his or her contemporaries;[1] or indeed in the oral origins of one of the key texts of contemporary Antillean

---

[1]   In addition to a plethora of interviews published in academic journals, it is striking to note the number of 'conversations' that appear in, or as, published books. To cite some of the most obvious examples: F. Pfaff, *Entretiens avec Maryse Condé* (Paris, Karthala, 1993), translated into English as *Conversations with Maryse Condé* (Lincoln and London, University of Nebraska Press, 1996); A. Césaire, *Nègre je suis, nègre je resterai. Entretiens avec Françoise Vergès* (Paris, Albin Michel, 2004); P. Louis, *Aimé Césaire: rencontre avec un nègre fondamental* (Paris, Arléa, 2004); P. Ginelli, *Archipels littéraires. Chamoiseau, Condé, Confiant, Brival, Maximin, Laferrière, Pineau, Agnant* (Montréal, Mémoire d'encrier, 2007). L. Gauvin's *L'Écrivain francophone à la croisée des langues* (Paris, Karthala, 1997), given its global geographic reach, includes a disproportionate number of interviews with French Caribbean writers (three out of eleven), while even standard critical studies such as D. Chancé's *L'Auteur en souffrance* (Paris, PUF, 2001) and R.-M. Réjouis's *Veillées pour les mots. Aimé Césaire, Patrick*

theory, the *Éloge de la créolité*.[2] At the textual level the foregrounding of
orality is conveyed in a recurrent emphasis on the enunciative moment, the
scene of storytelling, in much Caribbean fiction, as well as in the literary
trope of a character 'passing on' or relaying a second-hand, orally-related
tale.[3] Perhaps most obviously, in thematic terms, it can be seen in the
centrality of the figure of the *conteur* and, latterly, the *marqueur de paroles*,
in many Antillean novels.[4] And yet given this privileging of orality, and
given, for example, the prestige that the writers of the *créolité* movement
afford the spoken word, the historical dominance in Martinique and Guadeloupe of the novel – a genre apparently more remote from the voice than
'performed' genres such as drama or poetry – may seem surprising. If the
earliest stirrings of a literary consciousness were expressed in poetry (notably
that of Aimé Césaire), since at least the 1960s the genre of choice in the
Antilles has been narrative prose fiction, and the islands have produced a
disproportionate number of world-class novelists.

The dominance of fiction is in keeping with a more widespread generic
proclivity in contemporary writing, a proclivity which is, if anything, even
more in evidence in postcolonial writing. But it could also be argued that
narrative fiction, as the most hospitable literary medium for storytelling,
holds an especially strong appeal for the *francophone* Caribbean writer
because of the privileged position of the folktale in the French-speak-
ing islands. The term 'conte', of course, describes a wide range of forms
– riddles, proverbs and lullabies, as well as stories – but the signifier is, as
Rolande Rostal-Honorien notes, 'avant tout un indice de *fictionnalité* avant

---

Chamoiseau et Maryse Condé (Paris, Karthala, 2005), end with an interview (as it
happens, in both cases, with Chamoiseau).

2   The *Éloge* is supposedly the transcript of a lecture delivered in Saint Denis in Paris,
in 1988.

3   Thus, as Gallagher notes, French Caribbean narrative 'asserts its oral foundation by
subverting the conventional distinction between *récit* and discourse, highlighting
the indices of direct speech'; M. Gallagher, *Soundings in French Caribbean Writing
since 1950. The Shock of Space and Time* (Oxford, OUP, 2002), 121.

4   See for example J. Zobel's *La Rue cases-nègres* and P. Chamoiseau's *Solibo Magnifique*.
Chamoiseau novels such as *Texaco* and *L'Esclave vieil homme et le molosse* also feature
the *marqueur de paroles*, a somewhat anxious avatar of the novelist.

de désigner un genre déterminé'.[5] The striking investment of Martinican and Guadeloupean writers in this broad field of *fictionnalité* may therefore be motivated and nourished, at least in part, by the extraordinary historical strength of the *conte* in the francophone islands, a strength attested by a number of observers. For example, in one of the earliest studies of folklore in the Caribbean, Elsie Clews Parsons makes a categorical distinction between the islands where 'French Creole is still spoken' (Martinique, Guadeloupe, Haiti, but also Dominica and Trinidad) and their Caribbean neighbours, stating that these francophone islands offer 'by far the richest fields for the folklorist'. In contrast, she notes the relative paucity of the oral tradition in the Danish, Dutch and the northerly British islands, islands in which 'the heavy hand of church and state' curtailed the development of the *conte*.[6] This notion that Protestantism created a less hospitable environment for the oral tradition is implicitly endorsed by the Guadeloupean writer Maryse Condé, who suggests that Catholicism, with its investment in mystery and the *merveilleux*, created a fertile terrain for the development of the *conte* in the French islands. She notes that the masters in a typical French Caribbean plantation tended to come from precisely the areas in France in which the oral tradition was strongest: the Vendée, Normandy and Brittany. As Condé observes, these were 'régions très catholiques', in which 'les contes et légendes, d'une grande richesse, mêlent un merveilleux et une philosophie chrétiens à un fond traditionnel plus ancien'.[7] We shall return to Condé, and more particularly to Parsons, later in this Chapter. Suffice it

---

5 R. Rostal-Honorien, 'Frontières du *kont* en Guadeloupe', *Études Créoles* 25.2 (2002), Special Issue on 'Le Kont créole: à l'interface de l'écrit et de l'oral', 15–62, 17, my italics.

6 E. Clews Parsons, *Folk-lore of the Antilles, French and English, Volume 1* (New York, The American Folklore Society, 1933–1943), vi, hereafter referred to as *Folk-lore*. Already in 1884, the Austrian linguist Hugo Schuchardt made a case for a certain type of 'exception française' in terms of the inherently literary qualities of French-based Creole: 'Parmi les idiomes créoles, ceux originaires du français occupent nettement le premier rang sous l'angle littéraire'. Quoted by J.C. Carpanin Marimoutou, 'Des Fables créoles', *Études créoles* 24.2 (2001), 7–14, 7.

7 M. Condé, *La Civilisation du bossale. Réflexions sur la littérature orale de la Guadeloupe et de la Martinique* (Paris, L'Harmattan, 1978), 42.

for now to note that – whether or not it is linked to a particular religious tradition – the exceptional strength of the oral tradition in Guadeloupe and Martinique has nourished the sense of an urgent, if problematic, connection between story and history, between orality and literature, and has contributed to the rise of both fiction and theoretical writing.

The present article is concerned with theoretical or essayistic pieces which have analysed and, very often, appropriated the *conte*. Caribbean writing in French has been enriched, but also over-determined and contained, by the various theories of identity that have emanated from the islands, and by the ideological posturing and in-fighting that seems to be a condition of their existence. 'Theory' tends to be seen as the preserve of male writers, although this perception depends both on a rather limited view of what constitutes theory, and on the fact that the essays of male authors, perhaps because of the prestigious publishing houses in which their work appears, seem to achieve greater prominence than those of their female peers. The gendering of theory also derives from the fact that the reflections of male writers – even, or perhaps especially, when they seek to criticise each other – carry a striking freight of intertextuality, which perpetuates the sense of a highly masculine frame of reference that is dismissive or ignorant of the work of women. It is against this general background that the *conte* has been harnessed or co-opted, by a number of male writers, to a succession of ideological perspectives; the epistemological or socio-cultural value attached to the form has therefore shifted according to the theory of cultural identity being promoted. I shall begin by showing how the *conte* has been adopted and appropriated by a number of Martinican theorists, before looking in more detail at *Les Maîtres de la parole créole*,[8] a text which, like so many of the key texts of the créolité movement, is a collaborative work by Martinican men,[9] and from which I draw my problematically gendered title.

8   R. Confiant, M. Lebielle and D. Damoison, *Les Maîtres de la parole créole* (Paris, Gallimard, 1995), hereafter referred to as *Maîtres*.
9   The tales were translated into French by Confiant, from a Creole transcription provided by Lebielle, and both men also contribute an introduction. Confiant and Lebielle were born and live on the island, while Damoison is the son of Martinican

II

Already in 1942, the fourth issue of the *négritude*-inspired periodical *Tropiques* devoted three articles to Martinican folklore. The volume included a number of *contes* by Georges Gratiant and Lafcadio Hearn, and an introductory essay, 'Introduction au folklore martiniquais', co-authored by Aimé Césaire and René Ménil.[10] Césaire and Ménil are relatively unconcerned with the orality or the *créolité* of the form, and are more concerned to distance it from European literary conventions. They caution at the outset of their piece that neither cosmogonies, nor metaphysics, nor even 'l'expression des grandes aventures sentimentales qui marquent l'homme' are to be found in the *conte créole*.[11] This is not a medium of introspection nor of psychological depth, they argue.[12] Rather the *conte*, as an expression of slave culture, and in contradistinction to the textual cultures of the West, articulates a world view in which 'la pensée, comme le sentiment, est un luxe'.[13] It gives expression instead to the urgent needs of a starving people, and its fundamental theme is 'le ventre vide'.[14] It is the only repository of resistance to the dominant order of the plantation, an order described in all the vivid carnality of *négritude* ('mains coupées, corps écartelés, gibets').[15] Césaire and Ménil continue: 'Quand on aura dépouillé toutes les archives, compulsé tous les dossiers, fouillé tous les papiers abolitionnistes, c'est à ces contes que reviendra celui qui voudra

---

parents born in Paris. Confiant and Damoison have collaborated on another photo-text, *Le Galion. Canne, douleur séculaire Ô tendresse* (Petit Bourg, Guadeloupe, Ibis Rouge, 2000).

10   A. Césaire and R. Ménil, 'Introduction au folklore martiniquais', *Tropiques* 4 (1942), 7–11.

11   Césaire and Ménil, 'Introduction', 8.

12   Of course, while the same can be said of the European *conte*, which frequently emerged from situations of poverty and hardship, the specific context of slavery gives the *conte créole* a very particular quality in terms of its stock themes, tone and characters.

13   Césaire and Ménil, 'Introduction', 8.

14   Césaire and Ménil, 'Introduction', 10.

15   *Ibid.*

saisir, éloquente et pathétique, la grande misère de nos pères esclaves'. In keeping with the rhetoric of *négritude*, Césaire and Ménil thus accentuate the misery of the slave past, identifying two cycles in the development of the *conte* (hunger and fear), and emphasise its undertow of suffering and brutality. The *conte* is, they suggest, a more reliable and 'direct' record of this suffering than the document or archive, because it is the only one capable of communicating the trauma of the African slave, a history excised from dominant (European) accounts.

If, for Césaire and Ménil, the *conte* represents a potential source of inspiration for Caribbean writers (it is to these that the writer *will* turn, 'reviendra', once the insufficiency of existing sources has been recognised), it is the generation of writers linked to the *créolité* movement, and in particular Chamoiseau and Confiant, who have most fully realised this move. Since the 1980s, as part of the revalorisation of Creole culture largely driven by the *créolité* movement and the GEREC (Groupe d' études et de recherches en espace créolophone), Martinique and Guadeloupe have seen a proliferation of socio-historical, cultural and linguistic studies of the conte.[16] In addition, French literary tales – notably those of La Fontaine – have been translated into Creole, and transcriptions of *contes* as told 'live' by local *conteurs*, often in parallel Creole-French text, have been published.[17] In literary histories such as *Lettres créoles*, the *conte* is presented as an authentic cultural form which, along with dances such as the *bélé*, testifies to a specifically Creole creativity.[18] The age of orality is positioned by the *créolité* writers – perhaps somewhat quixotically – as a fertile transitional stage:

16   It is of course no coincidence that in Haiti, where oral culture is much less threatened than in the *départements d'outre-mer*, this phenomenon was much less in evidence.

17   Notable examples of parallel texts include: I. Césaire, *Contes de nuits et de jours aux Antilles* (Paris, Éditions caribéennes, 1989); F. Kitchenassamy, *Les Contes à dormir debout/Kont pou dômi doubou: contes bilingues français-créole* (Paris, L'Harmattan, 2000); C. Colombo, *Ti Jean et Monsieur le Roi/Ti Jan é Misié liwa. Contes de la Martinique bilingue créole-français* (Paris, L'Harmattan, 2006). Within a more strictly literary context, see also R. Ludwig's collection, *Écrire la parole de nuit* (Paris, Gallimard, 1994).

18   P. Chamoiseau and R. Confiant, *Lettres créoles: tracées antillaises et continentales de la littérature 1635–1975* (Paris, Hatier, 1991).

the 'temps de la parole' is located between two potentially alienating stages, *le cri*, the primal scream of the slave ship, and *l'écrit*, literature, which has been historically bound up with the French language, and with the master texts of colonialism.

In addition to its political significance, there are other reasons why the *conte* holds such a strong appeal for these contemporary writers. It is intimately linked to the two ages privileged by the *créolité* programme: childhood (a time when, traditionally, children are immersed in the oral tradition passed on by mothers and grandmothers) and old age (the few remaining *conteurs* are, according to Confiant and Chamoiseau, predominantly elderly men, and for obvious cultural reasons this generation has had a more direct experience of the oral tradition). The rehabilitation of the *conte* can also be read in the context of a growing interest in memory, now that what Chamoiseau, in a striking expression, calls the 'époque de mémoire en bouche', is over.[19] The *conte* harnesses together both collective and individual memory; as Jean Bernabé has argued, it is one of a number of 'genres dits mnémoniques, c'est-à-dire structurés selon une logique mémorielle',[20] while Confiant notes that the *conteur* is a 'personnage doué d'une mémoire fabuleuse'.[21] This interplay between a heroic individual who personifies memory, and a community which depends on his stories because of the amnesiac blow dealt by slavery, is frequently at the core of the contemporary Caribbean novel; in turn, many critics have attacked such texts for their nostalgia, privileging as they do community and ancestral wisdom to the exclusion of any real engagement with contemporary issues.[22]

---

19   *Solibo Magnifique* (Paris, Folio, 1988), 223.
20   J. Bernabé, '*Fènwè* et *wè klè*, le syndrome homérique à l'œuvre dans la parole antillaise', in J. Bernabé et al. (eds), *Au Visiteur lumineux. Des îles créoles aux sociétés plurielles. Mélanges offerts à Jean Benoist* (Petit Bourg-Schœlcher, Ibis Rouge-GEREC, 2000), 633–650, 637.
21   Confiant, *Maîtres*, 13
22   See for example R. and S. Price, 'Shadowboxing in the mangrove' *Cultural Anthropology* 12.1 (1997), 3–36.

Both Chamoiseau and Confiant have produced anthologies of *contes* which accentuate a sense of nostalgia for this 'golden age'. The title of Chamoiseau's collection, *Au Temps de l'antan*, averts to a bygone yesteryear, while the sepia-toned photographs which adorn Confiant's *Les Maîtres de la parole créole* serve to romanticise the featured *conteurs*. There is, however, a distinction to be drawn – perhaps of degree rather than of essence – in the way in which both writers have engaged with the form, a distinction due at least in part to the growing influence of the *créolité* movement in the mid-nineties. Chamoiseau's *Au Temps de l'antan* appeared in 1988: thus it preceded by a crucial year the *Éloge de la créolité*, which was to become such an influential cultural manifesto. The *Éloge* is notoriously critical of Césaire, and the *créolité* writers – particularly Confiant – have been criticised for their 'patricidal' attacks on him. And yet Chamoiseau's description of his own discovery of literature as having been mediated through the spoken rather than the written word strongly echoes Césaire's prediction in the *Tropiques* article quoted above. Chamoiseau observes, 'Lorsque j'ai commencé à écrire, que j'ai voulu me tourner vers des archives littéraires [...] je n'ai pas trouvé de bibliothèque, mais j'ai trouvé un conteur créole, des chansons, des proverbes, des comptines, et surtout la masse extraordinaire des contes créoles qu'on n'a pas encore fini d'explorer'.[23] In his introduction to *Au Temps de l'antan*, although he quotes Glissant, Chamoiseau's primary intertextual engagement is with Césaire. He opens the collection reverentially, with a Césaire poem, an unusually extended intertextual citation on the younger writer's part. The poem, 'Beau sang giclé', juxtaposes images of the horror of the plantation ('tête trophée membres lacérés/dard assassin beau sang giclé/ramages perdus rivages ravis') with the notion of childhood *as* folktale ('enfance enfance conte trop remué/l'aube sur sa chaîne mord féroce à naître').[24] Chamoiseau's introduction refers directly

---

23 In C. Détrie (ed.), *Poétiques du divers* (Montpellier-Praxiling, Université Paul Valéry-Montpellier III, 1998), 14.

24 P. Chamoiseau, *Au Temps de l'antan. Contes du pays Martinique* (Paris, Hatier, 1988), 11. This association between a primary orality and childhood will of course be explored at greater length in Chamoiseau's trilogy of *récits d'enfance*, *Une enfance créole* volumes I, II and III.

to the 1941 *Tropiques* article cited above, and strongly echoes the *négritude* poet's views.[25] He emphasises the intolerable conditions of the plantation, and like Césaire and Ménil, underlines that the *conteur* has 'érigé la faim comme une lancinance du conte créole, et la nourriture, comme un obsessionnel trésor'.[26]

If his position is thus close to that of the *négritude* writers some forty years earlier, in one respect Chamoiseau prefigures the *créolité* manifesto of which he will be a co-signatory the following year. Instead of distancing the *conte* from Europe, as Césaire and Ménil had done, Chamoiseau notes that it emerges from the cross-fertilisation of two distinct, or even polarised, traditions, Old World and New, in that the symbolic bestiary of Africa (elephant, tortoise, tiger) meets the European imaginary (the Devil, the Good Lord, Ti-Jean l'Horizon). This sense of a dual anchoring will be accentuated and extended in Confiant's two 1995 collections, *Contes créoles des Amériques* and, our main focus in what remains, *Les Maîtres de la parole créole*. These works appeared at the height of the *créolité* movement, and in them Confiant goes further than Chamoiseau in stressing the range of cultural elements fused in the *conte*.[27] In *Maîtres* Confiant acknowledges that the most significant source of the repertoire is 'celle qui provient de l'Afrique-Guinée',[28] and like Chamoiseau emphasises the European heritage. But rather than seeing the *conte* as a meeting point for two diametrically opposed cultures, the main thrust of the introduction is to celebrate the heterogeneity of the *conte*, its importance as a vector of transcultural exchange. This process has produced an entirely distinct

---

25   Without wanting to push the significance of the *Tropiques* article for Chamoiseau too far, it is worth noting that in this piece Césaire and Ménil highlight the suffering of the runaway slave during 'l'époque où les molosses fouillent ravins et montagnes': this narrative will be explored in Chamoiseau's 1997 novel *L'Esclave vieil homme et le molosse*, much of which unfurls in a ravine.

26   Chamoiseau, *Au Temps de l'antan*, 13.

27   R. Confiant, *Contes créoles des Amériques* (Paris, Stock, 1995), 9. *Contes créoles*, like the *Éloge*, emphasises the geographical reach of Creole culture, showing how the *conte* extended from the bayous of Louisiana to the Amazonian shores of Guyana.

28   Confiant, *Maîtres*, 7.

product which is much more than the sum of its diverse parts: the *conte* is 'un tout, pas un assemblage composite d'éléments africains, européens et amérindiens'.[29] Indeed the influences extend beyond the geographical and temporal span of the plantation, bearing the traces of pre-slavery (Amerindian) and post-slavery (Hindu and Tamil) cultures.[30] By thus detaching the *conte* from the matrix of the plantation, and from the painful context of slavery, Confiant departs from the *négritude*-inspired view of the *conte* as articulating only hunger and fear, and plays down the political resistance which was at the core of the medium for Césaire and Ménil. This version transforms the *conte* into a catch-all medium for the many diverse strands of Antillean identity, pre- and post-slavery strands being woven into the plantation context, so that the *conte créole* is pressed into the service of the rhetoric of *créolité*, and presented as the privileged avatar of a somewhat idealised hybrid identity.

III

This idealised hybrid identity has, however, an obvious blind spot in terms of gender. By focusing exclusively on the rhetorical functions of the public *conteur* who performed at rituals such as the wake, Confiant fetishises the *parole de nuit* to the detriment of the much more widespread, and still vibrant, *parole de jour*, passed on by women, often in the private space of the home. His introduction carries through the twinning of masculinity and *créolité* heralded by the title of, and introduction to, *Maîtres de la parole créole*: 'la créolité [...] témoigne de l'emprise, à chaque époque différente, de l'homme antillais sur le processus qu'est la créolisation. La

---

29   Confiant, *Maîtres*, 10.

30   After the abolition of slavery in Martinique and Guadeloupe in 1848, indentured labourers were brought from India.

créolité est donc à la créolisation ce que l'humanité est à l'hominisation'.[31] Each *conte* is accompanied by a black and white photograph, by Damoison, of the (usually elderly, invariably male) *conteur* who narrated the tale. These portraits of the artist as an old man add an elegiac quality to the project, accentuating the sense of nostalgia and of the waning of an exclusively masculine tradition.

Of course to identify a masculine bias in the work of the *créolité* writers is far from new, and the subject has been analysed in detail by critics such as A. James Arnold, Thomas Spear and Lorna Milne.[32] These critics have shown how a writer like Confiant, by positioning himself as a direct descendant of the *conteur*, the *maître de la parole*, occludes the female storyteller, and by extension the female writer, who cannot find a place within this masculine paradigm. So it is perhaps unexpected that *Maîtres* situates itself with explicit reference to the work of a female predecessor; in the introduction, the authors declare that the text 'parachève et complète l'œuvre de transcription du conte créole fort bien menée par l'Américaine Elsie Clew-Parson' (sic).[33] Elsie Clews Parsons (1875–1941), a feminist sociologist and anthropologist, was the author of a pioneering, if sadly unfinished, three-volume work, published between 1933 and 1943, *Folk-lore of the Antilles, French and English*.[34] In this painstaking and extensive study, which established her as the key authority in the field, she transcribed a vast number of tales from islands throughout the Caribbean. Parsons had taught herself many different Creoles, and spent years collecting the data which would fill three dense volumes. Her monumental task is here damned with faint praise (it has been 'fort bien menée'), as the

---

31 Confiant, *Maîtres*, 10–11.
32 See A.J. Arnold, 'The gendering of créolité. The erotics of colonialism' and T. Spear, 'Jouissances carnavalesques: représentations de la sexualité' in M. Condé and M. Cottenet-Hage (eds), *Penser la créolité* (Paris, Karthala, 1995), respectively 21–40 and 135–152. For a more nuanced view, see L. Milne, 'Sex, gender and the right to write. Patrick Chamoiseau and the erotics of colonialism', *Paragraph* 24.3 (2001), 59–75.
33 Confiant, *Maîtres*, 20.
34 *Op. cit.* Parsons's death on 19 December 1941 meant that the work remained unfinished.

contemporary writers, with unmistakable arrogance, identify their work
as completing and superseding hers. With this sleight of hand they fail to
acknowledge the very significant differences in the two projects, differences not only of scale and ambition but also of methodology. Parsons's
geographical scope (she visited twenty-one islands, including Montserrat,
Nevis and Anguilla) is matched by the breadth of the sample taken from
each island; her project runs to over 1600 pages, as opposed to the 202
pages (photographs included) of the 1995 work. While Parsons collected
twenty-seven tales in Martinique alone, and 283 in total, Confiant and
Lebielle's entire sample runs to twenty-six tales. Moreover, within this
fairly restricted corpus, twenty-one *contes* in *Les Maîtres de la parole créole*
emanate from Martinique, and only one each from Guadeloupe, Guyana,
Sainte-Lucie, Haiti and Dominique. This geographical imbalance betrays
the extent to which Martinique is the dominant case study in this supposedly inclusive, geographically varied narrative of Creole culture.[35]

Most significantly of all, however, no mention is made by the contemporary writers of the fact that Parsons's work is one of genuine linguistic
diversity, conforming to the hybrid, linguistically capacious version of
créolité celebrated in the *Éloge* and elsewhere. *Maîtres*, despite its rhetoric
and even its title, includes only one (token?) Creole tale, while *Folk-lore of
the Antilles* – a transcription of the *contes* as they were relayed to Parsons
– includes Haitian, Martinican and Guadeloupean Creoles, alongside, for
example, the regional English of Barbados and Jamaica. Parsons refuses to
'clarify' her stories through translation, and ensures that the Creole original
is privileged throughout. She explains in the introduction that 'a translation
into English of the first tale of all the larger collections' has been provided,

---

35   In fact, Confiant's *Contes créoles des Amériques*, which also alludes to Parsons in
     the introduction (and mentions two other female folklorists, Ingrid Neumann and
     Marie-Thérèse Lung-Fou), would seem to be a more worthy successor to *Folklore of
     the Antilles*, not least because it includes tales from fifteen islands, and is much less
     Martinique-centric than *Maîtres*. If ten of the stories emanate from Martinique,
     there are thirteen from Trinidad, eight from the Grenadines and seven from Guyana.
     Although the volume claims to shift ground from the Antilles to the Americas, how-
     ever, only six *contes* from Louisiana are included.

but argues that the summaries which accompany the transcriptions ensure that 'further translation has seemed unnecessary'.[36] Parsons is sensitive, moreover, to the compromises and distortions involved in transcription. She notes for example that one of her Martinican informants has 'contributed a somewhat literary flavour' to stories forwarded to her after her departure, although she concedes that this stylised version 'is of itself interesting as a transition from the folktale to literature'.[37] Parsons, then, like Hearn before her (also acknowledged by Confiant, in *Contes créoles* and elsewhere, as a major influence), was resistant to translation and conscious of the shortcomings of transcription;[38] such sensitivity prefigures the concerns of a contemporary writer such as Chamoiseau, whose fiction, since *Solibo Magnifique* in 1988, is shot through with metadiscursive reflections on the complex relationship between orality and textuality.

Against this general background, Confiant's apparent lack of anxiety in taking the process a stage further, by translating Lebielle's transcriptions of the *contes* into French, is all the more interesting. He deals with the issue in a short paragraph near the end of his introduction:

> C'est pourquoi, en traduisant en français la parole créole de ces vieux conteurs [...] nous avons voulu *demeurer au plus près* de celle-ci. Nous nous sommes efforcés de mouler le français dans la rythmique du créole, de calquer les images et les métaphores qui ornent ces contes, en évitant toute espèce de littérarisation qui ne ferait *qu'accentuer la trahison qui est au cœur de toute traduction*. On n'a donc pas affaire, ici, à des contes arrangés, réécrits ou clarifiés, mais à un matériau brut *qui se veut le reflet*

---

36 Parsons, *Folk-lore of the Antilles*, v.
37 Parsons, *Folk-lore of the Antilles*, vii.
38 Hearn observes that when transcribing contes, 'Afin de garder toute leur simplicité primitive et la naïveté harmonieuse des détails, il faudrait les noter sténographiquement à mesure qu'on vous les raconte. L'Esprit simpliste du conteur est embarrassé par les interruptions et contraintes inévitables de la dictée: le conteur perd sa verve, se lasse et raccourcit volontairement la dictée'. Quoted by S. Denis in his 'Introduction' to Hearn's *Trois fois bel conte* (Paris, Mercure de France, 1939), 14–31, 19. It could be argued that Hearn, with his emphasis on simplicity and naivety, promotes a rather reductive view of the language of the *conte*. For a very full discussion of Hearn's work on the *conte créole*, see M. Gallagher's contribution to this volume.

le plus fidèle possible d'une parole ou d'une langue encore vivantes, quoique contrariées dans leur évolution. Ceci par *devoir de fidélité* en quelque sorte.[39]

Confiant here reprises a number of conventional disclaimers: translation is inherently a form of betrayal; his French versions eschew logic and clarity in order to emphasise their distance from the Cartesian language through which they are conveyed. However, as a key figure of the *créolité* movement, and one who has always been much more heavily invested in the promotion of the Creole language than, for example, Chamoiseau, Confiant's position as translator of the texts into French is an uncomfortable one. With the exception of the opening tale, 'Demoiselle Criquet la devineresse' – whose Creole original, 'Devinè Kritjèt', seems to have been included for local colour, and is placed, revealingly, after the French version – *Les Maîtres de la parole créole* is entirely in standard French. This token Creole inclusion effects, of course, the reverse manoeuvre to Parsons, who as we saw above included a single English version in each main section of her work. And yet the act of translation is undoubtedly a more charged cultural mediation than the Creole-Creole transcription carried out by Lebielle, given the power dynamics at work in the diglossic relationship between Creole and French. This tension is perhaps most strikingly registered in the thrice-stated desire to remain 'au plus près' or 'fidèle' to the oral original; by over-stating his 'devoir de fidélité', Confiant betrays his own discomfort at the absence of an original Creole version that has been definitively written out of this glossy Gallimard coffee table book. So, while the title of *Maîtres* foregrounds the 'parole créole', Creole is strikingly absent from the work, in a manner that parallels the language's notorious occlusion from the *Éloge*.[40] Meanwhile the linguistic integrity and diversity of Parsons's volume, the compromises of transcription notwithstanding, means that her three volumes, published in the 1930s and 1940s, are in fact much

---

39   Confiant, *Maîtres*, 14, my emphasis.
40   On this and other contradictions in the *Éloge*, see M. McCusker, '"This Creole culture, miraculously forged": the contradictions of *créolité*, in C. Forsdick and D. Murphy (eds), *Francophone Postcolonial Studies. A Critical Introduction* (London, Arnold, 2003), 112–121.

closer to the vision of *créolité* which Confiant claims to endorse in his 1995 text than *Maîtres* itself.

Of course it could be argued that the differences outlined above are at least in part explicable by the necessary empiricism of the ethnologist versus the freer polemicising of the literary author and essayist; or by the incompatible demands of a commercial publisher such as Gallimard and an academic press such as the American Folklore Society. Moreover, it is undeniable that Confiant's 'insider status', as a local Martinican and Creole native speaker, gives him a licence that is not available to an outsider such as Parsons, whose literal distance from her subject matter, as a white American woman, may have generated a greater sense of critical distance. But if I have spent some time outlining the ways in which *Maîtres*, while claiming to bring its acknowledged 'mother text' to completion, diverges quite radically from *Folk-lore of the Antilles*, it is because this rather cavalier approach is in fact symptomatic of a more general occlusion of women, both as producers and as analysts of the *conte créole*. In systematically gendering as masculine the *conte* and the *conteur*, Confiant radically departs from almost all pre-existing accounts, and from even his own acknowledged influences. It is well known, for example, that Lafcadio Hearn drew most of his tales from female informants. In the section Parsons devotes to Martinique, out of twenty-seven informants, eight are unambiguously female, and throughout her collection the female voice is well represented. Indeed Thérèse Georgel's canonical collection of folktales, now in its third reprint, *Contes et légendes des Antilles*, makes no mention at all of the male *conteur*, attributing all the stories included to the 'dâ': 'On s'installe dehors, autour de la vieille "dâ" – servant qui fait partie de la famille. Elle met son vieux chapeau "bakoua" contre le serein. Et elle commence: "Bonbonne fois! Trois fois bel conte"'.[41]

---

41   T. Georgel, *Contes et légendes des Antilles* (Paris, Pocket Junior, 1994), 8. This collection was originally published in 1955 and again in 1962 by Nathan; its re-issue in the mid-nineties, in a format specifically targeted at children, is no doubt connected to the rise in interest in the *conte* in this decade.

And if *Maîtres*, like other works by the *créolité* authors on the subject of the *conte*, excludes the *conteuse*, it is also blind to the contributions that women writers have made to the study of the *conte*. It misreads, and seriously downplays the importance of, Elsie Clews Parsons, as we have seen, and ignores a number of other well-known works. Georgel, for example, already in 1955, was claiming a heterogeneous heritage for the *conte*, prefiguring the vision promoted by Confiant forty years later.[42] Other figures such as Condé, Dany Bebel-Gisler and Ina Césaire, who have produced important scholarship on the *conte*, are similarly sidelined. This fairly systematic oversight is all the less excusable given the extent to which these works by women are carefully grounded in terms of historical, linguistic or anthropological data, and deploy research methodologies that the more polemical interventions of their male colleagues ignore. Space does not permit a full analysis of this body of work, but Condé's *La Civilisation du bossale* (1978), which I quoted above in tandem with Clews Parsons, illustrates the general point. Condé's meticulous study, replete with copious bibliographical references, is diachronic and historically informed. She tracks important stages in the evolution of the form, analysing in minute detail the relationship between the African tale and the Antillean. Rather than considering the *conte* as a timeless and static form, such an approach allows her to make important distinctions and to nuance received critical wisdom. Hence, for example, she concludes that the theme of illegitimacy, identified by many as a stock trope of the Antillean *conte*, only emerged as a feature of the Ti-Jean cycle, and therefore with the second generation of slaves. The African slaves, as first generation immigrants, did not experience the sense of loss and amnesia which would haunt future generations, and which would find expression in an obsession with 'bâtardise' in the folktale. A similar attention to history, taxonomy and tradition can be

---

42 'Ils [les contes] sont venus aux isles avec les conquérants d'Europe, avec les esclaves enlevés à leur belle Afrique libre, avec les coolies transplantés, et même les Chinois attirés par le gain dans le petit commerce des boutiques. Ils se sont mêlés aux récits des Caraïbes qui, alors, peuplaient les isles et vivaient paisibles auprès des volcans qui dormaient'; Georgel, *Contes*, 5.

found in the work of Ina Césaire and Dany Bebel-Gisler among others.[43] And it is for this very reason, perhaps, that the writings of women writers on the *conte*, in their empirical and historically grounded sensitivity, and their attentiveness to archives and historical accounts, have had less purchase in contemporary critical debate. The privilege afforded to male writers – a privilege which the current piece, of course, perpetuates – is due at least in part to the 'sound-bite' nature of their observations, and to the theoretical spin which surrounds their pronouncements. Not only do these interventions lack the nuance and subtlety to be found in women's work, but their appropriation of the *conteur* risks displacing him into a timeless mythical Creole past, in a way that smacks of the exoticism which they decry in other writings.

Conclusion

In a recent study, Christine Colombo notes that the few storytellers who remain in Martinique and Guadeloupe have become more and more sought after by eager transcribers and recorders, to the extent that they now display a 'méfiance grandissante, craignant que l'on fasse un usage lucratif des contes recueillis'.[44] Like so many other aspects of Creole culture in the contemporary Antilles, then, the *conte* appears to find its most enthusiastic audience within one of two – some would say not unrelated – circuits, tourism and academia. A text such as *Maîtres*, which is at once a revivalist tract and a nostalgic and wistful lament, can be seen to have participated in a more general commodification of the folktale, and

---

43 Ina Césaire extends and reworks her father's taxonomy, identifying 'trois grands thèmes qui paraissent nullement incongru en pays colonisé: thème de la ruse, thème de la faim et thème de la révolte'. See *Contes de mort et de vie aux Antilles* (Paris, Nubia, 1976), 12–13.
44 C. Colombo, *Ti Jean et Monsieur le Roi/Ti Jan é Misié liwa*, 10.

ultimately, then, to have further endangered the *conte*. The elderly *conteurs* lovingly photographed by Damoison are usually in rural settings, surrounded by the traditional paraphernalia of Creole culture: horses, sugar cane, rum. Many are photographed in fragile *cases créoles*, often bearing classic icons of Catholicism, and most wear the traditional 'bakoua', the straw hat associated with the plantation. While the static poses of these men, who are literally stilled, suggest power, strength, dignity and individuality, their mouths remain resolutely, almost defiantly, shut. In this staged act of preservation, they stand, paradoxically, as mute witnesses, talismanic icons of a lost time. To this extent *Maîtres* could be seen to effect a further silencing of the tradition it seeks to celebrate and to resuscitate. Only the younger *conteurs* – a small minority of those pictured – appear to be actively engaged in storytelling: one emerges dramatically from behind a curtain, apparently on stage in a theatre, another performs to young children in a modern classroom, another appears to be at home, surrounded by family. But even these images, while conveying a sense of vibrancy, simultaneously point to the institutionalisation, domestication or containment of the *conte* in the contemporary context, set as they are in the symbolic sites of state, home and 'official' entertainment.

From having been at heart a performance of resistance to the dominant order, then, the *conte* today risks being evacuated of any political content and being subdued to feed a tourist market hungry for a spurious 'authenticity'. Tony Delsham, for one, questions the relevance of the *conte* when it is divorced from the plantation context: 'on admire compère Lapin, pique-assiette sans foi ni loi et sans ambition. On admire Débwuya pa péshé illusioniste cachant son désarroi sous une faconde de gagneur, avant d'être arrêté par les gendarmes'.[45] Delsham suggests that the values promoted in the contemporary appropriation of the *conte* – abdication of responsibility, dishonesty – are debilitating and regressive ones, and anachronistic in a post-slavery environment. The critical distance exhibited by women

45   T. Delsham, *Cénesthésie et l'urgence de l'être* (Schœlcher, Martinique Éditions, 2005), 14.

writers in their analysis of the *conte*, their reticence, their non-identification and their historical attentiveness, as well as their refusal to generalise or to appropriate, should undoubtedly be read in the context of this problematic revivalist ideology that is linked to, but ultimately transcends, an excessively masculinist poetics.

The politics of orality and allegory in the African *conte*

ANDY STAFFORD

According to Jean Cauvin the African *conte* 'ne peut être étudié avec des méthodologies conçues pour l'étude de textes écrits et montrant la pensée d'un auteur individuel'.[1] Though this *caveat* is helpful in understanding the specificity of African story-telling, it suggests a paradox at the heart of the folk-tale in the modern era. Our access to Francophone African tales is dependent largely on their written and published versions, and these are most commonly attributed to one single author. How then does the 'reader' of the African tale negotiate the difficulty of appreciating its performed meaning once outside of the context of an assembled audience? Can African stories, once written down, maintain a collective and oral character in the way that Senghor claimed in his notion of the 'dialectique' inherent in the African tale?[2]

This Chapter aims to show then that one way to reinstate, if only provisionally and tentatively, the orality of an African tale is to allegorise; that is, to suggest a means of returning oral stories to the moment of their transcription, by considering the historical and ideological landscape at the time when the stories were frozen into it. Naturally, the 'freezing' of a living African tale into a historical moment through the reader's attempt at allegorising it looks like a denial of the polyvalence of a village tale across time and place. Yet allegorisation allows, at the same time, for the written-down oral tale to be re-interpreted by different readers at different moments in time, with different sets of perspectives and horizons. In

---

1   J. Cauvin, *Comprendre les contes* (Paris, Les Classiques africains, 1992 [1980]), 3.
2   L.S. Senghor, cited in R. Colin, *Les Contes noirs de l'Ouest africain. Témoins majeurs d'un humanisme* (Paris, Présence Africaine, 2005 [1957]), 22.

other words, allegorisation – as an active, polemical move by the reader –
re-introduces a dialectic that the writing-down of the tale seems, in relation
to its ever-changing oral version, to have suppressed. Allegorisation of the
written-down oral tale, anchoring a story into the historical context of its
transcription, might be then, paradoxically, a way to explore its polyvalence.
In order to explore this idea, this Chapter takes two sets of tales, from the
period immediately before African independence – by Bernard Dadié and
Birago Diop – to establish the extent to which allegories of colonisation,
decolonisation and independence can be found in story-telling. How then
might the (African) *conte* invite allegorisation (especially political)?

We might suggest, in the first instance, that it is the form itself: we
tend, in post-Hellenist, post-Biblical Europe, to expect allegory in a tale.
Eric Auerbach's influential theory of mimesis insists on 'situation' as the
generator of allegory (such as Christians in the Roman Empire); we could
read New-Testament allegory (to continue with the Christian example) as
non-typological and 'situated', rather than parabolic and timeless. However,
as Cauvin argues, 'L'étude d'un conte relève à la fois de l'étude du texte et
de l'étude de la société'.[3] Is there something specifically 'African' contained
in this claim? Is it only, specifically, in the *conte* genre that this stricture of
Cauvin's pertains? Suggesting that we tend to allegorise following a *conte*'s
'Africanness' raises questions of definition, if not the danger of stereotype
and to which we will return in a moment. Finally, we could suggest that
allegory comes to impose itself by circumstance, in what Roland Barthes
calls 'le texte de la vie'. In his (radically) infamous analysis of Balzac's chill-
ing tale 'Sarrasine' (made across the context of May 1968 in France and
published as *S/Z* in 1970), Barthes mobilised Mallarmé's notion of the
'Book' to show that we come to a story, that we read a story (Barthes did
not mention its oral performance) with a knowledge of life drawn from
books, with all of life already inscribed as a book; in this sense, for Barthes,
all reading (at least of a tale, such as Balzac's) is itself an act of 're-writing',

an active re-inscription of the story into its moment of reading: '*dans le texte*', as Barthes highlighted in italics, '*seul parle le lecteur*'.[4]

There is then, this chapter wishes to show, following Barthes's *post-structuralist valorisation of active forms of reading, something outside of Vladimir Propp's theories and of structuralist accounts of narrative, in any political allegory found in the *conte*. But do all the above, as a quick survey of European traditions, cover the African counterpart? Not wishing to appear Eurocentric or unnecessarily beholden to structuralism, this Chapter aims to suggest that some of the elements above do nevertheless help us to approach political allegory in the post-war African written *conte*.[5] However, one dangerous pitfall that this analysis aims to avoid is that opened up by Fredric Jameson in 1986, in a now (in)famous sweeping generalisation about third-world literature and allegory.

Discussing and supplying a rather simplistic definition of allegory, and suggesting that the tale in particular enjoys a 'polysemic' relationship to meaning, Jameson's main claim has made not a few postcolonial critics shudder. Rather than insist upon the radical singularity of different literatures emerging from different parts of the world, Jameson sweepingly asserts that third-world literary texts 'are to be read as "national allegories", particularly when their forms develop out of predominantly Western machines of representation.'[6] Though one could argue cogently that the African tale is not a European 'machine of representation', its written version in a collection of stories published by a Europe-based publisher is surely more so. Indeed Jameson's sweeping generalisation – '*The story of the private individual destiny is always an allegory of the embattled situation of the public third-world culture and society*' (author's italics) – may be of more use when

---

4   R. Barthes, 'S/Z', in *Œuvres complètes* (Paris, Seuil, 1994 [1970]), II, 553–741, 657.

5   See for example the structuralist mantra: 'il n'y a pas, il n'y a jamais eu nulle part aucun peuple sans récit', in R. Barthes, 'Introduction à l'analyse structurale du récit', *Communications* 8 (1966), 8–27, 8.

6   F. Jameson, 'Third-world literature in the era of multinational capitalism', *Social Text* 15 (1986), 65–88, 73–74, 69. See P. Hallward, *Absolutely Postcolonial: Writing between the Singular and the Specific* (Manchester, Manchester University Press, 2001) however for a critique of post-colonialism's insistence upon 'singularity'.

we consider the tale within this paradox (African form but in European clothing). With its wholly generalised (even stereotyping) ambit, Jameson's assertion does little to encourage a Marxist critique of postcolonial theory worth its salt.[7] But it does have the advantage of pointing to a certain positioning of the Western reader confronted with an oral African performance that is now written down. Allegory, or better, allegorising, allows us to see that a story is now being re-'consumed' individually, in an act of reading of a tale that appears in the very same form every single time (because it is written down), but which is then confronted with the collective, variable, versions that are the living tale, as told by a series of live *griots* who make the story differ across time and space.

At the same time it is important to recognise that the critic is often left with an invidious choice when dealing with an African tale. There does not seem to be a middle way between either 'allegorising' (as we shall do in a moment), or, worse perhaps, according to the Moroccan poet Abdellatif Laâbi writing in the radical journal *Souffles*, 'folklorising'.[8] It is here that Jameson's *faux pas* becomes useful. What Jameson fails to acknowledge is not only the potentially dangerous nature of what he is saying with respect to 'diversity', but also what the Western reader has learnt to do with a written-down tale. This Chapter suggests that there is not *necessarily* anything inherently or recognizably allegorical of a political situation in any one tale, but that the individualised nature of the reading (from a book, in a room, in a library, as opposed to the *paroles de nuit* in an African village) offers the Western reader what is (as this chapter attempts to prove) the opportunity of making a productive (that is, agitational, polemical, counter-intuitive) 'misreading', thereby (re?)politicising, even recollectivising, (oral) literature in a way that Jameson's approach fails to maintain. It is almost as if the reader is invited to bracket the intention of the story precisely because it has already been traduced by being written down. In each case here then

7   Though, as T. Kelley reminds us, Jameson's critique of allegory is aimed more at the 'political unconscious' of Western (not African) allegory; see *Reinventing Allegory* (Cambridge, CUP, 1997), 11.

8   See A. Laâbi's review of a Khaïr-Eddine novel in the reviews section of *Souffles* 13/14 (1968), 36–37, 37.

the 'intention' of the narrator, writer, has been bracketed, though note has been taken of the analysis of power relations that Louis Marin makes in his study of the folk-tales collected in the seventeenth century by Charles Perrault.[9] In a sense, this is inevitable if we are to ask *how* we allegorise, and in which case it is perhaps worth presenting the two *conteurs* whose stories will form our two examples. Bernard Dadié and Birago Diop are two very different writers: the first from Côte d'Ivoire who never left Africa (for France nor elsewhere), the other a student who studied in Paris but returned regularly to Senegal as a veterinary surgeon.[10]

It is well known that Dadié was a militant anti-colonialist. Lilyan Kesteloot describes this excellent *conteur* as the writer of 'poèmes polémiques insignifiants', and Dadié continued his political messages in *Le Pagne noir*, written in 1953 and published in 1955, and in other stories included in *Légendes et poèmes*.[11] However it is the story 'Le Chasseur et le boa', collected in *Le Pagne noir*, on which we shall concentrate here. In this moral story of Faustian proportions, in which the opposition of wealth to poverty is linked to happiness and longevity, Africa is shown to be prone to a catalogue of disasters. The understanding between humans and animals is part of traditional Africa's utopian dreams, and the story is distinctly 'oral'

---

9   L. Marin's account of Perrault's relationship in his stories to social and political power structures in seventeenth-century France would be a useful starting point for a study (well beyond the scope of this Chapter) of the *griot* as positioned in the postwar African tale; see *Le Portrait du roi* (Paris, Editions de Minuit, 1981), 169–205.

10 C. Wake reminds us that Dadié took his secondary education in Senegal and then worked at the IFAN in Dakar; see 'Negritude and after: changing perspectives in French-language African fiction', *Third World Quarterly* 10.2 (1988), 961–965, 962.

11 L. Kesteloot, *Les Écrivains noirs de langue française: naissance d'une littérature* (Brussels, Université libre de Bruxelles-Institut de sociologie, 1963), 294. As N. Vincileoni points out, stories appearing in Dadié's *Légendes et poèmes* such as 'La Légende baoule', 'Le Règne de l'araignée', 'L'Aveu', 'Le Crocodile et le martin-pêcheur', and 'L'Homme qui voulait être roi', are all concerned with power; see *Comprendre l'œuvre de Bernard Dadié* (Paris, Les Classiques Africains, 1986), 118.

in its narration: the audience/readership is left at the end to answer the
question and to solve the moral problem.[12]

Diop's *Contes d'Amadou Koumba*, published in 1947, were written in
1942 and co-won the 'grand prix littéraire de l'A.O.F'.[13] The final story,
'Sarzan', rather atypical of the collection, was based on his 1939–42 veterinary tours.[14] Adapted for the stage in 1955 by Lamine Diakhaté, it is the
story of Thiémokho Kéita, a *tirailleur sénégalais* (clearly a sergeant, hence
the corruption 'Sarzan'), who, on his return from the Rif War in Morocco
and from France and Syria to his native village in colonial French Soudan,
tries to impose on his compatriots the Western values considered superior,
though badly assimilated, by Kéita. But in trying to overcome traditional
and ancestral beliefs, and in trying to get a road built in the village, he
goes slowly but surely mad. According to one critic, the moral of Sarzan is:
'nul ne peut impunément renier ou mépriser sa nationalité et sa culture au
profit de celles d'autrui', thereby warning Africans of cultural alienation and
defending the relativity of cultures when confronted with Western ethno-
centrism.[15] For Dorothy Blair, Diop's 'Sarzan' is a lesson in tolerance, and
the only tale in the collection addressing the Western reader directly.[16]

12   Of the four levels of allegory – the literal (historical), the Christ-linkage (typo-
      logical), the tropological (or moral) and the anagogical (towards heaven) – Dadié's
      story-telling is most probably tropological, concerned with the living of life; see
      J. MacQueen, *Allegory* (London, Methuen, 1970), 49.

13   Written, ironically, whilst Diop was living in Paris and published by Fasquelle, in
      a series 'Ecrivains d'Outre-Mer' coordinated by Léon Damas; see J. Chevrier, *La
      Littérature nègre* (Paris, Armand Colin, 2003), 85. The 1947 prize was shared with
      Ousmane Socé's novel *Karim*.

14   B. Diop, 'Sarzan', in *Les Contes d'Amadou Koumba* (Paris, Présence Africaine, 1961
      [1947]). First called 'Polyeucte Puni' when published in *La Revue du Monde* and
      written during the Occupation at the behest of Ramón Fernandez; see D. Blair,
      African Writing in French (Cambridge, CUP, 1976), 38.

15   Yet, Eurocentrism notwithstanding, Diop did not hide his debt to European story-
      tellers and short-story writers: Kipling, Rabelais, La Fontaine, Maupassant; Kane
      cited in G.O. Midiohouan, *La Nouvelle d'expression française en Afrique noire* (Paris,
      L'Harmattan, 1999), 41, 80, 84.

16   Though Diop, unlike Dadié, is not a moralist; see Blair, *African Literature*, 43, 50.

Guy Ossito Midiohouan underlines the 'actualité' and 'fraîcheur' of the stories in Diop's collection, to the point that the Senegalese scholar of Diop, Mohamadou Kane, has suggested: 'ces contes gardent des rapports particulièrement étroits avec la réalité', which he attributes to Diop's knowledge of the area as a veterinary surgeon.[17] Indeed, Midiohouan claims that the African 'nouvelle' was 'clairement' the most 'précocement nationaliste' of all the literary forms in Black Africa; and he cites the cycle of three short stories by Bernard Dadié, published in *Présence Africaine* in 1948, the year after Diop's collection of *contes* is first published.[18]

However, Kesteloot has famously insisted that the African *conte* is 'sans parti pris' in its depiction, and more 'désintéressé' than the novel:

> Le *conte* est [...] dépourvu de tout engagement polémique. Il ne revendique pas, il ne vise nullement à opposer noirs et blancs, il décrit simplement la vie traditionnelle, le folklore, les coutumes et les mœurs, et c'est chez lui que nous trouvons les traces les plus authentiques de la vie nègre.[19]

Indeed, like Kesteloot, A. C. Brench insists that Diop's stories 'are not militant affirmations, are not dependent upon African colonial subjugation for their effect', but stories 'independent of the colonial conflict', and thus all the 'more effective than any "committed" work of militant African nationalism'.[20] It was apt for Brench to assert this in 1967 – we are at the peak of negritude, black power and consciousness, when to assert African tradition was itself a political act. But now that the dust has settled on Negritude and fifty years have passed since the end of European colonialism in Africa, we need to consider how these stories are now interpreted, retroactively as it were, in the new context of twenty-first century literature and politics. *How* then do Diop's stories manage, as Brench puts it, to satisfy his audience's desire for justice?

17 See, for example, the social parasitism and religious mystification highlighted in 'Le Jugement' and in 'Le prétexte', and changes in lifestyle and beliefs in 'Sarzan'.

18 Midiohouan, *La Nouvelle d'expression française*, 44.

19 Kesteloot, *Les Écrivains noirs de langue française*, 309.

20 A.C. Brench, *Writing in French from Senegal to Cameroon* (London, OUP, 1967), 5–6.

Orality and *écriture*: allegorical orature

Even if the two stories discussed here are 'trop littéraires' for Jacques Chevrier, the oral origins and constraints on the *conte* seem to be important in our discussion of the politics of allegory.[21] Melissa Thackway makes the link between the *conte* and the cinema, in her chapter on 'orature', and quotes the Burkinabe director Dani Kouyaté whose 1995 film *Kéïta* features the African Griot:

> Griots [...] address everyone. They take fateful, fundamental stories and turn them into amusing legends. All those with experience, who are perspicacious, who read between the lines, will understand their meaning.[22]

As Thackway points out, Western viewers (and we could say also readers of African *orature*) do not find it easy to read characterisations in African stories as they are often 'trickster archetypes'.[23] However, she does not say how orature and satire are 'read'.

In his study of allegory John MacQueen describes how allegory becomes satire, though stresses that it is a facile simplification to say that allegory is general and satire particular:

> [T]he particularities of satire [...] acquire more than passing relevance when they are seen in terms of a system of moral ideas which is generally acceptable [...]. If one combines the narrative form and thematic content of allegory with the detailed

21 J. Chevrier, *L'Arbre à palabres. Essai sur les contes et récits traditionnels d'Afrique noire* (Paris, Hatier, 2005), avant-propos.

22 Kouyaté cited in M. Thackway, *Africa Shoots Back. Alternative Perspectives in Sub-Saharan Francophone African Film* (Bloomington-Oxford-Cape Town, Indiana University Press-James Currey-New Africa Books, 2003), 69.

23 Thackway, *Africa Shoots Back*, 83. For Thackway 'orature' in Africa allows a smooth passage from *conte* to film version to be made that loses none of the allegorical content, her example being Djibril Diop Mambety's 1991 film *Hyènes*, an adaptation of Friedrich Dürrenmatt's play *Der Besuch der alten dame* (*The Visit*).

richness and stylised point of view found in good satire, one discovers literary forms of great potential.[24]

MacQueen's example is morality plays. But we could equally speak of this blending of allegory and satire in African *contes*. Indeed, for Ngugi Wa Thiong'o, 'satire is certainly one of the most effective weapons in oral traditions', and which allows the griot to avoid the wrath of the object of satire, and to 'encourage reflection through laughter'.[25] However, classical allegory and biblical versions differ in one key area: the latter are linked to 'the divinely operated movement of history'.[26] Is there then a sense of the inevitability, even justness, of African independence in those *contes* written down during the 1940s and 1950s, and more generally in animist African culture and religion?

This leads to another paradox. One could say that the written version of a story invites political allegory by the reader, more so than the performed tale, as the transcribed story is infinitely re-readable, commentable, analysable.[27] And yet the infinitely 'rewritable', performed tale can connect contemporaneously with its political moment of retelling in a way that the ossified, written version cannot:

> Le conteur doué ne récite pas un texte qu'il sait par cœur. Son travail associe étroitement mémoire et création. L'histoire qu'il raconte fait partie d'un répertoire qu'il possède à fond et qui est d'ailleurs bien connu du public; mais il ne cesse de l'adapter,

24   MacQueen, *Allegory*, 68–69. According to the Ancient Roman Quintilian, the word allegory describes either 'one thing in words and another in meaning', or 'something absolutely opposed to the meaning of the words'; the former is akin to modern allegory, the latter to irony, sarcasm, contradiction or proverbs; Quintilian cited in MacQueen, *Allegory*, 49.

25   Thiong'o, cited in Thackway, *Africa Shoots Back*, 69, 70.

26   MacQueen, *Allegory*, 28–29.

27   The famous example being Barthes's radical re-reading of a Balzac tale in *S/Z* (1970). Though Barthes is right perhaps to see the act of re-reading as in opposition to the 'read/heard-only-once', is he correct to suggest that the 'intertext' is the mechanism by which the external world enters our reading?

c'est-à-dire de le modifier plus ou moins profondément pour tenir compte de l'attente et des réactions de son auditoire.[28]

It is clear here that there is common ground between the spoken and the written *conte*, but also marked differences in their respective modes of delivery and consumption. One way to look at how the written version is able, potentially, to re-inscribe the oral performance is to see how *contes* have travelled.[29] Another is to consider the narrative tropes themselves.[30]

28   M. Soriano, cited in D. Couégnas, *Introduction à la paralittérature* (Paris, Seuil, 1992), 63n1.
29   This is a topic that I have started to research within the Black Atlantic, looking at how African tales 'travelled' with slavery, and making very tentative conclusions on the Caribbean tale; see A. Stafford, 'De la causticité à la politique: "Paroles de nuit" en voyage à travers l'Atlantique', *Revue des arts de l'oralité* 1 (2008), 11–20. In fact, the most graphic example of the allegorical nature of the *conte* (and the short story) comes in Sembene Ousmane's 1962 story 'Le Voltaïque', in the figure of the treacherous African slave-driver Momutu. One could argue that changing one letter from Mobutu, the ruthless leader of newly independent Zaire who had been complicit in the murder of anti-colonial leader Patrice Lumumba in 1961, is only one element in a story that is clever for so many other, narratological reasons.
30   Dadié's stories seem deeply conscious of their open-ended status, whose democratic aim is also a clever *asteismos*, the 'wit of an urbane, refined sort' in ancient Greek (Athenian) culture; see MacQueen, *Allegory*, 50; and though not urbane, Dadié's stories also have a universal, worldly-wisdom. The African 'conte', both written and oral, gestures to, or leans on, its mythic status, but has no, or only a very particular, social status. We as readers know (but have to imagine how) the 'arbre-à-palabres' is not simply a story-telling place in the village, it embodies also all the ideas of African community and discursive expression, that is, the word 'parliament' in European culture and its distinctly oral etymology.

Narration, voicing and genre

Let us turn first to Diop's story of madness, 'Sarzan'. According to Kane the non-traditional nature of 'Sarzan' compared to the other tales in the 'recueil', is reflected in the fact that Diop 'porte témoignage et prend parti' and 'raconte, envahit la scène, l'accapare, confisque la liberté de son personnage'.[31] And according to Janos Riesz, in contrast to the other *contes* in the collection where Diop uses Koumba's narration to establish a distance between story and narrated reality, Diop loses all 'retenue': here, in 'Sarzan', Diop intervenes directly.

Riesz points out that there is a historical prologue to 'Sarzan' in which we learn how the inhabitants of Dougouba had, in the past, removed all Islamic traces and returned to ancestral teachings, thereby setting up a parallel between the Islamists and the West's trying (via Kéita) to 'civilise' the Bambara animists in the village.[32] If this is the *first* 'intervention' by Diop, the second, an indirect one this time, is when Kéita insultingly calls the Koteba ceremony 'sauvage', in sharp contrast to Diop's own defence of these 'manières de sauvage'. Returning a year later the narrator-author finds the road built but Kéita gone mad, and, Riesz insists, the narrator sees the madness of Kéita as a punishment meted out by the genies and the ancients, and thus the narrator 'avenges himself', says Riesz, on Kéita.[33] Given the 'fureur' of Diop's commentary, Riesz thinks that many critics

---

31 Cited in J. Riesz, 'La "Folie" des Tirailleurs sénégalais', in J.P. Little and R. Little (eds), *Black Accents. Writing in French from Africa, Mauritius and the Caribbean* (London, Grant and Cutler, 1997), 139–156, 146. Given its mix of realism, 'actualité', magical or fantasy elements, universality and particularity, 'Sarzan' is a 'conte-nouvelle', even a 'conte romanesque' according to the Senegalese scholar Mohamadou Kane, cited in Midiohouan, *La Nouvelle d'expression française*, 27 and 86. With its eclectic mixture of prose, dialogue and song, alternating between narrator and audience in non-linear sequences, 'Sarzan' would seem to deploy a form that is alien to the artistic traditions of Europe, though pantomime in Britain displays at times a genre-bending element.

32 Riesz, 'La "Folie" des Tirailleurs sénégalais', 146.

33 Riesz, 'La "Folie" des Tirailleurs sénégalais', 148.

lack the courage to explain this. Rather than a plaything of the gods and a
symbol of their force, 'Sarzan' Kéita is shown by Diop, argues Riesz, to be
punished twice, once when he is brainwashed and recruited to fight for the
French and thereby taking on France's civilising ideology against the life he
has abandoned, and then a second time for not being able to find his way
back to the life he should have had. The 'madness' then is perhaps an act of
salvation, a return by force of a (prodigal) son who could not be recuper-
ated by his kin any other way.[34] In this way the allegory is both directed
and controlled by Diop (from beyond the grave, as it were), but ironically
it is open to wide interpretation. This is perhaps helpful in understanding
allegory. On the one hand the narrator's intervention suggests that it is not
the narration itself (in written form) which guarantees allegory.[35] On the
other, the form itself is not a jealous guardian of allegory, but rather allegory
is a literary, creative form helped by, but not exclusive to, the *conte*.

   In Dadié's 'Le Chasseur et le boa' the narrative style is more traditional
than in Diop's 'Sarzan'. But these two very different stories are both able to
illustrate the range of allegory; and if allegory is not restricted purely to a
(dominant) type of African oral story, we can see also in these two stories
that allegory is performed by the narration in conjunction with the reader
(or listener). Thus Dadié's more innocent story – containing no *inherent*
link to the West, to colonialism nor to French rule in Côte d'Ivoire – is,
as we shall see, all the more acerbic in its allegorical parallels.

   Dadié places his story within the Ivorian theatrical and narrative tradition of the hero-hunter, the *Didiga*, but which he subverts quite overtly
(and humorously for those locals steeped in the tradition); for the hunter
is anything but a hero in 'Le Chasseur et le boa'. He is, as the narrator of

34   Riesz, 'La "Folie" des Tirailleurs sénégalais', 149. For Mohamadou Kane the key to
     'Sarazan' resides in the poems; but for Riesz the underlying reality that the poems
     impugn to the author-narrator does little to highlight the historical experience for
     the *tirailleurs* in which they become the scapegoats for the situation.
35   Though one could easily imagine 'Sarzan' as an oral *conte* and as theatre (see above),
     in which a distance could be introduced.

the *conte* never stops telling us, 'bien pauvre'.[36] But also Dadié's story is polemical in that the hunter is both weak and corruptible in the face of this poverty. This is not to say that the story does not have several levels. Given the caution advocated with regard to snakes, the *conte* is clearly destined for younger members of the village. Nevertheless, the story deploys a careful wink towards the adult viewer/reader; Dadié's *conte* is not a simple and ludic *mise en abîme* (a knowing parody and ironic allusion towards the status of the story being narrated), but, we might suggest, a distinctly marked critique of the colonialism of the moment, or rather a valorisation of those African traditions confronted with a rapacious and hypocritical colonial Europe.

This allegory – of an Africa that is honest, opposed to a Europe both modern and deceitful – can be best seen in the dialogue between the hunter and the boa. The boa is having difficulties and offers a choice to the hunter: free him and become rich (this is the faustian ruse of the boa), or ignore his cry for help and remain in poverty; and to the hunter's question 'Si je te détachais, m'épargnerais-tu?', the response from the boa is as clear as it is ambiguous: 'Depuis quand les animaux de la brousse se conduisent-ils comme vous?'. In other words, animals, unlike humans, keep their word: 'Nous aimons prouver notre bonté'.[37] Given Senghor's insistence upon the moral superiority of the African *conte* over Europe's deployment of fiction, it becomes even harder not to read this exchange as a commentary on, an allegory of, the links between Africa and Europe at the time, especially when, in order to persuade the hunter, the boa in Dadié's tale describes the respectful (read: compliant?) manner in which animals treat others:

[N]ous les animaux, nous attaquons franchement, face à face, et aussi franchement encore, nous récompensons nos bienfaiteurs. Nous n'envions jamais leur bonheur.

---

36   B. Dadié, 'Le Chasseur et le boa', in *Le Pagne noir* (Paris, Présence Africaine, 1970 [1955]), 97–106, 97.
37   Dadié, 'Le Chasseur et le boa', 99.

Nous ne sommes jamais jaloux des situations qu'ils peuvent avoir par la suite. Au contraire. Plus ils sont heureux, plus nous sommes fiers.[38]

This rather perfidious and obsequious speech betrays the role of the boa in this story. Instead of our seeing the boa, the animal, as Africa, and the hunter, man, as Europe, the contrary seems to arise. This can be seen in the discussion, chorus-like, between the two dogs.

The visit by the hunter 'au pays des génies' to see the riches that he could have if he helped the boa, and his tendency afterwards to 's'enrichir de la détresse des autres' (those in his village), is narrated by two dogs, the hunter's own and another dog 'sans maître'. The dog 'sans maître' maintains, like the boa, that all men live in an immoral way, but the hunter's dog rejects this suggestion: 'J'ai un bon maître et qui est devenu très généreux depuis qu'il est revenu de chez le Boa'; this opinion could easily have come out of the mouth of someone who thought they benefited in Africa from the colonial set up (the *évolués* perhaps?), and then the response of the dog 'sans maître' would seem to represent an attitude that was more Africanist and independentist, even cynical, towards Europe: 'moi, je préfère la brousse, ma liberté et mes gales'.[39]

It is difficult then not to see the 'chien galeux', 'sans maître', as an idealised image of an Africa that is traditional and not eaten up by a Europe that is deeply mercantilist. And this same dog says a little later: 'Les misères ne sont que les instants. Ce dont il faut tenir compte, c'est la joie qui est permanente, c'est l'harmonie, le bonheur qu'on sent un peu partout. Ton maître ne voit que son petit bonheur'.[40]

This idea of harmony fits exactly with what Léopold Senghor wrote about the African *conte* in 1958, in his preface to Diop's *Nouveaux contes d'Amadou Koumba*:

---

38   L.S. Senghor, Preface to B. Diop, *Les Nouveaux Contes d'Amadou Koumba* (Paris, Présence Africaine, 1958); Dadié, 'Le Chasseur et le boa', 99.
39   Dadié, 'Le Chasseur et le boa', 101–102.
40   Dadié, 'Le Chasseur et le boa', 105.

La *Paix*, si chère aux cœurs négro-africains, c'est-à-dire l'ordre, finit toujours par triompher. La Paix, par l'effet de ces vertus typiquement nègres que sont la piété, le bon sens, la loyauté, la générosité, la patience, le courage.[41]

But what Senghor does not mention in his description of the African *conte*, is the 'souci démocratique'. Dadié's narration is not only theatrical, in that the narrator addresses themselves directly to the audience, here the reader, by using the 'vous'.[42] But also the *conte* ends on a question with regard to the dilemma of the hunter that is addressed to us: 'Vous à sa place, quelle décision prendriez-vous?'. In many of Dadié's stories, we are led towards a 'democratic' ending: 'paroles de nuit' in Africa often leave the conclusion to the audience in Africa, and to the readership in the written-down version.

Conclusion

We have suggested that the oral and collective nature of the African *conte* can be maintained by a politicised 'audience' reading the stories both hermeneutically and retrospectively.[43] In both cases – Dadié's democratic tale and Diop's positioned story – the narration of the *conte* seems to invite political allegory. We have seen also how allegory, following Marin, appears like a vector (a 'voyage'), only and always moving, despite the written-down version being what he calls a *'terminus a quo'*.[44] The allegory appears also to be

---

41   Senghor, Preface to B. Diop, *Les Nouveaux Contes*, 17–18.
42   At one point the narrator interpellates us: 'vous le devinez'; see Dadié, 'Le Chasseur et le boa', 100.
43   See, for example, the chapter on allegory in D. Attridge, *J. M. Coetzee and the Ethics of Reading: Literature in the Event* (Chicago and London, Chicago University Press, 2004).
44   See L. Marin's discussion of a Perrault tale, 'La Peau d'Âne', and then of La Fontaine's story from Aesop, where Marin suggests that an important element of the folktale's allegorising is found in the *beast that speaks* (highly relevant to our two dogs here in

'polymorphic', which allows it to cross unceasingly, in a singular fashion, between story and world, between two texts.[45] Furthermore, Dadié has shown how a tale can be both typological (the hunter is a stock character in West Africa) *and* 'situated' (that is, contingency forces the hunter to make a choice); and contingency seems to be a key mechanism in suggesting allegory. Indeed, not unlike the manner in which poststructuralists proclaimed that *all* language is metaphor, might we not hazard, with the *caveat* regarding Jameson's pan-allegorical theory, that *all* narrative is in fact allegorisable, since contingency works on both sides of the divide between text and reader?

These concerns are clearly part of much wider literary-political debate. The crucial question in this chapter that hopefully we can answer, tentatively, in the affirmative is: given that all literature (oral or written) is socially and historically rooted, could we say therefore that some literature is 'more rooted' than others? If so, how? It may be that allegory is (paradoxically) *more* rooted if, like both Dadié and Diop's story, it 'hides', encodes or dramatises its political message.

---

the Dadié story), thereby linking eating and narrating in a *clinamen* (or tangent) of allegory; see L. Marin, *La Parole mangée* (Paris, Klincksieck, 1986), 39–60, 40. In his discussion of Félibien's *ekphrasis* of Le Brun's portrait of the King, Marin speaks of the 'distance constitutive de l'allégorie' that sits between the King on horseback and the three aerial figures which allegorise his goodness, power and majesty, a gap which the reader/viewer spots as a mystery, and across which we must 'voyager'; see L. Marin, *Le Portrait du roi*, 254 and 226.

45   Perhaps also the *conte*, with its allegorical tendency, finds its contemporary expression in *African* magical realism; but it remains to be seen to what extent magical realism is 'allegorical'.

SECTION FOUR

Storytelling in contemporary France: linguistic strategies

Autour de quelques contes maghrébins en situation interculturelle: création d'un texte à l'interface oral-écrit

NADINE DECOURT

En 1995, paraissait, chez Karthala, dans une collection à visée anthropologique, le recueil *Contes maghrébins en situation interculturelle*. Le dessin sur la couverture est l'illustration par l'une des conteuses d'un motif de conte de mensonge: un personnage majestueux porte un jardin sur la tête, comme une invitation à entrer dans un monde merveilleux.

Ces contes de tradition orale ont été collectés en France, en région lyonnaise, dans un contexte d'immigration, dans le cadre d'une formation par alternance intitulée: 'Contes et récits de la vie quotidienne'. Il s'agissait de donner un statut scientifique à une oralité vivante peu prisée dans le domaine de la littérature académique, puisque collectée auprès de femmes d'origine maghrébine ne possédant pas la maîtrise du français. Comment passer de l'oral à l'écrit sans trahir la saveur d'un parler vernaculaire métissé d'expressions en arabe ou en berbère? Comment communiquer le plaisir neuf de conter entre les langues et les cultures, de passer d'une version à l'autre, d'inventer de nouvelles formes de sociabilité *hic et nunc*? Comment relever le défi d'une mise en écriture qui brouille les normes de l'édition et entend moins restituer une mémoire que 'donner la parole' à ceux qui ne l'ont guère? En quoi le travail éditorial participe-t-il à un tissage hybride où le conte apparaît non seulement comme opérateur de lien, mais aussi comme catalyseur de coopérations d'un nouveau type entre conteurs et chercheurs?

Si, comme le définit P. Zumthor, en matière d'oralité, les circonstances déterminent l'œuvre en sa totalité, il importe tout d'abord de présenter la situation même de contage dans le contexte plus large du renouveau du conte en France et en Europe.[1]

I Contes et immigration

En septembre 1993, lorsque le groupe se met en place, la France, comme d'autres pays d'Europe, connaît un phénomène spécifiquement urbain, apparu dans les années 70: des conteurs font profession d'oralité. Le mouvement naît paradoxalement en France dans les bibliothèques, comme s'il fallait retrouver la parole vive consignée dans des livres et réinventer, chemin faisant, des voies d'accès à la lecture. La question de la médiation culturelle est donc centrale, comme l'atteste le titre du recueil, choisi en définitive par le responsable de la maison d'édition comme le plus juste, ce qui mérite déjà ici un éclaircissement quant aux relations entre les textes publiés et leurs contextes d'énonciation et d'émergence.

I.1 Apports de la culture maghrébine au renouveau du conte

Veronika Görög-Karady est l'un des rares chercheurs, en 1982, à s'être intéressée à ce renouveau qu'elle situe aux lendemains des événements de mai 68, comme un véritable projet de réhabilitation de l'oralité et des arts naïfs, et qu'elle rattache à la fois aux mouvements régionalistes et à la science ethnologique.[2] À travers une enquête menée sur une quinzaine de nouveaux conteurs, elle analyse leur trajectoire et montre leur idéal d'une relation esthétique immédiate: il n'y a pas d'écran entre le conteur et son public, dit-elle, les contenus des messages sont puisés dans une matière commune

---

1   P. Zumthor, *La Lettre et la voix* (Paris, Seuil, 1987), 282.
2   V. Görög-Karady, 'Qui conte en France aujourd'hui? Les nouveaux conteurs', *Cahiers de Littérature Orale* 11 (1982), 95–116.

sinon ordinaire, du moins accessible, les artistes ne s'enferment pas dans un rôle d'artiste particulier. Ils ont bénéficié aussi, selon elle, du long travail de réhabilitation du fantastique qui se poursuit dans la culture européenne depuis les romantiques. Ces résultats n'auraient pu être acquis sans des préalables savants, depuis la fondation de l'Académie Celtique sous l'Empire jusqu'aux travaux de Van Gennep et Sébillot. Un rapport nouveau, intime, actif, voire participant, entre créateurs et publics se crée, faisant appel à un domaine de l'imaginaire généralement refoulé chez les adultes dans le rêve, le jeu, l'inconscient. Il s'agit bien de reconquérir un public d'adultes.

Le colloque international, *Le Renouveau du conte en France et ailleurs*, organisé en février 1989 par le CNRS et l'association *L'Âge d'or*, fera date. Mais, en 1984 déjà, Bruno De La Salle, le principal artisan de ce renouveau en France, s'interroge, lui aussi, sur les raisons du retour inattendu d'une oralité promise à la disparition, avec la fin des terroirs. Parmi les différents facteurs, il pointe tout particulièrement l'apport de la culture maghrébine et l'influence des premiers conteurs maghrébins.[3] Ces derniers firent connaître les répertoires et les techniques dont ils étaient dépositaires. L'aspect exotique de leur style, note Bruno De La Salle, ne fut pas étranger à leur succès auprès du public adulte, par-delà leur qualité et l'adéquation du patrimoine oral musulman à la transmission populaire. Certains, comme Mohamed Belhalfaoui, furent particulièrement engagés dans une action de transmission ambitieuse. Quoi qu'il en soit, l'immigration concourt à ce que Roger Bastide, au Brésil, avait déjà désigné, en 1948, comme un 'folklore urbain'.[4] À l'exemple des États-Unis, des conteurs investissent donc les bibliothèques, les écoles, les quartiers dits difficiles. C'est là que s'inscrit le renouveau du conte, au cœur des politiques de la ville, dans le cadre des missions de lutte contre l'illettrisme, contre la violence, l'exclusion, la précarité, dans une histoire de 'l'interculturel', dont le sens et les enjeux demandent à être précisés.

3   B. De La Salle, 'La Culture maghrébine dans le renouveau du conte', *Grand Maghreb* 35 (1984).
4   R. Bastide, 'Opinions sur le folklore', *Bastidiana* 19–20 (1997), 35–39. Le folklore est nettement présenté dans sa fonction d'instrument d'assimilation des étrangers (notamment via les enfants d'immigrants).

I.2 Problématiques interculturelles

'La France a eu ses Juifs, ses Polonais, ses Italiens, ses Espagnols, ses Portu-gais, elle a aujourd'hui ses Maghrébins', écrit Sami Nair en 1984.[5] Avec 'la seconde génération' et les problèmes des banlieues imputés au déferlement des nouveaux arrivants, il analyse à Marseille l'apparition d'une véritable arabophobie.

Les travailleurs migrants venus du Maghreb et plus particulièrement d'Algérie dès le début du XXe siècle, loin de repartir au pays, ont fait venir massivement leurs familles par mesure de regroupement familial (suite à l'arrêt de l'immigration en 1974). Ces familles ont apporté avec elles des pratiques plus ou moins fragmentées de cultures dites alors d'origine, cultu-res encore en prise avec une oralité vivante. Comme j'ai pu le vérifier moi-même dans un premier travail de collecte, la mémoire des contes est restée très présente, notamment dans les familles de culture berbère (notamment kabyles d'Algérie).[6] Ces dernières ont été d'autant plus attachées à leur héritage qu'il fut systématiquement occulté par les divers dispositifs scolai-res mis en place, dans les années 1970, pour faciliter tant l'intégration des primo-arrivants dans le pays d'accueil que le retour au pays d'origine.[7] La logique de repérage par langue-nation restait très loin des réalités linguis-tiques et culturelles locales. Si les accords avec l'Algérie, pour des raisons politiques, n'ont été signés qu'en 1981, la langue berbère, elle, n'a jamais eu droit de cité.

Par-delà les considérations linguistiques, la question est bien celle de l'accueil dans le système français d'un monde déroutant, sous les traits de l'*homo islamicus*. Les confusions et les amalgames font le succès d'un mot

---

5   S. Naïr, 'Marseille: chronique des années de lèpre', *Les Temps modernes* 452–453–454 (1984), 1592–1615, 1601.

6   N. Decourt, *La Vache des orphelins. Conte et immigration* (Lyon, Presses Universitaires de Lyon, 1992).

7   Notamment les cours de langues et cultures d'origine dispensés par des ELCO, Enseignants de Langues et Cultures d'Origine employés par les pays d'émigration. Sur ces questions voir R. Berthelier, *Enfants de migrants à l'école française* (Paris, L'Harmattan, 2006).

qui s'impose et englobe toute une nébuleuse autour de l'immigré: 'maghrébin' se substitue à 'nord-africain', trop entaché de colonialisme. D'autres mesures seront prises pour valoriser les enfants de migrants dans le sillage de la circulaire du 25 juillet 1978:[8] il s'agit d'ouvrir l'école française à ce que Jacques Berque appellera, en 1985, 'les cultures d'apport de l'immigration'.[9] Les jeunes, eux, se revendiquent 'beurs', selon un mot de verlan (arabe transformé en rebeu etc.) et rompent avec le discours de l'origine, tandis que des parents de la première génération sont sollicités pour venir dire leurs contes à l'école. Le conte se trouve au cœur des pédagogies dites interculturelles, pris dans l'entre-deux, outil de médiation privilégié, au risque de nouvelles formes d'instrumentalisation et de ghettoïsation.

Il s'agit de faire marcher le modèle d'intégration à la française tout en prenant en compte une altérité qui résiste à l'assimilation. Le mot 'interculturel' fait donc figure de mot-outil, de mot-problème. Il révèle un débat de société et signale l'émergence d'une conscience qui met en cause l'universalisme abstrait et la hiérarchie des civilisations, c'est-à-dire l'inconscient des sciences sociales occidentales, pour reprendre les termes de Claude Liauzu.[10] Sa légitimité tient à ce qu'il nous révèle de notre propre diversité; elle tient à la nécessité de solidariser des 'présences culturelles', de passer du 'problème de l'immigration' à une problématique ouverte sur l'avenir. Ces enjeux, considérables, donneront lieu à des politiques chaotiques, alors que les sciences sociales françaises se tiennent à l'écart, selon C. Liauzu, du fait d'une vieille répugnance à l'interethnique et au minoritaire. L'interculturel reste dans la sphère de l'expérientiel; multi-, pluri-, inter-, les dénominations et dérivations sont nombreuses. Interculturalisme, interculturalité, interculturel: le terme, dans l'oscillation du suffixe, alimente les polémiques.

---

8   Circulaire 78–238, Ministère de l'Éducation Nationale, 'Scolarisation des enfants immigrés', recommandant 'la valorisation des langues et cultures d'origine' de l'école maternelle au collège.

9   J. Berque, *L'Immigration à l'école de la République* (Paris, La Documentation française, 1985).

10   C. Liauzu, 'L'École et l'immigration: enjeux culturels d'une société plurielle', *Travaux et documents de l'IREMAM* 3 (1987), 10.

C'est dans ce contexte de débats parfois violents qu'un corpus de contes a émergé, à travers un dispositif expérimental qui a déterminé en grande partie la nature de la collecte et les choix méthodologiques d'une édition respectueuse du style oral.

II Un dispositif expérimental de contage

Le pari était bien de travailler à l'édition scientifique de textes doublement illégitimes, aux yeux d'une littérature canonique, parce que contes-maghrébins, c'est-à-dire non seulement oraux, mais, qui plus est, saisis entre deux ou plus de deux langues, dans les formes impures des parlers vernaculaires. À cela s'ajoute la question de la variation qui apparaît ici sous les traits spécifiques et grossissants d'une situation interculturelle expérimentale de collectage.

II.1 La Variation in vivo

Les contes ont été collectés dans le cadre d'une formation par alternance conçue par Odile Carré, enseignant-chercheur à l'Institut de Psychologie (Université Lyon 2).[11] Ce dispositif expérimental touchait la formation et la recherche.

Odile Carré avait déjà travaillé avec des groupes de femmes autour d'autres objets culturels de relation (massage des bébés, pratiques du hammam). Le groupe 'Contes et récits de la vie quotidienne' est donc un groupe interculturel composé de seize femmes ayant en moyenne quarante ans, venant d'Algérie, de Tunisie et du Laos, et de cinq animatrices d'horizons professionnels différents: formation, service social, recherche. Les

11   O. Carré, *Contes et récits de la vie quotidienne. Pratiques en groupe interculturel* (Paris, L'Harmattan, 1998).

participantes du groupe appartiennent toutes à une première génération d'immigrées. Certaines d'entre elles sont analphabètes, les autres ont un niveau proche ou équivalent du certificat d'études. Toutes sont mères de familles parfois nombreuses.

Le travail du groupe visait à la fois au développement personnel de chaque participante et à l'acquisition d'un certain nombre de connaissances ou d'expériences susceptibles de développer les liens sociaux autour du conte, particulièrement entre les familles et les enseignants dans l'environnement urbain du quartier. Chaque participante a effectué un stage pratique dans un équipement social proche de son domicile (centre social, bibliothèque d'école ou de quartier, bibliothèque de rue, et même halte-garderie) et participé à une journée de regroupement par semaine. Cette journée se déroulait en deux temps: le premier était consacré à une analyse des pratiques de terrain, le second au contage, le français servant de langue véhiculaire.

Ainsi, pendant un an et demi, chaque vendredi, avons-nous tenu un salon de littérature orale, avec tous les rituels de bouche pour passer agréablement le temps. La rigueur observée dans la mise en place de règles de fonctionnement a permis une régularité particulièrement précieuse pour les processus de mémorisation. Deux participantes originaires du Laos, moins à l'aise dans la pratique du français, ont en tout cas stimulé l'exercice de la confrontation culturelle (comparaison de rituels de mariage, de naissance, de mort). De conte en digression, le groupe s'est petit à petit constitué sur le mode du 'nous', non sans larmes ni émotions à l'évocation des souffrances de l'exil et de la guerre.[12]

Petit à petit la honte de mal parler le français a pu être levée, des censures sont tombées: des contes facétieux et même licencieux sont apparus. Les séances de devinettes ont libéré la parole et les imaginaires. Certaines conteuses ont découvert, dans leur bibliothèque de quartier, des livres de contes de leur pays, avec fierté. L'écrit a servi de faire-valoir à leur mémoire. Celles qui intervenaient dans les écoles ont pris la mesure de leur savoir-faire. Les contes ont émergé par bribes sur le mode du 'moi, je le connais,

---

12   Pour plus de détails sur la vie du groupe, voir Carré, *Contes et récits*.

mais ce n'est pas tout à fait pareil'. Repris de séance en séance, par le jeu des interactions, ils se sont étoffés. Ainsi des motifs enfouis ont-ils ressurgi, dessinant une formidable méthode d'apprentissage de la langue. Des aides à la traduction se sont improvisées, lorsque surgissait une difficulté linguistique. Les solutions, trouvées *in situ*, seraient à prendre en compte dans le passage de l'oral à l'écrit. L'intention était bien de transmettre une nouvelle mémoire au fur et à mesure de son élaboration tant à l'intérieur du groupe qu'à l'extérieur, dans les divers lieux de voisinage.

II.2 Un projet éditorial partagé

Lorsque la formation s'achève, un corpus de conte s'est construit dans la circulation, certains contes étant immédiatement repris, d'autres restant la propriété de la conteuse-source, tel 'Ahmed fumeur Hachaïchi', version chaouïa du 'Chat botté'. Il est devenu évident pour toutes qu'il fallait faire un livre: *verba volant, scripta manent*. Prestige et commodité de l'écrit, qui à la fois conserve et diffuse.

Commence la partie proprement éditoriale, à laquelle les 'conteuses' ont apporté toute l'aide nécessaire, telle était en effet la nouvelle identité que les participantes se sont donnée, même si certaines étaient restées plutôt dans une position d'écoute. Odile Carré avait besoin de respecter l'anonymat de chacune pour rédiger la chronique du groupe, tandis que l'édition des contes me semblait exiger la publication du nom propre. Ainsi nos chemins d'écriture, déontologie oblige, ont divergé et donné lieu, pour l'établissement du recueil, à un autre partenariat devenu indispensable non seulement avec les participantes concernées par l'opération, mais avec une linguiste. Il s'agissait dès lors de croiser des regards et des expertises entre praticiens (chercheurs et conteurs) embarqués dans une même entreprise textuelle.[13]

---

13   Sur la nouvelle attention portée à ce type de collaboration, voir R. Finnegan, *The Oral and Beyond. Doing Things with Words in Africa* (Chicago, Chicago University Press, 2007), 194–195.

Les seuls recueils disponibles à cette période (et encore aujourd'hui) étaient des mises en écriture sans prétention scientifique, réalisées le plus souvent par des animatrices de bonne volonté, dans le 'style instituteur' que l'on a parfois reproché aux premiers écrivains de la francophonie. Or l'édition visée devait être menée dans un esprit de rigueur et de méthode, garant du respect du texte oral. Selon la formule de P. Galand-Pernet, tout travail d'édition scrupuleux sauve l'objet littéraire en établissant sa forme.[14] Naïma Louali-Raynal m'avait déjà aidée dans un travail de traduction et de transcription portant sur trois versions kabyles d'une 'Vache des orphelins' saisies en migration, celles de la grand-mère, de la mère et de la fille.[15] Son aide allait se révéler particulièrement précieuse dans un nouveau défi, dont on retiendra ici les aspects majeurs tenant à la performance dans ses dimensions à la fois verbales et non-verbales – 'performance of something', selon l'expression de Ruth Finnegan, ce quelque chose relevant d'un objet-texte détachable du contexte.[16]

Il y a bien, qu'on le veuille ou non, une différence entre oralité et écriture, au sens où le texte oral est infixé, 'imparfait' (selon le mot de Nicole Belmont) – ce qui n'exclut pas la répétition, alors que le texte écrit est définitivement fixe, ce qui n'exclut pas la variation.[17] Comme le montre Paul Zumthor, il y a *mouvance*: le texte oral, ou *œuvre performée*, met en relation un conteur, des auditeurs et une mémoire collective en partage.[18] Comment faire le choix entre les différentes versions qui s'étaient transformées au fil des séances? Fallait-il choisir la meilleure, la plus complète, voire la reconstituer, à l'instar de la méthode adoptée par les frères Grimm, mais comment? Quel sort faudrait-il ménager aux hésitations, aux essais de traductions, aux irruptions de la langue source? Quel statut donner aux variantes qui participaient au plaisir et à l'organisation du contage?

14   P. Galand-Pernet, *Littératures berbères. Des voix, des lettres* (Paris, PUF, 1998), 17.

15   Voir N. Decourt et N. Louali-Raynal, 'Les Procédés du contage: du contage traditionnel au néocontage', *Littérature orale arabo-berbère* 21 (1990), 121–152.

16   Finnegan, *The Oral and Beyond*, 193.

17   N. Belmont, *Poétique du conte. Essai sur le conte de tradition orale* (Paris, Gallimard, 1999).

18   Zumthor, *La Lettre et la voix*, 160, 269.

L'aporie demeure bel et bien, par-delà les nouvelles technologies, d'une *raison graphique*, qui fige et réifie. Comment étudier l'oral avec le seul outillage de l'écrit, comme le dénonçait Jack Goody, comment prendre en compte la voix, la gestualité, les effets d'interactions avec l'auditoire, sans perdre sur le papier le charme particulier que lui confère la performance?[19] À défaut d'enregistrements de qualité suffisante (audio), à défaut de caméra (étant donné les réserves culturelles des participantes quant à l'utilisation de l'image), le choix du livre seul s'imposait. Il relevait également d'une volonté d'appropriation d'un mode pérenne et prestigieux: l'écrit, dans ses modes de libre circulation. Il faudrait donc utiliser les ressources de la littérature pour respecter le rythme de l'énonciation et, par-delà les procédés littéraires du genre, saisir le style oral de chacune, selon les recommandations de Geneviève Calame-Griaule, au risque de briser les normes habituelles de l'acceptabilité et de la lisibilité.[20] Comment trouver les 'aménagements' qui puissent garantir l'efficacité du texte collecté sans l'affadir ni l'aplatir, quelles hybridations proposer entre l'oralité et l'écriture?[21]

III Choix methodologiques de transcription et de traduction

L'enjeu majeur n'était pas de restitution ni de sauvegarde, répétons-le ici, mais de partage du plaisir des variantes expérimenté dans le groupe interculturel. D'où la recherche d'une *écriture de la variance*.

---

19   J. Goody, *La Raison graphique* (Paris, Les Éditions de Minuit, 1979).
20   G. Calame-Griaule, 'Un itinéraire en ethnolinguistique', *Cahiers de littérature orale* 50 (2001), 15–33.
21   Terme emprunté à J. Derive, *Collecte et traduction des littératures orales. Un exemple négro-africain: les contes ngbaka-ma'bo de R.C.A.* (Paris, Selaf, 1975), 53.

III.1   Le Choix du corpus

Plutôt que de publier l'intégralité des contes collectés, le choix a été fait de privilégier ceux qui avaient créé une mémoire commune et pour lesquels nous disposions d'un nombre suffisant de versions enregistrées. Deux types de corpus ont donc été élaborés:

> un *corpus intra-conteur* (les différentes versions du même conte racontées par la même conteuse): les variables tiennent ici à la situation de contage et sont liées à la performance;

> un *corpus inter-conteur* (plusieurs versions d'un même conte racontées par des conteuses différentes): les variables tiennent ici plus particulièrement au style de chaque conteuse, à sa trajectoire propre entre deux langues et deux cultures.

'Les deux vieux et l'âne' (Djorah Chefai) ouvre le recueil sur un registre facétieux. Les trois autres contes sont des contes merveilleux racontés par Khoukha Nasri, dont la version du Chat Botté '(Ahmed Hachaïchi)' fait la charnière entre les deux corpus, compte tenu de variantes narratives qui ont été traitées sur le mode d'un conte à parcours multiples. La deuxième partie comporte, par ordre croissant de variantes: trois versions de 'La femme stupide' (autre conte facétieux), quatre versions des 'Œufs du serpent' (conte très présent dans les mémoires maghrébines) et cinq versions d'un conte de randonnée particulièrement répandu en Tunisie: 'Oum Sissi' (la chatte qui a perdu sa queue pour avoir dérobé de la viande ou du lait). Chaque version comporte un élément-titre spécifique, choisi au terme du travail d'analyse, comme son aboutissement et sa vérification même.

III.2   Analyse comparative et carte linguistique

Chaque ensemble de versions a d'abord fait l'objet d'une analyse comparative qui a permis de dégager l'architecture du récit et d'approcher le style de chaque conteuse. Pour chacune, une carte linguistique a été établie à partir des éléments récurrents du corpus:

- temps du récit,
- constructions syntaxiques,
- lexique,
- procédés narratifs.

Cette carte a joué un rôle déterminant dans le travail de mise en écriture, servant de véritable guide dans les cas les plus difficiles de ce que l'on peut appeler, avec les écrivains de la créolité (Glissant, Chamoiseau, Confiant), une traduction de la parole. Dans l'une et l'autre tâche (schéma de récit, carte linguistique), une étude minutieuse a été faite des 'signaux démarcatifs', tels que les définit Paulette Galand-Pernet.[22] Par 'signaux démarcatifs', il faut entendre les verbes introductifs du discours (si nombreux dans l'énoncé oral), les verbes de mouvement, les noms de personnages, les locutions de temps ou de lieux, les formules et répétitions diverses, système assez souple qui guide l'auditeur dans sa perception de l'histoire et permet à l'exécutant d'y imprimer sa marque artistique. Leur réseau contribue non seulement à l'agencement du texte, mais aussi à sa poétique, à son rythme propre, – élément essentiel selon Henri Meschonnic pour approcher la littérature même comme mouvement, comme l'oralité dans l'écrit.[23] S'ils passent parfaitement à l'oral, leur mise en écriture alourdit le texte au point de le rendre quasi illisible, notamment dans l'introduction des dialogues où s'accumulent les 'il dit', 'elle dit'.

En ce qui concerne les temps du récit, notons que rares sont les emplois du passé simple, temps quasi absent chez les conteurs professionnels, qui lui préfèrent le présent de narration. Lorsque la conteuse emploie une alternance entre le présent et le passé composé, nous avons fait le choix du présent et réservé le passé composé aux gloses, où il apparaît régulièrement comme le temps du commentaire.

Les constructions syntaxiques ont fait l'objet des changements qui nous semblaient indispensables au confort de la lecture. La fréquence de

---

22   Galand-Pernet, *Littératures berbères*, 184.

23   L'oral, pris dans cette acception, est ainsi opposé au parlé. Le texte est conçu comme mouvement. Voir H. Meschonnic, *Critique du rythme* (Lagrasse, Verdier, 1982), 705–713 et *Poétique du traduire* (Lagrasse, Verdier, 1999), 168–171.

phrases courtes, selon le schéma canonique (sujet, verbe, complément) – phrases sans connecteurs, portées par un débit rapide – nous a posé maints problèmes de ponctuation. Si la parataxe est caractéristique de la narration orale, comme l'ont rapporté maints linguistes et spécialistes de littérature orale,[24] notons qu'elle s'est légèrement atténuée au fur et à mesure où les conteuses gagnaient en aisance linguistique et en remémoration du répertoire, passant à un usage que l'on pourrait dire plus formel. Il convenait d'en respecter scrupuleusement les occurrences.

Le lexique enfin a posé des problèmes de compréhension et de traduction liés à la situation d'entre-deux langues. Plusieurs cas se sont présentés. Soit le mot intraduisible, après une première explication avec le groupe, se trouvait naturalisé (cas de *kedid*, la viande séchée) et se trouve maintenu: le lecteur pourra lui aussi prendre plaisir à l'acquisition d'un mot étranger. Soit le mot avait trouvé, au fil des variantes, une traduction admise par le groupe et a progressivement disparu au profit du français ('le mors du cheval'). Soit il s'est maintenu dans la traduction simultanée et s'est incrusté dans le contage, d'où l'usage de la parenthèse: 'elle garde le *lebçour* (les abats)', '*lakercha* (comme on dit les tripes)' – il s'agit des tripes du vieux mouton dont la femme stupide se pare en guise de bijoux. La bi-langue vient ici amplifier l'expression du dégoût.

III.3 L'Art de la glose

Les difficultés de traduction n'ont pas été seulement linguistiques, mais aussi culturelles. Elles ont donné lieu à des gloses qui se sont, elles aussi, incrustées au point de faire partie intégrante du procès de la narration. Peut-être même est-ce le procédé narratif qui spécifie la qualité du contage en situation interculturelle: le conte sert de support prétexte à la connaissance d'une autre culture, d'autres techniques, d'autres coutumes, d'autres usages.

---

24   Voir notamment Zumthor, *Introduction à la poésie orale*, 136–137; U. Baumgardt et J. Derive (éds), *Littératures orales africaines. Perspectives théoriques et méthodologiques* (Paris, Karthala, 2008), 297.

Dans le contage traditionnel, la glose existe: elle peut servir à clarifier l'action, à commenter un effet psychologique, à renforcer la connivence, car point n'est besoin d'expliquer ce qui va de soi. En situation interculturelle, elle prend plus d'ampleur et fonctionne comme nouveau signal démarcatif. Ainsi la conteuse se fait-elle un plaisir d'expliquer ce qui pourrait à ses yeux faire obstacle à la bonne compréhension de son récit, qu'il s'agisse de *realia* (objets, techniques) ou de coutumes, quand bien même le public pourrait être plus ou moins averti:

> Chez nous en Tunisie, dans chaque maison, il y a un puits. (Fathma)

> Un jour, elle a reconnu la voix de son frère, c'était son frère, l'invité, parce que, dans le désert, c'est une coutume, si quelqu'un passe, on l'invite. (Fatima)

> Vous savez, enfin, nous, on lave les morts, il faut qu'ils soient propres. (Fatima)

Deux formules généralement les introduisent: '(parce que) chez nous' et 'vous savez'. Cette dernière formule peut apparaître comme un opérateur de connivence: elle crée de toutes pièces un savoir ethnographique supposé absent.

L'oralité intègre ici la note de bas de page de l'édition savante dans le fil de la narration même. Le conteur négocie pas à pas le sens du texte compte tenu du contexte présumé de l'énonciation *hic et nunc*. Les gloses des premières séances sont bel et bien restées, elles ont pris en quelque sorte valeur littéraire. Le plaisir du conte en situation interculturelle, qu'il soit maghrébin ou autre, tient à ce pari de la rencontre, à la négociation (toujours périlleuse) d'un espace ludique d'intercompréhension. Le conte accomplit ici la fonction qui lui est traditionnellement dévolue de cohésion sociale et de connaissance; il ne s'agit pas seulement d'entretenir des connivences, mais bien de les fabriquer, de faire société. Le conte à cet égard fonctionne non seulement comme 'matrice de reconnaissance' au sens où l'entend Jean-Noël Pelen, mais comme espace d'ouverture et de bigarrure culturelles. Certes nous avons tous à peu près les mêmes contes et éprouvons le plaisir de nous replonger dans le temps mythique de l'enfance, mais cette matrice de reconnaissance est précisément ce qui autorise et stimule le jeu du même et de l'autre, dans une société qui s'éprouve de plus en plus plurielle.[25] Le plaisir de la réitération en ce sens n'exclut pas le plaisir de la variation, mais en est la condition même: la formule 'pas tout à fait pareil', qui a servi dans le groupe à l'introduction de la variation ('je le connais, mais ce n'est pas tout à fait pareil'), prend ici toute sa valeur anthropologique.

III.4 Langues et interlangue ou la petite musique de l'altérité

La recherche du mot juste, gloses comprises, procède d'un contage entre les langues et les cultures. Elle signe une esthétique métisse qui fait la part belle aux refrains en langue source. De version en version, ces refrains ont pris de l'assurance, de l'étoffe. Ils ont pu être vérifiés et complétés, grâce à des enregistrements en langue-source réalisés au domicile de chaque conteuse, en situation authentique de contage (avec des voisines, des amies). Ils constituent de précieux îlots de mémoire, qu'ils soient chantés ou psalmodiés, et introduisent une voix différente, celle d'une langue quasi archaïque et magique, dont le plaisir est assurément de réitération.

Par exemple, le refrain de la jeune femme, chassée par des belles sœurs, jalouses, qui lui ont fait avaler des œufs des serpents. Ainsi fera-t-elle reconnaître son innocence, à travers la voix de Fatima Mekki:

> Grain, Grain de Grenade
> Grain, Grain de Grenade, tes oncles sont sept
> Grain, Grain de Grenade, leurs armes sont sept
> Grain, Grain de Grenade, leurs chevaux sont sept
> Grain, Grain de Grenade, leurs maisons sont sept
> Grain, Grain de Grenade, leurs femmes sont sept.

Ces poésies, incrustées dans le conte, résistent à la traduction, quand elles n'engendrent pas leur propre transposition créatrice. Ainsi, désespérant de pouvoir traduire la formule d'ordalie qui opère le dénouement du conte

---

25 J.-N. Pelen, 'Le Simple Fait de raconter toujours la même histoire: réflexion sur l'en-deçà du sens dans la tradition du conte', dans A. Petitat (éd.), *Contes: l'universel et le singulier* (Paris, Payot, 2002), 197–213.

(littéralement 'le pur sort du pur'), Fatima se lance-t-elle un jour dans l'improvisation suivante, qu'elle adoptera par la suite: 'Je suis pure comme le lait, je suis pure, je n'ai rien fait', sautant par-dessus la difficulté linguistique comme l'innocente belle-sœur au-dessus du feu.

Il en est de même des motifs qui font image et qui, par leur répétition, prennent valeur de paroles formulaires. L'image de la délivrance en particulier frappe d'autant plus l'imaginaire que le conteur en répète le récit. Le voici dans la version d'Auguste Mouliéras:[26]

> Ô grand-père, j'ai chez moi une femme. Il y a un serpent dans son ventre. Alors, que dois-je lui faire?
> Le vieux sage lui répondit:
> Va, mon fils, donne-lui à manger de la viande salée, ne lui donne pas d'eau, quatre jours durant, suspends-la au toit par les pieds; mets-lui la tête en bas. Emplis une écuelle d'eau; remues-y tes mains. Il sortira. Toi, tue-le.

Comme dans cette version traditionnelle traduite par Camille Lacoste-Dujardin, Fatima déroule toute la scène et prépare de subtiles reprises (ce qui est conseillé sera exécuté, puis narré *in fine* au frère retrouvé, à des fins de reconnaissance):

> Il monte sur son cheval, en courant, il va voir le conseiller et lui dit:
> J'ai trouvé une belle jeune-fille, mais elle est triste, elle est malade. Que dois-je faire?
> L'homme ouvre son livre où il voit l'avenir et il dit:
> La femme est très malade, elle a sept serpents dans son ventre et vous pouvez faire quelque chose pour elle, c'est facile.
> Que dois-je faire?
> Va dans la forêt, prends une biche, une jeune gazelle. Mets beaucoup de sel, fais-lui avaler beaucoup de viande, jusqu'à ce qu'elle n'arrive pas à manger. Mets une grande bassine d'eau. Attache-lui les jambes en haut et la tête en bas et, attention, il y a sept serpents dans son ventre et chaque serpent qui sort, il faut le tuer tout de suite, parce qu'ils sont très grands.

---

26   C. Lacoste-Dujardin, *Traduction des légendes et contes merveilleux de la Grande Kabylie, recueillis par A. Mouliéras* (Paris, Geuthner, 1965), I, 128–135.

Si l'on retrouve la poétique du nombre sept si fréquent dans le conte kabyle, la biche (qui traduit la gazelle) est peut-être un emprunt à l'univers des frères Grimm, mais le lecteur retrouve l'imagerie du conte, à peu près avec les mêmes mots, dans ce flottement qui caractérise la 'remémoration créatrice' selon Goody, avec la part d'invention propre à chaque conteur.[27]

Refrains et motifs formulaires sont donc ces 'perles et coraux' que l'on a parfois la chance d'aller cueillir dans les profondeurs inexplorées de la mémoire.[28] Joyaux intangibles, ils traversent le temps et l'espace, à la manière des pierres inscrites que traquent les archéologues de terrain, et dont les formules restent lisibles, même à l'état de fragments endommagés. Les retrouver éveille les souvenirs du temps jadis avec une précision prous-tienne. On pourrait les appeler les intraduisibles de la littérature orale, ceux qu'on a envie d'écouter dans la langue, l'autre langue, 'l'outre-langue', pour reprendre une notion définie par Alexis Nouss dans son élaboration de la pensée métisse.[29] Leur surgissement suppose en tout cas réussie l'épreuve de la confiance. Il faut du temps, mais aussi des oreilles estimées propres à les accueillir. Les pratiques de lecture ne sont pas habituées à la voix chantée. Il en faut du courage pour oser un refrain dans sa langue et dans une langue que l'on ne maîtrise pas, en des lieux où règnent la littérature écrite et les règles du bien parler. Une glose, d'abord de précaution oratoire, puis de coquetterie littéraire, a disparu dans cette lente émergence d'une connaissance littéraire de soi: 'Je ne peux pas le traduire, c'est tellement plus beau en arabe!'.

De même les trouvailles de l'interlangue ont été gardées, dans la mesure où elles aussi se sont incrustées, participant à la rythmique du conte, au plaisir de la narration. Elles opèrent une poétique du code restreint (versus élaboré, pour reprendre les catégories de Basil Bernstein), en parfaite adé-

---

27   J. Goody, *Entre l'oralité et l'écriture* (Paris, PUF, 1994), 198.
28   Je reprends ici la métaphore du collectionneur qu'Hanna Arendt utilise à propos de Walter Benjamin dans H. Arendt, *Vies politiques* (Paris, Gallimard, 1974), 291–306.
29   Voir F. Laplantine et A. Nouss, *Métissages. D'Arcimboldo à Zombi* (Paris, Pauvert, 2001).

quation avec l'économie du style oral.[30] Par exemple: 'en courant' (ci-dessus) ou encore ce 'fou d'amoureux d'elle', décrivant le transport amoureux de l'homme qui a trouvé la belle, ensevelie sous le sable (seule une touffe de cheveux dépassait), et enceinte: à ce point fou d'amour, il saura la délivrer des œufs du serpent, c'est-à-dire braver la peur du déshonneur, lui faire confiance et en faire sa femme.

Autre exemple: l'emploi du mot 'miracle' dans une version du conte-type 'L'apprenti magicien' (T325). Le jeune héros reçoit l'ordre d'aller 'chercher du miracle': 'Si ton fils ramène du miracle, je te donne ma fille en échange, c'est promis'. Et il revient victorieux: 'Vous avez demandé du miracle. Voilà du miracle'. 'Bravo, ça c'est du vrai miracle,' réplique le roi. Le mot, qui fait écho au mot *prodige*, si présent dans la littérature du XVIIIe siècle, mais également dans la bouche de certains jeunes pratiquant un 'parler-banlieue,' revêt une efficace étrangeté dans ce nouvel emploi. Il a donc été retenu comme élément-titre, c'est ainsi que le conte était désigné dans le groupe.

IV Conclusion

Le recueil de ces quelques *Contes* saisis *en situation interculturelle* témoigne d'une volonté concertée de laisser entendre des voix singulières, sous le double contrôle des conteuses (sollicitées tout au long du travail d'édition) et de la variation elle-même, au risque d'une certaine rugosité. Le texte produit s'inscrit dans un écrit intermédiaire entre deux oralités: l'oralité de départ et l'oralité virtuelle supposée celle d'un lecteur qui, à son tour, racontera, puisera dans sa mémoire, rendra à l'oralité des récits passés par le cribble d'une édition savante et rendus à la dignité littéraire de passeurs de mémoire. Cet ouvrage de fait a valeur d'aide-mémoire, à la manière des textes médiévaux, fonction dont l'oralité contemporaine retrouve pleinement

---

30 B. Bernstein, *Langage et classes sociales* (Paris, Les Éditions de Minuit, 1975).

l'utilité. Création hybride entre l'oralité et l'écriture, la mise en écriture participe pleinement à *l'épreuve de la traduction*, en ce qu'elle dessine non pas une opposition entre l'oralité et l'écriture, mais un entre-deux, un espace dévolu au passage, à l'interface. Elle n'est pas sans interroger l'hypothèse d'Antoine Berman pour qui la traduction, qu'il s'agisse de littérature, de philosophie ou même de science humaine, joue un rôle qui n'est pas de simple transmission, ce rôle est tendanciellement constitutif de toute littérature, de toute philosophie et de toute science humaine.[31]

Ainsi des contes arrachés à leur contexte n'en véhiculent-ils pas moins une poétique expérimentale mettant en jeu le dialogue des cultures, le plaisir de la rencontre, par-delà la vie éphémère d'un groupe. Puissent-ils aussi garder trace d'un partenariat créatif, d'un tressage de paroles constitutif d'un penser/créer/vivre ensemble toujours ouvert, inachevé.

---

31   A. Berman, *L'Épreuve de l'étranger* (Paris, Gallimard, 1984), 293.

The oral-written dynamic in 'new' storytelling in French

JANICE CARRUTHERS

I Introduction

This Chapter focuses on the *conte* in the context of performed oral story-telling by professional and semi-professional *conteurs* in contemporary France.[1] As we shall see in Section II, this variety of oral narrative, known as new storytelling or *néo-contage*, is of particular interest as an interface between oral and written modes of discourse. Through the analysis of three linguistic phenomena – tense usage, speech and thought presentation, and levels of parataxis/coordination/subordination – I shall attempt to point up the complexities of the oral-written dynamic in the case of oral story-telling and the limitations of approaching the data via a binary oral-written divide.[2] The last part of the Chapter will explore other theoretical models, assessing to what extent they offer a viable alternative.

---

1   There are a number of fundamental differences between traditional and new sto-rytelling in terms of sources, choice of stories, performance context, sociolinguistic background of storytellers, and the relationship between oral and written versions of stories. For a discussion, see J. Carruthers, *Oral Narration in Modern French. A Linguistic Analysis of Temporal Patterns* (Oxford, Legenda, 2005), 4–7.

2   My thanks to the *Conservatoire de Littérature Orale* in Vendôme (Director: Bruno De La Salle) for generous access to their recorded collection, and to the AHRC who funded the research leave connected with this project.

II New storytelling and the oral-written divide

As anthropologists and ethnolinguists such as Finnegan have pointed out,
the term 'oral' when applied to storytelling, whether traditional or new,
is problematic in itself, raising issues around composition, transmission
and performance.[3] There are, in fact, different degrees of 'oral-ness'. Oral
composition can refer both to 'composition before performance' and 'composition in performance', neither process involving written texts as part of
the composition process – at least in theory. Transmission refers largely
to dissemination, although a story 'heard' through the oral medium can
of course subsequently be disseminated in written form and vice versa.
Crucially, oral performance implies oral delivery, although as we shall see,
oral delivery can nonetheless involve a relationship with a written text,
and this relationship can take many different forms. With oral storytelling, the question of memorisation is also fundamental to the discussion,
and it too can be variable across different cultures, different types of story
and different storytellers. In rare cases, stories are learnt verbatim. More
common is memorisation of key elements in the storyline (such as themes
or episodes), and of certain lexical items, phrases or formulae which are
deployed at particular points, but where the story is nonetheless performed
'spontaneously' in a given performance context. As Belmont puts it, *conteurs* 'discernent clairement les deux règles qui gouvernent la vie du conte,
la stabilité et le changement, et les deux facultés entre lesquelles ils doivent
trouver une balance, la mémoire et l'invention'.[4]

How does 'new storytelling' align itself in terms of the relationship
between oral and written modes? Unlike traditional storytelling, where
sources are often oral, the sources in the case of new storytelling consist
predominantly of written texts which range across a variety of historical

3   See the discussion in R. Finnegan, *Oral Poetry: Its Nature, Significance and Social
    Context* (Cambridge, CUP, 1977), and P. Zumthor, *Introduction à la poésie orale*
    (Paris, Seuil, 1983).
4   N. Belmont, 'La Tradition orale du conte, la transcription et les contes littéraires',
    Cahiers de littérature orale 52 (2002), 133–144, 137.

periods, continents and cultural traditions. These written sources are read, absorbed, imbibed, worked and reworked into an oral performance which, with very few exceptions, is not memorised verbatim.[5] There is thus, to use Lyons's term, an important element of 'medium transferability':[6] the composition process involves both written texts (as sources and working documents) and oral composition (in terms of the spontaneity of the performance). Transmission is complex, in that both written and oral versions of many of the stories tend to be in circulation and it is not uncommon for *nouveaux conteurs* to publish written versions of their stories. In Zumthor's terms, new storytelling represents a variety of 'oralité seconde', a type of orality functioning in contemporary Western society alongside the potentially powerful influence of written texts.[7]

III   Oral narrative: the research context

As far as work on the 'orality' of oral storytelling is concerned, the greatest advances have been made by folklorists, anthropologists and ethnolinguists, who have documented many of the key stylistic features of this type of narration in different languages and traditions.[8] Amongst these features figure, for example, the use of repetition (of themes, of phrases, of syntactic

---

5   Exceptions would include stories recounted in verse form for example.
6   J. Lyons, *Language and Linguistics* (Cambridge, CUP, 1981), 11.
7   See the discussion in Zumthor, *Introduction à la poésie orale*, Chapter 2.
8   For discussion of the stylistic and poetic features of oral narrative, see R. Bauman, *Story, Performance and Event: Contextual Studies of Oral Narrative* (Cambridge, CUP, 1986); Finnegan, *Oral Poetry*, in particular Chapter 4; W. Ong, *Orality and Literacy. The Technologising of the Word* (London and New York, Routledge, 1982), 23–27; D. Tannen, 'Spoken and written narrative in English and Greek', in D. Tannen (ed.), *Coherence in Spoken and Written Discourse* (Norwood NJ, Ablex, 1984), 21–40; P. Delarue and M.-L. Tenèze, *Le Conte populaire français. Catalogue raisonné des versions de France* (Paris, Maisonneuve et Larose, 2002), 7–99; A. de Félice, *Essai sur quelques techniques de l'art verbal traditionnel* (Thèse de doctorat, Université de

structures, of particular sounds, of particular lexical items), parallelisms, and, of course, the use of formulae of all sorts. Other linguistic features that have been the subject of debate include the use of certain figurative tropes such as metaphor and simile, and the integration of verse form and song into the narrative. Given the ethnolinguistic approaches involved in most of the published research, the features discussed have been less the subject of linguistic analysis *per se*, than important elements in cultural and anthropological debates. In any case, there is much variation in how these linguistic features operate; the type of story is relevant, as is the cultural tradition involved, and the nature of the performance context, especially in terms of the relationship between the storyteller and the listener(s).

In terms of narratology, there have also been major advances in the field of oral narrative, beginning with Labov and Waletsky's seminal work in 1967.[9] Their legacy was not only to have defined a minimal narrative (i.e. the juxtaposition of two temporally ordered clauses), but also to have developed a model for the structure of oral narrative in terms of its constituent sections, i.e. the orientation, complication, evaluation, resolution and coda. This model in turn has informed the work of linguists such as Fleischman, Wolfson and Polanyi.[10] The dominant subject for linguistic investigation has been conversational narrations, and concepts such as 'story' and 'performance' have both been defined sufficiently inclusively as to include spontaneous conversational stories, in that these are held to exhibit story features such as a 'point', a sense of evaluation, as well as classic performance features such as large quantities of direct speech,

Paris, 1957); N. Belmont, *Poétique du conte* (Paris, Gallimard, 1999); N. Guézennec, this volume.

9   W. Labov and J. Waletsky, 'Narrative analysis: oral versions of personal experience', in J. Helm (McNeish) (ed.), *Essays on the Verbal and Visual Arts. Proceedings of the 1966 Annual Spring Meeting of the American Ethnological Society* (Seattle, University of Washington Press, 1967), 12–44.

10   S. Fleischman, *Tense and Narrativity. From Medieval Performance to Modern Fiction* (London, Routledge, 1990); L. Polanyi, *Telling the American Story. A Linguistic and Cultural Analysis of Conversational Storytelling* (Norwood NJ, Ablex, 1982); N. Wolfson, *The Conversational Historical Present in American English Narrative* (Dordrecht, Foris, 1982).

asides, gestures, sound effects etc.[11] Alongside work on conversational narratives, Fleischman has explored the temporal patterning in medieval narrative texts, drawing a number of parallels with contemporary conversation, the comparison predicated on their common definition as 'oral story performance'.[12] However, although the *conte* has long been a central preoccupation for narratologists (witness the importance of Propp's *Morphologie du conte*), it is only recently that contemporary performed storytelling has entered the debate on the language of oral narrative. As Bres puts it, 'il est pour le moins significatif que les nombreuses études de contes – genre à réalisation orale par excellence – se soient dévelopées, à de rares exceptions près, à partir de versions écrites'.[13]

Any study of oral storytelling must also take on board broader research within linguistics on the structure of oral discourse. Much recent corpus-based research focuses on particular phenomena in the oral medium such as negation, detachment, inversion, relative clauses, subordination versus parataxis, tense usage, discourse markers, connectors and, more recently, speech and thought presentation.[14] Equally, there has been considerable work on the differences between oral and written language, often based on corpora of so-called 'prototypical' oral discourse (i.e. informal spoken language) and 'prototypical' written forms such as 'informational exposition'.[15] Theoretical perspectives are diverse, and include the *approche pronominale* (adopted by the leading CNRS team working on oral French, i.e. the

11 For discussion of performance features, see D. Hymes, 'Breakthrough into performance', in D.B. Amos and K. Goldstein (eds), *Folklore, Performance and Communication* (The Hague, Mouton de Gruyter, 1974), 11–74; Fleischman, *Tense and Narrativity*, 8–9; Wolfson, *The Conversational Historical Present*.

12 Fleischman, *Tense and Narrativity*.

13 J. Bres, 'Avant-propos', in M. Laforest (ed.), *Autour de la narration* (Quebec, Nuit Blanche, 1996), 7.

14 For an *état-présent*, see J. Carruthers, 'The syntax of oral French', *French Studies* 40.2 (2006), 251–260.

15 See the discussion in M.A.K. Halliday, *Spoken and Written Language* (Victoria, Deakin University Press, 1985); D. Biber, *Variation across Speech and Writing* (Cambridge, CUP, 1988), 37 and 47 *et seq.*; K. Jahanderie, *Spoken and Written Discourse* (Connecticut, Ablex, 1999), Chapter 8.

DELIC in the University of Aix-en-Provence),[16] conversational analysis (e.g. Kerbrat-Orecchioni), discourse-pragmatics (e.g. Fleischman), variationism (e.g. Coveney, Ashby, Armstrong).[17]

IV The oral-written dynamic: three linguistic phenomena

What do key linguistic features tell us about issues around the oral-written dynamic in new storytelling? This section will focus on three areas of the French language, where the *néo-conte* shows particularly interesting patterns. The data is taken from a larger study which explores temporal patterns in new storytelling, traditional storytelling and in informal conversational narrations.[18] The new storytelling data involves live performances by contemporary storytellers, most of which took place at the *Conservatoire de Littérature Orale* in Vendôme.

---

16   The DELIC team was founded by Claire Blanche-Benveniste and is now directed
      by Jean Véronis. For more details, see www.lif.univ-mrs.fr/spip.php?article353
17   See for example C. Kerbrat-Orecchioni, *La Conversation* (Paris, Seuil, 1996) and *Les Actes du langage* (Paris, Nathan, 2001); Fleischman, *Tense and Narrativity*; C. Blanche-
      Benveniste et al., *Pronom et syntaxe: l'approche pronominale et son application à la langue française* (Paris, SELAF, 1990); W. Ashby, 'Un nouveau regard sur la chute du *ne* en français parlé tourangeau', *Journal of French Language Studies* 11 (2001), 11–22;
      A. Coveney, *Variability in Spoken French: A Sociolinguistic Study of Interrogation and Negation* (Exeter, Elm Bank, 1996); N. Armstrong, *Social and Stylistic Variation in Spoken French: A Comparative Approach* (Amsterdam, Benjamins, 2001).
18   Carruthers, *Oral Narration*. Full details of the corpus can be found in the Appendix.

IV.1 Tense usage in narrative clauses

The question of tense usage in narrative clauses in oral narration is one of the most widely-researched cross-linguistic topics in contemporary work on tense and aspect.[19] The issue is particularly interesting in the case of new storytelling in French. If we begin by positing an oral-written divide, then of course the point can be made that the *passé simple* (PS) is the unmarked past tense used to mark bounded events in narrative clauses in French literary texts, and as such, the classic signal that the discourse is indeed a narrative.[20] It is widely attested in literature as well as many written versions of *contes*.[21] The PS has of course been all but eliminated from the spoken medium, where the *passé composé* (PC) is the unmarked narrative past tense.

However, given the number of types of text where this apparent spoken-written divide does not account satisfactorily for tense usage (e.g. informal letters), early theoretical models such as Benveniste's were already proposing alternative binary models. Benveniste posits two *plans d'énonciation*, *histoire* and *discours*, the former where the PS is the classic narrative tense (and which, by definition, mostly concerns written texts), and the latter which is fundamentally grounded in the present of the speaker and where the PC is used to mark past-time bounded events on the narrative line (which includes almost all varieties of spoken discourse and some varieties

---

19   The notion of 'narrative clause' is generally taken to refer to the clauses which express the bounded events recounted in sequence in a narrative (see Labov and Waletsky, 'Narrative analysis'). However, establishing which clauses in a narrative are actually narrative clauses is not always straightforward, as there are a number of problematic types of clause. See the discussion in J. Carruthers, *Oral Narration*, 13–14 and 30–31.

20   For discussion of the PS in this role, see W. Ayres-Bennett and J. Carruthers, *Problems and Perspectives. Studies in the Modern French Language* (London, Longman, 2001), 178–179. For further discussion of the term 'bounded events' (i.e. events which have clearly delineated beginnings and ends), see C. Smith, *Modes of Discourse. The Local Structure of Texts* (Cambridge, CUP, 2003).

21   See D. Malrieu, 'Linguistique de corpus, genres textuels, temps et personnes', *Langages* 153 (2004), 73–85.

of written texts).[22] Narrative discourse for Benveniste is primarily associated with *histoire* (precisely because it is thought of as 'written'), leaving oral narrative to sit rather uncomfortably in the *discours* category.[23] Revaz's classification turns Benveniste's model into a tripartite one, arguing that narrative should be divided between a *plan d'énonciation* where the speaker is involved (*liée*) and where the main narrative tense is the PC, and one where the speaker is not involved (*autonome*, main narrative tense PS), thus separating out oral discourse that is non-narrative (i.e. *interaction*) from that which is narrative (*diégétisation liée*):

Figure 1

Categorisation by ...			
Plan d'énonciation (Benveniste)	Histoire PS	Discours PC	
Plan d'énonciation (Revaz)	Diégétisation autonome PS	Interaction PC	Diégétisation liée PC

When we look at the patterns found in new storytelling against these categorisations, we find that no one of the above models applies neatly to the genre. Rather, there are a number of possible patterns of tense distribution, listed here in order of frequency:

- PC/PRN: alternation on the narrative line between the PC and the *présent narratif* (PRN) (i.e. Benveniste's *discours* or Revaz's *diégétisation liée* with the widely-attested oral feature of tense switching to the PRN)
- PC as the main narrative tense (the classic pattern for Benveniste's *discours*, or Revaz's *diégétisation liée*)

22   E. Benveniste, 'Les Relations de temps dans le verbe français', *Problèmes de linguistique générale* (Paris, Gallimard, 1966), I, 69–82.
23   Weinrich posits a similar division in terms of 'attitudes de locution'. See H. Weinrich, *Le Temps* (Paris, Seuil, 1973).

- PS/PC alternation on the narrative line (a pattern not normally attested in oral French, not accounted for in models such as Benveniste or Revaz, but common in contemporary journalistic narratives and attested in literature)[24]
- PRN/PC/PS alternation on the narrative line (a very rare pattern generally in Modern French which is also rare here)
- PS as the sole narrative tense (i.e. the classic pattern for written literary narrative, of histoire or *diégétisation autonome*)
- PRN as the sole narrative tense (a very rare pattern here).

The two dominant patterns are fundamentally those found in *diégétisation liée*. Moreover, tense switching between PC and PRN is extremely common and is a well-attested feature of oral narration across many languages.[25] It is used in new storytelling for functions which have been explored by a large number of scholars of contemporary oral French and medieval narratives alike, notably for foregrounding of particular events, for marking

24 PS/PC alternation is well-attested in journalistic discourse, where much research has been done on the pragmatic effects produced by certain temporal strategies, e.g. foregrounding particular events using the PS in an otherwise PC text, using the PC to 'frame' certain sections of text. See D. Engel, *Tense and Text. A Study of French Past Tenses* (London, Routledge, 1990); L. Waugh and M. Monville-Burston, 'Aspect and discourse function: the French simple past in newspaper usage', *Language* 62 (1982), 846–877. However, a number of observations on PS/PC alternation in literature can be found: see H. Boyer, 'L'Opposition passé simple/passé composé dans le système verbal de la langue française', *Le Français moderne* 47.2 (1979), 121–129; A. Judge, 'Choix entre le présent narratif et le système multifocal dans le contexte du récit écrit', in S. Vogeleer et al. (eds), *Temps et discours* (Louvain-La-Neuve, Peeters, 1998), 215–235. Note that all the apparent cases of three-way alternation in the corpus (i.e. PRN/PC/PS) are not in fact clear-cut. Rather than finding all three tenses in the same sections of discourse, in some stories the patterns involve two-way alternation (PRN/PC or PC/PS) in any given section. Moreover, this group of stories raises the problematic issue of the form 'dit' (i.e. third person singular of both PRN and PS) which is notoriously difficult to classify with absolute certainty (the classification is normally based on the alternation patterns in the surrounding text). We seem therefore not to be dealing with Judge's 'système multifocal' in these stories. For more discussion, see Carruthers, *Oral Narration*, 56.

25 The literature on this topic is vast. For discussion and further references, see Fleischman, *Tense and Narrativity* and Carruthers, *Oral Narration*, Chapter 3.

borderlines between narration and direct discourse, for the *verba dicendi* in direct discourse, for structural shifts between sections in the discourse, for events where there is heightened subjectivity, and for narrative peaks.[26] Several of these functions appear in (1) below, a narrative peak which occurs at the end of a *conte*:

> (1)   il y avait une petite mare **elle s'est penchée** sur la mare pour se remettre ses cheveux en place/ je vous passe les détails/ **il l'a poussée** *il noue* [il a noué] un voile tout blanc autour d'un cœur tout palpitant/ il faut dire la vérité il le regrettait déjà mais c'était déjà trop tard/ il rentrait chez lui il voyait plus le chemin **il est arrivé** dans l'impasse *il pousse* la porte **il a trébuché** sur le palier ça lui a fait tellement mal qu'*il s'écrie* aïe mon pied/ et le cœur de la mère lui *dit*/ tu t'es fait mal mon fils. (*Couple*)[27]

Tense-switching of this type is a hallmark of interactive narrative, of stories told by a narrator to an audience, both present in the discourse context, and both involved in the communicative context of storytelling.

The remaining four patterns, although not characteristic of oral discourse, are attested in other types of narrative, be they literary or journalistic. There does thus appear to be a significant difference between narrative and non-narrative discourse, whether we adopt a minimal definition of a narrative such as Labov and Waletsky's in Section III above, or a definition which focuses on larger stretches of discourse such as Carlota Smith's, where it is broadly accepted that narrative discourse mode is characterised by a dominance of structures (narrative clauses) conveying events that take

---

26   For a detailed discussion with examples, see Carruthers, *Oral Narration*, Chapter 3.
27   Transcription conventions:
Bold and underline = Passé composé on narrative line
Bold and italics = Narrative present
Italics = Free indirect discourse
[ ] = repetition of narrative verb
/ = pause
// = long pause
\ = falling intonation
® = laughter
M = music

place in anaphoric sequence.[28] In other words, within the options found in different types of narrative in French, while patterns attested in a communicative context of interactive narrative dominate, there are instances where tense patterning is more typical of *histoire*, or *diégétisation autonome*, where the PS is the main narrative tense, or where there is PS/PC alternation. We shall return to this in Sections V and VI.

IV.2 Speech and thought presentation

Speech and thought presentation (STP) concerns the ways in which events and discourses are reported in a narrative and is closely connected to the question of point of view, or focalisation. Leech and Short present the range of STP forms as a continuum, with a high degree of narratorial control at one end, and the voice of the characters at the other, presented either without any introduction by the narrator (free direct discourse) or with accompanying *verba dicendi* (direct discourse):[29]

Figure 2

Narrator apparently in total control		Narrator apparently in partial control + ∏ –		Narrator apparently not in control at all	
Narrative Report of Action NRA	Narrative Report of a Speech Act NRSA	Indirect Discourse ID	Free Indirect Discourse FID	Direct Discourse DD	Free Direct Discourse FDD

28 See Smith, *Modes of Discourse*, and the discussion of 'Narrative' in S. Marnette, *Speech and Thought Presentation in French. Concepts and Strategies* (Amsterdam, Benjamins, 2005), Introduction.

29 Figure 2 is adapted from G. Leech and M. Short, *Style in Fiction: A Linguistic Introduction to English Fictional Prose* (London, Longman, 1981), 324.

To use Rimmon-Kenan's terminology, 'focalisation' concerns the way in which events and discourses are focalised – either through the narrator's perspective (external focalisation) or directly through the perspective of a character in the narrative (internal focalisation).[30] External focalisation can be further subdivided into 'external focalisation from without' (i.e. the narrator presents outward manifestations of the objects (things, appearances, discourses)), whereas with 'external focalisation from within', the narrator-focaliser can present the thoughts or feelings of characters. In new storytelling, external focalisation tends to be the norm, and the STP categories that dominate reflect this: NRA and NRSA dominate the narrative line, with Direct Discourse (DD) used to convey the character's discourse, and verbs such as 'se dire' used to present thoughts and feelings. This type of patterning is evident in various types of interactive performed narrative, including medieval 'texts' as well as modern conversational data, the crucial defining feature of the discourse being that it is not the 'absent-author communication' of many literary texts, but 'narrative designed for interactive oral performance'.[31] Like the tense patterns we have observed, contextual factors relating to interactive performance between a narrator and audience are important.

Exceptionally however, patterns can be detected that are more typical of self-conscious, pre-planned discourse, notably literary techniques for internal focalisation, or for creating ambiguity with respect to narrative voice. Internal focalisation is usually conveyed using strategies such as interior monologue, free direct discourse, subjective description and free indirect discourse (FID), the last two often being difficult to distinguish from

30   For detailed explanation of these categories, see Marnette, *Speech and Thought Presentation*, Part I, Chapter 1.

31   For a discussion of this patterning in contemporary conversational narration, see J. Carruthers, *Oral Narration*, and for a comparison of patterning in the *chanson de geste* and new storytelling, see J. Carruthers and S. Marnette, 'Tense, voices and point of view', in E. Labeau, C. Vetters and P. Caudal (eds), *Sémantique et diachronie du système verbal français* (Amsterdam, Rodopi, 2007), 177–202. The quotation is from Fleischman, *Tense and Narrativity*, 91.

each other.[32] Interior monologue is not found in this corpus of *néo-contes*, and free direct discourse (FDD) is not in fact normally used for internal focalisation.[33] However, although rare, there are nonetheless potential examples of FID and subjective description which correspond to the classic type found in literary texts, where focalisation can be shifted from that of the narrator to that of the character, or, as is often the case, ambiguity can be created with respect to point of view.[34] Examples are not only rare, but almost always ambiguous, in the sense that although some FID features might be attested in a given context (notably lexical items, exclamations or questions associated with the subjectivity of the character), in the absence of deictics attributable unequivocally to the character (explicit markers of the character's 'here and now'), it is not always possible to be certain that the subjective elements are not attributable to the narrator:

> (2)   il achevait de charger son fidèle camion Sam d'un casier de limonade et de quatre-vingt-dix-neuf casiers de vin rouge/ cuvée Sénéclauze appellation non contrôlée au grain fleuri ®/ à livrer d'urgence au débit de boissons du canton de Port Louis\ était-ce l'opacité de la brume/ / M le silence des ténèbres / / la moiteur du brouillard / / il y avait quelque chose de pas normal de pas naturel de pas catholique dans l'air. (Camion)

Here it is especially the series of three questions and the repetition of 'pas + adjective' which suggest free indirect discourse, although it is of course possible to interpret these as the direct discourse of the narrator asking the

---

32   For a discussion of the linguistic properties of these categories with examples, see Marnette, *Speech and Thought Presentation*; and Carruthers and Marnette, 'Tense, voices and point of view'.

33   In practice, FDD in the oral *conte* functions in a similar manner to DD. Instances of FDD are separated out in terms of intonation and pitch from the narrative line, and often involve the *conteur* adopting features of the 'voice' of the character in question.

34   Note that FID has been attested in spoken discourse and in medieval texts, though it often differs in a number of ways from the classic FID found in modern literary texts. See L. Polanyi, 'Literary complexity in everyday storytelling', in D. Tannen (ed.), *Spoken and Written Language: Exploring Orality and Literacy* (Norwood, Ablex, 1982), 155–170; Marnette, *Speech and Thought Presentation*, Part II, Chapter 1.

questions. There are also many examples of phrases such as 'que faire?' and 'quoi faire?' which are arguably cases of FID, i.e. of the character's internal focalisation, the equivalent of 'que fallait-il faire?'. Here again, though, these could be considered direct discourse (of the narrator), or as cases of free direct discourse (of the character). We shall return in Sections V and VI to the implications of this.

IV.3 Linking constructions[35]

It is common in linguistic research to find the observation that the oral medium makes heavier use of parataxis and of adverbs, connectors and coordinators, than of complex subordination:

> One of the most widely recognised features of *oral* narrative, artistic or conversational, is its paratactic organization. Formal apparatus for textual cohesion, in particular for coordination and subordination, is often at a minimum, with clauses merely juxtaposed asyndetically or linked by the minimal connectives 'and' or 'then'.[36]

These views have not gone unchallenged and certainly need to be nuanced. In conversational French, Jeanjean quotes evidence of complex subordination in young children's speech.[37] Elsewhere, scholars have focused on the reason why the patterns observed by Fleischman might be found, i.e. that they are not a reflexion of a less sophisticated form of discourse, but rather a function of patterns of information structuring in different types of discourse, media and registers.[38]

---

35   The results presented in this section are a summary of those in Carruthers, *Oral Narration*, Chapter 4. See also the discussion in J. Carruthers, 'Oralité et expression de la séquence temporelle', in P. Caudal and J. Carruthers (eds), *Temporalité et structuration dans la narration orale* (Amsterdam, Rodopi, forthcoming).

36   Fleischman, *Tense and Narrativity*, 185. See also M. Riegel, J.-C. Pellat and R. Rioul, *Grammaire méthodique du français* (Paris, PUF, 1994), 473.

37   C. Jeanjean, 'À propos de l'utilisation des conjonctions chez les enfants', *Recherches sur le français parlé* 5 (1983), 191–209.

38   For example, Blanche-Benveniste, drawing on Halliday, demonstrates that the differences in the way in which narrative events are recounted between oral discourse

What then does the data in new storytelling suggest about this type of discourse? First of all, iconic sequence dominates and temporal sequence is the default interpretation. The key distinction here is that between narrative and non-narrative modes of discourse, since the default interpretation of temporal sequence is a fundamental characteristic of narrative discourse across many different theoretical perspectives.[39] Second, as some commentators predict, the two dominant types of structure between narrative clauses are parataxis (51% of instances), and minimal connectives (i.e. *et, et puis* and *alors*: c. 41% of instances), together accounting for over 90% of structures.[40] Factors relating to the 'composition in performance' aspect of storytelling are highly relevant here in terms of the way in which information is structured: the 'additive' nature of composition in a context of live performance encourages the accumulation of a series of narrative clauses, rather than the non-linear patterns created by many subordinating constructions. Moreover, it is possible that issues around register are important: as we have seen, the connectors attested in new storytelling (*et, et puis, alors*) tend towards the informal end of the spectrum.

Although they are rare (there are only eleven examples in the entire corpus used), there are some interesting features about the subordinate

---

and newspaper *faits divers*, is largely attributable to the demands of information structuring in the two media, the oral medium being much more likely to recount the events in iconic sequence. See C. Blanche-Benveniste, 'De la rareté de certains phénomènes syntaxiques en français parlé', *Journal of French Language Studies* 5 (1995), 17–29. See also P. Koch, 'Subordination, intégration syntaxique et "oralité"', in H.L. Andersen and G. Skytte (eds), *La Subordination dans les langues romanes: actes du colloque international, Copenhague* (Copenhagen, Munksgaard, 1995), 13–42.

39   See for example Smith's definition of 'Narrative' mode (Smith, *Modes of Discourse*), or Moeschler's directional model which draws on Relevance Theory and on Segmented Discourse Representation Theory (J. Moeschler, 'L'Ordre temporel dans le discours: le modèle des inférences directionnelles', in A. Carlier, V. Lagae and C. Benninger (eds), *Passé et parfait* (Amsterdam, Rodopi, 2000), 1–11). Note that all such theories allow for circumstances where an interpretation of narrative sequence can be overridden.

40   Similar patterns are attested in conversational narration and in traditional *contes*, but with a different distribution of particular connectors. See J. Carruthers, *Oral Narration*, Chapter 4, for a detailed discussion of the statistics.

clauses which are in fact attested. First, all but one preserve iconic sequence. Second, there is a much greater variety of subordinators than in the conversational narrations and the traditional *contes* with which they are compared in Carruthers (2005), where *quand* is the main temporal subordinator. Also, tense patterning in the subordinate and main clauses is highly standardised; non-standard pairings, such as a PS in the subordinate clause and a PRN in the main clause (examples of which are attested in the traditional storytelling data) are not found in the new storytelling data, nor are grammatically controversial forms such as the *passé surcomposé* which also occur in the traditional *contes*. Again, we will return to these observations in Sections V and VI.

As the discussion in Section II implies, although the 'oral' status of new storytelling is a vital part of its description, a binary oral-written divide is unhelpfully reductive and is limited as a tool for linguistic analysis. In Sections V and VI, I shall explore two other models, one where the approach is based on continua, and one which integrates a binary divide, continua, and a multi-parametered dimension.

V Biber (1988): a continuum-based model

In one of the first attempts to quantify differences between oral and written discourse, Biber takes as his starting point a set of 67 linguistic features identified as potentially important by other surveys of oral-written differences, and falling into sixteen major grammatical categories. So, for example, under the category of 'tense and aspect markers', Biber includes 'past tense', 'perfect aspect', and 'present tense'; under 'passives', he includes 'agentless passives' and 'by-passives'. From the statistically significant co-occurrence of these features, Biber posits a series of 'textual dimensions' related to the function of the texts in his corpus, i.e. continua that run from one pole of the dimension to the other, e.g. 'informational vs involved production', 'narrative purpose vs non-narrative purpose', 'explicit vs situation-dependent reference', 'overt expression of persuasion', 'abstract vs non-abstract information', 'on-line informational elaboration'.[41] Different types of text can then be positioned along each dimension. For example, for Dimension 1, 'Involved vs Informational Production', Biber proposes the following (Figure 3).[42]

We can see along this dimension that some types of discourse have a very high score in the 'involved' direction (e.g. telephone conversations), whereas others tend towards the 'informational' pole (e.g. official documents), with many varieties of discourse at points in between.

What Biber finds, when all six dimensions are analysed, is that there are no dimensions where there is an absolute dichotomy between spoken and written genres. There are some dimensions with clearer patterns (spoken genres tend to have high scores for involved productions, situation-dependent reference, and non-abstract information), but there are no clear-cut divides and many cases of overlap, where types of 'spoken' discourse can be positioned on the continuum close to 'written' forms and vice versa. As Biber puts it, 'no

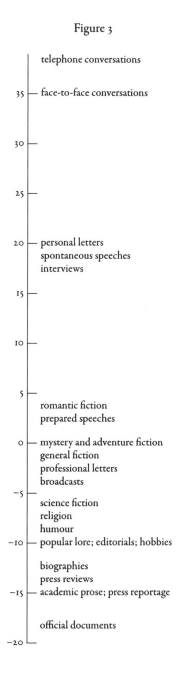

Figure 3

telephone conversations

35 — face-to-face conversations

30 —

25 —

20 — personal letters
spontaneous speeches
interviews

15 —

10 —

5 —
romantic fiction
prepared speeches

0 — mystery and adventure fiction
general fiction
professional letters
broadcasts

−5 —
science fiction
religion
humour

−10 — popular lore; editorials; hobbies

biographies
press reviews

−15 — academic prose; press reportage

official documents

−20

41   See Biber, *Variation*, Chapter 6.
42   Biber, *Variation*, 128.

absolute spoken/written distinction is identified [...]. Rather, the relations among spoken and written texts are complex and associated with a variety of different situational, functional, and processing considerations.'[43]

The strengths of this type of model are obvious. First, it is evidence-based, building the model from a quantitative analysis of the attested features. Second, it allows for a more fine-grained analysis according to quantities of features rather than a black-and-white categorisation. Third, it allows the properties of different spoken and written genres to be analysed and explored according to relevant factors, without imposing an assumed linguistic divide such as an oral-written one. Performed oral narrative is not one of the genres included in Biber's project, but in principle, the same methodology could be used to analyse its linguistic features, and to place new storytelling along each of Biber's six textual dimensions. It is difficult to assess, without doing the analysis, how well this would work for new storytelling and how the results would look, but it would be interesting to analyse the positioning of a 'genre' that is particularly complex in terms of its relationship with oral and written discourse. For example, we would expect 'informational vs involved production' to be important, with new storytelling likely to be placed at the 'involved' end of the spectrum; 'narrative vs non-narrative purpose' is crucial, and we would expect the discourse to show 'narrative' features. But other dimensions may be more difficult to score; for example, 'on-line informational elaboration' produces some unexpected cooccurrences for Biber (i.e. features associated with very formal informational discourse cooccurring with features associated with very informal spoken discourse), and could be particularly interesting for new storytelling given the blend of 'pre-planned' and 'spontaneous'. 'Explicit vs situation-dependent reference' is also complex in the case of new storytelling, since there are two levels of reference – that of the storytelling context (shared with Biber's 'face-to-face conversation'), and that of the story itself (shared with Biber's 'general fiction' and 'romantic fiction'). Moreover, Biber's model could be enhanced greatly by incorporating the findings of recent research, notably the possibility of tense-switching rather

---

43   Biber, *Variation*, 24–25.

than consistent past tense usage in narrative discourse (the latter is one of Biber's features).

VI Koch and Oesterreicher (2001): combining binary, continuum and multi-parametered factors

Following on from Söll's work,[44] Koch and Oesterreicher propose a model that posits three distinct but interrelated notions, i.e. 'réalisation médiale', 'conception' and 'comportement communicatif'.[45] Of these, 'réalisation médiale' is a binary divide concerned with an objective categorisation of the medium as either 'oral' (phonique) or 'written' (graphique). The idea of 'conception' involves a continuum associated with formality and register. 'Conception orale' would be placed at one end of the continuum, Koch and Oesterreicher citing a spontaneous conversation as an example; a legal text is cited as an example of a type of discourse at the 'conception écrite' end of the spectrum. 'Comportement communicatif' is the most complex of the three notions, and is of particular interest in the case of new storytelling since it involves situational and contextual factors that pertain to the performance. It is a multi-parametered notion, where each parameter allows for a continuum running from one pole to the other. The following figure shows the sorts of parameters involved, with the two poles of the continuum shown for each parameter:

---

44 L. Söll, *Gesprochenes und geschriebenes französisch* (Berlin, Schmidt, 1983).
45 P. Koch and W. Oesterreicher, 'Gesprochene Sprache und geschriebene Sprache (Langage parlé et langage écrit)', in G. Holtus, M. Metzeltin and C. Schmitt (eds), *Lexikon der romanischen Linguistik* (Tübingen, Max Niemeyer Verlag, 2001), I.2, 584–627.

Figure 4[46]
Paramètres pour caractériser le comportement communicatif des interlocuteurs par
rapport aux déterminants situationnels et contextuels

①	communication privée	communication publigue	❶
②	interlocuteur intime	interlocuteur inconnu	❷
③	émotionnalité forte	émotionnalité faible	❸
④	ancrage actionnel et situationnel	détachement actionnel et situationnel	❹
⑤	ancrage référentiel dans la situation	détachement référentiel de la situation	❺
⑥	coprésence spatio-temporelle	séparation spatio-temporelle	❻
⑦	coopération communicative intense	coopération communicative minime	❼
⑧	dialogue	monologue	❽
⑨	communication spontanée	communication préparée	❾
⑩	liberté thématique	fixation thématique	❿
etc.			etc.

So for example, 'communication privée' is opposed to 'communication publique', 'ancrage actionnel et situationnel' is opposed to 'détachement actionnel et situationnel' and so on.

What might this model offer an analysis of the *néo-conte*? In the case of 'réalisation médiale', and notwithstanding the caveats expressed above, a new storytelling performance is clearly a case of 'réalisation orale', normally involving a medium transfer from 'réalisation écrite' to 'réalisation orale'. As far as 'conception' is concerned, this is variable according to a number of factors such as individual performance context, storyteller, nature of the story etc., with certain types of oral performance close to the 'conception écrite' end of the spectrum and others less so. The approach taken in training sessions at centres such as the *Conservatoire de Littérature Orale* in Vendôme, and works on the art of oral storytelling such as Bruno De La Salle's *Plaidoyer pour les arts de la parole*, suggest strongly that the desired goal is an oral performance where the language is 'un usage élaboré de la parole', closer to a literary text than a conversational narration.[47]

46 Koch and Oesterriecher, 'Gesprochene Sprache', 586.
47 See J. Carruthers, *Oral Narration*, 58–60, for a discussion of attitudes in training to linguistic issues such as tense usage and subordination vs parataxis/adverbials. See

The picture as regards 'comportement communicatif' is more complex, but it is here that Koch and Oesterreicher's model may have most to offer. An oral storytelling performance is almost always in a context of 'communication publique', a case of 'co-présence spatio-temporelle' (narrator and audience are present) and 'fixation thématique' (in the sense that a particular storyline is followed), but the other parameters can vary to differing extents. For example, in public performances, the audience is often unknown to the storyteller, but this is not always the case; there is often strong emotionality, but not necessarily; parameters 4 and 5 would normally suggest 'détachement', but storytellers have a number of techniques for creating an impression of reducing that detachment; stories are often, but not always, monologues;[48] and, as our earlier discussion suggests, new storytelling lies somewhere on the spectrum between 'communication préparée' and 'communication spontanée'.

The challenge with respect to the *néo-conte* is to see whether the linguistic patterns attested can be mapped against the model, and in particular, to explore to what extent there are correlations between co-occurrence of features and particular configurations of the 'comportement communicatif' parameters, the latter determined by a host of factors influencing the performance context such as audience size, intimate versus impersonal relationship with the audience, degree of spontaneity, emotional content of the specific story etc. So for example, the dominant temporal patterns of PC and PC/NPR alternation, as well as the dominant STP patterns, the high levels of parataxis and the particular connectors used, may be related both to questions of 'conception', and to issues around some of the parameters under 'comportement communicatif', such as high degrees of emotionality, 'co-présence spatio-temporelle', 'co-opération communicative intense' etc. A very important question would be whether, for example, use of the *passé simple*, or of particular subordinating clauses, or of particular STP strategies such as FID, may be linked to a set of 'conception' features

---

also B. De La Salle, *Plaidoyer pour les arts de la parole* (Vendôme, CLIO, 2004), 26.

48 In most cases, the speaking subject remains constant, even though the *locuteur* changes regularly. However, in some cases, there is audience participation.

and/or different configurations of the parameters in 'comportement communicatif'. One interesting observation is that in the corpus used for my initial 2005 study, there is evidence of the cooccurrence of some of these features. For example, classic examples of FID tend to occur especially in *contes* where the main narrative tense is the PS, thereby perhaps suggesting that it is a feature likely to occur alongside other markers of 'conception écrite', and/or of a 'comportement communicatif' which may show a different distribution of parameters from the majority of *néo-contes*. Similarly, the proportion of subordinators occurring in *contes* where the main narrative tense is the PS is also high relative to the low use of the PS overall in the corpus.

In order to attempt to map linguistic features in the *néo-conte* against a model such as Koch and Oesterreicher's, a method for evaluating 'conception' and the parameters under 'comportement communicatif' would have to be developed, that would take into account objectively measurable criteria. Otherwise, there would be a danger of circularity in the argument. Moreover, in the particular case of the *néo-conte*, a way of including factors such as the type of *conte* (*conte merveilleux vs légende vs randonnée* etc.) would have to be incorporated into the version of the model used. Alongside the issues raised in this Chapter around medium and performance context, there are of course a host of sociolinguistic issues concerning the gender, age and background of the *conteurs*. So far, from the initial survey in 2005, there is no strong evidence that story type, or gender, or age influences the patterns found, but these variables too would need to be tested on a larger corpus. If a method for measuring some of the criteria included in Koch and Oesterreicher's model could be developed, not only could we see whether clear correspondences emerge, but we might also be able to investigate some of the apparently more problematic patterns, such as PS/PC alternation, or, more rarely, PS/PC/PRN.

VII Conclusions

A brief survey of three linguistic phenomena in the *néo-conte* points not only to a complex oral-written dynamic, but also to the need for an analysis that goes beyond the limitations of that binary divide. Approaches such as Biber's, and more especially Koch and Oesterreicher's, offer models that incorporate key elements of the performance context in new storytelling, and through which the complex positioning of the *néo-conte* with respect to factors connected to the oral-written dynamic might be captured more satisfactorily. Crucially, once the mapping of linguistic features against such a model is complete, a fuller analysis could be undertaken of *why* the patterns operate as they do.

Tense switching in French oral narratives

PATRICK CAUDAL

Tense switching is a very widespread phenomenon in oral narratives. Observed patterns suggest linguistically motivated choices on behalf of the narrator rather than a random distribution. Metaphorically, tenses are used by narrators pretty much as colours by painters – they are used to signal a wide range of communicative purposes, and therefore are crucial to achieving a number of narrative aesthetic effects. The goal of this Chapter is to make use of formal concepts elaborated around tense, aspect and discourse structure, so as to account for these distributional phenomena.

I Introduction: theoretical prerequisites

I.1 On some essential aspectuo-temporal concepts

Since the present paper proposes to analyse the distribution of tenses in oral narrative through the prism of contemporary research on tense and aspect, it is necessary to define some basic aspectuo-temporal concepts.

I will define event structure as the aspectual contribution of a clause (which is independent of the tense used). Event structures are determined by several parameters, namely (i) telicity (which refers to the existence of a natural and necessary endpoint for a given event description, tested by 'in <duration>' phrases – the modifier must then measure the duration of the event, not (at best) some preceding interval); (ii) dynamicity (dynamic events involve a 'controller', and are non-stative; dynamicity is tested with progressives (including periphrastic progressives such as *être en train de* in French), as stative predicates are known to be marginally compatible with such tenses):

(1)   Mona ate the pancake in five minutes. (telic sentence)
(2)   #/*Erwan was sick in five minutes. (atelic sentence)

I will define the aspectual contribution of tenses in terms of 'aspectual viewpoints' (AVPs), distinguishing three canonical classes of AVPs:[1]

- Imperfective AVPs focus on a sub-part of the 'core' stage of an eventuality, cf. so-called 'imperfect(ive)s' (e.g. the French *imparfait*);
- Perfective AVPs focus on the whole 'core' stage of an eventuality; cf. so-called 'aorists' (e.g. the French *passé simple*);
- Resultative AVPs focus on result stages/states; cf. perfects (e.g. the English present perfect).[2]

Besides these canonical AVPs, there exist a host of 'hybrid' non-canonical AVPs, which can be either underspecified AVPs or AVPs of a given canonical class whose contextual uses are starting to exhibit traits normally associated with another canonical class.[3]

---

1   The term is borrowed from C. Smith, *The Parameter of Aspect* (Dordrecht, Kluwer, 1991); it conveys the speaker's perspective on the development of an eventuality (as described by a verb, its complement and modifiers). However, the typology of viewpoints I defend here differs from Smith's. For more, see P. Caudal and L. Roussarie, 'Aspectual viewpoints, speech act functions and discourse structure', in P. Kempchinsky and R. Slabakova (eds), *The Syntax, Semantics and Acquisition of Tense and Aspect* (Dordrecht, Kluwer, 2005), 265–290.

2   See Dahl's 'perfect questionnaire' in Ö. Dahl, *Tense and Aspect in the Languages of Europe* (Berlin, Mouton de Gruyter, 2000); and also P. Caudal and L. Roussarie, 'Brands of perfects and the semantics/pragmatics interface', in P. Denis, E. McCready, A. Palmer and B. Reese (eds), *Proceedings of the 2004 Texas Linguistics Society: Issues at the Semantics-Pragmatics Interface* (Somerville, Cascadilla Press, 2006), 13–27.

3   See V. Nedjalkov, *Typology of Resultative Constructions* (Amsterdam, Benjamins, 1988); J. Bybee, R. Perkins and W. Pagliuca, *The Evolution of Grammar: Tense, Aspect and Modality in the Languages of the World* (Chicago, University of Chicago Press, 1994); Dahl, *Tense and Aspect*; and P. Caudal and C. Vetters, 'Passé composé et passé simple: sémantique diachronique et formelle', in E. Labeau, C. Vetters and P. Caudal (eds), *Sémantique et diachronie du système verbal français* (Amsterdam, Rodopi, 2007), 121–151.

I.2　Semantics and pragmatics of tenses in discourse

The present account will rely on a two-layered conception of linguistic interpretation, involving (i) propositional contents (which cover the compositional semantic contribution of an expression) and (ii) illocutionary force/ speech acts (which correspond to the communicative purpose pursued by the speaker by using a certain linguistic device. Thus the illocutionary force of an utterance can be classified in three broad categories: assertive, interrogative or jussive).[4]

The fact that semantic phenomena are primarily tested through the distribution and interpretation of explicit morpho-syntactic markers (e.g. aspectual or temporal phrases), will be here regarded as a key methodological principle. It will be an equally important methodological principle that vice versa, semantico-pragmatic or pragmatic phenomena can be tested through discourse structure. Following the work carried out by Asher and Lascarides, discourse structure will be determined here through discourse relations (DRs), $R(\alpha, \beta)$, connecting discourse segment α (roughly speaking, an utterance), to the discourse context via an attachment site β (another, previously uttered discourse segment).[5] If, following again Asher and Lascarides, we view DRs as 'relational speech acts', then whatever linguistic expression contributes to establishing discourse structure is an illocutionary force indicator (IFI), in the sense proposed by Bierwisch.[6]

It is now a well-known fact that the semantic and pragmatic content of tense markers are key parameters in calculating discourse relations and temporal ordering in discourse – two mutually dependent processes.[7]

4　See, for example, A. Papafragou, 'Epistemic modality and truth conditions', *Lingua* 116 (2006), 1688–1702; and M. Faller, 'The Cusco Quechua reportative evidential and rhetorical relations', in P. Austin and A. Simpson (eds), *Endangered Languages* (Hamburg, Helmut Buske Verlag, 2007).

5　N. Asher and A. Lascarides, *Logics of Conversation* (Cambridge, CUP, 2003).

6　See M. Bierwisch, 'Semantic structure and illocutionary force', in J.R. Searle, F. Kiefer and M. Bierwisch (eds), *Speech Act Theory and Pragmatics* (Dordrecht, Reidel, 1980), 1–35.

7　The idea, held for many centuries, that tenses encode *per se* instructions about temporal ordering has been proven to be inaccurate in the early 1990s, but attaching

To illustrate this, consider the DR *Narration*. *Narration*(α, β) connects discourse segments α (= attachment site) and β (= new segment to be attached to the discourse context) such that the eventuality e_α underlying α precedes and causes the eventuality e_β underlying β. Thus, in (3), we have *Narration*(π_1, π_2) and e_{π_1} causes and precedes e_{π_2}.[8] If we replace the *passé simple* in (3)/π_2 with the *imparfait* as in (4)/π_4, then we get a very different temporal ordering: e_{π_4} overlaps with e_{π_3} $(e_{\pi_3} \subseteq e_{\pi_4})$ – and we must now establish *Background*(π_3, π_4):

(3) Yannig *pressa* l'interrupteur (π_1). Il *fit* noir dans la pièce (π_2).
(4) Yannig *pressa* l'interrupteur (π_3). Il *faisait* noir dans la pièce (π_4).

As they constrain DRs, i.e. relational speech acts, tenses can therefore be regarded as IFIs.[9] This conclusion also fits nicely with the notion of AVPs, as they express the speaker's subjective perspective on the development of eventualities: such a perspective can hardly lack an illocutionary dimension.

Following Caudal and Roussarie, I will define *Illocutionary Viewpoints* (IVPs) as the semantico-pragmatic content of tenses.[10] IVPs are trans-categorical insofar as they cut across the domains of time, aspect, modality and evidentiality (four semantic categories to which tense affixes contribute); they reflect the *polyfunctional nature* of tenses. IVPs convey a 'light',

---

the contribution of tenses to their deep discursive function is an already ancient hypothesis. For more, see E. Benveniste, *Problèmes de linguistique générale, tome 1* (Paris, Gallimard, 1966) and H. Weinrich, *Le Temps* (Paris, Seuil, 1973). For a detailed discussion about the interaction of DRs with tense-aspect in computing temporal order in discourse, see W. de Mulder and C. Vetters, 'Temps verbaux, anaphores (pro)nominales et relations discursives', *Travaux de linguistique* 39 (1999), 37–58; and Asher and Lascarides, *Logics of Conversation*.

8 A speech act referent, often noted π within the SDRT framework, is an abstract object of discourse endowed with an underlying propositional content K.

9 See Caudal and Roussarie, 'Aspectual viewpoints'; and P. Caudal and C. Vetters, 'Les Temps verbaux: des connecteurs temporels qui s'ignorent?', in E. Moline, D. Stosic and C. Vetters (eds), *Les Connecteurs temporels du français* (Amsterdam, Rodopi, 2007), 105–137.

10 Caudal and Roussarie 'Aspectual viewpoints'.

pragmatic kind of linguistic convention, through discourse structure – cf. the so-called 'perfective' or 'narrative' uses of the French *imparfait*, which are triggered by the establishment of *Narration*, cf. (5a) vs (5b):

(5) a. Maigret *descendait* les escaliers. (imperfective viewpoint reading only)
b. L'instant d'après, Maigret *descendait* (e_1) les escaliers et *traversait* (e_2) le couloir pour sortir. (perfective viewpoint reading: $e_1 < e_2$)

These illustrate a recent change in IVP (such uses are not attested before early modern French).

II Tense alternations in epic narratives

We will now apply the theoretical tools discussed in section I to tense alternations in oral narratives (I will assume the reader to be familiar with common SDRT DRs), starting with a corpus of oral performances of epic narratives by French professional storytellers.[11] It comprises fragments of *L'Odyssée* by B. De La Salle (BDLS), *Le Kalevala* by G. Bizouerne, *La Geste hilalienne* by N. Aceval, and *L'Exil des fils d'Uisliu* by P. Caudal.[12]

Of course, we must bear in mind that tense alternations have been identified as a widespread phenomenon in written communication too,

---

11   I will rely here mainly on evidence stemming from discourse structural properties captured by DRs to characterise the semantic and pragmatic behaviour of tenses, unlike some existing works on tense alternations which lack such a concept as DRs. See, for example, L. Waugh and M. Monville-Burston 'Aspect and discourse function: the French simple past in newspaper usage', *Language* 62 (1986), 846–877; and S. Fleischman, *Tense and Narrativity. From Medieval Performance to Modern Fiction* (London, Routledge, 1990).

12   Note that the first performance of this particular epic was given in 2004, long before I undertook the present work as a linguist; my present theoretical concerns did not play any role in the shaping of this narrative.

particularly in literary fiction, cf. Judge's concept of 'multifocal tense systems', exemplified in (6):[13]

> (6) Il *nota* l'information. Le téléphone *sonna*. Non, il n'avait rien à déclarer pour le moment, l'enquête suivait son cours. On ferait un point presse dans la soirée. Je me demandais s'il allait parler de moi aux journalistes. Il *a décroché* un autre téléphone et *a ordonné* qu'on le fasse entrer. Et celui qui *entra*, l'air complètement perdu, c'était Daniel Lescure, le père de Magali. (Marie Nimier, 'Une enfant disparaît', in *Le Monde – Nouvelles de l'été* 13.07.2003, 11)

One of the notable characteristics of multifocality in (6) is that dialogues are generally fused with the body of the text – thereby achieving an apparent 'oralisation'. However, such a 'style' should be dubbed as 'polyphonic' (in the sense used by Ducrot) rather than as 'oral(ised)', in a traditional sense.[14] Indeed, 'multifocality' as in (6) is in fact characterised by the absence of a clear distinction between the narrator's contribution and 'true' dialogue; and this, by definition, is what Ducrot called polyphony – a highly literary device which Flaubert initiated in French in his famous 'style indirect libre' ('free indirect style'). Moreover, it should be noted that in oral narratives, attempts at polyphony, i.e. at blurring the dialogue/narration distinction, are limited and very sparingly used, for fear of causing the audience to fail to recognise whether the narrator is 'incarnating' some character or not at a given point of the narrative. Incarnations are often marked by multiple, simultaneous means in storytelling performances: direct speech, physical/vocal cues, variation of tone, disruption of eye-contact, etc. Storytellers cannot afford to mix up different possible sources for a given utterance;

---

13   A. Judge, 'Le Passé simple: un retour aux sources dans le contexte du mélange des temps?', in Labeau, Vetters and Caudal (eds), *Sémantique et diachronie*, 153–176. It is worth noting that 'multifocal' implicitly makes reference to Genette's theory of focalisation and point of view. See G. Genette, 'Discours du récit', in *Figures III* (Paris, Seuil, 1972), 65–278; and *Nouveau discours du récit* (Paris, Seuil, 1983). In turn, these should be related to Ducrot's notion of 'polyphony'. See O. Ducrot, *Les Mots du discours* (Paris, Minuit, 1980); and *Dire et ne pas dire* (Paris, Hermann, 1991). These two theories centre on the creative instability of the actual source of a given utterance, which is almost a defining characteristic of modern and post-modern fiction.

14   Ducrot, *Les Mots* and *Dire*.

they must carefully signal whenever they alternate between their own voice and that of a character. Polyphony is therefore at best marginal.[15] In other words, the (almost) *sine qua non* condition for the apparition of Judge's 'multifocal system' is ... written communication. Calling it 'oral' is rather ironic, as Judge's 'multifocality', far from being born of the conversion of written codes to oral codes, actually casts a text's small remnants of orality (i.e. dialogues) into a literary, written mould.

One must therefore look for explanations other than multifocality in order to account for tense system alternations in oral narratives. A close study of these alternations within the present corpus of epic narratives will reveal some telling linguistic regularities in the contextual and discourse-structural conditions governing them.

II.1 Distributional facts: tenses in epic narratives

A detailed survey of this present corpus suggests that the *passé simple* (PS) system is the main tense system used in epic narratives; it alternates locally with the *présent* (PR) system, cf. (7), and more rarely with the *passé composé* (PC) system:

> (7) Seul le divin Ulysse et son fils Télémaque, / Restaient en la grand'salle à songer aux manières / D'assurer leur vengeance. / Alors, sans qu'un seul mot s'envolât de leurs lèvres, / Ils *s'élancent* tous deux, *portent* au trésor / Les casques et les lances et tous les boucliers. / Puis, leur tâche achevée, Télémaque *rentra* / Vers son logis, à la lueur des torches. (BDLS, *Odyssée*)

---

15 I have conducted a brief corpus study of this phenomenon, and noted that whatever could count as instances of 'polyphony' generally resulted from mishaps in the narration – i.e. when the storyteller failed to make it clear she had alternated between dialogue and narration. Almost inevitably, the narrative segment at stake sounded confusing to the audience. For detailed observations on 'polyphony', see J. Carruthers, *Oral Narration in Modern French. A Linguistic Analysis of Temporal Patterns* (Oxford, Legenda, 2005), 92 *et seq.*

Now the fact that this corpus only comprises isometrically versified narratives might be a tempting explanation for the rarity of analytical tenses (i.e. those presenting a discontinuous morphology, e.g. the PC). However, analytical forms are attested within epic narratives, notably in dialogical passages. Some such instances can be found in (8)–(10):

> (8) Mais, dès lors que l'on *eut quitté* la ville sainte, / Jamais plus tu ne vins, je ne te sentis plus / Embarquée à mon bord pour me garder des maux. (BDLS, *Odyssée*)
>
> (9) Puisqu'ils n'en *ont* rien *fait*, que Zeus les récompense (...) ! (*ibid.*)
>
> (10) Athéna s'avança. Elle *avait pris* les traits / D'un jeune pastoureau. (*ibid.*)

Tense alternation therefore raises deeper issues than metrical economy. I will try here to demonstrate that it is mostly governed by the function of tenses at the semantics/pragmatics interface (via IVPs), which interacts closely with utterance parameters.

One apposite example is that there appears to exist a correlation between the sort of utterance situation at stake and the occurrence of analytical tense systems, particularly a mixed tense system, comprising the PC, the PR and the *imparfait*, a system which often occurs within direct appeals to the audience. Consider the introductory part of an epic tale. It is generally characterised by such a direct address to the audience, and possibly to heroes, or mythical authors (bards/scalds...) of the tale (see (11) below).[16] Such passages typically involve dialogical discourse relations, or at least bear on requests rather than on mere propositions (e.g. *Elaboration*(π_2, π_3) in (11)):[17]

> (11) Voici qu'un désir me *saisit*, / L'idée m'*est venue* à l'esprit / De commencer à réciter (...) / D'entonner le chant de famille (...) (π_1). / Frère aimé, compagnon chéri / Beau camarade de jeunesse, / *Viens* vite chanter avec moi (π_2), / *Approche*-toi pour réciter, (π_3) / Puisque nous voici réunis, / Provenant de lieux différents (...). (*Le Kalevala*, G. Bizouerne)

16   These are thus symbolically invoked.

17   See Asher and Lascarides, *Logics of Conversation*, 293.

Most of the turning points of an epic tale (climax/conclusion/opening of an episode...) can potentially be treated as dialogical 'interfaces', where the narrator-speaker/audience-addressee relation is foregrounded in the narrative. The nature of the speaker's discourse is altered; it leaves the realm of the (epic) narrative *stricto sensu* to enter that of a (sometimes formally more relaxed) dialogical/conversational narrative, characterised by the more abundant use of the PR and PC (as opposed to their relative rarity in other parts of epic tales).[18] And in fact, such dialogical/conversational passages are not exceptional at all, and are not even limited to turns in the narrative, particularly within folk tales, as we will see below.

Utterance parameters can trigger tense alternations in other contexts, e.g. with actual incarnations/dialogues. The fact that two verbs (a) and (b) (often *verba dicendi*) are separated by a direct discourse segment seems to makes it easier for tense alternations to occur, such as the PS (a) / PR (b) alternation in (12):[19]

> (12) Et puis [Athéna] *reprit* (a) / ses beaux et nobles traits de jeune femme habile:/
> « ...Il serait astucieux, celui qui, par les ruses, / Pourrait te surpasser, inlassable trompeur ! (...) » / Elle *rit*, il *répond* (b): « Quel mortel, ô Déesse, / Pourrait te reconnaître ? » (BDLS, *Odyssée*)

In addition to dialogues and dialogical contexts, tense alternations can be triggered by other contextual or discourse-structural factors, such as segmentation in sub-episodes, or changes within information structure.[20]

---

18 See Carruthers, *Oral Narration*, 49–50, for more on the characterisation of the PC as a conversational tense.

19 The existence of a strong correlation between PS to PR or PR to PS alternations with *verba dicendi* in oral narratives was first noted in Fleischman, *Tense and Narrativity*, 60, who saw in it the signal of a shift from *diegesis* to *mimesis*; see also Carruthers, *Oral Narration*, 72: '[such shifts] help to transform the narration into performance'. Indeed, it is important for the storyteller to 'smooth the edges' of changes in voice – these cannot be performed in quick, snappy successions for obvious reasons; hence the anticipated or prolonged use of the PR around a piece of dialogue within a narrative in a past tense (a fact also mirrored by prosody).

20 The relation between tense alternation, discourse segmentation and change in discourse topic (and more generally, information structure) is a hypothesis dating back

Thus the PR/PS alternation is often associated with a temporal connective such as *alors* (13), or a temporal adverbial, more rarely a gerundive or past/present participle apposition such as *saisissant* in (14), or some other non-finite temporal expression, functioning like a 'lock' between two different aspectuo-temporal systems (note that shifting back to the PS after a PS/PR alternation seems not to require any specific factor; I will assume this to be a consequence of the fact that the PS is the base, unmarked tense). Such expressions typically mark the beginning of a new sub-episode; and indeed, at least some have been described as 'temporal discourse frame introducers', setting up a new discourse topic, that is, a sub-episode within a narrative[21] – somehow comparable to 'turn-taking' in dialogue.[22]

> (13) Et d'où il arrivait. Mélanthios leur *dit*: / « Deux mots! O prétendants de la plus noble reine! / L'étranger, que voici, je l'ai vu tout à l'heure, / Mené par le porcher, mais j'ignore son nom. » / Antinoos, **alors**, *fait* querelle au porcher: / « Porcher te voilà bien! » (BDLS, *Odyssée*)
>
> (14) «Il te fallait encore amener celui-là ! / Que chacun des convives lui donne autant que moi, / Et pour trois mois entiers, il videra les lieux !» / Il *dit*. Et, **saisissant** un tabouret, le *lance*. / Ulysse *fut atteint* en pleine épaule droite. (BDLS, *Odyssée*)

These configurations facilitating tense alternation are all more or less based on combinations of contextual factors and discourse structural parameters. For example, switching from narration to dialogue alters (i) the source of an utterance (ii) discourse structure; discourse markers such as *plus tard* ('later') or *le lendemain* ('the day after') are either deictic or

---

at least to Wolfson. See N. Wolfson, 'The conversational historical present alternation', *Language* 55.1 (1979), 168–182. Also see Carruthers, *Oral Narration*, 83 *et seq.*, for a recent discussion.

21   See L. Vieu et al., 'Locating adverbials in discourse', *Journal of French Language Studies* 15 (2005), 173–193, 178–179. See also Carruthers, *Oral Narration*, 123, for a discussion of the interest of 'frame adverbials' as discourse structuring devices in different oral genres: Carruthers found that these are more frequent in conversational discourses, and less frequent where events proper are the main driving force behind the story line.

22   See H. Sacks, *Lectures on Conversation* (Oxford, Blackwell, 1992).

comparative items – and therefore crucially involve some relation to the speaker's perspective, beliefs, and communicative attitudes. This supports the hypothesis that a study of the distribution of tenses in oral narratives should be undertaken at the semantics/pragmatics interface.[23]

II.2 Tenses at the semantics/pragmatics interface in 'general' narratives

In order to make sense of the deep nature of the semantic/pragmatic factors underlying tense alternations in oral epic narratives, we need first to have some general notions about their behaviour in unmarked narrative contexts.

I will begin with alternations between a PR-centred tense system (including the periphrastic progressive 'être en train de') and a PS-centred tense system (alongside the *imparfait*), as these are fairly common in general narrative discourse.

The PR is very underspecified and capable of many diverse communicative uses, spanning both the domains of conversation/dialogue and narration (where we find the so-called 'historical present', generally described as a 'perfective' tense, and functioning very much like the PS). Narrative uses of the PR are widespread, and have attracted considerable attention.[24] They are often explained in terms of 'narrative proximity' or 'zooming'.[25] This intuitive analysis captures an essential characteristic of this particular

---

23 See Fleischman, *Tense and Narrativity*; and Carruthers, *Oral Narration*, for a similar interim conclusion.

24 See Fleischman, *Tense and Narrativity*; H. Chuquet, 'Construction d'événements et types de procès dans le récit au présent en français et en anglais', in J. Guillemin-Flescher (ed.), *Linguistique contrastive et traduction* (Gap, Ophrys, 1994), III, 1–56; and J. Bres 'De l'alternance passé composé/présent en récit conversationnel', in A. Borillo, C. Vetters and M. Vuillaume (eds), *Variations sur la référence verbale* (Amsterdam, Rodopi, 1997), 125–136.

25 See Fleischman's 'visualising' PR in *Tense and Narrativity*. I am putting aside the alleged 'dramatising' function of the narrative PR (see, for example, Fleischman's 'action' PR in *Tense and Narrativity*), which does not correspond to the fact observed here – namely, sequences of PR in oral storytelling are often used to convey sequences

alternation: it is clear that the PS and the PR differ in terms of temporal order with respect to the speech time interval (i.e. R<S vs R=S within a Reichenbachian framework); in the case of the narrative PR, the speaker effectively acts as if the speech time interval was shifted into the past; this is part of the narrative PR 'zooming' effect.

Following Bres's analysis, a more general 'enunciative zooming' function could even be ascribed to the narrative PR.[26] Bres noticed that the PR becomes omnipresent if the narrative is very informal and addressed to a familiar person; he argues that this fact supports the view that the narrative PR marks a (relative) 'neutralization of the speaker/addressee distinction.'[27]

However this should not lead us to conclude that the narrative uses of the PR involve a relative non-implication of the speaker, as in the case of the PS: although the speaker/addressee relation is arguably affected with narrative uses of the PR, it does not vanish. Additional evidence further dividing the narrative PR from the PS can be found in their respective semantic content. While the perfective viewpoint content of the PS is semantically inherent to this tense, it is only (pragmatically) conferred by the discourse context to the PR; this suggests that the two tenses express very different IVPs/AVPs.[28] The PR patterns like the *imparfait* in this respect, insofar as

---

of 'microscopic events', and not at all 'peak' events. See Bres, 'De l'alternance', 128, for a related analysis.

26   Bres, 'De l'alternance'.

27   I believe that an additional argument in favour of Bres's analysis in 'De l'alternance' can be in the found in the fact that generic uses of the PR can be modelled as involving *modals*, or modal-like functions (i.e. functions *à la Kratzer* quantifying over possible worlds – see G. Carlson and F. Pelletier, *The Generic Book* (Chicago, Chicago University Press, 1995)); they are in this sense evaluative (and subjective), while also conveying the belief that the 'rule' or 'law' expressed in this way is indiscriminately veridical for both speaker and addressee.

28   I will assume here a unified, monosemist approach to the semantics of tenses in general, following Caudal and Roussarie's methodology in 'Aspectual viewpoints' (but see also Bres, 'De l'alternance'). I will therefore not distinguish several separately conventionalised instances of PR, as Fleischman does in *Tense and Narrativity*. Thus Fleischman's distinction between the 'action' vs 'visualising' PR is not a matter of there existing

it requires a temporal succession context to achieve its narrative, perfective-like interpretation, as shown in the following example:[29]

(15) Il fait nuit maintenant $(\pi_{\scriptstyle 1})$. Brian tourne une page dont l'ombre balaie lente-ment la table $(\pi_{\scriptstyle 2})$. L'entendant soupirer à nouveau, il *lève* la tête vers sa femme $(\pi_{\scriptstyle 3})$. Elle regarde fixement devant elle, de ses yeux aux cernes bleu pâle $(\pi_{\scriptstyle 4})$. Enfin Erica tourne la tête $(\pi_{\scriptstyle 5})$. Un instant, leurs regards se croisent $(\pi_{\scriptstyle 6})$; et puis ils baissent les yeux l'un et l'autre $(\pi_{\scriptstyle 7})$.

Narration$(\pi_{\scriptstyle 2}, \pi_{\scriptstyle 3})$ is licensed by the addition of the adjoined participle *entendant*, which provides a causal event for $e_{\pi 2}$, and forces a perfective viewpoint interpretation of the PR; without this participle, we could have established *Background*$(\pi_{\scriptstyle 2}, \pi_{\scriptstyle 3})$. And vice versa, without *fixement* in $\pi_{\scriptstyle 4}$, which causes $e_{\pi 4}$ to be treated as an imperfectively viewed event and trig-gers *Background*$(\pi_{\scriptstyle 3}, \pi_{\scriptstyle 4})$, we could have established *Narration*$(\pi_{\scriptstyle 3}, \pi_{\scriptstyle 4})$. The availability of such imperfective readings for the PR contrasts with their impossibility for the PS (which blocks *Background*): the PR is not a seman-tically perfective viewpoint tense.

Also, the use of the narrative PR within sports reports is characteristic of the conversational flavour of the PR, as opposed to the PS. In this sort of interactional context, the speaker acts as a 'witness' to the unfolding action, lending her perspective to the addressee (they are one, so to speak). In a sense, the narrative PR marks both a dialogue and a monologue, as opposed to narratives in the PS (which mark neither, strictly speaking). And *contra* the PS, it is rather easy to combine the PR with explicit dialogical markers (interjections etc.) and, more generally, with direct discourse markers.[30]

---

several distinct PRs, but rather a matter of discourse structure (DRs) and other contextual interpretative phenomena operating on a unified semantics: the 'action' PR clearly involves *Narration*, while the 'visualising' PR involves *Background*.

29   The example is borrowed from Chuquet, 'Construction d'événements', 51.

30   In contrast to the 'zooming effect' of the PR, the alleged 'remoteness effect' of the PS will be explained by two mutually dependent facts: (i) it does not have any form of present relevance nor marks anything about the speaker/addressee relationship, and (ii) it is a non-conversational narrative tense (thus blocking dialogical and argu-mentative DRs, such as *Explanation*; see below).

Let us move now to the contrast between the PS and the PC. Recent linguistic literature has firmly established a number of crucial differences between these tenses. For instance, while the PC can be ascribed both perfective viewpoint and resultative viewpoint readings, the PS can only receive perfective viewpoint readings.[31] Thus, the PS blocks reverse causal order in discourse (18b) while the PC allows it (18a).[32] Allowing reverse causal ordering is a well-known typological property of perfects[33] (cf. Östen Dahl's 'perfect questionnaire'), which can introduce abductive, argumentative, subjective ordering of events in discourse:

(16) a. La maîtresse *a giflé* mon fils. Il *est arrivé* en retard.
       b. #La maîtresse *gifla* mon fils. Il *arriva* en retard.

By and large, then, the PS can be described as the narrative tense *par excellence*; of course, it most readily appears within a formal/elevated type of discourse, generally reflecting some sort of conscious norm, as much of its morphology is by now hardly mastered by average native speakers of French. However, it is not completely proscribed, even from less formal oral narratives, as we will show.[34] The PS can be regarded as a 'non-subjective'

---

31   It is a perfect tense with 'aoristic' features – see Caudal and Vetters 'Passé composé et passé simple'. See also A. Borillo et al., 'Tense and aspect', in F. Corblin and H. De Swart (eds), *Handbook of French Semantics* (Stanford, CSLI Publications, 2004), 233–348; and Caudal and Roussarie, 'Aspectual viewpoints'. The PC is indeed compatible with quite a few aspectuo-temporal adverbials expressing the present relevance of the resultant state (cf. *Jean a quitté son bureau* **maintenant** / **depuis une heure** ; *Jean n'a pas faim, il a déjà mangé*, etc.), and is generally capable of present relevance readings (cf. *A: Est-ce que je peux voir Jean? B: Non, il a quitté son bureau*), on top of being able to combine with past temporal modifiers (cf. *hier*) to introduce past events – a complex capacity which designates the PC as a 'double tense-aspect', both present resultative (present perfect) and past perfective.

32   See L. De Saussure, 'Quand le temps ne progresse pas avec le passé simple', in A. Carlier, V. Lagae and C. Benninger (eds), *Passé et parfait* (Amsterdam, Rodopi, 2000), 37–48; and P. Caudal, 'Reverse causo-temporal ordering and perfective viewpoint tenses', talk given at *Chronos 8* (University of Texas at Austin, 2008).

33   Dahl, *Tense and Aspect*.

34   See also Carruthers, *Oral Narration*.

narrative tense: it allows the speaker to present a flow of eventualities 'as is', without subjectively, argumentatively re-arranging its causo-temporal ordering. Most importantly, the PS remains incompatible with abductive, argumentative discourse structures even in the presence of certain connectives normally licensing it, such as 'donc'. Thus in (17) and (18), although 'donc' has a strong illocutionary force-level and subjective content, the preferred interpretation remains based on normal (and not reversed) causal order.[35] The PS even rejects the sort of argumentative inference illustrated in (19a) and (19b):

(17) a. Pierre *est tombé*. Donc Jean l'*a poussé*.
     b. Pierre *tomba*. #Donc Jean le *poussa*.
(18) a. Il *a reçu* un pot de fleurs sur la tête. Donc il *est passé* sous un balcon.
     b. Il *reçut* un pot de fleurs sur la tête. #/??Donc il *passa* sous un balcon.
(19) a. On *a vérifié* HR(1), HR(2), HR(3), donc on *a fondé* la récurrence. (web corpus)
     b. ??On *vérifia* HR(1), HR(2), HR(3), donc on *fonda* la récurrence.

This confirms again that the PS has purely non-argumentative, non-conversational/dialogical illocutionary functions. When used in narration, it causes the skein of eventualities to unwind itself, the speaker refraining from interposing her subjectivity in the narrative process. As a matter of fact, during their training years, most storytellers are taught that causal/temporal ordering of events is the keystone of narratives; it is no surprise

---

35   See L. Degand and H. Pander Maat, 'Scaling causal relations and connectives in terms of speaker involvement', *Cognitive Linguistics* 12 (2001), 211–245. The discourse structural notion of *discourse relations* used here to capture the essence of the PC/PS opposition contrasts with Carlota's Smith's notion of 'discourse mode' in *Modes of Discourse* (Cambridge, CUP, 2003) used in Carruthers, *Oral Narration*. Smith's model suffers from the fact that it does not apply to identifiable elementary discourse units, so that its empirical and theoretical predictions are impossible to verify (this also follows from the fact that it has not been formally implemented). However, as a very general textual tool (somewhat like the traditional Benveniste or Weinrich approaches), Smith's 'discourse modes' suffice to formulate certain important empirical generalisations. Thus, Carruthers's characterisation of the PC as a 'conversational tense' in *Oral Narration* is extremely similar to the present analysis.

then that the PS remains well alive within oral narratives even nowadays, as we will see, although it is generally associated with the more elaborate and formal kind of narrative (or pertaining to a culturally well-established genre, such as fairy tales).[36]

In sharp contrast, being a resultative tense (as a former perfect) among other things, the PC can get back to the speaker's *hic et nunc*, i.e. to the utterance parameters at the heart of a conversational discourse setting.[37] In narratives in which the PS or the PR are the non-marked tenses of narration, we will see that the PC is clearly connected with this sort of communicative shift (comments and digressions often appear in the PC; and indeed, these are inherently conversational). Owing to its 'present relevance' nature, it is quite clear why the PC is the favoured tense for casual narratives, which are closer to conversation than to formal/sustained narration. And indeed, narratives in the PC hardly belong to 'sacred language' – legendary, epic and/or mythological.[38] I believe that this is the only sound explanation for a phenomenon traditionally described in terms of register. The PS is not so much a 'noble', archaic tense (although some forms of that tense arguably are, such as the 1st and 2nd person) as a non-conversational tense, which therefore, cannot be used within matter-of-fact contexts, as these almost always turn out to be conversational, for obvious communicative reasons. On the other hand, a proper, sustained narrative cannot be structured altogether like an informal neighbourhood chat. The apparent register difference between the PC and the PS is in fact mostly a by-product of deep semantic and pragmatic differences between these tenses.

36   It is thus unsurprising that Carruthers found that the PS was rare in contemporary performances of 'néo-contes'. See Carruthers, *Oral Narration.*

37   Borillo et al. even argue in 'Tense and aspect' that the semantics of the PC introduces an *Elaboration* relation upon a topic event corresponding to the utterance time. While this notion is somewhat problematic when a past topic event is elaborated upon by an utterance in the PC, there is nevertheless something appealing about such an analysis, as it clearly marks the PC as a conversational tense.

38   'Grand parler' in the sense used by P. Clastres in *Le Grand Parler. Mythes et chants sacrés des Indiens Guaranis* (Paris, Seuil, 1974).

II.3 Back to tenses in epic narratives and the semantics/pragmatics interface

Now if we get back to the analysis of tense alternations in epic tales initiated in section II.1, it seems natural that the PS/PC or PS/PR alternation is mostly triggered within dialogical and conversational passages, rather than within purely narrative passages. With both alternations, the PC and PR are manifestations of a speaker's *hic et nunc* (the narrator or some character). It is for instance very telling that the narration by Odysseus (to Athena) of his arrival in Ithaca should be in the PC (20), and not in the PS; this demonstrates the speaker-centred, conversational nature of the passage (which is in fact yet another lie on the part of Odysseus!):

> (20) (...) Je ne fais que passer / Avec mon chargement, pour aller à Pylos. / Perdus dans la tempête, les rameurs *ont* enfin / *Découvert* cette rade. Du creux de leurs navires, / Ils *ont tiré* mes biens et m'*ont abandonné*. (BLDS, *Odyssée*)

And when Odysseus addresses his son Telemachus in order to reveal his true identity, again he resorts to the PC, a fact which highlights the eminently personal (and emotional) nature of that exchange:

> (21) Je ne suis pas un dieu, c'est moi qui suis ton père ! / Celui qui t'*a coûté* tant de pleurs et d'angoisses. / Tu ne verras jamais d'autre Ulysse que moi ! (...) / Tu m'*as vu*, tout à l'heure, sous les traits d'un vieillard, / Tu me vois, maintenant, un homme jeune encore. / Il est facile aux dieux de donner gloire ou honte ! (*ibid.*)

Similarly, interpolated clauses in the PC within a narrative using the PS-system acquire a very speaker-centred status; they directly express the narrator's subjectivity. This is for instance the case for the following comparison, which, being evaluative, is indeed subjective:

> (22) Il leur *prit* à tous deux un besoin de sanglots, / Sanglots plus déchirants que celui de l'oiseau / Auquel un paysan *a ravi* ses petits. (BDLS, *Odyssée*)

More generally, the PS/PC alternation is triggered whenever the speaker's utterance stance is altered. Thus in (23), the utterances in the PC represent comments, i.e. argumentative speech acts at a 'meta-discursive' level, in so far as the bard is taking his own narrative as the object of this section of discourse. The narrator is standing back from his earlier, narrative discourse stance; indeed, the PC is used in (23) to convey some sort of causally-reversed discourse relation between α and β – the SDRT *Explanation* discourse relation. And while the PC is perfectly compatible with such a meta-discursive (and in fact meta-narrative) illocutionary function, the PS is not. In (23), *es tombée* cannot be replaced by *tombas*:

> (23) Pendant seize ans, chaque nuit, / Ils lancèrent du Connaught / Des attaques vengeresses. / Ces coups de mains incessants / Firent que pendant seize ans / L'Ulster pleura et trembla. / Mais la prophétie funeste / N'est pas encore accomplie. Deirdre femme feu brillant ! (...) / Je dois te chanter encore (α) ! / Tu *es tombée* dans les mains / Du Roi d'Ulster Conchubur (β). (*L'Exil des Fils d'Uisliu*, P. Caudal)

To summarise, PS/PC alternations again reveal the gap between the PS (used for non-conversational narrative purposes, and excluding inter-sub-jective adjustments in communication) and the PC (which has a set of complementary uses in narration).[39]

III Generalising the analysis: tenses in folk tales

I will now try to generalise the above results by analysing a corpus of tra-ditional folktales in French, mostly originating from the 'Pays Gallo' (a French speaking area of Brittany where Breton was never used).

The first important observation we can make about this corpus, is that the PR and the PC are generally the default, unmarked tenses.[40] The PS

---

39 This point should be related to another empirical generalisation, namely that the PS and the PC have very different distributions with certain discourse connectives. See P. Caudal, 'Tenses, connectives and narration(s)', talk given at *Chronos 7* (University of Antwerp, 2006); and Caudal and Vetters, 'Passé composé et passé simple'.

40 See Carruthers, *Oral Narration*, 54, for similar observations.

is not proscribed, though; it alternates with the PR-system in some tales, in a manner that almost looks like free variation. However I will try and show below that these alternations are again linguistically self-conscious choices obeying deep communicative concerns.

The fact that the PS is not the most frequent 'base' tense for folk tales is already meaningful in itself: it corresponds to a correlation between narrative registers and the semantic/pragmatic function of tenses (see section II.2). By and large, three main narrative registers can be distinguished (and interestingly, some oral traditions are based on a similar tripartite classification):

    (i)   Conversational narration (i.e. anecdotes, jokes, informally told folk tales – e.g. 'menteries' ('tall tales'), etc.). This is daily-life narration; it shares many common features with plain dialogical interaction (the most notable of which is the possibility to construe abductive (causally reverse) discourses);

    (ii) Sustained prose narration; this is the register of most folk-tales, which reflect more or less conventionally established genres;

    (iii) Sustained 'formal' narration (involving verse and/or conventional formulaic devices, and/or some form of musical arrangement / singing / chanting / scansion...): e.g. epic or mythological tales.

We will see that the PS is ruled out in (i), (mostly) marked in (ii) and (mostly) unmarked in (iii). Vice versa, the PC is dominant and unmarked in (i), frequent and alternatively marked or unmarked in (ii), (relatively) rare and marked in (iii).

III.1 On the intrusions of the imparfait in PR-based traditional tales

It is obvious that one should carefully distinguish between 'truly present', speaker-centred uses of the PR (which refer to her *hic et nunc*) and narrative uses of the PR, which report past eventualities (see II.2). Indeed, narrative uses of the PR trigger tense sequence effects (very much like a 'covert' past tense), e.g. in commentative/evaluative clauses in the *imparfait* such as π_1 in (24) and (π_4) in (25):

(24) Il prend la galante en selle, et le voilà parti à la recherche de la bête. Dame, c'*était* pas facile (π_1)! I marche, i marche longtemps (π_2), i regardait partout (π_3). Et puis, il la trouve près d'une grande caverne. ('La Bête à sept têtes', in *Contes populaires du pays de Guérande*, 39–44)

(25) Il [Jean] aperçoit des arbres (π_1). C'étaient (??ce sont) des noyers (π_2). On avait gaulé les noix et un bonhomme essayait de les ramasser (...) (π_3). Il *arrivait* (π_4) (??arrive) pas, bien sûr ! (*ibid.*)

It is obvious that in (24) / (25), it would have been impossible for the speaker to make her comment in the PR, since it would have resulted in confusing the actual *hic et nunc* of the narration with the shifted, fictional, past temporal location of the described events. From a 'covert' past, one is forced to move towards an 'overt' past. Note also that using the PR 'regarde' in (24) would have licensed *Narration*(π_2, π_3) (i.e. the walking and the looking events would not have overlapped) since it could have described a non-iterated change-of-state event. This observation confirms that lexical aspectual factors also play a role in tense alternations (albeit marginally).

The requirement to use the *imparfait* within such commentative/evaluative clauses plus deictic constructions (such as exclamatives) should not surprise us; the former are, according to Potts, conventional implicatures, and crucially involve the speaker's subjectivity intruding within the narrative.[41] Deictics too are speaker-centred markers. Again, we are led to the conclusion that tense alternations are communicatively grounded.

III.2   Tales with mixed systems PR/PS

Let us turn now to tales where the PR/PS systems co-exist in an apparent free-variation manner, such as (26) and (27):

(26) Par ma foi, je *vais* vous raconter les aventures de Bras-de-Fer qu'était un bonhomme pas ordinaire. Dès son plus jeune âge, il désirait connaître le monde. Il lui fallait un solide bâton. Il le COMMANDA chez jagu, le fogeron (...) et SURVEILLA la confection de la canne. *Et puis, en route !* (...)

41   C. Potts, *The Logic of Conventional Implicatures* (Oxford, OUP, 2005).

Il enjambait les rivières, sautait les montagnes (...). Il APERÇUT (...) un autre géant comme lui, qui essayait d'abattre un moulin avec une meule de grès.
– Que fais-tu là ? lui *crie* Bras-de-Fer.
– Tu le vois, je détruis mon moulin qui ne me rapporte plus rien. (...)
– Veux-tu me suivre ? (...)
Et les voilà partis à l'aventure (...).
À quelques jours de là, un fleuve très large leur BARRA le passage. Un troisième géant y prenait un bain. (...) Bras-de-Fer le HÉLA (...). Les deux colosses S'EMPOIGNÈRENT. Bras-de-Fer TERRASSA son adversaire qui lui DIT :
– Tu es un rude combattant ! (...)
– Veux-tu nous suivre ? DEMANDA Bras-de-Fer.
– J'accepte !
Ils *partent* tous les trois, et marchent très longtemps... Ils *entrent* dans un grand bois et *s'arrêtent* dans une clairière, devant une maison silencieuse. Ils *frappent*... Rien! Ils *entrent*... Personne! (...) Ils *décident* de séjourner quelque temps. (...) Le premier jour, Meule-de-Moulin *pose* la marmite sur trois pieds et *souffle* le feu...(...) Au tour de Bras-de-Fer. Plus malin, il *examine* d'abord le foyer, et tout-à-coup *découvre* (...) une petite bête (...). Nos trois géants *suivent* cette trace (...). Un lion maître de la ville, *passe* chaque soir dans les rues et *choisit* une proie parmi les habitants. Bras-de-Fer *se sent* de taille à le combattre. Le lion *arrive* en rugissant. Un vigoureux coup de bâton l'*étend* raide mort. Les géants *entrent* dans la maison et y *trouvent* trois jeunes et belles femmes (...). [Bras-de-Fer] *est* maintenant maître des trois belles filles et de leur troupeau. Il ÉPOUSA la plus belle et l'EMMENA dans sa maison forestière. Il y VÉCUT désormais heureux à faire des fagots et à garder des moutons.
Il y est encore, s'il n'est pas mort!
('Bras-de-Fer', in *Contes populaires du pays de Guérande*, 45–48)

(27) C'étaient un bonhomme et une bonne femme qu'avaient une fille Jeannette.
Un soir, son galant VINT la voir:
– Comme t'es belle et biscornette, ma Jeannette. Qu'il lui *DIT*.
Alors vous pensez si la fille était contente, les parents aussi!
– Dame! que dit la mère, j'vas toujours ben aller chercher un cruchon de vin à la cave.
Elle *descend*, *met* la bue sous la clé de la barrique, *ouvre* le robinet. Mais elle pensait dans sa fille. (...) elle S'ASSIT le menton dans la main.
Au bout d'un moment, le bonhomme *SE DIT*: (...). Il S'ASSIT à côté de sa bonne femme. Et la piquette coulait toujours. La galande s'ennuyait pas trop là-haut, mais tout de même, elle *DIT* : (...) elle S'ASSIT à côté de ses parents, le menton dans la main. Et la piquette coulait toujours. Mon Jean s'ennuyait là-haut, tout seul.
– Qu'est-ce qui lui arrive? I remontent pas! (...) Faut que j'aille voir.

Dame qu'est-ce qu'i *voit* ? Les trois pauvres innocents, assis dans un coin, le
menton dans la main, et la piquette qu'avait coulé partout (...). Il *s'en va* chez
lui, selle son cheval, et le voilà parti dans le monde (...). Il n'ALLA pas loin,
parce qu'il y a pas mal d'innocents dans le monde. Il VIT d'abord un homme
(...). Il faisait chaud, et mon Jean avait envie de se mettre à l'ombre. Il *aperçoit*
des arbres. C'étaient des noyers (...).
– Et voilà mon troisième innocent! que pensait Jean. Après ça, il me reste plus
qu'à épouser Jeannette.
Et il le FIT. J'étais à la noce: c'est comme ça que *j'ai appris* cette histoire.
('Les Trois Innocents', in *Contes populaires du pays de Guérande*, 61–64)

The opening and closing utterances of (26) involve direct addresses in the
PR. The narration thus starts anchoring discourse within the speech time
interval S, then shifts it to some overt or covert past interval, and finally
anchors it back to S before closing the narrative. We again find a discourse
pattern already identified in epic tales (see also the end of (27)), with communicative purposes governing tense alternations. Communicative purposes thus explain the formulaic passage in the PS ('il epousa ...' etc.) which
precedes the closing line, and which effectively gives the final (meaningful)
event of the sequence.[42] Formulaic utterances in the PS are nevertheless not
limited to the opening and closing of folk tales. In (27) for example, the
repeated utterances of the verb *s'asseoir* in the PS are formulaic in nature.[43]
We also find abundant uses of the PS signalling an important and sudden
turn in the narrative (e.g. 'il vit ...'), or the conclusion of a sub-development
of the storyline, e.g. 'il n'alla pas loin' ..., and 'et il le fit', the latter PS being

---

42   This contrasts sharply with the use of the PR for a close succession of events involving
      the *Narration* DR, i.e. 'Bras-de-Fer se sent de taille... Le lion arrive...' in (27), which
      illustrates the 'zooming effect' of the PR discussed in II.2. These events do not con-
      stitute turns in the narrative; they are in this sense 'microscopic'. These covert past,
      narrative uses of the PR also contrast with the closure function of the (truly present)
      PR in (26) or of the PC in (27); such 'interface' uses correspond to data discussed
      above, cf. (11). On the 'changing section' and closure functions of the PR and PC,
      see Carruthers, *Oral Narration*, 83. These functions have been well-identified in the
      literature.
43   On the formulaic nature of repetition in oral narratives, see J. Derive (ed.), *L'Épopée.
      Unité et diversité d'un genre* (Paris, Karthala, 2002).

also formulaic, in that it illustrates the commonplace conclusion of many fairy tales: 'ils se marièrent et vécurent heureux jusqu'à la fin de leurs jours'. Both types of usage capitalise on the change-of-state, perfective viewpoint meaning of the PS by contrasting it with the semantically non-perfective PR. Such alternations put into effect a deliberate communicative strategy on the part of the speaker.[44]

III.3 Tales where the PS is marked and the PC unmarked, and vice versa

Similar observations can be made about tales where the PC is the base tense. The corpus studied here contained few such tales (mostly of a 'jokey' nature), but PC/PS alternation seemed to pattern very much like PR/PS alternation in the data I analysed. However, when the PS is the unmarked tense, the PC serves to signal the end of an episode, or a comment, by putting forth the speaker's *hic et nunc* again. Example (28) illustrates such uses of the PC.[45] The closing/summarising function of the PC obtains as we have *Result*(π_4, π_5) (triggered by the deictic construction 'ça fait que', with 'ça' referring to a substantial prior segment of discourse), and *Result*(π_1, π_2) (triggered by the deictic construction *velà que* ('voilà que') plus world-knowledge based inferences). Note that the PS would be incompatible with such deictic constructions; they involve a speaker-centred, conversational discourse structure:

(28) Y avait une fois une bonne femme qu'avait deux bœufs qui s'appelaient 'Tout-seul' et 'Tousdeux'. Velà le boucher qui vient pour les acheter. (...) Le boucher trouve que c'est pas cher. Tope pour 300 francs, qu'i dit. Mais les velà qui se disputent car il veut emmener les deux bœufs, et la bonne femme ne veut lui en donner qu'un. (...) La bonne femme est embêtée. A va trouver son voisin qui lui dit (...). Velà donc la bonne femme devant le juge. (...) que dit le juge. (...)

44   See Carruthers's notion of 'turbulence at narrative peaks' (*Oral Narration*, 77), which are indeed characterised (notably) by repetitions, and sudden tense alternations, as in (26)–(27).
45   See also Carruthers, *Oral Narration*, 83–85, for similar data and observations.

que dit le juge (π_1). *Velà la bonne femme qu'a gagné le procès* (π_2). Velà son voisin qu'arrive (π_3) (...). *Ca fait* (π_4) *qu'la bonne femme a gagné les deux fois* (π_5). ('Le Procès gagné', in *Contes du pays de Guérande*, 33–34)

The corpus of folktales studied here has revealed one interesting fact about short, 'jokey' tales (this is true of actual jokes, too): they cannot involve the PS at all, and can only appear with a PC (or marginally with a PR) tense system.[46] This is actually not a surprise, since obviously jokes/'jokey' tales are a highly dialogical, interactional sort of narrative (note in (29) the multiple occurrences of the adjective 'petit', with its strongly dialogical 'hypocoristic' meaning):

> (29) Un hiver, c'était glacé. Un loup *vient* trouver [Renard] pour trouver un moyen de calmer sa faim. Renard, inquiet, ne savait pas si un jour il n'allait pas leur faire un repas [sic]. Il lui *dit:* « Ben, écoute, compère (...) ». Alors ils *ont attrapé* un peu de poissons, et le petit renard *a emporté* tout chez lui, dans sa petite tanière. (...). Eh! oui, le loup *est resté* mais la glace *a grossi, forci, serré, serré* la queue du pauvre loup restée dans l'eau glacée... Il *est resté* là mourir de faim, il ne pouvait plus s'arracher. ('Le Renard de Stanego', recording, Claude LECOZ, Kerbligot, Péaule, K18, in *Contes et Légendes de Haute Bretagne*, 266 *et seq.*)

IV Conclusions

I hope to have demonstrated that tense alternations in oral narratives primarily reflect the communicative goals pursued by the speaker; that is, they depend largely on the function of tenses at the semantics/pragmatics interface, and on how the narrator/speaker makes use of them to achieve particular narrative purposes. If we add to this fact the obvious (although not predominant) presence of linguistic constraints on certain tense alternations (notably due to aspectual lexical factors; e.g. the use of the *imparfait* in (28)), then it appears that the room left for free variation is actually quite

46   See Bres, 'De l'alternance'.

limited. Crucially, tense alternations only make sense with respect to each other; the communicative virtues of a given alternation is, to a large extent, a function of the 'dominant', 'unmarked' tense system in which it occurs, the notion of 'unmarkedness' being local rather than global.[47]

I also hope to have established that a typological approach to oral narratives (even within the apparently unified realm of storytelling) is necessary.[48] According to the observations made about epic versus folk tale narratives, the following generalisations seem to hold:

- In epic narratives:
  o The alternation between PR and PS is relatively frequent, while the PC is relatively rare, and used only to switch back to a conversational communicative strategy (i.e. to express comments, judgments, and generally get back to the speaker/narrator's *hic et nunc*);
- In folktales:
  o Folktales generally exhibit fairly mixed tenses systems, where the PC and PR are the most frequent 'base/unmarked' systems (in such cases, the PS tends to receive 'punch line'/'catastrophic'/formulaic uses) and the PS is comparatively rare, particularly with an unmarked status.[49]

This general contrast between PC/PR and PS reflects the inherent conversational bias of many folktales, which pertain to a less formal/poetic, more conversational genre than epic tales. But these genre-driven generalisations also seem to stem from more fundamental generalisations, related to *marked uses* for each specific tense in a specific context. Thus marked PRs (i.e. when the PC or the PS dominates) are associated with 'narrative zooming' effects (particularly in close successions of events). Marked uses of the PC (with a dominating PS or PR) tend to be meta-discursive/narrative or argumentative/conversational (expressing comments, evaluations,

---

47 See Carruthers, *Oral Narration*.
48 Carruthers reached a related conclusion for what she calls 'report' vs 'stories' – see *Oral Narration*, 121 *et seq*. She showed that the distribution of tenses and discourses connectives was strongly correlated to oral genre considerations; she also highlighted the strong conversational bias of the PC.
49 See Carruthers, *Oral Narration*, for similar observations on an extended corpus of oral storytelling performances.

or closures of local narrative units, by coming back to the speaker's *hic et nunc*). Finally, if the PR or the PC dominates within a narrative sequence, then the PS exhibits marked uses conveying a 'dramatic' turn in the storyline (possibly the end of a sequence), or signalling a formula (often with a liminal function too).

Discourse connectives and other discourse structural items (e.g. frame adverbials) have not been discussed here for want of space; but of course, their interaction with tenses should be studied in a detailed way, as it appears in section II above that tenses exhibit striking differences in that respect.[50] Finally, discourse structural factors have been reduced here to a simplified view of DRs. For instance, the distinction between *coordinating* and *subordinating* DRs has been neglected,[51] although it is undoubtedly an important discourse structural notion; and other important categories such as parataxis vs hypotaxis (i.e. syntactic subordination) have been completely ignored. A thorough study of tense alternations in oral narratives would clearly require the impact of such discourse structural parameters to be clarified, but it remains an open issue for future investigations.

50 See Carruthers's *Oral Narration* for a large number of interesting empirical generalisations with respect to tense distribution with discourse connectives, frame adverbials and other discourse markers in oral narratives. Carruthers mentions the fact that such devices are much more frequent in reports than in conversational narratives such as folk tales. As she suggests, a continuum of discourse genres is at play here, just as epic tales vs traditional folk tales form some sort of empirical continuum. See *Oral Narration*, 123.

51 See L. Vieu and L. Prévot, 'Background in SDRT', in *Proceedings of TALN 2004* (Workshop volume, Fez, 2004), 485–494.

Parallélismes et contes oraux bas-bretons: niveaux, rôles et fonctions

NATHALIE GUÉZENNEC

I Introduction

Les traditions orales utiliseraient – parmi d'autres procédés rhétoriques – le parallélisme comme moyen de création orale.[1] Jakobson définit ce phénomène: 'la correspondance d'une ligne avec une autre, je l'appelle parallélisme. Quand un second élément textuel vient s'inscrire à côté ou au-dessus d'un premier, et qui lui est équivalent, ou opposé, du point de vue du sens, ou qu'il lui est apparenté du point de vue de la construction grammaticale, alors je parle de vers parallèles, et les mots ou syntagmes qui se répondent d'un vers à l'autre, je les appelle termes parallèles.'[2] Le parallélisme peut se rencontrer à chaque niveau de la langue (de la phonologie et la prosodie à la structure syntaxique) mais également à chaque niveau du texte.

Les questions que pose le parallélisme ne se réduisent pas à une compréhension purement stylistique du phénomène. Celui-ci amène à s'interroger sur les rapports entre les constructions parallélistiques, les valeurs

---

1 Voir R. Bauman, *Story, Performance and Event: Contextual Studies of Oral Narrative* (Cambridge, CUP, 1986); J.J. Fox, 'Introduction', dans J.J. Fox (éd.), *To Speak in Pairs: Essays on the Ritual Languages of Eastern Indonesia* (Cambridge, CUP, 1988), 1–28; J. Goody, *La Raison graphique: la domestication de la pensée sauvage* (Paris, Les Éditions de Minuit, 1979); A.B. Lord, *The Singer of Tales* (Cambridge, Mass. et London, Harvard University Press, 2000); M. Parry, *L'Épithète traditionnelle dans Homère* (Paris, Les Belles Lettres, 1928); et J. Vansina, *De la tradition orale, essai de méthode historique* (Belgique, Tervuren, 1961).

2 R. Jakobson, *Questions de poétique* (Paris, Seuil, 1973), 250.

culturelles[3] et les liens qu'unissent les unités parallèles de même niveau et de niveaux différents mais aussi sur la création et la mémorisation orale et sur ses rapports avec la création écrite.[4]

En effet, les genres littéraires oraux et écrits ont été distingués à partir de ces constructions. Même s'il y a des parallélismes dans la littérature écrite, la littérature orale se caractériserait par la présence plus importante de 'répétitions' et de constructions parallélistiques. Goody considère qu' 'il peut y avoir différents degrés de formalisation dans l'expression orale, et il est certain que le recours aux "formules" ou aux effets de parallélisme sémantique est un trait caractéristique de la création orale'.[5]

En suivant Fox qui fait un tour d'horizon des études sur le parallélisme, ces moyens de création orale concerneraient moins les traditions orales indo-européennes, hormis slaves, notamment russes: 'Undoubtedly parallelism of various sorts is a significant feature of other Indo-european poetic traditions as well, but often its occurence is optional, sporadic, or at times subordinate to the requirement of rhyme, alliteration, assonance, and a variety of complex metrical rules'.[6]

---

3   Voir Fox, 'Introduction'; A. Monod Becquelin, V. Vapnarsky, C. Becquey et A. Breton, 'Decir y contar la diversidad: paralelismo, variantes y variaciones en las tradiciones mayas', dans A. Monod Becquelin, A. Breton et M.H. Ruz (éds), *Formas mayas de la diversidad* (Mérida, Universidad Nacional Autónoma de México, à paraître); et A. Rumsey, 'Yaga Kange: a metrical narrative genre from the New Guinea highlands', *Journal of Linguistic Anthropology* 11.2 (2001), 193–239.

4   À partir de leur étude sur les épopées homériques et yougoslaves, Parry (*L'Épithète traditionnelle*) et Lord (*The Singer of Tales*) ont formulé des hypothèses sur la création orale en montrant comment les répétitions facilitaient la composition orale, idée développée par des ethnologues tels que Goody (*La Raison graphique*) et Ong. Ce dernier considère ces textes comme un prototype de l'oralité 'primaire', c'est-à-dire non touchée par l'écriture. Voir W.J. Ong, *Orality and Literacy, The Technologizing of the Word* (London, Routledge, 1982).

5   Goody, *La Raison graphique*, 261. Toutefois, Tedlock (cité par Rumsey, 'Yaga Kange') remet en cause les travaux de Parry (*L'Épithète traditionnelle*) et de Lord (*The Singer of Tales*) en soutenant que les vers métriques sont apparus par l'influence de l'écriture alphabétique ou syllabique.

6   Fox, 'Introduction', 11.

Le parallélisme n'est pas spécifique à la tradition orale poétique, on le trouve dans le conte oral, récit en prose, comme l'illustrent les travaux sur les contes mayas.[7] En outre, les travaux de Bauman sur les contes anglo-américains attestent la présence de parallélismes dans les traditions orales en langues indo-européennes.[8]

Qu'en est-il des contes oraux français? Nous faisons l'hypothèse que:

– Les contes français ont des parallélismes à différents niveaux textuels.
– Les parallélismes ont des fonctions dans la distinction des genres, fonctions mnésique et pragmatique.
– La tradition orale en France, bien qu'ayant été traversée par l'écrit, n'est pas si éloignée des traditions orales non indo-européennes par la présence d'un procédé universel de composition, le parallélisme, qui permet une transmission à long terme des objets immatériels.[9]

Notre corpus, enregistré en Bretagne, est constitué de 11 contes proprement dits et facétieux dont certains ont été créés par leur narrateur et d'autres transmis de bouche à oreille en breton. Tous les contes ont été enregistrés au cours de performances en français.[10]

---

7   Monod Becquelin, Vapnarsky, Becquey et Breton, 'Decir y contar la diversidad'.
8   Bauman, *Story, Performance and Event*.
9   Un certain nombre de contes ont été diffusés par la littérature de colportage puis transmis de bouche à oreille. Aujourd'hui, les conteurs construisent essentiellement leur répertoire à partir de l'écrit (recueil, création individuelle).
10 On parlera de contes français et non de contes bretons, car hormis certains motifs, leur extension dépasse la Bretagne.

II Le Conte et les parallélismes

II.1 Les Formes de parallélisme du conte

Lorsque l'on s'intéresse au parallélisme, on est face aux questions suivantes: 'les entités qui se correspondent par leurs positions ont-elles entre elles un lien de similarité? Jusqu'à quel point? De quelle façon?'. Ces propos attirent l'attention sur les liens tissés entre les unités parallèles, de même niveau et de niveaux différents.[11] Le modèle séquentiel d'Adam semble adéquat pour les dégager, car il définit les relations entre les unités et le texte, lequel est considéré comme une structure hiérarchique comprenant n séquences de même type et de types différents. En tant que structure, la séquence est vue comme:[12]

> – Un réseau relationnel hiérarchique: grandeur décomposable en parties reliées entre elles et reliées au tout qu'elles constituent.
> – Une entité relativement autonome, dotée d'une organisation interne qui lui est propre et donc en relation de dépendance/indépendance avec l'ensemble plus vaste dont elle fait partie.[13]

Une séquence est composée de macro-propositions qui sont des paquets de propositions. La proposition, unité minimale de jugement, est constituée d'un sujet (thème) et d'un prédicat. Adam en dénombre cinq: état initial, complication, évaluation, processus de dégradation, dégradation (dégradation évitée). Une macro-proposition peut être actualisée par une seule ou plusieurs propositions.

Bien qu'intéressant, son modèle présente une certaine rigidité. Notre sujet étant le parallélisme, certaines unités textuelles peuvent être reprises d'une séquence à l'autre et donc être dans une relation d'équivalence. Dès

---

11   Jakobson, *Questions de poétique*, 234–235.
12   J.-M. Adam, *Le Texte narratif* (Paris, Nathan, 1994).
13   Adam, *Le Texte narratif*, 111.

lors, pour nous, les macro-propositions ne constituent pas des catégories finies et s'appliquent à un récit particulier. Ainsi, la macro-proposition, 'L'homme dit au héros qu'il est juste' (*Rismodell an Den Just*), a été dégagée à partir des phrases (et/ou propositions) parallèles se situant dans trois séquences différentes (1,2 et 3):

1. oh ben répond l'homme plus juste que moi tu trouveras pas;
2. en ben plus plus que moi vous trouverez pas;
3. plus juste que moi tu trouveras pas qu'il dit.

Il s'agit donc d'une paraphrase de propositions rendant compte de l'équivalence sémantique des unités parallèles sans les variantes (e.g. identité du narrateur).[14]

Ces parallélismes d'un micro-niveau peuvent composer des parallélismes de niveau supérieur, au niveau de la séquence, les parallélismes séquentiels. À ce modèle, nous ajoutons un niveau supérieur à la séquence, la macro-séquence, composée de plusieurs séquences.[15] Celle-ci permet de rendre compte des suites que l'on peut donner au récit et/ou aux différents développements que l'on peut insérer. Les macro-séquences, plus ou moins autonomes,[16] peuvent se 'répliquer' une, deux ou n fois comme le montre la comparaison des versions des contes recueillies avec celles du répertoire français de Delarue et Tenèze.[17]

Pour dégager ces parallélismes et observer à quel niveau ils se situent et leurs relations avec les autres unités structurelles du récit, notre choix s'est

---

14 Voir la section II.3, 'Les Parallélismes phrastiques et répétitions'.

15 Voir N. Belmont et G. Calame-Griaule, 'Éditorial', *Cahiers de littérature orale* 43 (1998), 7–23. Elles parlent de 'répétitions d'épisodes' qui semblent correspondre aux parallélismes séquentiels et macro-séquentiels. Nous préférons le terme de 'réplication' à celui de 'répétition' qui induit l'idée d'identité, alors qu'il s'agit plutôt d'équivalence.

16 Le schéma 2 montre que le conte peut s'arrêter à chaque frontière de macro-séquence signalée par une ligne horizontale.

17 P. Delarue et M.-L. Tenèze, *Le Conte populaire français. Catalogue raisonné des versions de France* (Paris, Maisonneuve et Larose, 2002).

porté sur le modèle des possibles narratifs de Brémond.[18] En partant du fait
que tout récit s'organise temporellement, un fait advient, se développe et
s'achève selon un rapport d'antécédent, Brémond établit une logique des
possibles narratifs, qui éclaire l'enchevêtrement des actions mais également
les virtualisations et les réalisations. À chaque moment, un choix s'opère
dans le devenir du récit. Son modèle repose sur une triade de base:

Schéma 1: séquence élémentaire reproduit de Brémond[19]

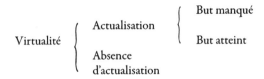

Ces séquences élémentaires se combinent pour engendrer des séquences
complexes. Les récits reposent sur l'alternance de phases d'amélioration et de
dégradation, d'équilibre et de déséquilibre successifs. À partir de ce modèle,
en analysant les bifurcations choisies par le narrateur, il serait possible de
dégager des genres. 'En construisant, à partir des formes les plus simples
de la narrativité des séquences, des rôles, des enchaînements de situations
de plus en plus complexes et différenciés, nous jetons les bases d'une classification des types de récit'.[20] Pour Brémond, tout récit répond à un projet
humain qui s'actualise dans des événements qui peuvent se classer en deux
types fondamentaux: amélioration à obtenir – dégradation à éviter.

En résumé, les différents niveaux de parallélismes peuvent être schéma-
tisés et hiérarchisés ainsi: macroséquence > séquence > macroproposition >
proposition. Le critère principal pour délimiter ces catégories est le niveau
de dépendance hiérarchique que les unités entretiennent les unes par rapport aux autres, de même niveau et de niveau différent. Certaines unités
linguistiques joueraient le rôle de frontière entre unités de même niveau.
Selon les psycholinguistes, le conte s'organiserait autour de l'archiconnecteur

18   C. Brémond, 'La Logique des possibles narratifs', *Communication* 8 (1981), 66–82.
19   Brémond, 'La Logique', 67.
20   Brémond, 'La Logique', 82.

'et' et des coordonnants temporels (puis, alors, ensuite ...). 'Alors' signale les changements d'épisodes (séquences et macro-séquences).[21] Les déplacements spatio-temporels semblent également avoir la même fonction.[22]

II.2 Les Parallélismes macro-séquentiels, séquentiels et macro-propositions

II.2.1 Les Contes proprement dits

Pour illustrer les parallélismes du niveau textuel, nous avons choisi un conte proprement dit,[23] intitulé *Rismodell an Den Just*.[24] Il a été transmis oralement en breton au conteur dans les années trente lors de veillées. Ce conte, appartenant au type T332 *La Mort Parrain*, est d'extension européenne et moyen-orientale. Divers folkloristes l'ont recueilli en Bretagne notamment Luzel, dont la version est très proche hormis la fin,[25] de celle dont nous disposons.[26] Les trois macro-séquences parallèles (en gris) relatent la quête d'un parrain juste. Le héros rencontre tour à tour Dieu, Saint Pierre et l'Ankou.[27] Seul ce dernier sera considéré comme juste et deviendra le parrain du fils du héros.

21   Voir Schneuwly, cité par P. Coirier, D. Gaonac'h et J.-M. Passerault, *Psycholinguistique textuelle. Approche cognitive de la compréhension et de la production des textes* (Paris, Armand Colin, 1996), 131. Pour lui, 'et puis' aurait également ce rôle. Dans notre corpus, il établit davantage des frontières entre les différents événements au sein d'un même épisode.

22   N. Guézennec, *Mémoire et transmission de la tradition orale en Basse-Bretagne. Approches ethno- et sociolinguistiques de la littérature orale, de la mémoire, de l'oral et de l'écrit* (Thèse de doctorat, Université de Paris X-Nanterre, 2005).

23   Quatre sur six contes proprement dits étudiés et tous les contes facétieux (cinq) présentent des parallélismes macro-séquentiels et séquentiels.

24   *Le Conte de l'Homme Juste* a été enregistré le 19–08–1997 au Huelgoat (Finistère, France) dans un café.

25   Dans cette version, l'amélioration n'est pas obtenue.

26   Delarue et Tenèze, *Le Conte populaire*, 367–368, version de 1878.

27   Personnification de la mort chez les Bas-Bretons.

Schéma 2: macrostructure de *Rismodell an Den Just*

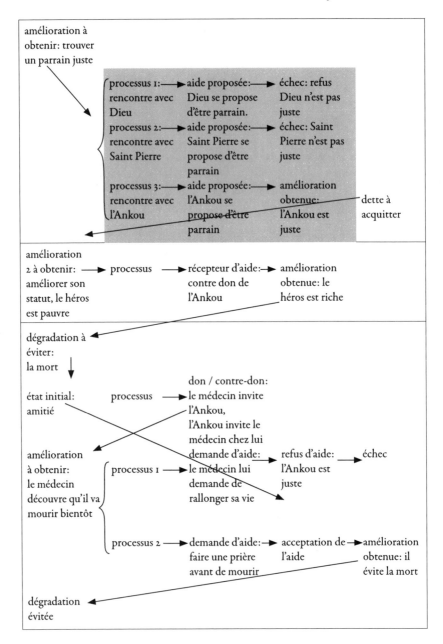

amélioration à
obtenir: trouver
un parrain juste

processus 1:——▶ aide proposée:——▶ échec: refus
rencontre avec   Dieu se propose   Dieu n'est pas
Dieu   d'être parrain.   juste
processus 2:——▶ aide proposée:——▶ échec: Saint
rencontre avec   Saint Pierre se   Pierre n'est pas
Saint Pierre   propose d'être   juste
                             parrain
processus 3:——▶ aide proposée:——▶ amélioration
rencontre avec   l'Ankou se   obtenue: dette à
l'Ankou   propose d'être   l'Ankou est   acquitter
                             parrain   juste

amélioration
2 à obtenir: ——▶ processus ——▶ récepteur d'aide:——▶ amélioration
améliorer son   contre don de   obtenue: le
statut, le héros   l'Ankou   héros est riche
est pauvre

dégradation à
éviter:
la mort

                                               don / contre-don:
état initial: processus ——▶ le médecin invite
amitié   l'Ankou,
                                              l'Ankou invite le
                                              médecin chez lui
amélioration   demande d'aide: refus d'aide: ——▶ échec
à obtenir: processus 1 ——▶ le médecin lui   l'Ankou est
le médecin   demande de   juste
découvre qu'il va   rallonger sa vie
mourir bientôt

                      processus 2 ——▶ demande d'aide:——▶ acceptation de ——▶ amélioration
                                              faire une prière   l'aide   obtenue: il
                                              avant de mourir   évite la mort

dégradation ◀
évitée

La macro-séquence qui se réplique trois fois est composée de trois séquences, elles-mêmes composées de macro-propositions communes. Toutefois, la dernière séquence (échec) présente le plus de différence avec les deux premières, car elle constitue la réussite de la quête du héros.

Schéma 3: macro-propositions et séquences communes aux 3 macro-séquences
parallèles de *Rismodell an Den Just*

MSq* amélioration à obtenir : trouver un parrain juste (X 3)	Macro-séquences 1 à 3	
Sq: rencontre avec X	Mp 1: indice spatial Mp 2: la rencontre d'un homme Mp 3: description physique Mp 4: l'homme lui demande où il va Mp 5: le héros lui explique sa quête	
Sq: aide proposée	Mp 1: l'homme se propose d'être parrain Mp 2: le héros lui précise qu'il recherche un homme juste Mp 3: l'homme dit au héros qu'il est juste Mp 4: le héros demande qui il est Mp 5: l'homme répond	
	Macro-séquences 1et 2	Macro-séquence 3
Sq échec: X n'est pas juste / amélioration: X est juste	Mp 1: le héros dit qu'il ne sera pas le parrain Mp 2: l'homme lui demande pourquoi Mp 3: le héros explique les raisons pour lesquelles il n'est pas juste	Mp 1: l'homme démontre qu'il est juste Mp 2: le héros accepte et l'homme devient le parrain

*   MSq: macro-séquence, Sq: séquence, Mp: macro-proposition.

Les macro-séquences parallèles sont plus ou moins autonomes comme le montrent les différentes versions d'un conte réaliste *Bilzic*, également transmis de bouche à oreille au même conteur. Les différentes épreuves du héros pour devenir voleur, parallèles, sont supprimables si elles ont la même fonction dans le récit (voler le cochon, le gâteau et le cheval). On peut supposer qu'elles peuvent également changer d'ordre.

Schéma 4: suppression d'épreuves selon les versions de *Bilzic*[28]

l'oncle envoie le héros faire une épreuve (amélioration déméritoire)	Version 1 18–08–1997	Version 2 27–07–2001	Version 3 17–08–2001
voler la bourse d'un voyageur (échec: augmentation des épreuves)	1	1	1
voler un cochon	2		2
voler un gâteau	3	2	3
voler un cheval		3	4
voler le drap du voleur (amélioration déméritoire augmentée: si succès devient le chef des voleurs)	4	4	5

II.2.2 Les Contes facétieux

Les contes facétieux, comme le souligne Lajarte, présentent une très grande hétérogénéité: 'structure de l'histoire, formes du récit et de la narration, thématique de l'histoire, nombre, attributs et fonctions des acteurs – toutes ces composantes textuelles varient considérablement d'un conte à l'autre.'[29]

Ceux recueillis utilisent plus ou moins systématiquement les réplications d'épisodes qui apparaissent comme un fondement de leur composition.

---

28   Version 1, enregistrée dans un café; version 2 et 3: dans une forêt au Huelgoat (Finistère, France).

29   P. de Lajarte, 'Du conte facétieux considéré comme genre: esquisse d'une analyse structurale', *Ethnologie française* 4 (1974), 319–332, 319.

C'est le cas de deux récits, *Le Moulin* et *Rismodell ar Miloar*.[30] Le premier, transmis oralement, n'est construit que sous forme de parallélismes, des dégradations en chaîne. Cette forme de construction est caractéristique des *formula tales* ou randonnées.

Schéma 5: macrostructure du *Moulin*

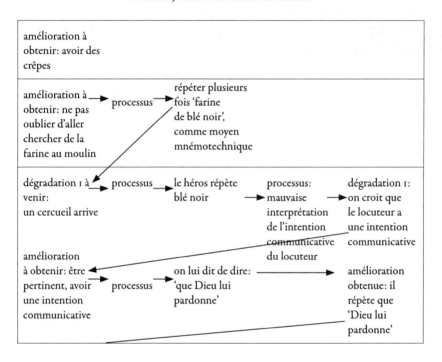

30   *Le Conte du miroir* a été enregistré le 08–07–2000 et *Le Moulin*, le 06–07–2000 lors d'une scène ouverte à Brennilis (Finistère, France) dans une auberge.

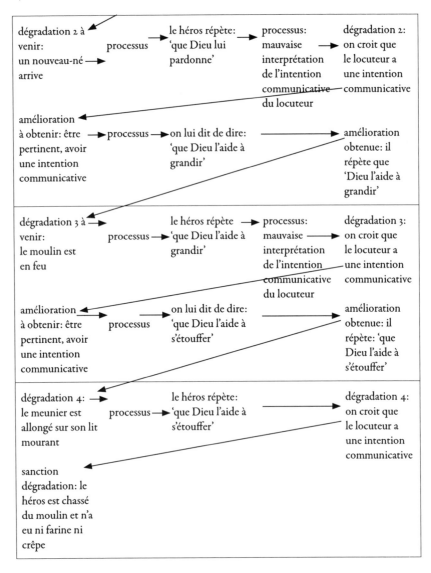

Ce conte qui commence par une amélioration à obtenir – aller chercher de la farine au moulin pour faire des crêpes – repose sur des dégradations en chaîne, parallèles, d'ordre sémiotique ou plutôt pragmatique, c'est-à-dire que l'identité entre les séquences se situe au niveau de l'interprétation des événements et des messages par les protagonistes du récit. Ce récit peut être analysé selon le principe de pertinence.[31] Un énoncé est pertinent dans un contexte donné s'il a au moins un effet dans ce contexte. L'interlocuteur interprète le message en faisant des hypothèses logico-déductives sur des données contextuelles et linguistiques et en recherchant des effets contextuels d'un énoncé.

Dans ce conte facétieux, chaque locuteur fait une mauvaise interprétation du discours de son allocutaire et se trompe sur son intention informative, c'est-à-dire l'intention d'amener son interlocuteur à la connaissance d'une information. L'anti-héros – qui ne s'adresse à personne – ne fait que répéter un énoncé comme moyen mnémotechnique et n'a donc pas d'intention informative. Les personnes que le garçon rencontre dans chaque situation pensent à tort que celui-ci a une intention communicative et parle à propos de la situation qui intervient dans l'interprétation du message. Les énoncés du 'héros' ne sont pas 'pertinents', car ils amènent les personnes à interpréter ses paroles avec une intention qu'il n'a pas. Celles-ci corrigent son message pour que celui-ci corresponde à leurs attentes, c'est-à-dire parler en fonction de la situation. Toutefois, le garçon ne comprend pas l'intention communicative de ses allocutaires et continue de répéter le message comme moyen mnémotechnique sans prendre en compte le contexte qu'il va rencontrer.[32] Dès lors, chaque discours répété devient non pertinent dans chaque nouvelle situation. Les personnes rencontrées déduisent que l'anti-héros a une intention impolie et néfaste (en souhaitant le mal), car les discours sont des expressions dotées d'une force performative: le souhait (non illocutoire de la part de l'enfant).

Le parallélisme pragmatique repose ici sur des parallélismes syntaxiques, c'est-à-dire que l'identité se situe au niveau de la construction phrastique. Chaque verbe du discours qu'on fait répéter à l'anti-héros est connoté positivement ou négativement en fonction de son sujet et objet.

---

31   D. Sperber et D. Wilson, *La Pertinence. Communication et cognition*, trans. A. Gerschenfeld et D. Sperber (Paris, Les Éditions de Minuit, 1989).

32   Selon Sperber et Wilson (*La Pertinence*), l'intention communicative est l'intention qu'a le locuteur de faire connaître à l'interlocuteur son intention informative.

Schéma 6: l'augmentation de la connotation des verbes en fonction de leur sujet et
objet dans *Le Moulin*

on dit: 'que Dieu lui pardonne' devant un mort on ne dit pas: 'que Dieu lui pardonne' devant un nouveau-né	pardonner: objet un mort + objet: un enfant −
on dit: 'que Dieu l'aide à grandir' devant un nouveau-né on ne dit pas: 'que Dieu l'aide à grandir' quand il y a un feu	grandir: sujet un enfant + sujet: un feu −
on dit: 'que Dieu l'aide à s'étouffer' devant un feu on ne dit pas: 'que Dieu l'aide à s'étouffer' devant un mourant	s'étouffer: sujet un feu+ sujet: un mourant −

Chaque amélioration obtenue dans une situation devient dans la suivante
une dégradation allant s'accroissant: dégradation 1 < dégradation 2 < dégradation 3 < dégradation 4. La sanction est donc plus importante à la fin du
récit. On ne corrige plus l'enfant verbalement, on le chasse.

L'autre récit, *Rismodell ar Miloar*, inventé par le conteur, est composé
de deux macro-séquences parallèles qui constituent la charnière du récit.
En échange d'un service, le couple reçoit un objet inconnu, un miroir, qui
entraîne des dégradations en chaîne, parallèles, illustrant la discorde dans
le ménage. Dans les deux dégradations, l'image reflétée est interprétée par
chacun des époux comme étant celle d'une autre personne. Le parallélisme,
pouvant être analysé pragmatiquement comme le conte précédent (mauvaise
interprétation des données contextuelles), rend compte de la stupidité des
protagonistes, un des thèmes définitoires du genre facétieux.

Schéma 7: macrostructure de *Rismodell ar Miloar*

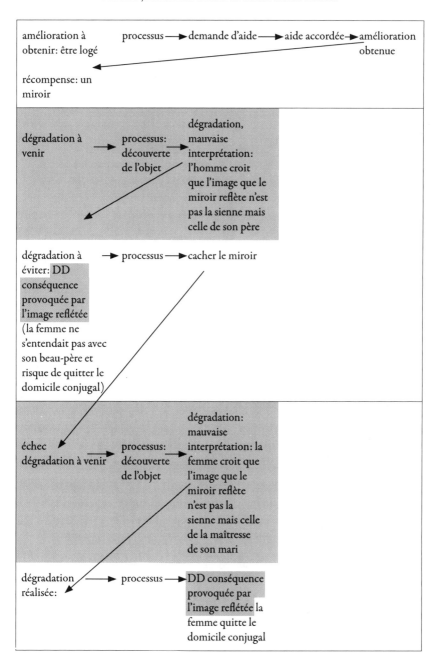

amélioration à
obtenir: être logé   processus ──▶ demande d'aide ──▶ aide accordée ──▶ amélioration
                                                                             obtenue

récompense: un
miroir

dégradation à   processus: dégradation,
venir   découverte   mauvaise
                    de l'objet   interprétation:
                                     l'homme croit
                                     que l'image que le
                                     miroir reflète n'est
                                     pas la sienne mais
                                     celle de son père

dégradation à   ──▶ processus ──▶ cacher le miroir
éviter: DD
conséquence
provoquée par
l'image reflétée
(la femme ne
s'entendait pas avec
son beau-père et
risque de quitter le
domicile conjugal)

échec   dégradation:
dégradation à venir processus: mauvaise
                    découverte   interprétation: la
                    de l'objet   femme croit que
                                     l'image que le
                                     miroir reflète
                                     n'est pas la
                                     sienne mais celle
                                     de la maîtresse
                                     de son mari

dégradation   ──▶ processus ──▶ DD conséquence
réalisée: provoquée par
                                     l'image reflétée la
                                     femme quitte le
                                     domicile conjugal

Les macro-propositions sont les suivantes:

Schéma 8: macro-propositions et séquences communes aux 2 macro-séquences
parallèles de *Rismodell ar Miloar*

	Macro-séquences 1 et 2
Sq: processus de la dégradation	– découverte de l'objet miroir
Sq: mauvaise interprétation	– mauvaise interprétation de l'image reflétée – les protagonistes décrivent l'image reflétée
Sq: dégradation à éviter (MSq 2) ou dégradation non évitée (MSq 3)	– discours direct: conséquence provoquée par l'image reflétée

II.3 Les Parallélismes phrastiques et répétitions

Certaines séquences communes ont les mêmes macro-propositions, elles-
mêmes composées des mêmes phrases sans aucune variation (répétition à
l'identique) ou avec un ou deux éléments qui varient. Dans ce cas, les éléments répétés jouent le rôle de structure à partir de laquelle sont repérés
les éléments variables, les paires.[33]

Dans *Rismodell an Den Just*, le conteur utilise pratiquement la même
phrase (la variation, 'juste', peut être déduite de la séquence précédente)
qui compose la macro-proposition 'L'homme lui dit qu'il est juste':

Schéma 9: répétition phrastique dans *Rismodell an Den Just*

Macro-séquence 1	Macro-séquence 2	Macro-séquence 3
oh ben répond l'homme plus juste que moi tu trouveras pas	en ben plus plus que moi vous trouverez pas	plus juste que moi tu trouveras pas qu'il dit

---

33   Monod Becquelin, Vapnarsky, Becquey et Breton, 'Decir y contar la diversidad'.

La variation peut être sensiblement plus importante lorsque le conteur utilise des paraphrases (schéma 10).

Schéma 10: phrases parallèles correspondant à la Mp 'découverte de l'objet miroir' dans *Rismodell ar Miloar*

Macro-séquence 1	Macro-séquence 2
c'est l'emballage	la planche est enveloppée
il défait l'emballage	la désenveloppe

Outre ces phrases répétitives ou similaires, d'autres peuvent avoir comme éléments variables des unités, des paires, qui apportent des informations nouvelles non déductibles contextuellement ou co-textuellement (schéma 11).

Schéma 11: phrases parallèles de la Mp 'les protagonistes décrivent l'image reflétée' dans *Rismodell ar Miloar*

Macro-séquence 1	Macro-séquence 2
il a la casquette sur le côté	
l'œil encore coquin	elle a l'œil poché qu'il dit
	le nez qui coule (rires)
la moustache qui frise qu'il dit	oh la la les cheveux ébouriffés
	sous sa coiffe de travers qu'il dit
	ah ouais regardez moi la rire
il chique aussi	eh elle a plus qu'une dent dans la bouche

Il est possible de dégager un niveau d'invariabilité qui fonctionnerait comme un modèle à partir duquel le conteur compose et insère les unités variables. Les descriptions physiques parallèles du couple de *Rismodell ar Miloar* (schéma 11) sont similaires du point de vue de la syntaxe, de l'ordre de présentation et des parties physiques ainsi que la façon dont celles-ci sont décrites. L'œil 'coquin/poché', puis les cheveux ou les poils 'moustache qui frise/cheveux ébouriffés', le chapeau 'casquette sur le côté/coiffe de travers' et la bouche 'chique/une dent', sont successivement dépeints dans les deux passages.[34] Le conteur paraît avoir en mémoire des indications mnémotechniques reposant sur une représentation spatiale du visage.

Le même type d'analyse, que l'on présente de façon plus schématique, peut être fait pour *Le Moulin*. Les caractères souligés représentent le niveau invariable des paires:

1er discours direct: loc 1: <u>blé noir</u>
<u>Description situation 1</u>
<u>Loc 1: 1er DD</u>
Loc 2: mais non ne dis pas + <u>reprise 1er DD</u> + dis + <u>2ème DD</u>: que Dieu l'aide à + syntagme verbal
Loc 1: 'je dis' + <u>2ème DD</u>
je continue ma route en disant (ou je dis) + <u>2ème DD</u>
<u>Description situation 2</u>
<u>Loc 1: 2ème DD</u>
Loc 3: mais non ne dis pas + <u>reprise du 2ème DD</u> + dis + <u>3ème DD</u>
etc ...

Chaque partie de l'histoire fonctionne de la même façon. Le conteur sait qu'il y a une situation dans laquelle l'anti-héros ne devra pas dire le discours précédent, car le verbe connoté positivement dans la situation antérieure sera connoté négativement dans la nouvelle situation. Pour *Rismodell an Den Just*, le premier exemple montre que seul le nom du personnage, la paire, varie. La structure de la phrase parallèle est donc dans le premier

---

34   Dans cette version, on observe de la variation au niveau du 'cadre', l'homme et la femme sont décrits de haut en bas du visage mais pour la femme, le conteur revient au haut du visage pour décrire la coiffe et les cheveux.

exemple 'moi je suis NP qu'il dit', et dans le second: 'ah c'est vous NP eh ben alors vous serez pas le parrain'.[35]

Schéma 12: parallélismes phrastiques dans *Rismodell an Den Just*

	Macro-séquence 1	Macro-séquence 2	Macro-séquence 3
Mp: l'homme répond	moi je suis le Bon Dieu qu'il dit	eh ben moi je suis Saint Pierre qu'il dit	moi moi je suis l'Ankou qu'il dit
Mp: le héros dit qu'il ne sera pas le parrain	ah c'est vous le Bon Dieu eh ben alors vous serez pas le parrain	ah c'est vous qui gardez les portes du paradis là-haut oui ah ben alors je pense que vous n'êtes pas juste qu'il dit vous serez pas le parrain	

Les parallélismes mettent en relief les éléments variables, les paires, qui font avancer le récit.

On peut également hiérarchiser structurellement les informations parallèles. Certaines appartiennent aux expansions, unités supprimables sans que le sens général du récit soit bouleversé comme des détails physiques, psychologiques (11) et spatio-temporels ou actions annexes (10). D'autres correspondent aux nœuds, c'est-à-dire aux éléments non supprimables qui font avancer le récit (schémas 9, 12).[36]

---

35   NP: nom propre.
36   Barthes, *Communication*.

III Rôles et fonctions

Nous avons vu que les parallélismes étaient un outil de composition du conte, mais quels sont leurs rôles mnésique, pragmatique et dans la distinction des genres?

III.1 Fonction pragmatique et genre du récit

A partir de l'analyse structurelle précédente, il est possible de rendre compte des sous-types de contes et de montrer en quoi ils se distinguent.[37]

> – **conte proprement dit:**
> 1. amélioration à obtenir – (dégradation – amélioration) – amélioration;
> 2. mérite appelle récompense;
> 3. démérite appelle châtiment.

> – **conte facétieux:** amélioration à obtenir – tentative d'amélioration (ou amélioration) – échec (dégradation).

Le récit apparaît comme une structure hiérarchisée, à plusieurs niveaux, comme l'ont suggéré les psychologues.[38] Les contes facétieux se caractérisent par la non-amélioration de la situation initiale et si elle a lieu, elle s'effectue par une dégradation.[39] Les contes proprement dits sont les plus complexes, car les événements se croisent, contrairement à la facétie, dont la structure est plus linéaire.

---

37 Guézennec, *Mémoire et transmission.*
38 A. Baddeley, *La Mémoire humaine: théorie et pratique* (Grenoble, Presses Universitaires de Grenoble, 1992).
39 Guézennec, *Mémoire et transmission.* Un autre type de conte facétieux a été dégagé: amélioration à obtenir – dégradation – amélioration.

Comme le souligne Monod Becquelin chez les Mayas, les parallélismes participent à la distinction des genres et à l'efficacité de la parole.[40] Dans le conte proprement dit, la structure d'une partie se voit reproduite plusieurs fois avec quelques changements. Les séquences parallèles sont souvent subordonnées à une séquence d'ordre supérieur. Dès lors, une réplication peut être supprimée ou changer d'ordre, car elle a la même fonction dans le récit (exemple: tentative d'amélioration).[41] Ce phénomène illustré dans le conte maya ne semble pas lui être spécifique et nuance l'idée des spécialistes littéraires d'une pure linéarité du conte européen.[42]

Le conte facétieux est formé de plusieurs structures de fonctions différentes complètement parallèles, qui rappellent l'expression de Lajarte 'l'équivalence d'ordre sémiotique' pour définir ce genre.[43] Ce type de parallélisme structurel crée une reproduction des événements. Pouvant construire tout le récit, les parallélismes apparaissent comme un moyen pour produire des facéties. Les parallélismes pragmatiques caractérisent ce genre. En effet, c'est à cause de leur mauvaise interprétation des événements que les protagonistes les reproduisent au lieu de changer leur cours. L'emploi de phrases parallèles accentue cette reproduction et dès lors, l'impact comique du récit.

Les réplications d'épisodes dans les contes proprement dits concernent les tentatives du héros, les différentes épreuves. Le parallélisme ralentit le moment du dénouement et crée ainsi du suspense, en permettant de construire un certain nombre d'autres tentatives. Contrairement à la facétie, la réplication n'empêche pas l'avènement des événements et l'aboutissement d'une fin attendue: l'amélioration de la situation.

---

40 Voir A. Becquelin, 'Le Tour du monde en quelques couplets. Le parallélisme dans la tradition orale maya', dans J. Fernandez-Vest (éd.), *Kalevala et traditions orales du Monde* (Paris, CNRS, 1987), 467–488; et A. Monod Becquelin, 'Polyphonie thérapeutique: une confrontation pour la guérison en tzeltal', dans A. Monod Becquelin et P. Erickson (éds), *Les Rituels du dialogue* (Nanterre, Société d'ethnologie, 2000), 511–553.

41 Voir schéma 4.

42 Monod Becquelin, Vapnarsky, Becquey et Breton, 'Decir y contar la diversidad'.

43 P. de Lajarte, 'Du conte facétieux'.

Outre son rôle dans la distinction des genres, le parallélisme est inséparable
de la performance. Dans le conte proprement dit, il permet aux conteurs
de s'adapter au public en augmentant ou en réduisant le récit par l'introduction ou la suppression d'une séquence ou macro-séquence. Le parallélisme facilite la compréhension du récit en servant de points de repère sur
lesquels l'auditeur peut s'appuyer. D'autre part, le parallélisme phrastique
aide les conteurs, selon leurs dires, à se remémorer le récit au cours de la
performance, surtout en cas de 'trous de mémoire'. La question des parallélismes est d'ailleurs inséparable de la question de la mémoire.

III.2 Rôle mnésique et support de la mémoire

Les parallélismes jouent un rôle important dans la transmission des genres
oraux et permettent de préserver et de transmettre le savoir.[44] On peut se
demander de quelle façon.

   Les psychologues et les ethnologues ont montré que plus un texte a de
règles qui se surimposent à lui, mieux il est rappelé.[45] On a souvent insisté
sur le rôle du niveau phonologique – le rythme et la rime – comme base
de l'encodage verbal, qui permettrait de réduire la variabilité.[46] Le rôle des
autres types de parallélismes l'a moins été. Toutefois, Severi montre que les
Cunas – Indiens du Panama – ont des discours rituels avec une structure
parallélistique apprise par cœur.[47] Les éléments variables du texte sont appris
séparément par le moyen des pictogrammes alors que la structure parallélistique commune est exclusivement confiée à 'la mémoire des sons'.[48] La
mémoire *verbatim* serait facilitée par les formules constantes de la structure.

---

44   Fox, 'Introduction'.
45   Voir Baddeley, *La Mémoire humaine*; Belmont et Calame-Griaule, 'Éditoral'; D.C.
      Rubin, *Memory in Oral Traditions. The Cognitive Psychology of Epic, Ballads and
      Counting-out Rhymes* (Oxford, OUP, 1995); et Vansina, *De la tradition orale*.
46   Rubin, *Memory in Oral Traditions*.
47   C. Severi, 'Paroles durables, écritures perdues. Réflexions sur la pictographie cuna', dans
      M. Détienne (éd.), *Transcrire les mythologies* (Paris, Albin Michel, 1994), 45–73.
48   Severi, 'Paroles durables', 61.

On peut donc se demander si les parallélismes sont des auxiliaires de la mémoire et si les unités concernées par ce phénomène varient moins que celles qui ne le sont pas. Pour le savoir, j'ai comparé plusieurs versions d'un même récit énoncées dans des laps de temps courts (de quelques jours à un mois) par le même conteur.

III.2.1 Les Réplications d'épisodes

Il apparaît que plus les contes présentent des réplications d'épisodes moins ils varient au cours du temps.

Conte facétieux: *Le Moulin > Rismodell ar Miloar > La Parole > Les Boules*
Contes proprement dits: *Bilzic > Rismodell an Den Just > Ar Zantic-Kozh*

Graphique 1: pourcentage de mots rappelés par genre

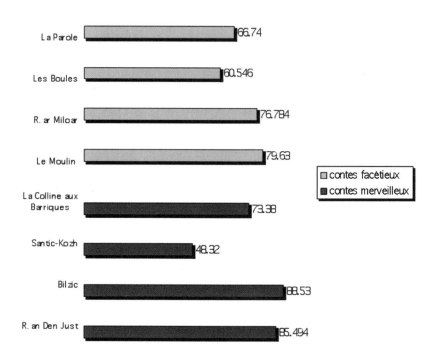

De plus, pour chaque récit, les séquences ou macro-séquences parallèles varient moins que celles qui ne sont pas parallèles ou qui ont moins de similitudes. On peut conclure que les macro-parallélismes impliquent un meilleur taux de rappel des mots.

III.2.2. Les Parallélismes de phrases

Qu'en est-il des phrases parallèles? Il apparaît qu'elles sont pratiquement rappelées mot pour mot (schéma 13).[49]

Schéma 13: variation dans le temps des phrases parallèles dans *Rismodell ar Miloar*

	Version 1 08–07–2000	Version 2 24–08–2000*
P. MSq 2	ah c'est lui la casquette sur le côté l'œil encore coquin la moustache qui frise qu'il dit c'est lui	ah c'est lui la casquette sur le côté la moustache qui frise l'œil encore coquin qu'il dit c'est lui
P. MSq 3	regardez moi celle-ci c'est une belle elle a l' œil poché le nez qui coule les cheveux ébouriffés sous sa coiffe de travers une dent dans la bouche (rires)	celle-ci elle est belle regardez moi sa coiffe de travers sous ses cheveux ébouriffés son œil poché son nez qui coule une seule dent dans la bouche

*   Pour la situation d'enregistrement, voir note 30.

49   Seules les unités parallèles ont été transcrites.

Les parallélismes de phrases ont tendance à être mieux rappelés que les unités non parallèles quel que soit leur statut: des nœuds (*Rismodell an Den Just*), des détails physiques et psychologiques, et même des descriptions spatio-temporelles, généralement plus sensibles à la variation situationnelle.[50]

Des psycholinguistes ont démontré le rôle des parallélismes dans les phrases coordonnées en ce qui concerne la rapidité de traitement.[51] Ce rôle a certainement des répercussions sur la remémoration et la production. On peut émettre l'hypothèse que les parallélismes permettent au locuteur de se concentrer sur ce qui varie. Du côté de la réception, l'auditoire s'imprègne de ces structures répétitives et peut ainsi se concentrer sur la dissemblance. Les parallélismes permettraient donc de hiérarchiser les informations. Par la ressemblance, les éléments variables sont mis en relief.

IV Conclusions

On peut postuler deux mécanismes de remémoration, un global: les macro-parallélismes fonctionneraient comme des matrices préalablement mémo-risées à partir desquelles le conteur compose. Et l'autre serait local, chaque macro-séquence appelle une séquence; une séquence, une macro-propo-sition etc. Le choix des paires est donc contraint en fonction de la pro-gression du récit, de la syntaxe etc. En suivant Rubin,[52] les parallélismes constitueraient un type de contrainte parmi d'autres – comme la structure sous-jacente, l'imagerie– qui facilite la remémoration et aide à discriminer les unités en mémoire en limitant leur choix lors du rappel.[53] Plus il y a de

---

50   Guézennec, *Mémoire et transmission*.
51   A. Dubey, P. Sturt et F. Keller, *Parallelism in Coordination as an Instance of Syntactic Priming. Evidence from Corpus-Based Modeling* (Vancouver, HLTC-CEMNLP, 2005).
52   Rubin, *Memory in Oral Traditions*.
53   Voir N. Guézennec, 'Pointer les lieux. Relation entre gestes, littérature orale et con-texte', *Cahiers de l'Association for French Language Studies* 13.2 (2007), 60–99; et 'La

contraintes moins la tradition orale varie.[54] Le parallélisme aurait donc un statut cognitif. Ceci pourrait expliquer pourquoi les contes recueillis en Bretagne montrent des points communs au niveau des macro-séquences et des séquences parallèles avec les versions répertoriées par Delarue et Tenèze.[55] Il est possible que ces structures aient un rôle dans la bonne transmission de certains motifs à long terme. Dès lors, les contraintes intrinsèques au genre paraissent jouer un rôle plus important dans la bonne transmission des contes à très long terme que l'écrit, souvent considéré comme un vecteur important dans la transmission des objets immatériels.[56] Ainsi, le conte français ne se distingue pas sur le phénomène parallélistique des contes à tradition orale en dépit de la présence de l'écriture dans cette tradition.

On peut s'interroger sur l'influence de la tradition écrite sur le parallélisme. Selon Tedlock, les contraintes formelles d'ordre métrique dans la poésie orale, telle que la poésie homérique, serait liée à l'écrit.[57] Or, il semblerait que ni l'écriture ni l'existence d'une tradition littéraire ne soit un préalable aux parallélismes. La conclusion de Rumsey à propos d'une tradition orale de Nouvelle Guinée va dans ce sens: 'In short, *pace* Tedlock, the development of formulaic poetry with long metrical runs does not depend on alphabetic or syllabic writing or on contact with literate traditions.'[58] Au contraire, dans le cas des contes, leur mise par écrit a une influence inverse sur les parallélismes. En témoigne l'édition des contes par les conteurs où l'écriture – qui permet de planifier le message en se corrigeant – tend à casser la 'répétition' en diversifiant davantage les structures phrastiques mais conserve les macro-niveaux. L'oralité préserve en revanche tous les niveaux de construction du conte.[59]

Mémoire des contes et légendes bas-bretons: réflexions sur la mémoire orale et la mémoire écrite', *Fabula* (à paraître).

54   Rubin, *Memory in Oral Traditions*.

55   Delarue et Tenèze, *Le Conte populaire français*.

56   Goody, *La Raison graphique*.

57   Cité par Rumsey, 'Yaga Kange'.

58   Rumsey, 'Yaga Kange', 216.

59   Voir Guézennec, *Mémoire et transmission*, 311; et Monod Becquelin, Vapnarsky, Becquey et Breton, 'Decir y contar la diversidad', 18.

On est donc amené à penser le parallélisme comme un phénomène de l'oralité mais en même temps à l'envisager au-delà de la problématique de l'oral et de l'écrit. En effet, son rôle dans la création, la mémoire et la transmission, et sa très probable universalité[60] comme l'attestent les divers travaux sur le parallélisme, amènent à l'interroger d'un point de vue cognitif.[61] Toutefois, bien qu'il s'agisse d'un phénomène universel, son actualisation ne l'est pas, car chaque tradition privilégie le parallélisme pour des raisons esthétiques et des valeurs culturelles, aspects que nous avons laissés en suspens.[62]

---

60 Jakobson, cité par Fox, 'Introduction', 11.
61 Fox, 'Introduction'.
62 Rumsey, 'Yaga Kange'.

Bibliography

Abrantès, Mme de, *Mémoires* (London, Edinburgh and Paris, Nelson, n.d.).

Ackermann, K., *Von der philosophisch-moralischen Erzählung zur modernen Novelle. 'Contes' und 'nouvelles' von 1760 bis 1830* (Frankfurt-am-Main, Klostermann, 2004).

Adam, J.-M., *Le Texte narratif* (Paris, Nathan, 1994).

Aikhenvald, A., *Evidentiality* (Oxford, OUP, 2004).

Anonymous, 'De la littérature conteuse', *Gazette de France*, 8 June 1833.

Arendt, H., *Vies politiques* (Paris, Gallimard, 1974).

Armstrong, N., *Social and Stylistic Variation in Spoken French: A Comparative Approach* (Amsterdam, Benjamins, 2001).

Arnold, A.J., 'The gendering of *créolité*. The erotics of colonialism', in M. Condé and M. Cottenet-Hage (eds), *Penser la créolité* (Paris, Karthala, 1995), 21–40.

Asfour, A., *Champfleury: Meaning in the Popular Arts in Nineteenth-Century France* (Frankfurt, Peter Lang, 2001).

Ashby, W., 'Un nouveau regard sur la chute du *ne* en français parlé tourangeau', *Journal of French Language Studies* 11 (2001), 11–22.

Asher, N. and Lascarides, A., *Logics of Conversation* (Cambridge, CUP, 2003).

Attridge, D., *J. M. Coetzee and the Ethics of Reading: Literature in the Event* (Chicago and London, Chicago University Press, 2004).

Aulnoy, M.C., Le Jumel de Barneville, Comtesse d', *Contes nouveaux ou Les Fées à la mode* par Mme D** [1698], in *Madame d'Aulnoy. Contes des fées suivis des Contes nouveaux ou Les Fées à la mode*, ed. N. Jasmin (Paris, Champion, 2004), I.

Ayres-Bennett, W. and J. Carruthers, *Problems and Perspectives. Studies in the Modern French Language* (London, Longman, 2001).

Baddeley, A., *La Mémoire humaine: théorie et pratique* (Grenoble, Presses Universitaires de Grenoble, 1992).

Bal, M., *Narratology: Introduction to the Theory of Narrative* (Toronto, University of Toronto Press, 1985).

Balzac, H. de, *La Comédie humaine*, 12 vols, eds P.-G. Castex et al. (Paris, Gallimard-Pléiade, 1976–81).

—— *Œuvres diverses*, eds R. Chollet et al. (Paris, Gallimard-Pléiade, 1990).

—— P. Chasles and C. Rabou, *Contes bruns*, ed. M. Milner (Marseille, Éditions des autres, 1979 [1832]).

Bandy, W.T., 'Baudelaire et Edgar Poe', *Revue de littérature comparée* 41 (1967), 180–194.

Barchilon, J., *Le Conte merveilleux français de 1690 à 1790: cent ans de féerie et de poésie ignorées de l'histoire littéraire* (Paris, Champion, 1975).

Barthes, R., 'Introduction à l'analyse structurale du récit', *Communications* 8 (1966), 8–27.

—— *S/Z*, in *Œuvres complètes* (Paris, Seuil, 1994 [1970]), II, 553–741.

Bastide, R., 'Opinions sur le folklore', *Bastidiana* 19–20 (1997), 35–39.

Baudelaire, C., *Correspondance*, eds C. Pichois and J. Ziegler (Paris, Gallimard-Pléiade, 1973).

—— *Fusées. Mon cœur mis à nu. Pauvre Belgique*, ed. A. Guyaux (Paris, Folio, 1986).

—— *Notes nouvelles sur Edgar Poe*, in *Curiosités esthétiques*, ed. H. Lemaître (Paris, Classiques Garnier, 1962), 619–639.

—— 'Théophile Gautier', *L'Artiste* 4, 13 March 1859, in *Œuvres complètes*, ed. M. Ruff (Paris, Seuil, 1968).

Bauman, R., *Story, Performance and Event: Contextual Studies of Oral Narrative* (Cambridge, CUP, 1986).

Baumgardt, U. and J. Derive (eds), *Littératures orales africaines. Perspectives théoriques et méthodologiques* (Paris, Karthala, 2008).

Beaumont, Madame Leprince de, *Le Magasin des enfants, ou Dialogues d'une sage gouvernante avec ses élèves de la première distinction, dans lesquels on fait penser, parler, agir les jeunes gens suivant le génie, le tempérament et les inclinations d'un chacun. On y représente les défauts de leur âge; l'on y montre de quelle manière on peut les en corriger; on s'applique autant à leur former le cœur qu'à leur éclairer l'esprit. On y donne un abrégé de l'histoire sacrée, de la fable, de la géographie, etc., le tout rempli de réflexions utiles, et de contes moraux pour les amuser agréablement; et écrit d'un style simple et proportionné à la tendresse de leurs années* (Paris, Champion, 2008 [London, n.p., 1756–1780]).

Becquelin, A., 'Le Tour du monde en quelques couplets. Le Parallélisme dans la tradition orale maya', in J. Fernandez-Vest (ed.), *Kalevala et traditions orales du Monde* (Paris, CNRS, 1987), 467–488.

Bekker, B., *Le Monde enchanté* (Amsterdam, P. Rotterdam, 1694).

Bellemin-Noël, J., *Les Contes et leurs fantasmes* (Paris, PUF, 1983).

Belmont, N., 'La Tradition orale du conte, la transcription et les contes littéraires', *Cahiers de littérature orale* 52 (2002), 133–144.

——*Poétique du conte. Essai sur le conte de tradition orale* (Paris, Gallimard, 1999).

—— and G. Calame-Griaule, 'Éditorial', *Cahiers de littérature orale* 43 (1998), 7–23.

Benjamin, W., 'The Storyteller: reflections on the works of Nikolai Leskov', in *Illuminations*, ed. H. Arendt, trans. H. Zohn (London, Fontana, 1983), 83–109.

Benveniste, E., *Problèmes de linguistique générale* (Paris, Gallimard, 1966), I.

Berman, A., *L'Épreuve de l'étranger* (Paris, Gallimard, 1984).

Bernabé, J., 'Fènwè et wè klè, le syndrome homérique à l'œuvre dans la parole antillaise', in J. Bernabé et al. (eds), *Au Visiteur lumineux. Des îles créoles aux sociétés plurielles. Mélanges offerts à Jean Benoist* (Petit Bourg-Schœlcher, Ibis Rouge-GEREC, 2000), 633–650.

——P. Chamoiseau and R. Confiant, *Éloge de la créolité* (Paris, Gallimard, 1993 [1989]).

Bernstein, B., *Langage et classes sociales* (Paris, Les Éditions de Minuit, 1975).

Berque, J., *L'Immigration à l'École de la République* (Paris, La Documentation française, 1985).

Berthelier, R., *Enfants de migrants à l'école française* (Paris, L'Harmattan, 2006).

Berthier, P., *La Presse littéraire et dramatique au début de la Monarchie de juillet (1830–1836)* (Villeneuve d'Ascq, Presses Universitaires du Septentrion, 1997), 1119–1133.

Biber, D., *Variation across Speech and Writing* (Cambridge, CUP, 1988).

Bierwisch, M., 'Semantic structure and illocutionary force', in J.R. Searle, F. Kiefer and M. Bierwisch (eds), *Speech Act Theory and Pragmatics* (Dordrecht, Reidel, 1980), 1–35.

Blair, D., *African Literature in French: A History of Creative Writing in French from West and Equatorial Africa* (Cambridge, CUP, 1976).

Blanche-Benveniste, C., 'De la rareté de certains phénomènes syntaxiques en français parlé', *Journal of French Language Studies* 5 (1995), 17–29.

—— et al., *Pronom et syntaxe: l'approche pronominale et son application à la langue française* (Paris, SELAF, 1990).

Bogniaho, A., 'Francophonie et diversité littéraire', in A. Huannou (ed.), *Francophonie littéraire et identités culturelles. Actes du colloque du Gelef (cotonou, 18–20 mars 1998)* (Paris, L'Harmattan, 2000), 29–45.

Böll-Johansen, H., 'Une théorie de la nouvelle', *Revue de littérature comparée* 5.4 (Oct.–Dec. 1976), 421–432.

Bordelon, L., *Histoire des imaginations extravagantes de Monsieur Oufle* (Amsterdam, E. Roger, P. Humbert, P. de Coup et les frères Châtelain, 1710).

——*L'Histoire des imaginations extravagantes de Monsieur Oufle*, in *Voyages imaginaires, songes visions et romans cabalistiques* (Amsterdam and Paris, n.ed., 1789), XXXVI.

Borillo, A. et al., 'Tense and aspect', in F. Corblin and H. De Swart (eds), *Handbook of French Semantics* (Stanford, CSLI Publications, 2004), 233–348.

Bottigheimer, R.B., 'Before *Contes du temps passé* (1697): Charles Perrault's "Grisélidis" (1693), "Souhaits ridicules" (1693), and "Peau d'Asne" (1694)', *Romanic Review* 99.2 (2009), 175–189.

——*Fairy Tales. A New History* (Albany NY, SUNY Press, 2009).

—— 'Perrault au travail', in A. Defrance and J.-F. Perrin (eds), *Le Conte en ses paroles: la figuration de l'oralité dans le conte merveilleux du Classisme aux Lumières* (Paris, Desjonquères, 2007), 150–159.

—— 'France's first fairy tales: the rise and restoration narratives of "Les Facetieuses Muictz du seigneur François Straparole"', *Marvels & Tales* 19.1 (2005), 17–31.

—— 'Fairy tales, old wives, and printing presses', *History Today* 54.1 (2004), 38–44.

—— *Fairy Godfather. Straparola, Venice, and the Fairy Tale Tradition* (Philadelphia, University of Pennsylvania Press, 2002).

—— 'Fairy tales and folk tales', in P. Hunt (ed.), *International Companion Encyclopedia of Children's Literature* (London, Routledge, 2004 [1996]), I, 261–274.

—— 'Marienkind (KHM 3): a computer-based study of editorial change and stylistic development within Grimms' tales 1808–1864', *ARV Scandinavian Yearbook of Folklore* 46 (1990), 7–31.

—— *Grimms' Bad Girls and Bold Boys: The Social and Moral Vision of the Tales* (New Haven and London, Yale University Press, 1987).

—— (ed.) *Fairy Tales and Society: Illusion, Allusion, and Paradigm* (Philadelphia and London, University of Pennsylvania Press, 1986), 75–94.

Boyer, H., 'L'Opposition passé simple/passé composé dans le système verbal de la langue française', *Le Français moderne* 47.2 (1979), 121–129.

Brakelmann, F. W. J., *Giovan Francesco da Straparola da Caravaggio* (Göttingen, E.A. Huth, 1867).

Brémond, C., 'L'Étymologie des contes', *Féeries* 3 (2006), 183–213.

—— 'Préhistoire de Schéhérazade', in J.-L. Joly and A. Kilito (eds), *Les Mille et une nuits. Du texte au mythe* (Rabat, Publications de la faculté des lettres et sciences humaines, 2005), 19–42.

—— 'La Logique des possibles narratifs', *Communication* 8 (1981), 66–82.

Brench, A.C., *Writing in French from Senegal to Cameroon* (London, OUP, 1967).

Bres, J., 'De l'alternance passé composé/présent en récit conversationnel', in A. Borillo, C. Vetters and M. Vuillaume (eds), *Variations sur la référence verbale* (Amsterdam, Rodopi, 1997), 125–136.

—— 'Avant-propos', in M. Laforest (ed.), *Autour de la Narration* (Québec, Nuit blanche, 1996), 7–8.

Brody, J., 'Charles Perrault, conteur (du) moderne', in L. Godard de Donville and R. Duchêne (eds), *D'un siècle a l'autre. Anciens et modernes. Actes du XVIe colloque du CMR* (Marseille, CMR 17, 1987), 79–90.

Brooks, P., *Reading for the Plot. Design and Intention in Narrative* (Cambridge, Mass. and London, Harvard University Press, 1984).

Bryant, D., *Short Fiction and the Press in France, 1829–1841* (Lampeter, Edwin Mellen Press, 1996).

Bybee, J., R. Perkins, and W. Pagliuca, *The Evolution of Grammar: Tense, Aspect and Modality in the Languages of the World* (Chicago, University of Chicago Press, 1994).

Bybee, J. and S. Fleischman (eds), *Modality in Grammar and Discourse* (Amsterdam, Benjamins, 1995).

Cabinet des fées ou Collection choisie des contes des fées, et autres contes merveilleux. Ornés de figures (Le), 41 volumes (Geneva and Paris, Barde, Manget et Compagnie-Cuchet, 1785–1789).

Calame-Griaule, G., *Contes dogons du Mali* (Paris, Karthala, 2006).

—— 'Un itinéraire en ethnolinguistique', *Cahiers de littérature orale* 50 (2001), 15–33.

—— (ed.), *Le Renouveau du conte* (Paris, CNRS, 1991).

Carlson, G. and Pelletier, F., *The Generic Book* (Chicago, Chicago University Press, 1995).

Carpanin Marimoutou, J. C., 'Des fables créoles', *Études créoles* 24.2 (2001), 7–14.

Carré, O., *Contes et récits de la vie quotidienne. Pratiques en groupe interculturel* (Paris, L'Harmattan, 1998).

Carruthers, J., 'Oralité et expression de la séquence temporelle', in P. Caudal and J. Carruthers (eds), *Temporalité et structuration dans la narration orale* (Amsterdam, Rodopi, forthcoming).

—— 'The syntax of oral French', *French Studies* 40.2 (2006), 251–260.

—— *Oral Narration in Modern French. A Linguistic Analysis of Temporal Patterns* (Oxford, Legenda, 2005).

—— and S. Marnette, 'Tense, voices and point of view in medieval and modern "oral" narration', in E. Labeau, C. Vetters, and P. Caudal (eds), *Sémantique et diachronie du système verbal français* (Amsterdam, Rodopi, 2007), 177–202.

Caudal, P., 'Reverse causo-temporal ordering and perfective viewpoint tenses', talk given at *Chronos* 8 (University of Texas at Austin, 2008).

—— 'Tenses, connectives and narration(s)', talk given at *Chronos* 7 (University of Antwerp, 2006).

—— and L. Roussarie, 'Brands of perfects and the semantics/pragmatics interface', in P. Denis, E. McCready, A. Palmer and B. Reese (eds), *Proceedings of the 2004 Texas Linguistics Society: Issues at the Semantics-Pragmatics Interface* (Somerville, Cascadilla Press, 2006), 13–27.

—— and L. Roussarie, 'Aspectual viewpoints, speech act functions and discourse structure', in P. Kempchinsky and R. Slabakova (eds), *The Syntax, Semantics and Acquisition of Tense and Aspect* (Dordrecht, Kluwer, 2005), 265–290.

—— L. Roussarie, and C. Vetters, 'L'Imparfait, un temps inconséquent', *Langue française* 138 (2003), 61–74.

—— and C. Vetters, 'Les Temps verbaux: des connecteurs temporels qui s'ignorent?', in E. Moline, D. Stosic and C. Vetters (eds), *Les Connecteurs temporels du français* (Amsterdam, Rodopi, 2007), 105–137.

—— and C. Vetters, 'Passé composé et passé simple: sémantique diachronique et formelle', in E. Labeau, C. Vetters and P. Caudal (eds), *Sémantique et diachronie du système verbal français* (Amsterdam, Rodopi, 2007), 121–151.

Cauvin, J., *Comprendre les contes* (Paris, Les Classiques africains, 1992 [1980]).

Cazotte, J., *La Patte du chat, conte zinzimois*, in A. Defrance and J.-F. Perrin (eds), *Hamilton et autres conteurs* (Paris, Champion, 2008 [Tilloobalaa [Paris], n.p., 1741]).

Césaire, A., *Nègre je suis, nègre je resterai. Entretiens avec Françoise Vergès* (Paris, Albin Michel, 2004).

—— and R. Ménil, 'Introduction au folklore martiniquais', *Tropiques* 4 (January 1942), 7–11.

Césaire, I., *Contes de nuits et de jours aux Antilles* (Paris, Éditions caribéennes, 1989).

—— *Contes de mort et de vie aux Antilles* (Paris, Nubia, 1976).

Chamoiseau, P., *Au Temps de l'antan. Contes du pays Martinique* (Paris, Hatier, 1988).

—— *Solibo Magnifique* (Paris, Folio, 1988).

—— and R. Confiant, *Lettres créoles: tracées antillaises et continentales de la littérature 1635–1975* (Paris, Hatier, 1991).

Champfleury, *Contes*, ed. G. Secchi (Rome, Bulzoni, 1973).

Chancé, D., *L'Auteur en souffrance. Essai sur la position et la représentation de l'auteur dans le roman antillais contemporain (1981–1992)* (Paris, PUF, 2001).

Chauvin, V., *Bibliographie des ouvrages arabes ou relatifs aux Arabes publiés dans l'Europe chrétienne de 1810 à 1855*, 12 vols (Liège, H. Vaillant-Carmanne, 1892–1922).

Chevrier, J., *L'Arbre à palabres. Essai sur les contes et récits traditionnels d'Afrique noire* (Paris, Hatier, 2005).

—— *La Littérature nègre* (Paris, Armand Colin, 2003).

Chuquet, H., 'Construction d'événements et types de procès dans le récit au présent en français et en anglais', in J. Guillemin-Flescher (ed.), *Linguistique contrastive et traduction* (Gap, Ophrys, 1994), III, 1–56.

Clastres, P., *Le Grand Parler. Mythes et chants sacrés des Indiens Guaranis* (Paris, Seuil, 1974).

Clausen-Stolzenburg, M., *Märchen und mittelalterliche Literaturtradition* (Heidelberg, C. Winter, 1995).

Clements, R. and J. Gibaldi, *Anatomy of the Novella* (New York, New York University Press, 1977).

Clouston, W.A., *Popular Tales and Fictions. Their Migration and Transformation* (Edinburgh and London, W. Blackwood, 1887).

Cogman, P., *Narration in Nineteenth-Century French Short Fiction* (Durham, University of Durham Modern Languages Series 22, 2002).

Coirier, P., D. Gaonac'h and J.-M. Passerault, *Psycholinguistique textuelle. Approche cognitive de la compréhension et de la production des textes* (Paris, Armand Colin, 1996).

Colin, R., *Les Contes noirs de l'Ouest africain. Témoins majeurs d'un humanisme* (Paris, Présence Africaine, 2005 [1957]).

Colombo, C., *Ti Jean et Monsieur le Roi/Ti Jan é Misié liwa. Contes de la Martinique bilingue créole-français* (Paris, L'Harmattan, 2006).

Condé, M., *La Civilisation du bossale. Réflexions sur la littérature orale de la Guadeloupe et de la Martinique* (Paris, L'Harmattan, 1978).

—— and M. Cottenet-Hage (eds), *Penser la créolité* (Paris, Karthala, 1995).

Confiant, R., 'Lafcadio Hearn: the magnificent traveller', Foreword to *Two Years in the French West Indies* (Oxford, Signal Books, 2001), ix–xii.

—— and D. Damoison, *Le Galion. Canne, douleur séculaire Ô tendresse* (Petit Bourg, Guadeloupe, Ibis Rouge, 2000).

—— *Contes créoles des Amériques* (Paris, Stock, 1995).

—— M. Lebielle and D. Damoison, *Les Maîtres de la parole créole* (Paris, Gallimard, 1995).

Cosquin, E., 'Le Prologue-cadre des *Mille et une nuits*, les légendes perses et le livre d'Esther', *Études folkloriques* (1922), 293–347.

Couégnas, D., *Introduction à la paralittérature* (Paris, Seuil, 1992).

Coveney, A., *Variability in Spoken French: A Sociolinguistic Study of Interrogation and Negation* (Exeter, Elm Bank, 1996).

Dadié, B., 'Le Chasseur et le boa', in *Le Pagne noir* (Paris, Présence Africaine, 1970 [1955]), 97–106.

Dahl, Ö., *Tense and Aspect in the Languages of Europe* (Berlin, Mouton de Gruyter, 2000).

Dayan, P., 'Baudelaire at his latrine: motions in the *Petits poèmes en prose* and in George Sand's novels', *French Studies* 48.4 (1994), 416–424.

Décote, G., *L'Itinéraire de Jacques Cazotte: 1719–1792: de la fiction littéraire au mysticisme politique* (Geneva, Droz, 1984).

Decourt, N., *La Vache des orphelins. Conte et immigration* (Lyon, Presses Universitaires de Lyon, 1992).

—— and N. Louali-Raynal, 'Les Procédés du contage: du contage traditionnel au néocontage', *Littérature orale arabo-berbère* 21 (1990), 121–152.

Defrance, A., 'Écriture féminine et dénégation de l'autorité: les contes de fées de Madame d'Aulnoy', *Revue des sciences humaines* 238 (1995), 111–126.

—— and J.-F. Perrin (eds), *Le Conte en ses paroles: la figuration de l'oralité dans le conte merveilleux du Classisme aux Lumières* (Paris, Desjonquères, 2007).

Degand, L. and H. Pander Maat, 'Scaling causal relations and connectives in terms of speaker involvement', *Cognitive Linguistics* 12 (2001), 211–245

Delarue, P., 'Les Contes merveilleux de Perrault. Faits et rapprochements nouveaux', *Arts et traditions populaires* 1 (1954), 1–22; and 2 (1954), 251–274.

——and M.-L. Tenèze, *Le Conte populaire français. Catalogue raisonné des versions de France* (Paris, Maisonneuve et Larose, 2002).

De La Salle, B., *Plaidoyer pour les arts de la parole* (Vendôme, CLIO, 2004).

——'La Culture maghrébine dans le renouveau du conte', *Grand Maghreb* 35 (1984).

Delsham, T., *Cénesthésie et l'urgence de l'être* (Schœlcher, Martinique Éditions, 2005).

Démoris, R., *Le Roman à la première personne. Du classicisme aux Lumières* (Geneva, Droz, 2002).

Denis, S., 'Introduction' to L. Hearn, *Trois fois bel conte* (Paris, Mercure de France, 1939), 14–31.

Derive, J., *Collecte et traduction des littératures orales. Un exemple négro-africain: les contes ngbaka-ma'bo de R.C.A.* (Paris, Selaf, 1975).

——(ed.), *L'Épopée. Unité et diversité d'un genre* (Paris, Karthala, 2002).

Derrida, J., *De la grammatologie* (Paris, Éditions de Minuit, 1967).

Détrie, C. (ed.), *Poétiques du divers* (Montpellier-Praxiling, Université Paul Valéry-Montpellier III, 1998).

Diderot, D., *Ceci n'est pas un conte*, in *Œuvres romanesques*, ed. H. Bénac (Paris, Classiques Garnier, 1961).

Diop, B., 'Sarzan', in *Les Contes d'Amadou Koumba* (Paris, Présence Africaine, 1961 [1947]), 167–181.

——*Les Nouveaux Contes d'Amadou Koumba*, pref. L.S. Senghor (Paris, Présence Africaine, 1958).

Dubey, A., P. Sturt, and F. Keller, *Parallelism in Coordination as an Instance of Syntactic Priming. Evidence from Corpus-Based Modeling* (Vancouver, HLTC-CEMNLP, 2005).

Duchêne, R., 'Signification du romanesque chez les mondains: l'exemple de Madame de Sévigné', *Revue d'histoire littéraire de la France* 77 (1977), 578–594.

Ducrot, O., *Dire et ne pas dire* (Paris, Hermann, 1991).

——*Les Mots du discours* (Paris, Minuit, 1980).

Dumasy, L., *La Querelle du roman-feuilleton* (Grenoble, Université Stendhal, 1999).

Dundes, A., 'Introduction to the Second Edition', in V. Propp, *Morphology of the Folktale*, trans. L. A. Wagner (Austin and London, University of Texas Press, 1986), xi–xvii.

Ellis, J.M., *One Fairy Story Too Many* (Chicago, University of Chicago Press, 1983).

Engel, D., *Tense and Text. A Study of French Past Tenses* (London, Routledge, 1990).

Faller, M., 'The Cusco Quechua reportative evidential and rhetorical relations', in P. Austin and A. Simpson (eds), *Endangered Languages* (Hamburg, Helmut Buske Verlag, 2007).

Farrant, T., *Balzac's Shorter Fictions* (Oxford, OUP, 2002).

Félice, A. de, *Essai sur quelques techniques de l'art verbal traditionnel* (Thèse de doctorat, Université de Paris, 1957).

Finnegan, R., *The Oral and Beyond. Doing Things with Words in Africa* (Chicago, Chicago University Press, 2007).

—— *Oral Poetry: Its Nature, Significance and Social Context* (Cambridge, CUP, 1977).

—— *Limba Stories and Storytelling* (Oxford, Clarendon Press, 1967).

Flaubert, G., *Écrits de jeunesse*, ed. M. Nadeau (Lausanne, Société Coopérative Éditions Rencontre, 1964).

Fleischman, S., *Tense and Narrativity. From Medieval Performance to Modern Fiction* (London, Routledge, 1990).

Fonyi, A., 'Nouvelle et subjectivité', *Revue de littérature comparée* 5.4 (1976), 355–375.

Forster, E.M., *Aspects of the Novel* (Harmondsworth, Penguin, 1966).

Fox, J.J. (ed.), *To Speak in Pairs: Essays on the Ritual Languages of Eastern Indonesia* (Cambridge, CUP, 1988), 1–28.

Frayling, C. (ed.), *Napoleon Wrote Fiction* (Salisbury, Compton Press, 1972).

Galand-Pernet, P., *Littératures berbères. Des voix, des lettres* (Paris, PUF, 1998).

Gallagher, M., *Soundings in French Caribbean Writing since 1950. The Shock of Space and Time* (Oxford, OUP, 2002).

Galland, A., *Le Voyage à Smyrne*, ed. F. Bauduen (Paris, Chandeigne, 2000).

Garcier, F., 'Du nom au genre: le cas de la *short story*', *La Licorne* 22 (1992), 19–27.

Gaster, M., 'The modern origin of fairy tales', *Folk-Lore Journal* 5 (1887), 339–351.

Gates, H.L., *The Signifying Monkey. A Theory of African-American Literary Criticism* (Oxford, OUP, 1988).

Gautier, T., *Les Jeunes France. Romans goguenards* (Paris, Éditions des autres, 1979 [1833]).

Gauvin, L., *L'Écrivain francophone à la croisée des langues* (Paris, Karthala, 1997).

Genette, G., *Nouveau discours du récit* (Paris, Seuil, 1983).

—— 'Discours du récit', in *Figures III* (Paris, Seuil, 1972), 65–278.

—— 'Frontières du récit', *Communications* 8 (1966), 152–163.

Georgel, T., *Contes et légendes des Antilles* (Paris, Pocket, 1994 [Paris, Nathan, 1957]).

Ginelli, P., *Archipels littéraires. Chamoiseau, Condé, Confiant, Brival, Maximin, Laferrière, Pineau, Agnant* (Montréal, Mémoire d'encrier, 2007).

Glissant, E., 'Le Chaos-monde, l'oral et l'écrit', in R. Ludwig (ed.), *Écrire la "parole de nuit". La nouvelle littérature antillaise* (Paris, Folio, 1994), 111–129.

Godenne, R., *Études sur la nouvelle de langue française* (Geneva, Slatkine, 2005).

—— *La Nouvelle* (Paris, Champion, 1995).

—— 'Pistes pour une étude de la nouvelle au XIXe siècle', in B. Alluin and F. Suard (eds), *La Nouvelle: définitions, transformations* (Villeneuve d'Ascq, Presses Universitaires de Lille, 1990).

Gomme, L., 'Presidential address', *Folk-Lore* 2 (1891), 1–30.

Goody, J., *Entre l'oralité et l'écriture* (Paris, PUF, 1994).

—— *La Raison graphique: la domestication de la pensée sauvage* (Paris, Éditions de Minuit, 1979).

—— and I. Watt, 'The consequences of literacy', in J. Goody (ed.), *Literacy in Traditional Societies* (Cambridge, CUP, 1968), 27–68.

Görög-Karady, V., 'French Study of African Folklore', in P. Peek and K. Yankah (eds), *African Folklore: An Encyclopedia* (London, Routledge, 2004), 138–141.

—— 'Qui conte en France aujourd'hui? Les nouveaux conteurs', *Cahiers de Littérature Orale* 11 (1982), 95–116.

Grätz, M., *Das Märchen in der deutschen Aufklärung. Vom Feenmärchen zum Volksmärchen* (Stuttgart, Metzler, 1988).

Grevet, R., *L'Avènement de l'école contemporaine en France (1789–1835)* (Villeneuve d'Ascq, Presses Universitaires du Septentrion, 2001).

Grojnowski, D., 'De Baudelaire à Poe: l'effet de totalité', in J. Gratton and J.-P. Imbert (eds), *La Nouvelle hier et aujourd'hui* (Paris, L'Harmattan, 1997).

Guériff, F., *Contes populaires du pays de Guérande* (La Crèche, Geste éditions, 2001).

Gueullette, J.E., *T.S. Gueullette, un magistrat du XVIIIe siècle* (Paris, Droz, 1938).

—— *Notes et souvenirs sur le Théâtre-Italien au XVIIIe siècle, publiés* (Paris, Droz, 1938).

Gueullette, T.S., *Contes mogols* (Paris, Les Libraires associés, 1765).

—— *Les Aventures merveilleuses du mandarin Fum-Hoam. Contes chinois*, 2 vols (Paris, J.-B. Mazuel, 1723).

Guézennec, N., 'La Mémoire des contes et légendes bas-bretons: réflexions sur la mémoire orale et la mémoire écrite', *Fabula* (forthcoming).

—— 'Pointer les lieux. Relation entre gestes, littérature orale et contexte', *Cahiers de l'Association for French Language Studies* 13.2 (2007), 60–99.

—— *Mémoire et transmission de la tradition orale en Basse-Bretagne. Approches ethno- et sociolinguistiques de la littérature orale, de la mémoire, de l'oral et de l'écrit* (Thèse de doctorat, Université de Paris X-Nanterre, 2005).

Guise, R., 'Le Roman-feuilleton (1830–1848): naissance d'un genre' (Thèse de doctorat, Université de Nancy, 1975).

Guissard, M., *La Nouvelle française. Essai de définition d'un genre* (Louvain-la-neuve, Bruylant Academia, 2002).

Halliday, M.A.K., *Spoken and Written Language* (Victoria, Deakin University Press, 1985).

Hallward, P., *Absolutely Postcolonial: Writing between the Singular and the Specific* (Manchester, Manchester University Press, 2001).

Hannon, P., *Fabulous Identities: Women's Fairy Tales in Seventeenth-Century France* (Amsterdam and Atlanta, Rodopi, 1998).

Hawwas, A.-E.-H., 'A prologue tale as manifesto tale: establishing a narrative literary form and the formation of the Arabian Nights', *Marvels & Tales* 21.1 (2007), 65–77.

Hearn, L., *Esquisses martiniquaises I*, ed. M. Gallagher (Paris, L'Harmattan, 2003).

—— *Esquisses martiniquaises II*, ed. M. Gallagher (Paris, L'Harmattan, 2003).

—— *Contes créoles II (inédits)*, collected by L. Hearn, trans. L. Solo Martinel (Lamentin-Martinique, Ibis rouge, 2002).

—— *Two Years in the French West Indies* (Oxford, Signal Books, 2001 [New York, Harper & Bros, 1890]).

—— *Trois fois bel conte*, trans. S. Denis, pref. C.-M. Garnier (Paris, Mercure de France, 1939).

—— *Contes des tropiques*, trans. M. Logé (Paris, Mercure de France, 1926).

—— *Esquisses martiniquaises*, trans. M. Logé (Paris, Mercure de France, 1924).

—— *Stray Leaves from Strange Literature* (Boston, James A. Osgood & Co., 1904).

—— *Youma* (New York, Harper & Bros, 1890).

—— *Chita: A Memory of Last Island* (New York, Harper & Bros, 1889).

—— *Some Chinese Ghosts* (Boston, Roberts Bros, 1887).

—— *La Cuisine créole: A Collection of Culinary Recipes* (New York, Will H. Coleman, 1885).

—— *Gombo Zhèbes: A Little Dictionary of Creole Proverbs* (New York, Will H. Coleman, 1885).

—— *One of Cleopatra's Nights and other Fantastic Romances by Théophile Gautier* (New York, R. Worthington, 1882).

Hell, V., 'L'Art de la brièveté', *Revue de littérature comparée* 5.4 (Oct.–Dec. 1976), 389–401.

Herbelot, B. d', *Bibliothèque orientale* (Paris, Compagnie des Libraires, 1697).

Herranen, G., '"A big ugly man with a quest for narratives"', *Studia Fennica* 33 (1989), 64–69.

Histoire Littéraire des Femmes Françaises... Par une Société de Gens de Lettres (Paris, 1769).

Hobbs, R., *From Balzac to Zola: Selected Short Stories* (London, Duckworth-Bristol Classical Press, 1992).

Hobson, M., *The Object of Art* (Cambridge, CUP, 1982).

Hymes, D., 'Breakthrough into performance', in D.B. Amos and K. Goldstein (eds), *Folklore, Performance and Communication* (The Hague, Mouton de Gruyter, 1974), 11–74.

Jacobs, J., 'The folk', *Folk-Lore* 4 (1893), 233–238.

—— 'The problem of diffusion: rejoinders', *Folk-Lore* 5 (1894), 129–149.

Jacques-Chaquin, N., 'La Passion des sciences interdites: curiosité et démonologie (XVè–XVIIIè siècles)', in S. Houdard and N. Jacques-Chaquin (eds), *Curiosité et Libido Sciendi de la Renaissance aux Lumières* (Paris, ENS, 1998), I, 73–107.

Jahanderie, K., *Spoken and Written Discourse* (Connecticut, Ablex, 1999).

Jakobson, R., *Questions de poétique* (Paris, Seuil, 1973).

Jameson, F., 'Third-world literature in the era of multinational capitalism', *Social Text* 15 (1986), 65–88.

Janin, J., 'Le Piédestal', *Revue de Paris* 43 (1832), 103.

Jasmin, N., *Naissance du conte féminin. Mots et merveilles: les contes de fées de Madame d'Aulnoy, 1690–1698* (Paris, Champion, 2002).

Jean, G., *Le Pouvoir des contes* (Tournai, Casterman, 1990 [1981]).

Jeanjean, C., 'À propos de l'utilisation des conjonctions chez les enfants', *Recherches sur le français parlé* 5 (1983), 191–209.

Jolles, A., *Formes simples* (Paris, Seuil, 1972 [1930]).

Judge, A., 'Le Passé simple: un retour aux sources dans le contexte du mélange des temps?', in E. Labeau, C. Vetters and P. Caudal (eds),

Sémantique et diachronie du système verbal français (Amsterdam, Rodopi, 2007), 153–176.

——'Choix entre le présent narratif et le système multifocal dans le contexte du récit écrit', in S. Vogeleer et al. (eds), *Temps et discours* (Louvain-La-Neuve, Peeters, 1998), 215–235.

Julien, E., 'Reading "orality" in French-language novels from sub-Saharan Africa', in C. Forsdick and D. Murphy (eds), *Francophone Postcolonial Studies. A Critical Introduction* (London, Arnold, 2003), 122–132.

Kelley, T., *Reinventing Allegory* (Cambridge, CUP, 1997).

Kennard, N., *Lafcadio Hearn* (New York, Appleton & Co. Ltd, 1912).

Kerbrat-Orecchioni, C., *Les Actes du langage* (Paris, Nathan, 2001).

——*La Conversation* (Paris, Seuil, 1996).

Kesteloot, L., *Les Écrivains noirs de langue française: naissance d'une littérature* (Brussels, Université libre de Bruxelles-Institut de sociologie, 1963).

Kitchenassamy, F., *Les Contes à dormir debout/Kont pou dômi doubou: contes bilingues français-créole* (Paris, L'Harmattan, 2000).

Koch, P., 'Subordination, intégration syntaxique et "oralité"', in H.L. Andersen and G. Skytte (eds), *La Subordination dans les langues romanes: actes du colloque international, Copenhague* (Copenhagen, Munksgaard, 1995), 13–42.

——and W. Oesterreicher, 'Gesprochene Sprache und geschriebene Sprache (Langage parlé et langage écrit)', in G. Holtus, M. Metzeltin and C. Schmitt (eds), *Lexikon der romanischen Linguistik* (Tübingen, Max Niemeyer Verlag, 2001), I.2, 584–627.

Krehbiel, H.E., *Afro-American Folksongs: A Study in Racial and National Music* (New York, G. Schirmer, 1914).

Kreilkamp, I., *Voice and the Victorian Storyteller* (Cambridge, CUP, 2005).

Labov, W., 'Some further steps in narrative analysis', *Journal of Narrative and Life History* 7 (1997), 395–415.

——and J. Waletsky, 'Narrative analysis: oral versions of personal experience', in J. Helm (McNeish) (ed.), *Essays on the Verbal and Visual Arts. Proceedings of the 1966 Annual Spring Meeting of the American*

Ethnological Society (Seattle, University of Washington Press, 1967), 12–44.

Lacambre, G. and J. Lacambre (eds), *Champfleury: son regard et celui de Baudelaire* (Paris, Hermann, 1990).

Lacoste-Dujardin, C., *Traduction des légendes et contes merveilleux de la Grande Kabylie, recueillis par A. Mouliéras* (Paris, Geuthner, 1965), I, 128–135.

Lagenevais, F. de, 'Le Roman dans le monde', *Revue des deux mondes* 13.2 (1843), 586–614.

Lajarte, P. de, 'Du conte facétieux considéré comme genre: esquisse d'une analyse structurale', *Ethnologie française* 4 (1974), 319–332.

Laplantine, F. and A. Nouss, *Métissages. D'Arcimboldo à Zombi* (Paris, Pauvert, 2001).

Latapie, S., 'Un dispositif intégré: le conte dans le *Magasin des enfants* de Mme Leprince de Beaumont', *Féeries* 1 (2003), 126–143.

Laurent, D., 'La Querelle du *Barzaz Breiz*' in J. Balcou and Y. Le Gallo (eds), *Histoire littéraire et culturelle de la Bretagne* (Paris, Champion-Coop Breizh, 1997).

LeClerq, C., 'De la croyance des Gaspésiens, touchant l'immortalité de l'âme', in C. LeClerq, *Nouvelle relation de la Gaspésie* (Paris, A. Auroy, 1691), 310–329.

Leech, G. and M. Short, *Style in Fiction: A Linguistic Introduction to English Fictional Prose* (London, Longman, 1981).

Lenglet Du Fresnoy, N., 'Contes des fées et autres contes merveilleux', *Bibliothèque des romans*, in N. Lenglet Du Fresnoy, *De l'usage des romans où l'on fait voir leur utilité et leurs différents caractères, avec une bibliothèque des romans accompagnée de remarques critiques sur leur choix et leur édition* (Amsterdam, Vve de Poilras, 1734), article XI.

Lhéritier de Villandon, M.-J., 'Œuvres meslées de Mlle L'H**', in *Contes. Mademoiselle Lhéritier, Mademoiselle Bernard, Mademoiselle de La Force, Madame Durand, Madame d'Auneuil*, ed. R. Robert (Paris, Champion, 2005 [Paris, Jean Guignard, 1696]), II.

Liauzu, C., 'L'École et l'immigration: enjeux culturels d'une société pluri-elle', *Travaux et documents de l'IREMAM* 3 (1987).

Loiseau, S., *Les Pouvoirs du conte* (Paris, PUF, 1992).

Loiseleur-Deslongchamps, A.-L.-A., 'Essai historique sur les contes orientaux et sur les Mille et une nuits' ('Introduction aux Mille et une nuits'), in *Les Mille et une nuits* (Paris, Édition du Panthéon littéraire, 1838).

Lord, A.B., *The Singer of Tales* (Cambridge, Mass. and London, Harvard University Press, 2000 [1960]).

Louandre, C., 'Statistique littéraire. De la production intellectuelle en France depuis quinze ans. Dernière partie. Littérature ancienne et étrangère, Poésie, Roman, Théâtre', *Revue des deux mondes* 20 (1847), 671–703.

Louis, P., *Aimé Césaire: rencontre avec un nègre fondamental* (Paris, Arléa, 2004).

Lucrèce, *De la nature, Livre III*, trans. H. Clouard (Paris, Garnier-Flammarion, 1964).

—— *De la nature*, trans. J.-B. de Boyer d'Argens, in *Mémoires secrets de la République des Lettres ou le théâtre de la vérité* (Geneva, Slatkine, 1967).

Ludwig, R. (ed.), *Écrire la parole de nuit: la nouvelle littérature antillaise* (Paris, Gallimard, 1994).

Lyons, J., *Language and Linguistics* (Cambridge, CUP, 1981).

MacQueen, J., *Allegory* (London, Methuen, 1970).

Magnanini, S., 'Postulated routes from Naples to Paris: the printer Antonio Bulifon and Giambattista Basile's fairy tales in seventeenth-century France', *Marvels & Tales* 21.1 (2007), 78–92.

Malrieu, D., 'Linguistique de corpus, genres textuels, temps et personnes', *Langages* 153 (2004), 73–85.

Marin, L., 'Les Enjeux d'un frontispice', *L'Esprit créateur* 27.3 (1987), 49–57.

—— *La Parole mangée* (Paris, Klincksieck, 1986).

—— *Le Portrait du roi* (Paris, Éditions de Minuit, 1981).

Marler, R.F., 'From tale to short story', in C.E. May (ed.), *The New Short Story Theories* (Athens, Ohio, Ohio University Press, 1994), 165–191.

Marnette, S., *Speech and Thought Presentation in French. Concepts and Strategies* (Amsterdam, Benjamins, 2005).

Marotin, F. (ed.), *Frontières du conte* (Paris, Éditions du CNRS, 1982).

Massol, C., *Une poétique de l'énigme. Le récit herméneutique balzacien* (Geneva, Droz, 2006).

Matthews, B., 'The philosophy of the short-story', in *The London Review*, 5 July 1884.

May, C.E. (ed.), *The New Short Story Theories* (Athens, Ohio, Ohio University Press, 1994).

[Mayer, C.-J.], *Le Cabinet des fées, ou Collection choisie des contes des fées, et autres contes merveilleux* (Amsterdam and Paris, Serpente, 1786).

McCusker, M., '"This Creole culture, miraculously forged": the contradictions of *créolité*, in C. Forsdick and D. Murphy (eds), *Francophone Postcolonial Studies. A Critical Introduction* (London, Arnold, 2003), 112–121.

Mérimée, P., *Théâtre, romans et nouvelles*, eds J. Maillon and P. Salomon (Paris, Gallimard-Pléiade, 1978).

Meschonnic, H., *Poétique du traduire* (Lagrasse, Verdier, 1999).

—— *Critique du rythme* (Lagrasse, Verdier, 1982).

Midiohouan, G.O., *La Nouvelle d'expression française en Afrique noire* (Paris, L'Harmattan, 1999).

Milne, L., 'Sex, gender and the right to write: Patrick Chamoiseau and the erotics of colonialism', *Paragraph* 24.3 (2001), 59–75.

Moeschler, J., 'L'Ordre temporel dans le discours: le modèle des inférences directionnelles', in A. Carlier, V. Lagae and C. Benninger (eds), *Passé et parfait* (Amsterdam, Rodopi, 2000), 1–11.

Monod Becquelin, A., 'Polyphonie thérapeutique: une confrontation pour la guérison en tzeltal', in A. Monod Becquelin and P. Erickson (eds), *Les Rituels du dialogue* (Nanterre, Société d'ethnologie, 2000), 511–553.

—— V. Vapnarsky, C. Becquey and A. Breton, 'Decir y contar la diversidad: paralelismo, variantes y variaciones en las tradiciones mayas', in A. Monod Becquelin, A. Breton and M.H. Ruz (eds), *Formas mayas de la diversidad* (Mérida, Universidad Nacional Autónoma de México, forthcoming).

Mulder, W. de and C. Vetters, 'Temps verbaux, anaphores (pro)nominales et relations discursives', *Travaux de Linguistique* 39 (1999), 37–58.

Müller, B., *Le Français d'aujourd'hui* (Paris, Klincksieck, 1985).

Murat, H.-J. de Castelnau, Comtesse de, 'Avertissement', in *Histoires sublimes et allégoriques* (Paris, F. and P. Delaune, 1699).

——*Ouvrages de Mme la comtesse de Murat* (Paris, Bibliothèque de l'Arsenal, manuscrit n 3471).

Murray, P., *A Fantastic Journey: The Life and Literature of Lafcadio Hearn* (Sandgate, Kent, Japan Library, 1993).

Musset, A. de, *Lettres de Dupuis et de Cotonne. Œuvres complètes*, ed. P. Van Tieghem (Paris, Seuil, 1979).

Naïr, S., 'Marseille: chronique des années de lèpre', *Les Temps modernes* 452–453–454 (1984), 1592–1615.

Naumann, H., *Primitive Gemeinschaftskultur. Beiträge zur Volkskunde und Mythologie* (Jena, E. Diederichs, 1921).

Nedjalkov, V., *Typology of Resultative Constructions* (Amsterdam, Benjamins, 1988).

Nettement, A., *Études critiques sur le feuilleton-roman* (Paris, Lagny frères, 1847).

Nisard, D., 'D'un commencement de réaction contre la littérature facile', *Revue de Paris* 57 (Dec. 1833), 211–218.

Okpewho, I., *African Oral Literature. Backgrounds, Character, and Continuity* (Bloomington, Indianapolis, Indiana University Press, 1992).

Ong, W., *Orality and Literacy. The Technologizing of the Word* (London and New York, Methuen, 1982).

—— 'Oral remembering and narrative structures', in D. Tannen (ed.), *Analyzing Discourse. Text and Talk* (Washington, University of Georgetown Press, 1982), 12–24.

Papafragou, A., 'Epistemic modality and truth conditions', *Lingua* 116 (2006), 1688–1702.

Parry, M., *The Making of Homeric Verse (Collected Papers of Milman Parry)* (Oxford, Clarendon Press, 1971).

——*L'Épithète traditionnelle dans Homère* (Paris, Les Belles Lettres, 1928).

Parsons, E., *Folk-lore of the Antilles, French and English*, 3 vols (New York, The American Folklore Society, 1933–1943).

Pasco, A., *Nouvelles françaises du dix-neuvième siècle* (Charlottesville, Rookwood, 2006).

Pelen, J.-N., 'Le Simple Fait de raconter toujours la même histoire: réflexion sur l'en-deçà du sens dans la tradition du conte', in A. Petitat (ed.), *Contes: l'universel et le singulier* (Paris, Payot, 2002), 197–213.

Perrault, C., *Griselidis, nouvelle, avec Le Conte de Peau d'Asne et celuy des Souhaits ridicules. Quatrième edition.* Rpt. as *Contes de Perrault, Fac-similé de l'édition originale de 1695–1697*, ed. J. Barchilon (Geneva, Slatkine Reprints, 1980 [Paris, J.B. Coignard, 1695]).

Perrin, J.-F., 'L'Invention d'un genre littéraire au XVIIIè siècle: le conte oriental', *Féeries* 2 (2004–2005), 9–28.

——'Petits traités de l'âme et du corps: les contes à métempsycose (XVIIè–XVIIIè siècle)', in R. Jomand-Baudry and J.-F. Perrin (eds), *Le Conte merveilleux au XVIIIè siècle* (Paris, Kimé, 2002), 123–139.

——C. Bahier-Porte, M.F. Bosquet, R. Daoulas and C. Ramirez (eds), *Les Contes merveilleux de Thomas-Simon Gueullette* (Paris, Champion, 2009).

Perrot, J. (ed.), *Les Métamorphoses du conte* (Brussels, Peter Lang, 2004).

Pfaff, F., *Entretiens avec Maryse Condé* (Paris, Karthala, 1993).

Pichois, C. and J. Ziegler, *Baudelaire*, trans. G. Robb (London, Vintage, 1991).

Pike-Conant, M., *The Oriental Tale in England in the Eighteenth Century* (London, Cass, 1966 [1908]).

Place-Verghnes, F., *Jeux pragmatiques dans les 'Contes et Nouvelles' de Guy de Maupassant* (Paris, Champion, 2005).

Poe, E.A., *Selected Writings*, ed. D. Galloway (Harmondsworth, Penguin, 1967).

Pöge-Alder, K., *"Märchen" als mündlich tradierte Erzählungen des Volkes? Zur Wissenschaftsgeschichte der Entstehungs- und Verbreitungstheorien von Volksmärchen von den Brüdern Grimm bis zur Märchenforschung in der DDR.* (Frankfurt-am-Main, Peter Lang, 1994).

Polanyi, L., *Telling the American Story. A Linguistic and Cultural Analysis of Conversational Storytelling* (Norwood NJ, Ablex, 1982).

—— 'Literary complexity in everyday storytelling', in D. Tannen (ed.), *Spoken and Written Language: Exploring Orality and Literacy* (Norwood, Ablex, 1982), 155–170.

Potts, C., *The Logic of Conventional Implicatures* (Oxford, OUP, 2005).

Poulain, A., *Contes et légendes de Haute Bretagne* (Rennes, Ouest-France, 1999).

Pratt, M.-L., 'The short story: the long and the short of it', in C.E. May (ed.), *The New Short Story Theories* (Athens, Ohio, Ohio University Press, 1994), 91–113.

Price, R. and S. Price, 'Shadowboxing in the mangrove', *Cultural Anthropology* 12.1 (1997), 3–36.

Propp, V., *La Morphologie du conte* (Paris, Seuil, 1970).

——*Les Racines historiques du conte merveilleux*, trans. L. Gruel-Apert, pref. D. Fabre and J.-C. Schmitt (Paris, N.R.F.-Gallimard, 1983 [1946]).

Reid, I., *The Short Story* (London, Methuen, 1977).

Réjouis, R.-M., *Veillées pour les mots. Aimé Césaire, Patrick Chamoiseau et Maryse Condé* (Paris, Karthala, 2005).

Revaz, F., 'Passé simple et passé composé: entre langue et discours', *Études de linguistique appliquée* 102 (1996), 175–190.

Rigolot, F., 'Prolégomènes à une étude du statut de l'appareil liminaire des textes littéraires', *L'Esprit créateur* 27.3 (1987), 7–18.

Riegel, M., J.C. Pellat, and R. Rioul, *Grammaire méthodique du français* (Paris, PUF, 1994).

Riesz, J., 'La "Folie" des tirailleurs sénégalais', in J.P. Little and R. Little (eds), *Black Accents. Writing in French from Africa, Mauritius and the Caribbean* (London, Grant & Cutler, 1997), 139–156.

Rimmon-Kenan, S., *Narrative Fiction: Contemporary Poetics* (London, Methuen, 1989).

Robert, R., *Le Conte de fées littéraire en France de la fin du XVIIe à la fin du XVIIIe siècle* (Paris, Champion, 2002 [1982]).

Roche-Mazon, J., '"Les Fées" de Perrault et la véritable Mère L'Oye', *Revue hebdomadaire* 41 (1932), 345–360.

Rosen, C. and H. Zerner, *Romanticism and Realism. The Mythology of Nineteenth-Century Art* (London, Faber and Faber, 1984).

Rostal-Honorian, R., 'Frontières du *kont* en Guadeloupe', *Études créoles* 25.2 (2002), Special Issue on 'Le *kont* créole: à l'interface de l'écrit et de l'oral', 15–62.

Rubin, D.C., *Memory in Oral Traditions. The Cognitive Psychology of Epic, Ballads and Counting-out Rhymes* (Oxford, OUP, 1995).

Rumsey, A., 'Yaga Kange: a metrical narrative genre from the New Guinea highlands', *Journal of Linguistic Anthropology* 11.2 (2001), 193–239.

Sacks, H., *Lectures on Conversation* (Oxford, Blackwell, 1992).

Sainte-Beuve, C.-A., 'De la littérature industrielle', *Revue des deux mondes* IV.19, 1 Sept. 1839, 675–691.

Sand, G., *François le Champi*, pref. A. Fermiger (Paris, Folio, 1976).

Saussure, L. de, 'Quand le temps ne progresse pas avec le passé simple', in A. Carlier, V. Lagae and C. Benninger (eds), *Passé et parfait* (Amsterdam, Rodopi, 2000), 37–48.

Schenda, R., 'Semiliterate and semi-oral processes', trans. R.B. Bottigheimer [from *Vom Mund zu Ohr. Bausteine zu einer Kulturgeschichte volkstümlichen Erzählens in Europa*], *Marvels & Tales* 21.1 (2007), 127–140.

—— *Vom Mund zu Ohr. Bausteine zu einer Kulturgeschichte volkstümlichen Erzählens in Europa* (Göttingen, Vandenhoeck and Ruprecht, 1993).

—— 'Telling tales – spreading tales: change in the communicative forms of a popular genre', in R.B. Bottigheimer (ed.), *Fairy Tales and Society: Illusion, Allusion and Paradigm* (Philadelphia and London, University of Pennsylvania Press, 1986), 75–94.

—— *Volk ohne Buch. Studien zur Sozialgeschichte der populären Lesestoffe 1770–1910* (Frankfurt, Klostermann, 1970).

Seifert, L., 'Entre l'écrit et l'oral: la réception des contes de fées "classiques"', in A. Defrance and J.-F. Perrin (eds), *Le Conte en ses paroles. La Figuration de l'oralité dans le conte merveilleux du Classicisme aux Lumières* (Paris, Desjonquères, 2007), 21–33.

—— 'Madame Le Prince de Beaumont and the infantilisation of the fairy tale', *French Literature Series* 31 (2004), 25–39.

Sempere, E., *De la merveille à l'inquiétude: le registre du fantastique dans la fiction narrative du XVIIIè siècle* (Thèse de doctorat, Université de Paris 3, 2006).

Senghor, L.S., 'Preface' to B. Diop, *Les Nouveaux Contes d'Amadou Koumba* (Paris, Présence Africaine, 1958), 7–22.

Severi, C., 'Paroles durables, écritures perdues. Réflexions sur la pictographie cuna', in M. Détienne (ed.), *Transcrire les mythologies* (Paris, Albin Michel, 1994), 45–73.

Sévigné, Marie de Rabutin Chantal, Marquise de, *Correspondance*, 3 vols, ed. R. Duchêne (Paris, Gallimard-Pléiade, 1973–78).

Simonsen, M., *Le Conte populaire français* (Paris, PUF, 1981).

Smith, C., *Modes of Discourse. The Local Structure of Texts* (Cambridge, CUP, 2003).

—— *The Parameter of Aspect* (Dordrecht, Kluwer, 1991).

Söll, L., *Gesprochenes und geschriebenes französisch* (Berlin, Schmidt, 1983).

Soriano, M., *Les Contes de Perrault: culture savante et tradition populaire* (Paris, Gallimard, 1968).

Spear, T., 'Jouissances carnavalesques: représentations de la sexualité', in M. Condé and M. Cottenet-Hage (eds), *Penser la créolité* (Paris, Karthala, 1995), 135–152.

Sperber, D. and D. Wilson, *La Pertinence. Communication et cognition*, trans. A. Gerschenfeld and D. Sperber (Paris, Éditions de Minuit, 1989).

Stafford, A., 'De la causticité à la politique: "Paroles de nuit" en voyage à travers l'Atlantique', *Revue des arts de l'oralité* 1 (2008), 11–20.

Starr, F., *Inventing New Orleans: Writings of Lafcadio Hearn* (Jackson, University Press of Mississippi, 2001).

Storer, M.E., *Un épisode littéraire de la fin du XVIIème siècle: la mode des contes de fées, 1685–1700* (Geneva, Droz, 1972).

Tannen, D., 'Spoken and written narrative in English and Greek', in D. Tannen (ed.), *Coherence in Spoken and Written Discourse* (Norwood NJ, Ablex, 1984), 21–40.

Tenèze, M.-L., '"Si Peau d'Âne m'était conté...". À propos de trois illustrations des *Contes* de Perrault', *Arts et traditions populaires* (April–Dec. 1957), 313–316.

Thackway, M., *Africa Shoots Back. Alternative Perspectives in Sub-Saharan Francophone African Film* (Bloomington-Oxford-Cape Town, Indiana University Press-James Currey-New Africa Books, 2003).

Trinquet, C., 'On the literary origins of folkloric fairy tales: a comparison between Madame d'Aulnoy's "Finette Cendron" and Frank Bourisaw's "Belle Finette"', *Marvels & Tales* 21.1 (2007), 34–49.

Vaillant, A., J.-P. Bertrand, and P. Régnier, *Histoire de la littérature française du XIXe siècle* (Paris, Nathan, 1998), 18–22.

Vansina, J., *De la tradition orale, essai de méthode historique* (Tervuren, Musée royal de l'Afrique centrale, 1961).

Velay-Vallantin, C., *L'Histoire des contes* (Paris, Fayard, 1992).

Verdier, G., 'Figures de la conteuse dans les contes de fées féminins', *XVIIe siècle* 180 (1993), 481–499.

Vernier, F., '*Nouvelle*, laboratoire expérimental? L'impossible définition', in V. Engel and M. Guissard (eds), *La Nouvelle de langue française aux frontières des autres genres, du Moyen Âge à nos jours* (Ottignies, Quorum, 1997).

Vertron, *La Nouvelle Pandore ou les femmes illustres du siècle de Louis le Grand*, 2 vols (Paris, 1698).

Vieu, L. and L. Prévot, 'Background in SDRT', in *Proceedings of TALN 2004* (Workshop volume, Fez, 2004), 485–494.

Vieu, L. et al., 'Locating adverbials in discourse', *Journal of French Language Studies* 15 (2005), 173–193.

Vigny, A. de, *Histoire du cachet rouge* and *La Veillée de Vincennes*, in *Servitude et grandeur militaires*, ed. F. Germain (Paris, Classiques Garnier, 1965).

Vincileoni, N., *Comprendre l'œuvre de Bernard Dadié* (Paris, Les Classiques Africains, 1986).

Voltaire, *Dictionnaire philosophique*, in *Œuvres complètes*, ed. L. Morand (Paris, n.ed., 1877–1885).

—— *Romans et contes en vers et en prose*, ed. E. Guitton (Paris, Livre de Poche, 1994).

Wake, C., 'Negritude and after: changing perspectives in French-language African fiction', *Third World Quarterly* 10.2 (1988), 961–965.

Warner, M., *From the Beast to the Blonde. On Fairytales and their Tellers* (London, Chatto and Windus, 1994).

Waugh, L. and M. Monville-Burston, 'Aspect and discourse function: the French simple past in newspaper usage', *Language* 62 (1982), 846–877.

Weber, H., *Tales of the East* (Edinburgh, J. Ballantyne, 1812).

Weinrich, H., *Le Temps* (Paris, Seuil, 1973).

Wesselski, A., *Versuch einer Theorie des Märchens* (Reichenberg in Böhmen, Sudetendeutscher Verlag Franz Kraus, 1931).

Wolfson, N., 'The conversational historical present alternation', *Language* 55 (1979), 168–182.

——*The Conversational Historical Present in American English Narrative* (Dordrecht, Foris, 1982).

Zimmerman, M., 'Baudelaire, Poe and Hawthorne', *Revue de littérature comparée* 39.3 (1965), 448–450.

Zobel, J., *La Rue Cases-Nègres* (Paris-Dakar, Présence Africaine, 1974).

Zuber, R., 'La Voix de la conteuse et le goût du merveilleux', *Commentaires* 40 (1987–88), 752–755.

Zumthor, P., *Introduction à la poésie orale* (Paris, Seuil, 1983).

——*La Lettre et la voix* (Paris, Seuil, 1987).

Notes on Contributors

RUTH B. BOTTIGHEIMER, Professor of Comparative Literature, teaches at Stony Brook University and researches the history of and the interrelationships among early modern Italian, French, and German fairy tales. Her monograph *Fairy Godfather* (2002) details Giovan Francisco Straparola's creation of the European rags-to-riches fairy tale and relates the inception and continuing popularity of poverty-magic-marriage-wealth to urban experiences and sensibilities. *Fairy Tales. A New History* (2009) offers a print-based paradigm for long-term stability in fairy tale plots, while her ongoing work considers fairy tales within the history of magic tales from the ancient world to the modern period.

JANICE CARRUTHERS is Senior Lecturer in French Studies at Queen's University Belfast. Her research interests are in Linguistics, where she has published widely on tense, aspect and oral narrative. Her 2005 book, *Oral Narration in Modern French*, appeared with Legenda, and she is annotating an AHRC-funded electronic corpus of new storytelling for deposit in the Oxford Text Archive. Her current interests are in syntax, temporal patterning, framing, and speech and thought presentation in contemporary oral *contage*.

PATRICK CAUDAL is a CNRS researcher in the *Laboratoire de Linguistique formelle* (Université Paris Diderot). He is assistant director of the Rodopi series 'Cahiers Chronos' and has published numerous articles on the semantics and pragmatics of tense, aspect and modality. He is currently director of a project, funded by Marie-Curie (TAMEAL), which analyses these concepts in Australian languages. Patrick Caudal is also a professional storyteller and author of a collection of ancient Celtic tales, *The Last Song of the Bard*. He is President of the *Centre de littérature orale* in Vendôme.

NADINE DECOURT teaches and researches at the CREA (Centre for Research and Studies in Anthropology), Université de Lyon. She works on the *conte* as a vehicle of communication in multicultural situations, and more broadly on the circulation of the spoken word and of cultural imaginaries. Her volumes of collected *contes* (*Contes maghrébins en situation interculturelle*), as well as her research on experimentation and variation (*Contes et diversité culturelle*), bring together anthropology and comparative literature. Her current research is in collaboration with *conteurs*, researchers and directors involved in multimedia projects.

ANNE DEFRANCE lectures in the Université Michel de Montaigne (Bordeaux 3), where she is a member of the CNRS team LIRE (Literature, Ideology, Representations), and a member of the editorial board of the journal *Féeries*. She works on the *conte merveilleux* of the seventeenth and eighteenth centuries. Her monograph, *Les Contes et les nouvelles de Mme d'Aulnoy*, appeared with Droz in 1998, and her critical editions of the *contes* of Pajon, Duclos, and Cazotte have appeared with Champion and BGF. She is currently working on a critical edition of Moncrif's *contes*.

TIM FARRANT is Reader in Nineteenth-Century French Literature at the University of Oxford and a Fellow of Pembroke College. His publications include *Balzac's Shorter Fictions: Genesis and Genre* (Oxford University Press, 2002) and *An Introduction to Nineteenth-Century French Literature* (Duckworth, 2007). He is currently writing a book on short fiction in nineteenth-century France.

RICHARD A. FRANCIS is Emeritus Professor of Eighteenth-Century French Studies at the University of Nottingham. His most recent work is the edition of *L'Ingénu* in the *Complete Works of Voltaire*; he has also published extensively on Prévost and has written a biography of Romain Rolland.

MARY GALLAGHER is Associate Professor of French and Francophone Studies at University College Dublin. She has published mainly in French Caribbean studies (chiefly on Saint-John Perse and on contemporary writing from Martinique and Guadeloupe), although her most recent book is entitled *World Writing: Poetics, Ethics, Globalization* (Toronto UP, 2007). She is currently working on a book on Lafcadio Hearn.

NATHALIE GUÉZENNEC completed a doctorate in linguistics and ethnology, and is a member of the CNRS LACITO laboratory in Paris X. She works on Breton oral literature and has a particular interest in the interplay of contextual, psychological and textual factors in narrative memory. She has published a number of articles in this area, notably 'La Mémoire des contes et légendes Bas-Bretons' in *Fabula* and 'Pointer les lieux. Relation entre gestes, littérature orale et contexte', in the *Cahiers de l'Association for French Language Studies*.

MAEVE MCCUSKER is Senior Lecturer in French Studies at Queen's University Belfast, where she is co-director of the interdisciplinary Postcolonial Research Forum. She has published widely on Caribbean writing in French. Her monograph, *Patrick Chamoiseau: Recovering Memory*, appeared with Liverpool University Press in 2007, and her current research focuses on early writing from the Antilles. Her scholarly edition of one of the first novels from the francophone Caribbean, Louis de Maynard's *Outre-mer* (1835), will appear in L'Harmattan's 'Autrement mêmes' series in 2010.

JEAN-FRANÇOIS PERRIN is Professor of French literature at the Université Stendhal, Grenoble 3. He has written widely on a number of seventeenth and eighteenth-century authors (Crébillon, Hamilton), and is particularly known for his work on Rousseau. He also specialises in the *conte merveilleux*, on which he has published many articles: his critical edition of Gueullette's *Contes merveilleux* (in collaboration with C. Ramirez et al.) is forthcoming with Champion.

SOPHIE RAYNARD is Assistant Professor at The State University of New York at Stony Brook. She has published a monograph on French *conteuses* – *La Seconde préciosité. Floraison des conteuses de 1690 à 1756* (2002) – as well as several articles on seventeenth-century *conteuses*. She also served as the guest editor for a Special Issue on fairy tales with the *Romanic Review* (in press), where she contributed the preface and an article. She is currently working on a second monograph, a study addressing the poetics of the *contes de fées* in paratexts.

ANDY STAFFORD is a member of the editorial group of *Francophone Post-colonial Studies* and teaches at the University of Leeds. A specialist in the work of Roland Barthes, he has also published pieces on Tahar Ben Jelloun, Aimé Césaire, Patrick Chamoiseau, Aziz Chouaki, Driss Chraïbi, Moham-med Dib, Frantz Fanon, Edouard Glissant, Sembene Ousmane, Edward Said, Leïla Sebbar and Philippe Tagli. He has just completed a study of the radical Moroccan journal *Souffles*, and recently co-edited a volume on Alge-ria (L'Harmattan, 2009). His next project is a book on the contemporary 'Photo-text' in French (Liverpool University Press, forthcoming).

Index